ETHICS
GENERAL AND SPECIAL

THE MACMILLAN COMPANY
NEW YORK · BOSTON · CHICAGO · DALLAS
ATLANTA · SAN FRANCISCO

MACMILLAN & CO., Limited
LONDON · BOMBAY · CALCUTTA
MELBOURNE

THE MACMILLAN CO. OF CANADA, Ltd.
TORONTO

ETHICS
GENERAL AND SPECIAL

9̶2̶

BY

OWEN A. HILL, S.J., Ph.D.

Lecturer on Psychology, Natural Theology, Ethics
and Religion, at Fordham University,
New York City, N. Y.

𝔑𝔢𝔴 𝔜𝔬𝔯𝔨
THE MACMILLAN COMPANY
1920

Imprimi potest.

JOSEPHUS H. ROCKWELL, S.J.,

Praepositus Prov. Marylandiae Neo-Eboracensis.

Nihil obstat.

ARTHURUS J. SCANLAN, S.T.D.,

Censor Librorum.

Imprimatur.

PATRITIUS J. HAYES, D.D.,

Archiepiscopus Neo-Eboracensis.

NEO-EBORACI, die 15 Aprilis, 1920.

PREFACE

The whole trouble with all Modern Philosophy is rank subjectivism, and subjectivism is, perhaps, most destructive in the domain of Ethics. Protestantism and Modern Philosophy grow on the same tree, and the root of the tree is subjectivism. This fact accounts for all the atheism, all the materialism, all the socialism in the world. It is to blame for all the irreligion, all the injustice, all the tyranny now afflicting large and small nations; and the World War did not settle matters, the Peace Conference, in spite of all its good intentions, practically left things where it found them. Evils persevere as long as their causes; and till men think right, till Modern Philosophy is killed from men's minds, till Scholastic Philosophy gets everywhere the hearing it deserves, these evils, far from being eliminated, will prosper, grow and multiply. No body of men can regulate mankind, unless mankind itself is amenable to direction, unless mankind entertains correct notions regarding God, the Soul, and the nature of authority. Laws are no better than the men who make them, and laws are little worth, unless subjects are minded to see and obey divinity in them. It is awfully hard, in fact it is impossible, to persuade anybody to think that any single man or any collection of men, whether a majority or a minority, possess independent right over the free wills of other men, and are empowered to make and execute laws on their own initiative. God alone holds that supreme prerogative; and this fact is clear proof not only that all authority is immediately from God, but also that all authority passes immediately from God to ruler, without effective interference with authority itself on the part of the people. God is immediate maker of the Natural Law, He is mediate maker of all civil law; and the presence of God in civil law makes civil law a sacred obligation. Unjust law is no law at all, because God has no part in its making. Unjust law has all the force men

can give it. It has physical force in its favor, because men
can contribute that; and physical force never binds men's
free wills. Unjust law has no moral force, the kind that God
gives; and free wills are servants to moral force alone. All
the moral force in civil law comes from God, men are able
to back it up with physical force; but moral force, because
it touches free wills, is beyond the jurisdiction of mere men,
and necessarily leans for its validity on God alone.

Consent of the governed is one thing before the establishment of government, it is an entirely different thing after
government is once established. Physical freedom is man's
birthright, and remains intact before and after the establishment of government. Civil law is made by the state, and
before government is constituted there is no state, and therefore no adequate human lawmaker. Before government becomes a fact, natural law is the one restraint on moral freedom; and natural law wants a multitude without government
to form a government at its earliest convenience. A people,
therefore, is not morally free to live with or without government. Nature wants men to live in a state, under law and
authority; and nature's wishes are what God wants, nature's
wishes are the Natural Law.

A government de jure and de facto is, of course, better
than a government merely de facto; but when a government
de jure is impossible without continuous strife and universal
bloodshed, a government de facto is better than no government at all. Even rights must be prosecuted with prudence,
and in case of such a government de facto, right must await
a more favorable opportunity to assert itself, it must not work
with headlong rashness to its own harm and the destruction
of order.

In common sense and the natural law legitimate conquest
is as just and secure a title to authority as inheritance or
suffrage or purchase; and in the words of Suarez nearly every
government in modern times traces its origin to right of conquest. This is far from meaning that modern states are built
on physical force for single title. They are built immediately
on physical force, mediately on moral right. Physical force
when employed to pursue a right has all the sacredness of

moral right itself. To take a familiar and up-to-date instance, the Allies had a perfect moral right to impose on Germany and Austria all the terms of the armistice. Whatever terms the Allies exacted from the defeated Germans they exacted by force; but this force was backed up by clear moral right, the indisputable right nations have to defend themselves against an open, bold and aggressive oppressor, to punish his crime with becoming penalties, and to make it effectively and forever impossible for him to repeat his dastardly act. When criminals are captured and convicted, they are not straightway liberated. They are fined light or heavy sums, they are imprisoned for short or long terms; and if the criminal happens to be a murderer, reason quite approves of his utter destruction. Conquest, of course, can be illegitimate or legitimate. Illegitimate conquest is no valid title. Illegitimate conquest, like everything else illegitimate, is of no value in the court of morality.

A government or State always implies a body of laws, or a constitution; and, prior to the establishment of a government, the people enjoy full moral freedom to select some set form of government and appoint a ruler. Moral freedom is removed by law, law is the denial of moral freedom, because law means obligation, and obligation means moral necessity, the diametrical opposite of moral freedom.

Self-determination implies full moral freedom to choose a form of government and select a ruler. Where no government exists, no civil law exists, no constitution exists, and this right to self-determination is sacred; where government is already established, civil law exists, a constitution or fixed body of civil laws, exists; and the principle of self-determination is all wrong. Correct Ethics recognizes no such independent right in ruler or subjects. Law restricts moral freedom, and the constitution is law. The constitution stands for the Royal Compact championed by Suarez. Neither ruler nor people must override the constitution. This constitution embodies the respective rights and privileges of ruler and subjects, and defines the method of procedure to be followed in case of a dispute between ruler and subjects. As long as the ruler keeps within the terms of the constitution, his right to author-

ity is beyond question, and subjects by themselves are not at
liberty to change the form of government or curtail the ruler's
prerogatives.   The ruler can at intervals make concessions to
his subjects, subjects can at intervals do the same favor to
their ruler; but every such transaction must be mutual and
agreeable to both parties.   The ruler can voluntarily abdicate
or forfeit his authority by abuse of his prerogative; and in
either case, unless succession is otherwise settled by the constitution, the multitude reverts to its original condition of
no government, and the people have full moral freedom to
select a form of government and choose a ruler.   In the prosecution of an unjust war the ruler can lose his authority by
legitimate conquest; and in this case ruler and subjects pass
under the authority of the conqueror.   In pursuance of this
truth the Allies at the Peace Conference imposed a form of
government on Germany and Austria, allowing them a small
measure of liberty in their selection of rulers, disarmed them,
taxed them, and in every way treated them as subject peoples.
The small states previously belonging to Germany and Austria got from the Allies, for purposes of peace, the right to
self-determination, and in granting this favor the Allies as
victors were clearly within their rights.

CONTENTS

PART I

GENERAL ETHICS

PART II

SPECIAL ETHICS

CONTENTS

CONTENTS

ETHICS, GENERAL AND SPECIAL

PART I

GENERAL ETHICS

INTRODUCTION

A WORD about the importance of our subject. This work is intended to throw some additional light on the topic of morality. For Ethics is our theme, and Ethics is the science of morality. And if any detail of thought has a vital bearing on man's destiny, if any branch of study helps shape his life, that detail of thought is suggested by Ethics, morality is that study. *Ethics is the science of putting order in man's free acts;* and, when you reflect that all sin, and much trouble, and hell itself are only varying phases of disorder, it must be evident that this science, theoretically mastered and systematically reduced to practice, could effect a revolution in the world. And the revolutionists would be hailed as the Emancipators of mankind. They would go down in history, and they do go down in history as the supremest benefactors of our race.

Witness the instance of our Lord and Saviour Jesus Christ. Even His bitterest enemies, even men who deny Him every other vestige of divinity, acknowledge that the world was made better by His presence among men, and attribute to His maxims and example an abiding influence for good. He was a teacher of Ethics for whom the world waited with longing for full four thousand years. He was a teacher of Ethics, whose like the world of to-day misses exceedingly. The wisdom of His utterances even from a purely human standpoint, without regard at all to the spirit of faith and grace's environment, in which they ought to be accepted, is as much a subject of concern to the learned of to-day as it was in His

1

own lifetime to the doctors in the temple, to the Scribes and
the Pharisees deeply read in the Law. The wisdom of His
utterances extorts praise from unbelievers, and compels the
attention of the universe. Men who will not worship Him
as God are unable, when face to face with His heavenly doctrine and precepts, to withhold the homage due superhuman
intelligence. I insist upon this point as a conclusive proof
of the deep importance attaching to Ethics, because Christ's
ethical teaching is the only claim Christ has on the reverence
and respect of men completely abandoned by faith, and not
wholly bereft of reason. He has other and far more cogent
claims on our homage; but we, as well as strangers to faith,
can learn with profit to appreciate the human side of the
God-man's character. And Christ, apart from His tran-
scending dignity as God, ranks first among the most consummate legislators the world ever entertained, and merits as
such unstinted praise from all mankind, from believer and
unbeliever alike. He owes the homage wrung from unwilling
unbelievers not to the influence of grace, nor yet to the
miracles of wonder He wrought in favor of suffering and
sickness, but mainly to the fact that His discourses breathe
an unerring love for rectitude; and half His lifework was
the ethical instruction of humanity.

Teachers, who appeal to the curious in human nature, will
hold the ears of men until supplanted by other teachers with
more startling novelties for wares; but teachers of morality
will never be without an audience, though they deal out
truths as old as time. Such is the passion of mankind for
what tends to put men in improved relations with themselves,
with one another, and with God, that, as long as a human
heart beats, due importance will be attached to problems of
morality, and propounders of morality will have their uses
in the universe. We men are eminently practical beings, and
the almost total absence of pure theory, and of the strictly
academic discussions common in Logic and Metaphysics from
Moral Philosophy, makes this branch of the science more interesting and absorbing. After all, we were equipped with
minds only to borrow light from them for the operations of
the will, the head is servant to the heart, and life takes all its
true color from action, not from knowledge. To this simple

fact must be ascribed the undoubted superiority of Ethics in the kingdom of study. Then, too, we are born with an inalienable and harassing love of happiness. We want to be happy here, we want to be happy hereafter, and the wish lives of our very life. Every glance of the eye aims at the discovery of happiness' hiding place, every throb of the heart is an invitation to happiness' pity, and every single thought of saint and sinner alike has happiness for mainspring and motive. There is no help for it; we were made that way; and, to lose the inclination, we should have to get outside of ourselves. Moral Philosophy professes to mark out the lines along which we can without loss pursue this fleeting phantom of happiness, and at the same time makes distinct record of blunders to which the history of our race bears witness. It puts on a solid basis principles, that, if practically fulfilled, can have but one result, the inward approbation of a conscience, working on and up to the right. And when conscience approves, remorse is still, this life knows no truer happiness than peace, and thorough blamelessness is bonded promise of eternal blessedness.

Moral Philosophy puts us right with the world of being in which we move, and does the thing in the neatest way conceivable. It first discusses general notions of morality; motives for action, standards of measure, methods and means of discovery, palliative circumstances, characteristics, responsibility, merit and blame, helps and hindrances, law. These abstract questions pave the way for more tangible and positive considerations. They partake of the nature of principles, that run through the second or practical part of Moral Philosophy. A man's duties and a man's rights are definitely settled in this second part, by applying to the different emergencies, in which a man may find himself, all the truths accumulated and made good in the first part. Thus, the first condition that confronts us, when brought into being, is that of dependence on God. Moral Philosophy takes hold of this condition, examines it in every detail, and sternly decrees the rigid demands of reason with regard to religion, worship and revelation. It then lays down rules for man's behavior towards himself and towards his fellow-men, taken as individuals. These rules are far reaching, and define exactly his obligations with respect to his body, his soul, his life, and his neighbor's body, soul and life. They determine the nature and fairness of private property, and establish the sanctity of contracts. Society in all its ramifications is the next study. The family and the State are the topics; and each meets with the fullest treatment. The family presents such vital questions as marriage, its oneness, its perpetuity, its obligations, its relations with the civil power, parents and children. The State leads to an analysis of men's inclination to band themselves together, of the purpose that actuates the inclination, of the elements entering into society's structure; of authority, its origin, its phases, its constituents, and of the mutual relations between ruler and subjects. Tongiorgi offers this other division of Ethics from its causes: 1, Final cause, or man's last end; 2, Material cause, or man's moral acts; 3, Formal cause, or good and evil; 4, Model cause, or Natural Law; 5, Efficient cause, mind, will and habits, behavior.

These, therefore, are some of the topics destined to occupy our attention. The field is so vast that we can hope to do anything like justice to only the leading points; and it shall be my endeavor, while making my treatment of the matter as thorough as possible, to omit nothing of primary importance. While devoting no little time to the forward part of Moral, or General Ethics, we intend to pay more special attention to the after-part, designated by some authors as Natural Right. The spirit of Catholicity will of course pervade our whole work. We shall never forget that we are men of faith, with the light of the Scriptures as interpreted by the Church for guide, with the traditions of two thousand years at our service, and the example of an army of saints before our eyes. We enter not into this enquiry in the disposition of Rationalists, who exercise to-day so wide an influence in the world of thought, outside the one true Church. We hesitate to remove God's messages to men from the field of morality. We refuse to regard man as an absolute, self-sufficient being, independent of his surroundings, accountable to no superior for his conduct, his own guide, his own reward, his own punishment. We maintain, on the contrary, that every instant of his life is beset with well defined relations; that he is poor, and weak, and erring; that he is affected by his environment, strictly responsible before an all-wise, an all-holy, and an all-powerful God for his thoughts, his words and his acts; and a candidate for the Heaven or hell of Scripture, for the place of delight with golden streets, or the prison house of fire that knows no surcease of pain. Reason with us is quite as important a factor in morality as it is with the Rationalists. We hold it in even higher esteem than they. We follow as far as it leads, accept all its legitimate conclusions, and allow neither prejudice nor passion to meddle with our loyalty to its counsels. We take no half-measures, we journey not to a certain point and then stop short. But, when reason makes clear the undoubted existence of a teaching Church, the reality of a code of law harassing in the extreme to human nature, we adopt its teaching with all the responsibilities and all the sacrifices implied. When reason proclaims in a loud voice its own proneness to confound the false with the true, its inability to cope with problems, capable of taxing even angelic minds, we take reason's word for the statement, and accept on God's authority what reason cannot even understand. Reason without a guide is not sufficient in the delicate task of arranging the moral details of a man's life. Reason was made to adopt the truth, not to fathom all truth; and reason is then exerting its proper activity, when in matters beyond its grasp it humbly submits to instructions from a superior. Reason is of its nature infallible, but it is by accident capable of mistake, and accidents are nowhere so likely to occur as in the domain of moral teaching. Intellectual pride is the forerunner of unbelief, unbelief gives loose rein to license, license kills conscience; and, when conscience is once dead, man sinks lower than the level of a beast, and becomes a veritable monster of iniquity.

There are certain basic truths we take for granted in all these discussions, not because they cannot be proved, but because they belong to other departments of philosophy. They are all abundantly proved elsewhere, and we are justified in carrying over truths made good in other portions of the study. Chief among these truths I should reckon the existence of God; His supreme ownership of all else, man not excepted; the immortality of the soul; free will; and man's ability to compass certainty in the domain of knowledge. Atheism, Ma-

terialism, Determinism, and Scepticism are theories opposed
to these several points of doctrine, and are overwhelmingly
refuted in Natural Theology, Psychology, and Logic. We
prove God a living reality from the need of one unproduced
actual being, to explain the produced beings that fall under
our experience. Deny God, and the universe of creatures is
without explanation, an effect with no cause. We prove God
a living reality from the wonderful order apparent in the
physical universe, written large across the sky, the earth, and
the sea. We prove God a living reality from a moral order
embodied in the voice of conscience, proclaiming aloud the
wishes of a superior compelling us with threats and promises
to cherish right and despise wrong, to do good and avoid
evil. We prove God a living reality from the common consent of mankind, dating back to the earliest ages of history,
and enduring with undiminished vigor down to our own times.
God is supreme owner of all else in virtue of the principle
that to the maker belongs the thing he makes; and God created, made from nothing, the world and all the minerals,
plants, brutes and men the world contains. Apart from other
compelling arguments, the soul's immortality is settled by its
simplicity and spirituality. It has no parts, and is, therefore,
in itself incorruptible or indestructible. It is intrinsically
independent of matter, and is, therefore, safe from accidental
corruption or destruction. The omnipotence of God cannot
annihilate a human soul without doing violence to God's other
attributes; and no one attribute in God runs counter to another. Every individual man is a living witness to his possession of free will. All human intercourse is based on this
quality of men; and in any other hypothesis law and social
order would have no meaning; honesty and virtue would
perish from the earth; reward and punishment would be idle
terms without a show of significance. Scepticism is a huge
joke in philosophy; a direct insult to the goodness and wisdom of God; and its own completest refutation. Therefore,
with perfect right we suppose everywhere in these discussions
that God exists, that man is His property to dispose of as He
pleases, that man's soul will live forever, that man is free,
and that all doubt is a diseased condition of the mind that
study and observation can cure.

THESIS I

Every agent works unto an end. This end is truly a cause. The will in all its deliberate movements has some definite last end, whether absolutely or relatively such. Jouin, 5–19; Rickaby, 3–6.

QUESTION

By a sort of paradox we begin our Ethics with the end. Ethics is a set of rules for conduct, man's conduct is a series of his deliberate acts, and the beginning of every deliberate act is some end or purpose the man proposes to himself to accomplish or effect. And so the paradox ceases. While true to its name in one order, the end is false to its name in another. It is last in the order of execution, first in the order of intention. The house as a finished product is the last thing to reward the builder's eyes, after weeks and months of work; the same house, as it existed in his mind and will, was the first thing to suggest plans and operations, running all the way from cellar to roof. We are therefore justified in beginning with the end, because intention precedes execution, and nobody builds a house without prior thought of plans, without prior wish of a habitation. People never build a house without caring what will be the result of their endeavors; they never build a house, when they want an automobile. Intention is end energizing the will, and on this account intentional and deliberate are practically synonymous. To energize the will, the end must first fall under the notice of the intellect; and a deliberate act is an act done with full knowledge and consent. Unintentional for the same reason is in our language an equivalent for indeliberate. The philosophy of the thing is plain in our expression, "Where no offense is intended, no offense can be taken." Wise men pay no attention to a hurt, when the wrong-doer has no desire to hurt, or hardly knows that his conduct causes pain. Intention, therefore, presupposes an intellect and a will working together in mutual har-

mony, and the use of the word is regularly restricted to man.
In brutes, plants and minerals the same phenomenon of
finality, or seeking an end, is verified in every exertion of
their energy, and is best named appetency, tendency, nature.
A brute has instinct for guide and appetite for root of desire, both are constrained faculties without a vestige of freedom; and they base a certain imperfect deliberation, a certain
show of intention, attributed in philosophy to brutes. Brutes
never in reality choose, when of two or more alternatives they
adopt or embrace one; the transaction is due not to choice or
selection, but to an inexorable law imposed on them by their
Maker, and instinct is with us a handy term for that law.
The whole process in brutes is not intention, but appetency;
and the perfect deliberation present in man's acts is always
absent from the acts of brutes. Plants enjoy neither sense nor
appetite; and they grow, nourish and reproduce themselves
without any knowledge whatever on their part, without any
desire whatever, but wholly in virtue of a tendency or bent
communicated to them by their Maker. In their case, all
knowledge of end and all desire of its accomplishment are
in God. And what is true of plants is true of minerals, with
this single difference that capacity for self-motion attaches
to plants, while it is absent from minerals. Minerals, therefore, prosecute their end by very nature, in virtue of obedience to the law of gravity, and to whatever other physical
and chemical laws obtain in creation, God imposing this duty
of obedience.

Every agent works unto an end; and the saying, when restricted to minerals, plants and brutes, is of small or no importance in Ethics, because every such agent is outside the
sphere of morality. In common with other creatures, man
works towards an end; and, what is more important in Ethics,
man in all his deliberate movements works towards a definite
last end, whether absolutely and unreservedly or only relatively such. God Himself is no exception to this rule of
finality; and in creation He must have purposed His own
glory, as nothing short of God is worthy of God, and God
can slave to no unworthy end. God's glory is, therefore,
the absolutely last end of all creatures; and, in the words
of our catechism, we are all here to praise, worship and serve

God, and to save our souls. God's glory is creatures' external last end, because it is primarily for God, not for creatures. Besides this external last end, we must recognize an internal last end; and in the course of our work we shall see that it is for man complete happiness, the vision of God, salvation. In the event of wishing to create, God simply had to intend creatures for His glory, and we know from man's natural craving for complete happiness that God meant man to compass this surpassing good.

And all morality dates back to this single fact. Man must respect his Maker's wishes, because it rests with the maker to dispose of his work as an owner; and God's wishes are plain; man must glorify God by a life of virtue here, and by complete happiness hereafter. Good and evil must, therefore, be differentiated, law must be kept under penalty of punishment, and duties must be fulfilled with scrupulous exactness. Hence, we begin with end, show that while God's glory is man's absolutely last extrinsic end, the possession of God is man's absolutely last intrinsic end; that virtue is his relatively last intrinsic end; that virtue can be differentiated from vice; that the objective order of things is the standard or measure enabling men to distinguish virtue from vice; that man is under strict law to avoid evil and do good, and satisfy every relation in force between himself on the one hand, and God, self and the neighbor on the other. Destiny is end viewed as an obligation imposed by a superior; and man's destiny, taking into account his present and future life, is complete happiness or the intellectual possession of God; man's destiny, restricting the question to this present life alone, is virtue, or a closer and closer approach to God by the introduction of moral rectitude into his conduct. And the enemies of finality want to feel free from all restraint, and escape responsibility for their misdeeds, on the plea of total and complete independence.

Finality is the most obvious phenomenon in nature; and yet, to escape the manifest responsibility resulting from finality, some philosophers have denied its existence. Epicurus and men of his stamp felt themselves hampered in their dreams of pleasure by the unwelcome notion of a final cause, and in their intellectual impotence strove to shake it off, by agreeing to regard it an empty fancy. They maintained that everything happened by a sort of unavoidable chance, and claimed that man trifled with himself in supposing that he had any destiny to fulfil. Of course the doctrine would prove convenient to men set on living at haphazard, unwilling to borrow any worry from possible consequences of their rash conduct. Whatever obscurity may cloak the truth in the case of inanimate and irrational agents, the thing is too plain in the case of man to admit of the slightest doubt. Man knows that he has a destiny to fulfil, and because of his power of choice, coupled with the inevitable conviction, that in his every act he is pursuing some definite purpose, he knows that he will be rewarded or punished according to his deserts.

TERMS

Every Agent. Agents can be separated into three classes, *beings without any knowledge whatever, beings with sensible knowledge or instinct, and beings with intellects and wills.* Agents of the first class work unto an end under direction; minerals without any motion of their own, plants with self-motion. Agents of the second class work unto an end apprehensively or with knowledge, and with motion of their own, but by instinct which is a necessary cause. Agents of the third class work apprehensively, with motion of their own, and with the power to select and reject means. Examples of all three are an arrow on its way to the target, a dog walking home, a man making money.

End. Finis est id propter quod aliquid fit, id cujus gratia aliquid fit. The end is that on account of which, for the sake of which something is done. It is what induces the agent to work; that towards which the agent strives, to rest in it, to quit the activity of seeking, not the activity of enjoyment. Ends are classified thuswise: *Last or farthest away; proximate or closest; and intermediate, between last and proximate.* Last is sometimes absolutely and unreservedly last, sometimes relatively last. *An end is absolutely last, when it cannot in reason be referred to any higher end, any end beyond or farther away; when the agent can in reason devote himself and all his endeavors to its accomplishment; when it is the possession of God, and only then. It is relatively last, when it is in reality referred to no end beyond, like money in the case of a miser, though it can be in reason, and in conscience ought to be referred to some higher end, like money in the case of a saint; when it cannot in reason claim all a man's endeavors, but only a certain corner of his energies and attention. A proximate end* is virtually a means to some last or intermediate end. *An intermediate end* is a means lying between a proximate and last, the first intermediate being a means to the second, and so on to the finish. In the present classification we distinguish two orders, that of execution and that of intention; and our division is in the order of execution. The possession of God, or complete happiness, is first thing in the order of intention, last in the order of execution. Thought of reward starts effort, reward stands to the winner after effort is over. Ends are likewise divided into *end which, end for which, and end in which.* They are, respectively, the good sought, the person advantaged, and possession. Examples are, learning, student and education, in the matter of study. *An end to be produced* is a good without physical existence prior to the agent's activity; *an end to be obtained* is a physical reality prior to the agent's effort. Health in the case of a sick man, and gold in the case of a miser are instances. *End of deed and end of doer,* in Latin, operis and operantis, are important. The first is that to which the agent's work is by its very nature suited and fitted; the other is whatever good the agent selects for purpose of his work. Ends of deed are, a house with a builder, a song with a singer, time with a watchmaker. Ends of doer are, worship, fame, money with all three.

Cause. Whatever produces another with influence on its very being, the influence issuing in dependence, is a cause. There are four leading causes, two of them internal, *material* and *formal;* two of them external, *efficient* and *final.* Each of the four has its own proper and peculiar activity, each producing the effect, each contributing in its own special way to the production of the effect or new existence. *An efficient cause* has direct bearing on the effect, without entering its intrinsic constitution, and contributes of its own to the effect, whether its activity be physical or moral. *A final cause* directly affects the efficient cause, and through it influences the effect, contributing of its own to the effect by moral activity alone. The influence of an efficient cause is exerted first and foremost on the effect; the influence of a final cause is exercised first and foremost on the mind and will of the agent, and through them on the effect. The difference between a physical efficient cause and a final cause is too plain to be missed, but the same is not true of a moral efficient cause and a final. Moral efficients are close images of finals, and yet the two must not be confounded together. A moral efficient has a more direct bearing on the effect than a final. One man bribes another with money to commit murder. The briber is moral efficient cause of the murder, the money offered is final cause of the murder. The activity of the briber bears on the murder, he uses the murderer as an instrument, and the moral phase of the affair passes to physical. The money bears on the mind and will of the murderer, and all its activity remains moral. Neither is a final cause a mere condition. Like all causes, it is a condition too; but to the notion of condition it adds the quality of a thing more intimately connected with the work or effect. *A condition as such enters into no part of the effect proper.* All its ultility ceases, when the effect proper begins. It makes things ready, and then disappears. The final cause, on the contrary, really sets the agent in motion by the influence it exerts on his will, if the agent is rational, or by the influence it exerts on the will of the First Cause, God, if the agent is irrational. Besides, *a condition is no sufficient reason for the effect.* In the process of burning compare the dryness of the waste burnt, and its juxtaposition, with a fire that consumes it. Some final cause must urge the builder to begin operations, and this final cause influences him all the way from beginning to finish, from cellar to roof. The end is a cause only in the order of intention; in the order of execution it is in proper language an effect.

The Will. A spiritual faculty, proper and peculiar to man, capable of seeking good by acts elicited under the direction of the intellect. Appetite is of three kinds; *natural,* proper to minerals and plants; *sensible,* proper to brutes; and *intellectual or rational,* proper to man. All three are in man, natural and sensible alone are in brutes, natural alone is in minerals and plants. The will is rational appetite, and meets with full and complete treatment in Psychology.

Deliberate. Man is capable of two kinds of acts, *deliberate and indeliberate.* Toying with the beard or aimlessly rubbing the chin, is the classical instance of an indeliberate act. Deliberate acts are so familiar that an example would be superfluous. The will aside, intellectual knowledge and a degree of attention are really the distinguishing characteristics of a deliberate act, as compared with an indeliberate act. Will separates it not from indeliberate, but from spontaneous acts. *Perfect deliberation* is itself defined to be an act of the reason, by which, at the instigation of the will, the mind compares together different ends, different means, with a view to making a choice. In deliberation it will be noted that the third operation of the mind, not merely the first or second, has play. In other words, a comparison is instituted, and this process necessitates the employment of argumentation. Philosophers recognize a kind of *imperfect deliberation,* which they attribute to brute animals. The knowledge requisite is limited to sole perception of the end by means of the external senses, aided principally by sensile discrimination. And men are as capable as brutes of this imperfect deliberation, or real indeliberateness. It nowise reaches, like the knowledge of perfect deliberation, to the nature of the end, or to the connection between a certain act and a certain purpose. In imperfect deliberation the motion of the agent is ordinarily quick and sudden; in perfect deliberation it is ordinarily slow and measured. *Human acts,* distinctively such, have three elements, *intellectual knowledge, desire and freedom, activities of intellect and will,* man's two specific functions. Desire and freedom can be expressed together by the one word, selection. Selection always presupposes knowledge, in much the same way as operations of the mind have operations of the senses for foundation. Hence the adage, "Nil volitum, nisi praecognitum," "Things unknown are not matter for wishes." Freedom in the same way has for support the two faculties of intellect and will; and, in the absence of either, freedom is impossible. *A voluntary or deliberate act is an act proceeding from the will accompanied by intellectual knowledge of the end sought.* Deliberate, or voluntary acts in strict sense, are arranged in different classes.

Perfectly voluntary acts are accomplished with full knowledge, and with full consent of the will.

Imperfectly voluntary acts imply that either knowledge, or consent, or both are imperfect.

Absolutely voluntary acts are accomplished with full deliberation, attention and bias.

Acts are relatively or after a manner voluntary, when consent is present, but mingled with a certain aversion and leaning of the will towards the opposite act. E.g., sailors throwing cargo overboard in storm.

A directly voluntary act turns on some immediate object of the will, intended in itself and for its own sake. E.g., theft, murder.

Indirectly voluntary acts turn on some object necessarily connected with immediate object. E.g., effect in cause, drunkenness in excessive drinking, death and a thrown stone.

In a positively voluntary act the will acts, as in a sin of commission.

In a negatively voluntary act the will refuses to act, as in a sin of omission.

Expressly voluntary acts are clear from words or signs.

Tacitly voluntary acts are gathered from facts.

An act is actually voluntary, when willed here and now, without question of break or interruption.

An act is virtually voluntary, when voluntary by force of an original actual voluntary, the actual wish being broken or interrupted, without detriment to its moral continuity and influence.

An act is habitually voluntary, when its original was actually willed once, and was never taken back; but the actual wish was broken or interrupted to such an extent by sleep, or delay, or something such that it no longer lasts or influences by way of an act, but only by way of a habit.

An act is interpretatively voluntary, when never actually willed, but would be willed if thought were had of the thing, e. g., desire of salvation combined with opposition to baptism.

Three parts. I. End. II. Cause. III. Last end.
PROOFS I, II, III

I. Every agent works unto some determined and well defined effect. Otherwise all effects would be indifferent, or of
the same attractiveness; and there would be no reason why
one effect should be produced rather than another. Very production is a sign that the effect produced was more attractive
to the agent than other effects. But such an effect has all the
constituents of an end, which is that on account of which the
agent works. Ergo, every agent works unto an end.

II. Whatever produces another with influence on its very
being, the influence issuing in dependence, is truly a cause.
But such is the end. Ergo, the end is truly a cause. *With
regard to the Minor*. The builder's purpose contributes even
more to the building of the house than his saw or hammer, because it starts things and stays with him to the finish. The
saw does its own work, the hammer its own; and that is all.
The end is responsible for their work and for the work of
everything else employed in the construction of the building.
In rational agents the end's influence is immediate; in minerals, plants and brutes it is mediate, directly influencing
God, their Maker and First Cause, to furnish them with such
and such natures, tendencies and faculties, or instincts, in
preference to others, because best suited and adapted to the
works He intends them to accomplish.

III. 1°. In every series of causes there ought to be a first
cause. But if the will had no definite last end, there would
be no first cause. Ergo.

With regard to the Major. The second cause, to be second,
would be an effect. But an effect without a cause is impossible. Ergo.

With regard to the Minor. The last end is the first cause.
Ergo.

With regard to this Antecedent. The first cause is what
first excites the agent to activity. But this is the office of the
last end. Ergo.

With regard to this Minor. Axiom—The end is first thing
in a man's intention, last thing in the order of execution.

2°. The last end, with regard to an act of the will, fills the place of motion's first principle. But remove the first principle of motion, and no motion exists. Ergo, in the event of no definite last end, no act of the will ensues.

3°. When one thing in nature is the reason why another thing receives such or such a denomination, the first of the two is more deserving of the denomination than the second, which actually receives it. But all intermediate ends owe their whole being, and consequently their every denomination, to some last end; and these intermediate ends, at least, are purposes worked unto by every agent. An intermediate is sought only with a view to some corresponding last end. Otherwise it is not an intermediate end. Ergo, the last end is all the more so such a purpose; that is, the will in all its deliberate movements has some definite last end, whether strictly or relatively such.

4°. Every particular or individual good tends of its nature to some common or universal good, as to its proper end. But God, the absolute good, is common or universal good, and every created good is particular or individual good. Ergo, every created good, or things in general tend of their nature to one good, God, as to their last end.

With regard to the Major. Parts exist for the sake of the whole.

With regard to the Minor. All good comes from, and depends for its being on God.

N.B. This last argument proves that nature wants man in all his deliberate movements to have God for definite last end. Man's every wish is implicitly, if not explicitly, an effort towards complete happiness, and complete happiness is the possession of God. Implicitly, therefore, this definite last end is always the absolutely last or God; and implicitly speaking God is necessarily the last end of every deliberate act or series of actions. What nature wants, God wants. We cannot improve on God, and when we try to do so we fail.

PRINCIPLES

A. The single difference between a means and an end is this, that the former is striven after merely for the sake of the end, while the latter is striven after for itself. In fact, a means is an end before it is compassed; it becomes a means only after it ceases to be an end only after it is compassed. Means in process of making, means in *fieri*, is an end; means formally taken, means in *facto esse* is not an end. Before it can be used, it has to be compassed or sought; and what the will seeks, is the man's end. Hence the absurdity of writers, who claim that Jesuit philosophers and moralists advocate the wicked theory, that a laudable end justifies any means whatever, no matter how immoral and wrong. Jesuits would be blind, indeed, if they failed to see at a glance that such a theory, because of the unimportant difference between means and end, would be a virtual advocacy of this evidently iniquitous principle, that all ends, good, bad and indefferent, are justified; and that murder and forgiving charity, robbery and alms-deeds are equally worthy of our aspirations and endeavors.

B. An intention is an act by which the will embraces the end as its peculiar good. Any reason urging the will to this act is called a motive. Whatever helps to the possession of the end is a means; and such means as simply remove impediments from the path are remedies.

C. The motion the end communicates to the agent is not physical, but of equivalent efficacy in another order, namely, in the logical order, the order of thought. Its whole efficiency lies in the love it stirs in the agent's will, after its presentation by the intellect of the agent; and this love contributes as much to the production of the effect as the physical efficient cause.

D. Man in his indeliberate actions, works unto an end much as brutes, apprehensively, with motion of his own, but by instinct. Such acts are called acts of the man, not acts of man or human acts.

E. The end, or final cause, considered in the order of execution, is no cause of the effect, since its place is behind that of the effect, and causes precede their effects. We maintain only this, that the end is a true and real cause, when considered in the order of intention. Objectively speaking, end in the order of execution is a built house, end in the order of intention is a thought house.

THESIS II

Man of his very nature desires complete happiness. Complete happiness is man's absolutely last end subjectively taken. This natural desire must be possible of fulfilment. No created good can secure to man complete happiness. The possession of God is alone complete happiness, and God is alone complete happiness, and God is man's absolutely last end objectively taken. Jouin, 5–19; Rickaby, 6–26.

QUESTION

Here on the threshold of morality a multitude of questions besets us. We know from Metaphysics that every agent, man included, works unto some end. We know, further, that man excels all other creatures in this, that he chooses his end and selects means to its accomplishment. He is not an accumulation of blind forces, working along lines mapped out for him by another. He thinks for himself, he decides for himself, he weighs, examines, approves, condemns. We have from our previous acquaintance with philosophy a fair insight into his faculties. From experience we have a fair knowledge of the motives, that clamor for his attention in the routine of everyday affairs. Some are money-makers, some are chiselling for themselves a niche in the temple of fame, some are in continual search for health or the means to preserve it, some keep busy nursing an appetite for palatable dishes, and others travel in pursuit of a good they can expect to come up with only after death. We have to range ourselves in some class. Nay, we are placed already. For the present we want to look at things with the cold, calculating eyes of reason, to profit by our own mistakes and the mistakes of others, and stand just where common sense would have us stand in life's struggles. We want to find out what craving is in reality at the bottom of human desires, and what one object in the universe can sate the craving. Our thesis is the answer. Hap-

18

piness is last in the series of wish-factors, and God is alone large enough, when possessed, to leave no room for further desire. We mean by wish-factors the reasons prompting our wishes; and money, pleasure, honor are wished in last analysis because they hold out promise of happiness. Man cannot in reason want anything beyond God, man cannot in reason rest in the enjoyment of anything this side of God.

TERMS

Happiness. This is the theme with which the Lord Christ opened His sublime discourse on the Mount. The beatitudes are eight steps in the ladder to God; and, when the wisest of men communicated the secret of success in life to the listening multitude, He knew best with what word to preface His remarks. Beati, He said, blessed, happy are the poor in spirit, and so on through the catalogue. His mission was in part the instruction of mankind and the conquest of souls. Redemption and merit aside, He aimed in all His movements at spreading the kingdom of virtue in the hearts of men. And the happiness born of virtue was the most tremendous motive at His command. He thought no reward a more appealing incentive to virtue than happiness, and God's ideas are right. He knew in His infinite wisdom that other rewards, while possibly exerting a temporary influence over men's minds, would in the last resort fail of effect. He knew that other rewards, from their very nature and the constitution of man, would prove only partial incentives, subject to all the varying phases of human conduct. He knew that wealth, for instance, with all its attractiveness for some, would act as a deterrent on others; that fame would appeal to the instincts of a circle limited indeed in numbers. But happiness is a universal good, it is at the root of all the world's wishes, it holds its own against the ravages of time, against all the vicissitudes with which humanity is acquainted. *Boethius thus defines complete happiness, "A lasting condition blessed with everything good." "The enduring possession of every good."* These are no idle words, and their right understanding will remove many difficulties. They vindicate to complete happiness at least two characteristic elements, *a heaped-up measure of good, and unending duration.* These elements are thoroughly wanting in all the varied joys this earth affords. Mundane or incomplete happiness has inseparably linked with itself a twofold curse. While it fills one corner of a man's heart with pleasure, it fills another with pain. Its near departure haunts its possessor like a spectre. Partial pain and possible loss are ingredients of all the happiness with which this earth is acquainted; and no amount of reasoning, no amount of care can quite eradicate them. St. Augustine, insisting on its fulness, thus describes complete happiness, *"That man is happy who has all that he wants, and wants only what he can have without sin."* Complete happiness is, therefore, an unending round of delights, in which no legitimate craving goes unfulfilled, in which no illegitimate craving has existence. This is *perfect bliss.* Philosophers besides recognize an inferior sort of blessedness, which for clearness' sake they call *imperfect bliss.* It is the only sort of incomplete happiness, truly deserving the name, this present life affords; *and it consists in a close union with our last end by the establishment of moral rectitude in our actions.* It is peace of conscience, it is holiness, it is the inheritance of the saints. It is the initial step in our progress towards complete happiness, or perfect bliss; and, while haunted with the fear of loss and mingled with misery, wretchedness and pain, it procures in the grand total of blessings and ills a preponderance of blessings. Philosophers likewise distinguish between *objective or material happiness, and subjective or formal happiness.* The first, or objective, is the object or thing, whose presence fills out man's every desire, God. The second, or subjective, is the actual possession of that object or thing. The first is called the end *which;* the second, the end *in which.* The definition quoted from Boethius tallies exactly with subjective complete happiness.

Of His Very Nature. This longing for happiness is therefore a natural craving, *and things may be natural to man in either one of two ways. They may be born and live with him in a manner entirely independent of his free will, or they may be in strict accord with his nature, and yet entirely dependent on his free choice for their existence within him.* The desire of which we at present speak is natural to man in the first way. It is a necessity of his nature, it cannot be schooled out of his thoughts, it cannot be shaken off or gotten rid of. It is as much a part of the man as upward motion is part of fire's essence. *It is different from an acquired desire,* which may of course be natural to man in the second way. Marriage is usually alleged by writers on the subject as an instance of something natural to man, with full dependence on his own free choice.

Desires. Many in their folly miss the proper means to make good this desire. Many seek its accomplishment in very dubious occupations, in pleasures decidedly illegitimate, and are sadly disappointed in their expectations. But, as it is possible of fulfilment, it must be within man's reach. There must be a line of conduct unfailingly able to lead to its consummation. It can never happen that complete happiness will fail him, who honestly does his utmost to win it, and steadily keeps his record clean of fault and defect.

No Created Good. The assertion is sweeping, and excludes from the dignity of man's last end everything but God. In the history of philosophy not a few ancients went astray on this point. *Epicurus* contended that *pleasure* was man's supremest desire, his highest good. He sometimes bestowed a scant praise on virtue, only because opposite vices interfered with the full enjoyment of physical pleasure. *Zeno,* a leader among the stoics, reckoned *wisdom combined with virtue* the summit of man's aspirations. *Aristotle,* the founder of the Peripatetic school, contended for *a union of virtue and pleasure.* It may be noticed that the dignity of last end, or highest good, is ascribed by no one to wealth. Misers alone love wealth for wealth's sake, and misers are not numerous. Practical men of sense regard wealth as only a useful commodity, a means to the acquirement of other blessings more eagerly coveted. As a merely useful good, wealth must of course yield precedence to virtue, pleasure, wisdom, and every good catalogued as either becoming or pleasurable.

Possession of God. In purely ethical discussions theology of course has no place, and statements advanced must be made good without any reference to Holy Scripture, as a source of argument. We Catholics know from our catechism that Heaven is our last end, and we know that Heaven is the accumulation of all good centered in the beatific vision, or closest kind of union with God. Bliss in Heaven consists entirely in seeing God face to face, and this intellectual possession of God, supernaturally accomplished, constitutes man's supremest happiness. Strip the beatific vision of its supernatural qualities, and you have at once the doctrine of philosophy concerning man's last end. Though able to make surmises, philosophy teaches nothing positive regarding the resurrection of the body; but in Psychology we saw how clearly it makes good the immortality of the soul. Therefore, the only possession of God, possible of conception to unaided human thought, is intellectual possession, based on an intimate union of intellect and will with Him.

Last End. This complete happiness, or possession of God, is therefore the ultimate purpose of man's every movement. His proximate and explicit purpose may be limited happiness, but his ultimate and implicit purpose is always complete happiness. Its influence is not always evident, because somewhat below the surface of things; but its influence is none the less present. *It has a twofold value, implicit and explicit.* Thus, when, for instance, knowledge because of its manifold advantages urges the student to labor, the hiding principle is that all-pervading desire of perfect happiness. Love of knowledge merely seems to be the sole motive. Complete happiness has in this case an implicit value, and its efficacy is none the less real than when it explicitly asserts itself.

Proofs I, II, III, IV, V

I. 1st. Complete happiness is the satisfaction of man's every legitimate wish. But man of his very nature desires the satisfaction of his every legitimate wish. Ergo, man of his very nature desires complete happiness.

With regard to the Major. Perfect or finished good is the all important and characteristic element of complete happiness; and since good is subject-matter of the will's legitimate wishes, complete happiness is the satisfaction of man's every legitimate wish. N.B. Nature prompts no illegitimate wish. Perverted passion, wrong prejudices, faulty education are responsible for such wishes.

With regard to the Minor. Man's will would be otherwise doomed to perpetual unrest, and would become an instrument of unending torture.

2nd. Nature, impediments aside, exerts its utmost activity. But human nature or man is capable of desiring complete happiness, and no impediment is conceivable. Ergo, man of his very nature desires complete happiness.

With regard to the Minor. Man's mind is able to grasp the highest truth. His will, to keep equal pace with his mind, must be able to desire the highest good, or complete happiness.

II. Man's last end must have these three qualities: It must be the supremest good, fully equal to all the wants of all his faculties, even vegetative and sensitive. Needless to say, it must satisfy vegetative and sensitive wants eminently, not formally. It must so contain within itself all the good resident in other conceivable ends, that these other ends be only stages in man's progress toward its acquisition. In other words, it must be of such sort, as to attract man's heart of its own single self, and be at the same time the thing of interest in every object of man's desires. It must be the desire of every man's heart, whether formally and explicitly, or materially and implicitly. But complete happiness is the only good answering this description. Ergo, complete happiness is man's last end.

III. A desire with nature for origin and author, cannot be impossible of fulfilment. But man's desire for complete happiness is a desire of this sort. Ergo, it is possible of fulfilment.

With regard to the Major. Denial of this Major would be an open denial of the axiom, that every effect demands a corresponding cause. For the effect, or natural desire, is admittedly alive in every man's bosom, and its cause is assuredly nothing short of at least possibility of fulfilment. Besides, God, the Author of our nature and all its inborn longings, would be, were complete happiness an empty dream, a most consummate torturer and executioner, not the beneficent creator reason requires Him to be.

IV. The good things, proposed by adversaries for man's last end, are signal failures. Thus, a, *physical pleasure* ministers to only senses of the body, and neglects the soul's interests;

b, *physical pleasure* likewise involves pain for some member or organ not actually participating in it, and nearly always threatens harm to the soul;

c, *physical pleasure* is an utter stranger to that endless duration, which is happiness' first requisite;

d, *spiritual delight* is at most an effect of the good we seek, and as such inferior to the good productive of this delight; and, therefore, an impossible last end;

e, *spiritual delight* would then be the motive for search after becoming good; and the becoming and the agreeable would be without distinctive characteristics;

f, *pleasure, whether physical or spiritual,* is change or motion; and man's last end is complete rest;

g, *the wisdom and virtue of this life* leave many things yet to be desired, health, wealth, beauty, strength, long years. Certainly wisdom and virtue, accompanied by these several blessings, are more an incentive to desire than wisdom and virtue, considered apart from them;

h, *pleasure, wisdom and virtue combined,* or the joint possession of all the blessings this earth affords, is so full of conflicting elements, as to be quite out of the question, and impossible of fulfilment;

i, *danger of change, fear of loss, actual loss, gnawing anxiety, toil and a thousand other evils* poison all the good things of this exile, and emphatically forbid man to look for satisfaction or rest in their acquisition;

j, *virtue alone excepted, every other good with which earth is acquainted, even life itself, may without discredit be sacrificed on the altar of patriotism.*

V. 1st. Some good, created or uncreated, is man's last end, or complete happiness. But no created good is equal to the task, and God alone is uncreated good. Ergo, God is man's complete happiness, his last end.

2nd. God, when creating man, necessarily appointed him an end wholly worthy of Himself. But God alone is wholly worthy of God. Ergo, God is the end appointed man, the end established in man's creation. But the end assigned by God to man is man's last end. Ergo, God is man's last end.

3rd. Nothing short of the universal and supreme good can be man's last end. But God alone is the universal and supreme good. Ergo, God, and nothing short of God, is man's last end.

With regard to the Major. Man's last end, from the very nature of things, must be a good, whose possession leaves nothing further to be desired; and universal or supreme good alone enjoys this prerogative.

With regard to the Minor. Were there another universal and supreme good, there would be two gods.

PRINCIPLES

A. Our every desire, if we follow the laws imposed upon us by our Maker, will be abundantly satisfied in the next life. Some of these desires will have their fulfilment *formally,* or exactly as they are shaped. Others, on account of the peculiar circumstances attaching to a future state, will be accomplished, as philosophers say, *eminently,* in a grander way, or *equivalently.* The possession of God will be the sum of our delights, and God is infinite in resources to make up for whatever pleasures our future condition will render impossible. Thus, there will be no eating, no drinking in Heaven; but, apart from the fact that our lower nature will then make no clamor for sweets it now so much covets, God will be able to pour into our souls a measure of happiness, more than able to atone for these paltry losses. Some philosophers think they see, in the completeness of good things involved in this natural desire of happiness, a proof of the future resurrection of the body. They contend that happiness would be incomplete, unless the body somehow shared after death in the joys accorded the soul. But the time-honored distinction between *intensity and extent* is an answer to their difficulty. Unless our Creator could in some way make up in intensity for the loss extent, or number of parts affected by bliss, suffers, the body would surely have to arise, and live forever like the soul, to enjoy its proper reward. Reason throws no light on the body's destiny after death, because, in the event of its total disappearance, though man's happiness would be less in extent, its intensity could be so multiplied, that his loss would become a gain.

B. God, because simple, and therefore without parts, must be known wholly, if known at all. This circumstance is, however, far from rendering it necessary for the blessed in Heaven to know Him totally or exhaustively, or in such a way that nothing in His nature escapes their knowledge. God is infinite, and to know Him totally is the work of an infinite, not a finite intellect like man's. The familiar example of a mountain seen in the distance may serve to elucidate the point. The whole mountain is seen, without being wholly seen.

C. We must in our language guard against making God a means to an end. He is not the instrument, through which we attain to happiness. He is our happiness. He is not a thing designed for our use or commodity, but we are things designed for His glory; and, in furthering His glory, we are filling out our destiny.

D. As a principle of activity, man's intellect is of course finite and limited; but, when the objects, to which man's intellect can reach, are taken into consideration, no finite or limited number can represent them. Because of the limitations inherent in its activity, man's intellect can know God in only a limited way; because of the multitude of objects, to which it can reach, man's intellect can be filled by nothing created, and therefore by God alone. All being is the adequate object of man's intellect, and created being is not all being. Created and uncreated are that, and created is contained in uncreated, or actual unproduced, or God.

E. Between the mind and its object some sort of proportion must have place. But this proportion, or likeness, need not necessarily be that of being, or nature. Proportion of fitness, constituted by the circumstance, that God as a being can fill a place in man's thoughts, is enough.

F. Pleasure is good sought on its own single account, and in this particular resembles a last end. It is not, however, a supreme good, able to satisfy every desire; and, in this particular, pleasure falls away from the requirements of an absolutely last end.

G. Individual men tend towards a last end, not that abstraction called human nature. Pantheists, therefore, are wrong, when they admit the existence of a last end for human nature, and deny last ends in connection with individuals.

H. Man's natural desire for happiness is a something he cannot lose. Its accomplishment, because dependent on the acts of his free will, can readily enough be frustrated.

I. God, pure and simple, is the *material object* of man's thoughts. God, as He assumes shape in man's mind, is the *formal object* of these thoughts. Since, therefore, God is infinite only in Himself, or as material object, man's mind, to have knowledge of Him, need not be infinite. The formal object of a faculty, not its material object, denominates it, puts it in the class of infinites or finites.

J. As long as man obeys the dictates of reason, so long is he tending towards God, if not formally, at least by interpretation. He may not advert to the fact that he is tending towards God, and that would be *formal tendency;* but in substance he is doing what he would do if he formally tended towards God, and this is *tendency by interpretation.*

THESIS III

Man's destiny in this life, his supremest happiness on earth, his relatively last end, consists in drawing closer and closer to his absolutely last end, by the establishment of moral rectitude in his actions. Between good and bad in the moral order, between right and wrong, an essential, intrinsic difference exists. The immediate measure of moral rectitude is the objective order of things, as understood by the intellect; the mediate measure is God's wisdom and goodness. Jouin, 5–19; Rickaby, 109–126.

QUESTION

Man's last end is eternal happiness in the possession of God Life is but a stage in our progress towards God, it is a period of proof or trial. We are from the outset vested with heads, and hearts, and hands; with all the needed light, and courage, and strength, to pursue our appointed journey without mishap. Our supremest happiness here below hinges entirely on our present destiny, and our present destiny is of a complexion with our destiny hereafter. Man's history extends beyond the grave, death is far from closing the record. This present life forms, as it were, the first chapter, the years without end to follow make up the rest of the story. But this first chapter is a thing of the utmost concern, it is a thing of the highest importance. All the succeeding chapters borrow from it their light and shade, with it all succeeding chapters must be fair or hideous. Union with God constitutes complete happiness; and, unless a man's last moments find him close by the ties of righteousness to his Maker, that man can hope for nothing but most wretched misery. Unless a man's every moment finds him struggling towards this happy consummation, misery will not wait till the hour of death to fasten its hold upon him. What for want of a better term we call imperfect misery, is the perpetual lot of the

28

wicked here on earth. The graduated scale of happiness and woe is the same. A life lived in preparation for supreme felicity constitutes imperfect beatitude, the supremest possible on earth. A life lived in preparation for supreme woe constitutes incomplete wretchedness, the most irksome possible on earth.

The comparison is between virtue and vice, and between things inseparably connected with both. Peace of conscience is the one thing inseparably connected with virtue, remorse is the one thing inseparably connected with vice. Wealth, pleasure and honor are inseparably connected with neither virtue nor vice; and must, therefore, be kept out of the comparison. Virtue with these three concupiscences of life is, of course, happier in point of extent or quantity than virtue without them, though their presence fails to affect necessarily the intensity or quality of virtue's happiness. Vice with these three goods of life is less unhappy in point of extent or quantity than vice without them, though their presence never diminishes the annoyance of remorse itself in point of intensity or quality. Poverty, pain and obscurity cannot destroy or diminish peace of conscience; money, pleasure and honor cannot cure or alleviate remorse. And again we are talking of normal minds, wide awake to their condition, with a practical realization of peace and remorse. In this whole business intensity or quality counts for more than extent or quantity. There is more money from the viewpoint of extent or quantity in five one-dollar bills than in a single hundred-dollar bill, and yet everybody knows what way a sensible person would look, if invited to choose. Intensity or quality is what makes the difference. A bad life with all the other goods of earth except virtue is more irksome in point of peace and remorse than a good life without all the other goods of earth; and this is sufficient for our present purpose. Peace of conscience is the hundred-dollar bill, wealth and the other goods of life without virtue are five one-dollar bills. Even if experience failed to bear us out in this statement, philosophy itself is witness that any contrary event would imperil the fitness of things. Preparation, then, for that absorbing union with God, at the root of every human desire, is the limit set by common sense for well directed activity. Virtue is as indispensable to happiness here below as it is to happiness in the world to come; and virtue is moral rectitude, the avoidance of evil, the accomplishment of good.

Unless we close our eyes to the light, and do to death the instincts implanted within us, we cannot mistake vice for virtue, we cannot confound evil with good. Between them there is an impassable chasm. No merely accidental, but an essential difference exists between one and the other. And the standard marking this difference is plain. It is the objective order of things, things as they are, things as they ought to seem to you and to me, things as they shall inevitably seem to you and to me, if we only follow the light vouchsafed us, and cherish conscience for a friend. This standard never shifts place. Styles of dress change with the season, the etiquette of to-day is other than that of our forefathers; but the measure of moral rectitude is the same to-day, yesterday and forever. It is founded on the goodness and wisdom of God, and partakes of their immutability.

TERMS

Destiny. End, when viewed as a something imposed on another by one in a position to exercise this prerogative, is called destiny. Man's last end is an inheritance of his nature, and as such proceeds from the author of nature, God. Its fulfilment is a law of nature, and the initial step towards the same, or the right ordering of his life, may with justice be called his destiny.

Happiness on Earth. We speak at present of incomplete, or imperfect happiness, which consists wholly in the fact that the sum of blessings enjoyed outweighs the sum of evils endured, considering only the blessings and evils inseparably connected with virtue and vice, with intensity not extent for standard.

Moral rectitude. Rectitude is straightness, and the figure of speech at the root of the word fits the thought. Moral rectitude is the shortest distance between two points, our present condition and the felicity of bliss eternal. Its duties lie along a path that never winds to right or left, but keeps straight on. Measured by its requirements, a man's exact position in the matter of living up to his destiny is easily and readily discernible. Morality is the badge of human nature. *A moral act necessarily calls for an intellect and a will in the agent.* Intellect and will in an agent necessarily call for moral acts. *Acts are first said to be moral, and then good or bad in the moral order.* They are moral from the mere circumstance that they have their origin in an enlightened reason, and a will free in its activity. They are good or bad, they derive their righteousness or their malice from their agreement with or divergence from some set standard. *This standard is primarily for us the objective order of things.* When an act falls away from this standard, it is bad; when it covers the standard, as the rule covers a straight line, the act is good. Men's minds of course differ, and allowance must be made for differences of views sanctioned by Providence. But no believer in God's wisdom, and power, and truthfulness, can for a moment suspect that men's minds in normal condition can confound evil with good, vice with virtue. Had God so constructed intellect, He would be inviting confusion into the universe of morality, He would be cursing our race more heavily than if He allowed the stars to drop from their places, the sun to depart from its course, and baleful comets to run hither and thither at random in the sky. Of course there are intellects, dependent on diseased organs, capable of confounding black with white; but these are beside the purpose. *Philosophy deals with what is the general rule, not with exceptions.* She discusses men taken from the busy walks of life, she does not go to madhouses for subjects. Neither does she pretend to make models of conduct the lives of unfortunates, who would be in strait-jackets, if the madhouse had its due. There is, however, such a thing as subjective morality; and we must recognize the part it plays in the affairs of life. But, be it remarked and well understood that *there is in truth no such thing as subjective morality, pure and simple.* My way of thinking, your way of thinking, when they fail to square with the objective order of things, are what I mean by subjective morality, pure and simple; and that kind of morality is a contradiction in terms. Such morality is as little deserving of the name as purely subjective adhesion to a false statement is deserving of the name of certainty. Certainty of that kind is perverse stubbornness, has no part with the truth, and is more lamentable than thorough uncertainty or ignorance. Even so, my way of thinking, your way of thinking, if not what they ought to be, are indications of either monstrous iniquity or ignorance. I can by repeated assaults on conscience reduce it to comparative silence, I can by repeated abuse of the light, set up within my bosom, practically extinguish it, I can by constant contact with men given over to a reprobate sense put on their ways, assume their habits of thought, and sin almost without remorse. But I cannot, no man can, make wrong right. No man can by any process of thought make the crooked line of wickedness identical with the straight line of virtue.

The man with a moral squint was either born that way, and took no pains to cure the defect, or acquired the habit later in life by repeated acts of disloyalty to conscience. If he was born that way, and honestly tried without any success to better himself, he is a moral imbecile, an idiot, and irresponsible. If he acquired the habit, he is a monster of iniquity; he has put himself into a hole from which he will never, perhaps, rise; and he is clearly responsible, indirectly or in cause, for every wrong he does the laws of morality. This *subjective morality* is a modification, extrinsic and superadded to the action of which there is question. It depends for all its force on the intention, and therefore the knowledge of the agent. It differs entirely from *objective morality*, which resides wholly in the deed done, which is a something intrinsic and essential to that deed, and is entirely independent of the agent's intention and knowledge. *One is morality of the man, the other is morality of his acts;* and, as a man is not good unless his acts are good, subjective morality of itself without objective morality is worth nothing.

And here new questions arise, those of *responsibility and merit*. The man whose morality is purely subjective, who does wrong without scruple, may be in one of three classes. He may be an idiot, and is no more responsible for his acts than brute animals. He deserves no reward for whatever is virtuous in his conduct; he deserves no blame for what would be in another highly reprehensible. He may be the victim of ignorance in no way imputable to him, of ignorance that can with no amount of reasonable endeavor be shaken off. In this case, if any such exists, he is again irresponsible for his condition, and for all the wrong it occasions. In neither of these two cases do the acts elicited cease to be immoral or wicked from an objective standpoint. Objective morality is something outside the agent's power, and no ignorance, no idiocy can destroy or change it. Of course the insane and the grossly ignorant are not responsible before the sovereign Judge for their deeds; but responsibility, imputability and demerit are not morality, and should not be confounded with it. Last of all, a man may be the willing victim of ignorance, that he could have easily remedied at some point in his downward career, that he on the contrary fostered and encouraged by every means at his disposal. Such ignorance is of course inexcusable; and purely subjective morality, or immorality, based on it is deserving of condign punishment.

By way of summary, therefore, we maintain that subjective morality of itself, without objective morality for foundation, is nothing. Subjective morality, combined with invincible ignorance, is of weight in moral questions; but such subjective morality is not subjective morality considered in itself. Invincible ignorance makes a wrong conscience right, it never makes an objectively evil act objectively good. The man's intellect is inculpably wrong, his will is right. His will embraces what his intellect represents as right, and the settlement of what is right and wrong, subjectively speaking, is with the intellect, not with the will. The cases in which subjective morality, or the agent's intention, can justify or condemn a course of conduct, are limited to such sort of acts as are indifferent in themselves to the denominations good and bad. Thus, walking is a healthful exercise for the legs, and depends entirely on purpose and circumstances for its morality. If a man uses his legs on an errand of robbery, walking becomes for him morally culpable. If he uses them on an errand of mercy, or for purposes of worship in the church, walking becomes a virtue. Wilful murder of the innocent will forever continue to be a crime, no matter what view deluded men take of the thing. Wilful murder of the guilty by any man or body of men, not vested with the right of life and death, resident in the State, will never be any-

thing short of murder. Lynching, for instance, is on the face
of the thing immoral. Circumstances may indeed render its
authors more or less responsible for their sin. Zeal for law
and order may palliate the crime, a spirit of indignation may
fan men's minds to a fury, and rob them for the time being
of common-sense; but their method of procedure is wrong,
and no amount of zeal, no degree of excitement, no influence
of early education can utterly transform the nature of things,
and invest crime with the properties of virtue, though invincible ignorance or insanity can free the criminal from
blame.

An Essential Difference. This is opposed to an *accidental
difference.* Another name for the same thing is an *intrinsic
difference,* as opposed to *extrinsic.* The difference between
good and bad is *essential,* inasmuch as no power can remove
this quality from good and bad actions. It is *intrinsic,* inasmuch as the acts denominate themselves, independently of all
outside interference. This difference would be *merely accidental,* if it were not wrapped up in the very being of the act;
if it could, the act remaining to all intents and purposes
identically the same, be present to it to-day and absent from
it to-morrow. It would be *merely extrinsic,* if it owed its
whole force to something foreign to the act. Some philosophers, whatever their motive, have seen fit to set up a merely
accidental and extrinsic difference betweeen good and evil.
Thus, *Hobbes, Rousseau and Hegel contended that civil law is
the standard of morality. Saint Lambert and Montaigne
thought public opinion and tradition the rule. Von Hartmann ascribed everything to the stage of evolution compassed
by individual consciences.* We are ready with good grace to
grant that these several standards are immense helps towards
detecting the difference between right and wrong. Civil
law, for instance, though not very universal in its applications, though it leaves untouched many emergencies liable to
occur in a man's daily conduct, is nevertheless uniformly fair
in its enactments, and draws a sharp line between good and
bad. Public opinion can generally be trusted, tradition is an
abundant source of correct moral notions, and conscience when
free from bias is unerring. But these measures are all open
to serious objection on more scores than one. *They are too*

limited in extent. They are too much subject to change. They are too liable to shift with the whims and fancies of fickle and unstable men. They are entirely subjective, and deliver over to the empire of man responsibilities, more dreadful than he can with justice be expected to acquit himself of, vesting him with God's prerogative as sole arbiter of right and wrong. Morality, unless it rests on the very nature of things, is settled on altogether too uncertain a foundation.

Immediate Measure. The measure nearest to hand for practical use. *The mediate measure* is the more remote, more difficult of access, the last reason and final support of the immediate measure, the model according to which the immediate measure is shaped. Room of Measures in the Tower of London, and measures throughout the kingdom can serve for illustration.

Objective Order of Things. Order is defined, *"the arrangement of two or more units according to certain definite relations."* The order spoken of in the thesis is *moral order, not physical;* the units composing it are *moral beings, with intellect and free will, God and men.* This moral order is twofold, *objective and subjective.* The first depends altogether on things themselves, the second adds to the first the further circumstance of reception into an intellect. The objective order of things is something established by nature, or more properly by the Author of nature. Subjective order is objective order grasped and recognized by the mind, or knowledge of things based on the relations in force between the multiplied moral units of creation. Thus, one element of objective order is the place God occupies towards men in the universe. This order, the very nature of things, requires that men acknowledge and worship God. His prerogatives as first cause and last end can be satisfied with nothing short of that twofold homage. Parents are such by nature that order is disturbed, unless children pay them the reverence, obedience and deference due their station. An innocent man has an inalienable right to his life, and only the rankest kind of disorder would refuse to respect his right. But this objective order would be of little avail as a rule of conduct, unless it became part and parcel of a man's intellectual wares by entering his mind. Hence, the standard of morality in its completeness, is said to be *the objective order of things as understood by the intellect.*

God's Wisdom and Goodness. God's wisdom, as far as we are at present concerned, is the mind of God made manifest to us in creation. His goodness is His will made manifest to us in the same mirror.

Proofs I, II, III

I. a, Man's destiny in this life consists in drawing closer and closer to his last end.

b, His destiny is made good by the establishment of moral rectitude in his actions.

c, This moral rectitude constitutes man's supremest happiness on earth.

a, This life and the future life are integral parts of man's whole duration. Ergo, man's destiny in this life should be as far as possible identical with that of his future life. But man's destiny in the life to come is complete happiness, or the secure enjoyment of God forever; and the only condition resembling this final state, and at present possible to man, is incomplete happiness, or a closer and closer union with his last end. Ergo, man's destiny in this life consists in drawing closer and closer to his last end.

b, Near union with God, as man's last end or destiny in this life, 1st, ought to imply man's highest perfection; 2nd, ought to be something in man's power; 3rd, ought to contribute its share towards the consummation of nature's universal end. But such is the establishment of moral rectitude in man's actions. Ergo, man's destiny in this life is the establishment of moral rectitude in his actions.

With regard to the Major. 1st, Because every end implies the agent's good, the last end implies the agent's highest good. 2nd, Because man is free, and the working out of his destiny must depend on his own efforts. 3rd, Because man is a unit in nature, and God's wisdom makes it necessary for the units in nature to work together in harmony.

With regard to the Minor. 1st, Man's highest good affects what is noblest in man, his reason; reason's most perfect work is order; and moral rectitude or virtue is a life in harmony with objective order. 2nd, Gifts of body like health, wealth, beauty, are independent of our wishes; but moral rectitude is the man's own handiwork. 3rd, Creatures inferior to man work unto their ends by nature, or instinct, and necessarily; man works unto his end by the use of free will, with full liberty; and so completes the graded scale of being in the universe.

c, Man's supremest happiness on earth consists in this, that in the sum total of evil and good, good preponderates. But moral rectitude in a man's life procures this result. Ergo, moral rectitude constitutes man's supremest happiness on earth.

With regard to the Minor. Apart from the fact that there are higher joys than delights of the body, just men are always the least unhappy. They own a peace the world knows not. Their wills are developed in the right direction by constant exercise in the pursuit of good. Their minds are sharpened by intellectual employment. They escape all the penalties of the law. They are strangers to the annoyance of remorse. They are free from the pains, diseases and early death that wickedness often engenders.

Confirmation. The happiness born of moral rectitude, is a figure and shadow of the happiness the blessed enjoy in Heaven. Ergo.

II. 1st, Were there no essential and intrinsic difference between right and wrong, there would be no acts essentially and intrinsically right and wrong. But many such acts in reality exist. Ergo, between right and wrong an essential and intrinsic difference exists.

With regard to the Minor. Love of God is an act essentially and intrinsically right. It is right now, it was always right, and will forever continue to be right, even if the whole world entered into a conspiracy to call it wrong. Hatred of God is in precisely the same way an act essentially and intrinsically wrong.

2nd, Right and wrong have characteristics essentially different. Ergo, between right and wrong an essential difference exists.

With regard to the Antecedent. From proof of next part it will appear, that right is harmony with the objective order

of things; and wrong, absence of this harmony. Harmony
and discord are essentially different.

III. *a, immediate measure; b, mediate measure.*

a, 1st, Acts are right, when in perfect agreement with the
dictates of reason; acts are wrong, when beside these dictates.
But the dictates of reason are objective order, as understood
by the intellect.   Ergo, the immediate measure of moral rectitude is the objective order of things, as understood by the
intellect.

With regard to the Major.   Reason is the guide vouchsafed
to man by God for his safe conduct, and reason's dictates are
the rule of morality.

With regard to the Minor.   Not to be a purely subjective
standard, the dictates of reason must be founded on the objective order of things.   Otherwise the dictates are vagaries
and hallucinations.

N.B.   The dictates of reason are moral obligations an-
nounced by reason, the herald of the Natural Law, and they
get fuller consideration in our next thesis.   They are practical judgments, not mere speculative statements, and always
involve moral necessity or strict obligation, denoted by the
word "must" or "ought."   God must be worshipped, parents must be obeyed.   "Must" means moral obligation or
necessity, not physical.   Free agents as such are incapable of
physical.   *Moral obligation means moral necessity of putting
or omitting a physically free act, absolutely required for the
procurement of a good absolutely necessary for the man in
the moral order.*   This good is his last end.   Moral obligation
arises *from objective order and divine command together.*
Kant derives it from objective order alone without God, and
this is what his *categorical imperative* in substance means.
Moral obligation arises *in part from objective order,* because
virtue is way to last end, and virtue is harmony with objective
order.   Not every good act is necessary to last end, but only
such good acts as cannot be omitted without detriment to objective order, and reason acquaints us with them.   Moral
obligation arises *in part from divine command,* because God
alone as Creator is empowered to set man a last end, tie him
with a perfect moral bond and give him by way of source and
origin virtue and every other perfection.

2nd, Right and wrong proceed from harmony and disagreement with nature; and the immediate measure of moral rectitude is what primarily enables us to distinguish with certainty between them. But to distinguish is to know, and this harmony and disagreement with nature can reach our knowledge only through the intellect, understanding things just as they are, or the objective order of things. Ergo, the immediate measure of moral rectitude is the objective order of things, as understood by the intellect.

With regard to the Minor. Nature means things as God made them, things just as they are, the objective order of things.

3rd, *Rejection of other standards. Not public opinion,* because opinion is rather measured by our standard; opinion is uncertain, changeable and unsafe. *Not civil law,* because law is rather measured by our standard; law cannot make certain acts good, certain acts bad.

b, The mediate measure of morality is that on which the immediate measure depends. But its immediate measure, the objective order of things, depends on the wisdom and goodness of God. Ergo, the mediate measure of moral rectitude is God's wisdom and goodness.

With regard to the Minor. All creation, signified by the objective order of things, proceeds from the wisdom and goodness of God.

PRINCIPLES

A. Man's supreme happiness is absence of pain, sickness, sorrow. *Answer.* Man is made up of body and soul. His body, or sense-appetite, seeks agreeable good, like animals, by instinct; his soul, or rational appetite or will, seeks becoming good, desirable in itself, without heed to pain and sorrow, when opposed to becoming good. Soul surpasses body, and man's will is man's highest faculty in the order of morality.

B. Senses ought to be consulted in this life. *Answer.* Complete happiness is impossible in this life. Man's highest good appeals to what is spiritual within him, because intelligence is his specific characteristic. When sense wars against reason, it must be repressed. Deficiencies will be more tolerable, if in the domain of sense. Of course, the less pain, the better; the more at ease the sense, the better; provided only that reason, or the spiritual element in man, suffers thereby no detriment. If pain of sense, want of bodily comfort, sorrow of soul, contribute to progress in morality, they are to be welcomed with the enthusiasm of fortitude.

C. Fear of loss is compatible with incomplete happiness, not with complete.

THESIS IV

A natural law, unchangeable, universal, eternal, has place in men; its complete and full sanction is reserved for the next life; and eternal punishment is not opposed to God's goodness. This natural law is the foundation and corner-stone of all positive law. Jouin, 36–48; Rickaby, 133–177.

QUESTION

We are now satisfied, that the promotion of morality's interests in himself and others, is man's present destiny. For the happiness, which righteousness alone can purchase for him, is the nearest possible approach to complete bliss this earth knows. It makes of life a veritable antechamber to a blessed eternity; it leads a man right up to the threshold of God's presence; and God's enduring presence is the ne plus ultra of man's hopes and desires. We are likewise the happy possessors of a standard sound and true, which will infallibly enable us to detect the ever present difference between right and wrong. The objective order of things, as grasped by the intellect, is our measure; and we feel secure in our position. For, in trusting our lot to this rule or measure, we are ultimately leaning on the wisdom and goodness of an all-wise and beneficent God.

But here a difficulty arises. We know that a shadow and image of complete happiness will result to us from steady compliance with the exactions of morality. We know that any falling away from rectitude will be visited with punishment, such at least that our days will be more acquainted with woes than with blessings. Incomplete happiness attaches to virtue; incomplete misery, to vice. But beyond this we are at sea. Unless we establish in this matter of morality the living presence of law, framed and backed by a being of high authority, rectitude becomes a thing of mere taste, choice between incomplete happiness and incomplete misery, its obli-

41

gations are trivial indeed, because self-imposed. Some philosophers venture an answer to the difficulty by setting up what they call *the autonomy of reason*. *They follow Kant.* They wish wickedness, pure and simple, to be its own full chastisement, and virtue its own reward. In other words, they want no external influence whatever brought to bear on man, in the problem of mapping out his conduct. They want the disgust experienced in deeds of crime, the mind's ill-ease, to be sole bar to the commission of wrong. They would recognize no sin but that superior airy sort of transgression styled philosophic. Theological sin, and the unrest it occasions by fear of some personal avenger, they cry down, and declare creatures of superstitious imagination. But the autonomy of reason is an afterthought of godlessness, and has atheism for single excuse. As a system, if reduced to practice, it would in one generation involve the world in moral ruin. If reason were its own law, and judge, and headsman, our cities would soon teem with cutthroats, thieves and assassins. They are not a polite crew, and the shock their better instincts experience, when engaged in wrong-doing, hardly restrains their hands. The noise made by mere consciousness of being out of harmony with nature, makes them lose no very appreciable amount of sleep. Such sanction might possibly exert a check on high-strung, very correct dispositions; but it would never reach the multitude in anything like an effective way.

Law alone, with its tremendous sense of obligation, with its terrifying dread of penalty, can hold our race to the observance of right and the avoidance of wrong. And God would be doing mankind an incalculable injury, He would be raining down evils upon our heads, did He not step into the breach as a legislator, and confirm us in rectitude by law and all the vast machinery of retributive sanction. Were man responsible to himself only for his misdeeds, he would escape with scant justice, and would deny himself in nothing. It is our business to prove that mere knowledge of wrong done, and the confusion springing from such knowledge, are not morality's naked sanction. We have to establish the existence of a law, born with the man, imperatively ordering the fulfilment of all justice, imperatively forbidding the accomplishment of any evil. We intend to vindicate to this law characteristics wholly its own, ranking it high above all the enactments of human positive law. We intend, further, to make good by positive argument the nature of its sanction, and show that it is the root, foundation and support of all positive law. Unless a man approaches the work of introducing rectitude into his conduct with the deepest respect for natural law, and with a live consciousness of its obligations, he is not fully equipped for the task imposed upon him by nature, and will inevitably miss his destiny. Hence the importance, the necessity, of setting these notions on a firm basis, of demonstrating their objective value, and placing it beyond the reach of dispute and cavil.

TERMS

Natural Law. Law, taken in its widest sense, is a standard or rule of action, directive of the agent to its proper end. The following table presents at a glance the various possible kinds of law.

Law, 1)
In widest sense, 2)
In less wide sense, 3)
In strict and proper sense, 4)
Divine, 5)
Human, 6)
Eternal, 7)
Natural, 8)
Positive, 9)
Ecclesiastical, 10)
Civil, 11)

1) The word *law* is a derivative from the Latin *ligare,* to bind; and invariably suggests the idea of *obligation.*

2) Standard or rule of action, *directive of agent to proper end.* E.g., laws of nutrition, &c., &c. Applicable not only to man and beasts, but to dead matter as well.

N.B. Action, or motion, from without is not life.

3) Standard or rule, *directive of artistic efforts.* E.g., laws

of painting, sculpture, poetry, oratory. Applicable to beings endowed with intellect, and therefore to man alone.

An ordinance founded on right reason, drawn up and promulgated for the common good by him who has charge of the community affected. Applicable to moral acts alone, to acts proceeding from an intellect and a free will. This definition is taken bodily from St. Thomas, Summa Theol. 1. 2; Q. 90; a. 4. *All four causes, material, formal, final and efficient, enter into its composition.* It separates law from every conceivable notion resembling the same. It observes due bounds, and keeps law within its own limits. On account of these several qualities the definition is all that can be desired, and commends itself to everybody. Thus, the *matter of law* is derived from principles vouched for by *right reason.* No other rule can be of binding force on men possessed of intellects. This is so true that a clearly unreasonable law is no law at all. It may be well, however, to remark that, commonly speaking, the only safe position to occupy in this matter is voiced in that saying of moralists, *"In doubt acquiescence in the will of the superior is a duty."* The care of a community is so complex a thing, affected by circumstances so far above the understanding and appreciation of individuals governed, that the superior alone, with multiplied advantages at his disposal, and a clear vision of intricate details, can best judge what ruling the exigencies of the case demand. He alone knows best the wants of his empire. He alone knows best what good results, in the long run, this or that enactment will, in spite of appearances to the contrary, effect. His practised eye is accustomed to look at things from a higher plane. Individuals in the state look not beyond personal convenience and inconvenience, and would, perhaps, in their selfishness little reck what fate befell the government, if only they escaped unhurt from the ruins. Hence, they are wide awake to detect in every new ruling some semblance of injustice. Men are born rebels, and are apt to be prejudiced judges, when passing on a law that interferes with their privileges, or cuts down the measure of their liberties. They easily lose sight of the circumstance, that legislation is primarily for the community's benefit; that the individual must on occasions retire into the background, and submit to the indignity of being trampled upon, just to push the community's interests to the front. Hence, a law is not to be set aside the very first moment a cry of injustice is raised against it. It must be viewed on all sides, its practical workings must be followed down to their minutest details, and the common good, not private advantage, must be the standard of measurement. If, however, it plainly offends against the demands of right reason, it can be rated no law at all, and neglected as such. *A law is not a precept.* The former affects equally the whole community, the latter is restricted to this or that individual. The distinction between the two is brought out in the definition. Of course law is binding, only when it proceeds from a legitimate source, *from the representative of authority,* who alone enjoys legislative rights, as means to the discharge of his duties. *Due promulgation* may be called a necessary *property of law.* Law is intended for human beings; and, as knowledge is the mainspring of all their deliberate acts, knowledge of the law must precede its fulfilment. This necessary condition must not be understood to run counter to that common saying in the courts, "Ignorance of the law is no excuse." A law may be thoroughly well promulgated, and yet escape the notice of stray members in the community. *Promulgation means simply advertisement sufficiently public and widespread to catch the attention of citizens blessed with the ordinary amount of prudence and care.* It by no means ensures knowledge of the law to such as are too ignorant or too indifferent to help themselves. *Sanction,* too, capable of frightening off violators, and creating in men a salutary respect for the law, is considered a requisite for every enactment meant to be seriously taken.

5, *Divine law* has God for author, and that too in an immediate sense. All law proceeds from God as origin. It is strictly divine, only when God is its framer, whether He accomplishes everything by Himself solely, or uses man as His mouthpiece.

6, *Human law* is framed by man without immediate interference on the part of God.

7, *Eternal law.* St. Augustine, contra Faustum, 122, c. 27., offers this definition, *"God's reason or will commanding the*

preservation of natural order, forbidding its disturbance."
God is the supreme Lord of nature. He is King, with the
universe for throne, and all the creatures of the universe for
subjects. He is, therefore, a legislator as well; and His
kingdom is under the sway of laws chosen and appointed by
Himself. But He is unchangeable, and what He is to-day,
He was and is from all eternity. This code of laws, therefore,
for the government of His creatures, had been in His thoughts
endless ages of ages before creation proceeded from the
strength of His hands. Every lawmaker first submits to his
mind for approval, whatever enactments he intends to later
on promulgate. He likewise lays before his will tentative
drafts of the same, for rejection or adoption. And, when the
work of inspection is over, he stands ready to acquaint the
world with his wishes. Barring whatever imperfection clings
to this method of procedure, God is no exception to the rule in
its fundamental points. The laws that now govern nature
were first passed upon by His wisdom, and constitute in that
stage of the process what we call eternal law.

§ *Natural law, objectively taken,* that is, viewed with reference to the source from which it proceeds, is eternal law in
its application to man, or become evident in rational nature;
it is man's half of God's eternal law. *Subjectively taken,* that
is, viewed with reference to man, it is *an inborn habit of
mind, enabling a man to detect the harmony or discord in
force between the notions that constitute morality's first principles.* By principles of morality we here mean statements
vouched for by reason, and indicative of right and wrong.
These principles are various, and are rated in importance
according to their different degrees of cogency. Thus, *first or
primary principles* are such as have in their favor the clearest
kind of evidence, and are so plain that even at first sight no
man of ordinary common sense can doubt their accuracy.
Instances are, "Man must do good and avoid evil; Man must
lead an orderly life; God must be loved." Principles of this
first class can under no conceivable supposition become void
of effect or untrue, and they admit of no ignorance, vincible or
invincible. And all this, simply because the above statements,
on account of relations intervening between subject and predicate, contain necessary truths. *Principles, immediately and*

with little effort derived from these first or primary principles, constitute a second class. The ten commandments of the Decalogue are said to be laws of this second class. Some writers except the third, because it singles out the Sabbath. These principles admit of vincible not invincible ignorance. *Finally, a third place is occupied by principles, flowing indeed from first or primary and secondary principles, but in a somewhat hidden and obscure way.* They become evident only after mature consideration, and on this account, perhaps, are thoroughly well grasped by only the learned. Polygamy and divorce are examples, alleged by some authors, of laws contained in this third class. These last principles admit of even invincible ignorance.

Eternal law provides for physical and moral order alike; natural law, because meant for men, provides for moral order alone. Substitute moral order for natural order in St. Augustine's definition of eternal law, add promulgated or made manifest in the light of reason, and you have at once natural law objectively taken. Objectively, then, natural law is a divine command issuing from God's reason or will, prescribing the preservation of moral order, forbidding its disturbance. *Natural law objectively taken* is natural law as it exists in God, its maker; subjectively taken, it is natural law as it exists in man, the person it affects or binds. *Subjectively taken,* natural law is an inborn habit of mind, enabling man to know what he must do and what he must avoid. Man must do only what is in harmony with moral objective order, he must avoid what is at discord with the same order; and we already proved that this objective order is the measure of morality. He must, therefore, be able to detect this harmony and discord, and natural law is the means put at his disposal by God. Natural law objectively taken is made up of what we call morality's first principles, commands issuing from the reason or will of God; each of the principles, like all judgments, contains a subject and predicate, and the harmony or discord the natural law subjectively taken helps the mind to detect is between these subjects and predicates in morality's first principles. Instances are, God is a person who must be worshipped by man. Parents are persons who must be obeyed by their children. Worship is in harmony with God, the creator. Obedience is in harmony with parents, makers and guides. Killing is at discord with innocent persons. Taking is at discord with what belongs to another. Untruth is at discord with the purpose of language.

These principles of morality are not mere speculative statements, they are practical judgments, with a must or an ought. *The harmony or discord is between the subject and predicate, the must or ought is from the divine command prescribing to human nature the preservation of order, forbidding its disturbance.* This is right or this is wrong, is a mere speculative statement; this ought to be done, or this ought to be avoided, is a practical judgment. Mind is not the maker of the natural law, but its herald. God is its maker, man is its subject, and his mind helps him to a knowledge of it, much as the medium that advertises state legislation. In this sense the natural law is said to be written or printed in the mind or heart of man. Therefore principles of morality are practical judgments vouched for by reason, and indicative of right and wrong.

"Do good and avoid evil," is the one first principle by excellence of the natural law, because it implicitly contains the whole law, and because from it all a man's duties are derivable. Other principles are variously classified by various authors *as first, second and third principles; as primary, secondary and remote conclusions from both; as immediate, proximate and remote.* First, primary and immediate admit of no ignorance, vincible or invincible; second, secondary and proximate admit of vincible ignorance; third principles and remote conclusions admit of even invincible ignorance. In every principle of the natural law the predicate is somehow contained in the subject. Otherwise some principles of the natural law would be false. In first or primary principles the predicate is contained in the subject, and its presence cannot be missed by normal minds; it can be seen at a glance. In second or secondary principles the predicate can be discovered in the subject with ease, with small or no study. In third principles or remote conclusions the discovery is made with difficulty and at the expense of considerable study.

Worship of God is a prescription of the natural law. Worship of God in general, without any qualifications, is a primary principle; external worship is a secondary principle; and worship on the Sabbath, as distinct from other days of the week, can be called a remote conclusion from the other two principles. No ignorance, vincible or invincible, regarding the need of worship in general is possible. Ignorance regarding the need of exterior worship is possible, but always vincible and inexcusable. Invincible ignorance regarding worship on the Sabbath is easily conceivable. Lies are forbidden by the natural law. The prohibition against lies in general, without any qualifications, is a primary principle. "Thou shalt not lie," is a secondary principle easily deduced from the first; and it leaves room for vincible ignorance. Thou shalt not lie, to save an important secret, to avert war, to prevent murder, is a remote conclusion deducible with some difficulty from primary and secondary, and it admits of even invincible ignorance. Theft and murder are against the natural law. Avoid theft, avoid murder are primary principles. Thou shalt not steal, thou shalt not kill are secondary principles. Thou shalt not steal from motives of kindness to the poor, from motives of religion or piety, to get an education, is a remote conclusion from primary and secondary. Thou shalt not kill at the request of your victim, to do your victim a favor, to benefit the race, to send your victim to Heaven, to propagate the true religion, is a remote conclusion from primary and secondary.

The nature or substance of the act forbidden by natural law suggests this other division. *Some principles turn on acts bad in themselves, on their own account, absolutely, in a way independent of every outside consideration.* Instances are, hatred of God, blasphemy, idolatry, a lie. *Others turn on acts bad in themselves, not on their own account, but on account of a violated right involved in the act itself; not absolutely, but conditionally; not independently, but with dependence on the right in question.* Instances are, theft and murder. *Others again turn on acts bad in themselves, not on their own account, but on account of moral risk or danger involved in the act.* Instances are, polygamy, divorce, heretical and impure reading. Things wrong the first way admit no change of matter and are always and everywhere wrong. Things wrong the second and third ways admit change of matter; and, the change made, they cease to be wrong. God can take away the right involved or the owner can lose it. God can remove the risk and danger or a proportionate cause can justify the risk or danger.

In their attempts to explain God's approval of polygamy in the Old Law, writers experience trouble, and have recourse to various interpretations of natural law. *One school recognizes three different types of precepts urged by the natural law.* These types are much the same in nature as the precepts just explained, and are called *most universal, remote and more remote; or, with Meyer, primary, secondary and more remote.* Examples are, "Do good, and avoid evil." "Honor thy father and mother." "Be a man of one wife." The Thomists, who insist on this classification, teach that God can dispense with the natural law in precepts of the third class. Suarez objects to the statement, that God is at liberty to dispense with the natural law in any of its enactments. Since we have agreed to regard the natural law as a mere manifestation of the eternal law, his position is well taken; and we hold with him that God in sanctioning polygamy nowise interfered with the operation of the natural law. He procured such a change of circumstances and conditions, that polygamy fell outside of matter under the ban of the natural law.

Another school, to meet the same difficulty, assigns three ways in which things can run counter to the natural law. It is agreed on all sides that natural law forbids whatever is in itself and intrinsically wrong, not merely in its consequences, not in virtue of some outside prohibition, like civil law or the injunction of a parent. Then come the distinctions. A thing, they say, can be in itself and intrinsically wrong in a threefold way. *First, it can be wrong in itself, and absolutely;* like blasphemy, idolatry and lying. The moral disorder in this case is something wrapped up in the physical being of the act. *Secondly, it can be wrong in itself, not on its own account, and not absolutely;* like theft and murder. The moral disorder results not precisely from the physical act, but from the presence of some right connected with it, and violated. The self-same physical act can be entirely blameless, when exerted to come into one's own property, or to kill a criminal condemned by the state to death. *Thirdly, it*

*can be wrong in itself, not on its own account, but on account
of moral risk or danger it involves,* like the perusal of un-
chaste or irreligious literature. The moral disorder results in
this case from the danger to faith and morals attendant on
such reading. With regard to these divisions, it must be
remarked that even natural law has no application, when the
matter of the act undergoes a certain change. Thus, the
forcible removal of what was another's property will cease to
be theft, if the intruder is first invested with a sound claim
to it. The midwives of Israel committed no wrong, when
they carried off the vessels and ornaments of the Egyptians,
simply because God, who is the absolute Lord of everything,
transferred to them through Moses dominion or ownership.
The same remark holds good in the case of an executed criminal. Students of theology and medicine are obliged by their
calling to read books, the mere curious perusal of which
would be highly sinful, and the need of such reading in their
case justifies the risk.

The first of the classes just enumerated includes only such
cases as admit no change of matter. God Himself cannot
render blasphemy, lying, idolatry commendable. With regard to polygamy, all writers grant, and must maintain, that
it is not a crime against the natural law in the first way, and
in the same sense as blasphemy, idolatry and lying. Some
contend that it resembles theft, inasmuch as the woman's
rights are not respected. It must be evident that, were this
supposition true, God could have made polygamy in the Old
Law legitimate by depriving the woman of whatever rights
it would otherwise violate. The most approved writers, however, agree to regard polygamy a wrong against the natural
law, inasmuch as it menaces the well-being of marriage, and so
damages the race in its origin. It is fraught with danger to
the stability and happiness of wedlock, and exposes children
to heavy evils. Discontent, jealousy and attendant quarrels
are, naturally speaking, sure to reign where polygamy is a
recognized practice. God favored the patriarchs and their
wives with dispositions above petty grievances of this sort,
and in removing danger rendered the condition legitimate.

*A third school professes to find all the sinfulness attaching
to polygamy in the single circumstance, that, God's prohibi-*

tion presupposed, the polygamist invades the rights of God, and runs counter to His express wishes. A Catholic eating meat on Friday, would in this supposition be no less an offender against the natural law than the Mormon with a house full of wives. *A fourth school, finally, distinguishes between enactments of the natural law strictly so called, and mere recommendations urged by nature as highly becoming, though not of binding necessity.* They group under enactments of the first class universal maxims, like, "Do good and avoid evil"; conclusions readily and plainly derivable from these maxims, like the Ten Commandments; and precepts ordaining the avoidance of things intrinsically and absolutely bad, like blasphemy. Under recommendations urging the proper they group conclusions derivable after some study from universal maxims, like the statutes against polygamy and divorce; precepts ordaining the avoidance of things bad in themselves, not because of themselves, but because of danger attached, like the perusal of immoral literature.

To choose, now, between the different schools, I venture to think that the explanation offered by the second school is clearest, best defined, and most to the point. Natural law, therefore, is a mandate of reason, ordering the performance of whatever is good intrinsically and in itself, forbidding things intrinsically and in themselves bad. Seeming exceptions made in the Old Law in the cases of Isaac's intended slaughter, the Hebrew midwives, and polygamy among the patriarchs were simply no violations at all of the natural law. God worked a change in the matter on which these acts turned. He invested Abraham with full dominion over his son's life; He transferred to the Hebrew women rights in property that once belonged to the Egyptians; He removed from polygamy all the dangerous abuses that naturally surround such a condition, and so rendered it as salutary and secure as monogamy.

Positive divine law is a decree, proceeding with full freedom from the mind of God, in the interests of common good. The ceremonial prescribed in the Old Law was positive divine law for the chosen people. The utterances in the gospels forbidding absolute divorce and polygamy, are positive divine law in the new dispensation. Natural law is separated from positive divine law by the absence of freedom in the legislator, and by the nature of the promulgation it demands. God is not free to make lying sinful or virtuous, and the same is true of theft, murder, polygamy and divorce, when no change of matter has taken place. While ordaining certain rites and ceremonies for use in His service, He remained entirely free to select some and reject others. The natural law is such that its actual promulgation has place in the very fact of a human being's existence. Up to that hour it is still possessed of what philosophy calls promulgation in aptitude. Knowledge of the natural law escapes a man during the period of infancy, but knowledge of the law must not be confounded with its promulgation. Positive divine law on the contrary has all its effect, only when received by the subject bound to its observance, and necessarily supposes some such subject actually existent, and capable at least of grasping its content. Natural law is a means indispensably necessary to the end of man. Positive divine law is, indeed, a means more or less necessary to man's end, but nohow indispensably necessary. This or that positive divine law need never have existed, and man could still compass his end. This or that positive divine law can at any time cease to exist, without in the least jeopardizing man's final interests.

Natural law is the eternal law in its application to creatures endowed with reason, and as such cannot long remain hidden from an enquiring mind. Its decrees are not inscribed on tablets of stone, or wood, or written pages, but on a man's heart. Its promptings are ever present, and defy forgetting. The light vouchsafed by nature to all her sons is able to convey notions of the natural law, and interpret its dictates. No training in the schools is needed, no labor over long lists of rules and regulations. These features, peculiar to natural law, constitute another vast difference between itself and positive law, whether human or divine. Positive law is of no avail whatever, unless promulgated or brought to man's notice by some such external sign as language, written or spoken. Any body of positive laws can of course include obligations and restrictions already imposed by the natural law. In fact, owing to the weakness inherent in men's minds and wills, it is eminently proper for legislators to insist in clearer terms

on points already defined by the natural law. This method
has a twofold advantage. It makes ignorance less excusable,
and adds to the sanction, already awaiting in the next life
every violence done the natural law, the further punishment
of immediate fine, pain or imprisonment. Law is only then
purely and simply positive, when it decrees things not previously settled by natural law; when it turns on acts, which,
in themselves indifferent, become right or wrong according to
the good pleasure or wishes of a superior. Positive divine
law has God for immediate author. Human positive law
has man for immediate author. This human law is either
ecclesiastical or civil.

10 *Ecclesiastical law is law uttered by the Church.*

11 *Civil law is law uttered by the state; or by him in whose
person the authority of the state resides.*

Unchangeable. The first or primary principles of natural
law are absolutely unchangeable. God Himself cannot reverse them. All its other principles, of an inferior order, are,
strictly speaking, as unchangeable as these first or primary
principles. God, however, as absolute Lord of the universe,
can introduce into the matter, with which these inferior principles are concerned, changes that modify the whole face of
things, and leave no room for the law's application. E.g.,
Isaac, midwives, capital punishment.

*Universal, in a Twofold Sense. It binds all without excep-
tion. It is within the reach of everyone's knowledge.* There
can be no ignorance of primary principles. Whatever ignorance exists regarding secondary principles, is due entirely to
personal and private negligence. It is therefore voluntary,
can be readily overcome, and is utterly inexcusable. Invincible ignorance is conceivable in the case of remote conclusions.
The essence of human nature is the same in all mankind, and
this essence is the foundation of the natural law. We contend merely that the natural law is within easy reach of every
man's knowledge. We by no means maintain that nations
made up of men, whom long centuries of crime have practically changed into beasts, necessarily retain a clear knowledge
of nature's requirements in the matter of morality. Neither
do we intend to prove that natural law is universally observed, or that its principles in their application invariably

fare well. These first principles of morality may be firmly fixed in the minds of a people, and theoretically respected, without at all hindering that people from making serious mistakes in their application and practical employment.

Eternal. It is of as long duration as its counterpart or model, eternal law. It had of course no practical application, until rational creatures appeared on the scene; but the law itself had being from all eternity in the mind of God. No enactment ceases to be a law, simply because actual subjects are wanting to observe it. It is enough if it can later on have such subjects; if, as a matter of fact, it is certainly going to have such subjects at some future period. Eternal law and natural law differ not in point of duration, but in point of subjects. The distinction between the two laws is real and inadequate. In point of subjects from eternity natural law is no worse off than eternal.

Sanction Means Reward or Punishment Fixed by the Lawmaker for the Observance or Violation of His Law. This sanction can be of many kinds. *It is internal,* when the reward or punishment is wholly within the man himself, not due to outside influences. E.g., joy of a good conscience, and remorse. *It is external,* when some outside agent rewards or punishes. E.g., Heaven or hell. With regard to its efficiency, a sanction may be *sufficient or insufficient,* and that too either *absolutely or relatively. It is absolutely sufficient,* when it is of itself motive enough to urge a man in every case to the law's observance. *It is relatively sufficient,* when, of somewhat less force, it avails only to urge certain kinds of men in certain kinds of cases to the law's observance. From this description one can easily derive the notion of absolutely and relatively insufficient sanction. Sanction is, besides, *perfect or imperfect. Perfect,* when the due proportions of justice are kept between a man's deserts and his reward or punishment. When the contrary happens, when sanction falls short of justice, it is called *imperfect.* All sanction has a twofold end or object. It is designed on the one hand to promote the reign of moral order, to keep men to their duty; on the other, to reinstate justice when dethroned by wrong; to discharge the debts of justice, when men deserve well of her by the performance of right. Meyer derives the difference in force between penalties inflicted from the object this or that sanction proposes to itself. All depends, he says, on the order at stake. If punishment is meted out with reference primarily and principally to procuring order in the moral affairs of a private individual, the sanction will consist of pains destined almost wholly to cure and correct. Sanction of this sort is proper to boys receiving instruction at the hands of a tutor, and is called *medicinal*. If punishment is meted out primarily and principally to procure social or political order in the state, the sanction will consist of penalties inflicted almost wholly with a view to avenging social wrongs, and is called *punitive*. The amendment of the transgressor, because the common good is in this case of paramount importance, occupies only a secondary place. It can be entirely neglected, if any attempt to secure it runs counter to the common good. This observation of Father Meyer is eminently correct, and can be of service later on, when the morality of capital punishment is in question.

Next Life. We are far from wishing to deny that violations of the natural law meet with heavy punishment in this life, or that compliance with its precepts has a reward even in this life. Seneca says, Epist. 22, "Wickedness takes a big swallow of its own poison." St. Augustine, Confess. I, "It is thy good pleasure, O Lord, and it is a fact, that every soul out of harmony with right is its own greatest tormentor." We merely hold that the sanction, as a matter of fact attendant on the natural law here below, is wholly inadequate, and far from satisfying the demands of justice. The immortality of the soul is warrant for the reality of a future existence; and reason, apart from revelation, even if solid proofs are wanting, hints darkly at a place of eternal torments. From revelation the prison-house of fire, denominated hell, is an established fact. Philosophy can proceed no farther than prove the need and the compatibility of such a place of torment with God's attributes.

Positive Law. About the justice and binding force of God's positive enactments there can be no controversy. He is infinitely wise, infinitely just, and cannot, in virtue of these two attributes, impose on men obligations lacking any essential or necessary characteristic. His true Church, strengthened by reiterated promises of guidance and assistance, can make no mistake in the field of legislation. But that branch of human positive law denominated civil, because subject to the immediate influence of men, swayed by prejudice and passion, open to moments of forgetfulness and ignorance, can readily enough admit of blunders, and can carry on its records rules and regulations decidedly wrong and opposed to reason. Such laws, as we have already seen, are laws only in appearance, and have in reality no binding force whatever. It may be well, then, to discuss what qualities are needed to render any positive law, notably civil, worthy of consideration, respect and obedience. A law, to be worthy of the name, must, along with due and sufficient promulgation, fulfil certain conditions classified under three heads. *Some affect the lawmaker; others, the matter contained in the law. The lawmaker must be possessed of genuine authority over the persons, for whom he legislates, in points the law touches.* The vitality of all law has its origin in God, and God can seal with His approval only such mandates as proceed from legitimately constituted superiors. *In the matter of its prescriptions the law must be just and possible.* It must be just, because otherwise it would not have natural law for foundation and support. It must be possible, in accordance with that worn truth, "Ad impossible nemo tenetur." "No man is bound to do the impossible." Justice brands as worthless whatever law conflicts with a citizen's higher duty, whatever law is neither necessary nor useful for the common good. Natural law cries out against anything like the sacrifice of a higher duty to lower offices, and the very essence of law, as set forth in its definition, makes the common good an indispensable requisite. The common good must be sought, too, in a fair way. To secure this fairness, the law must with an impartial hand distribute burdens over the whole commonwealth. It must not enrich the wealthy at the expense of the poor. It must not rob the rich, to confirm the idle in their wicked ways. But everything must, as far as possible, be so nicely adjusted that neither the rich, nor the poor, nor the idle can with justice complain. Justice likewise brands as worthless whatever law imposes obligations impossible of fulfilment. Impossibility is either phys-

ical or moral. An obligation is physically impossible of fulfilment, when it simply surpasses the physical strength at a
man's disposal, e.g., a law ordering subjects to push moun-
tains into the sea. It is morally impossible of fulfilment,
when its observance is beyond measure difficult. Liberty can
have no play, when a man's physical force is unequal to some
task assigned; and law without liberty is a dead letter.
Suarez remarks that the difficulty involved in compliance with
voluntary poverty, chastity and obedience, induced God, perhaps, to make these several virtues matter of counsel, not law,
in the new dispensation. Several maxims well worth re-
membering flow as corollaries from the doctrine just made
good. A human enactment at open variance with God's law
is no law at all, and entirely void of value. An enactment
favoring injustice is no law. Rulers have no right to impose
unjust laws on their subjects. *Despotism and absolutism* are
species of government opposed to these maxims; and some
philosophers, untrue to their calling, have upheld systems
favoring these crimes. *Machiavelli,* for instance (1469–1527),
allows the advantage of men in power to usurp the place of
justice. *Hobbes* (1588–1679) is of opinion that supreme authority can make no mistake, incur no blame. *Spinoza* (1632–
1677), because of his pantheistic notions, is guilty of the same
folly. *Rousseau* (1712–1778) attributes to democracy the
prerogatives ascribed by Hobbes to monarchy. *Hegel* and
his followers make the state God, and pass by easy steps to
the absurdity of a public conscience, the standard and rule
of private morality. We who advocate the right are accused
of introducing into public affairs baneful subjectivism, derogatory to the majesty of the law, and subversive of its efficacy.
But the accusation is a vile slander. Our enemies are, on
the contrary, subjectivism's most steadfast allies, they degrade
law to the level of conscienceless bullying, substitute might
for right, and, robbing law of all moral efficacy, arm it with
the force and violence of unprincipled coercion and tyranny.
Our platform rests on the eternal principles of justice, founded
on the eternal law of God, and manifest to man in his reason.
These principles are certainly a more objective reality than
the empty whims and selfish enactments of greedy rulers.
To clothe an unjust enactment with a majesty borrowed from

so sacred a thing as law, is like blasphemy; and to set might over right is to step from civilization to savagery. To avoid mistakes in practice, too much stress cannot be laid on that principle advanced earlier in the course of these remarks, *"In doubt, acquiescence in the will of a superior is a duty."* Duly constituted authority is always in possession, and its rulings must be considered just and fair, until their injustice and unfairness are solidly and incontrovertibly proved. If, however, there can be no doubt about a law's injustice, resistance to the law may become a duty or a privilege. If it antagonises some divine good, if it stands up against some law of God, we enjoy no liberty in the matter; we are bound to disregard the unjust law, and die martyrs rather than observe it. "We must obey God rather than men." A.A.4. If it plainly antagonises some human good, whether it tends to promote private greed at the expense of the public welfare, or oversteps the bounds of authority to work harm, or fosters favoritism to the detriment of justice, disobedience becomes a privilege, of which subjects may avail themselves or not, as they please. Such a law certainly has of itself no claims on the conscience. Conscience, however, may exact the personal inconvenience, arising from obedience, as a lesser evil than the consequent scandal and disturbance. But in that case the obligation arises not from the unjust law, but from the natural duty men lie under of at times sacrificing their own interests to further the interests of society.

Foundation and Corner-stone. This question has a more important bearing on Ethics than might at first sight be supposed. We are at present grounding ourselves in principles, that will afterwards serve us in the solution of difficulties, arising from the post we occupy in affairs. As citizens, we shall be amenable to the law; and, unless we recognize God in the law, we shall be possessed of only half the truth, and little able to faithfully discharge our duties. Every enactment emanating from legitimate authority has God at its back, and philosophy is witness to the fact. If, as we hope to prove, natural law is the foundation and corner-stone of all positive law, and if natural law is God's own decree, men cannot do violence to civil or ecclesiastical law without dishonor to God. Law, therefore, has a double avenger, God and the

State; and good citizenship becomes a matter of conscience. Law owes only half its efficacy to the legislator's will, the other half descends from Heaven. Fear of God's wrath must act along with dread of fine and imprisonment, to exercise a salutary restraint on the passions of men.

In law, as in everything else, we can, with the Scholastics, consider matter and form. Its matter is the substance of the order it contains. Its form is that binding force it possesses, that moral necessity it imposes. We cannot contend that the body or substance of every positive law is contained in the natural law. Many positive laws have for object the performance of acts in themselves quite indifferent, about which natural law has not a word to say. But no matter how indifferent in itself an act prescribed by positive law may be, we hold that natural law, after human legislation has spoken, vests the act with all the binding force any dictate of the natural law owns. We further hold that, by a process of reasoning, every ruling made by positive law is reducible to a principle hidden somewhere in the natural law.

Proofs

I. *A natural law has place in man.*
II. *This natural law is,* [a] *unchangeable,* [b] *universal,* [c] *eternal.*
III. *Its complete and full sanction is reserved for the next life.*
IV. *Eternal punishment is not opposed to God's goodness.*
V. *Natural law is the foundation of all positive law.*

I. 1st, Experience is witness, through the medium of conscience, that certain rules of conduct, exacting obedience, wring acknowledgment from the mind by their clearness. But laws of the kind constitute what we call natural law. Ergo, natural law has place in man.

With Regard to the Major. Worship God, honor parents, do unto others as you would have others do unto you.

With Regard to the Minor. These rules have their origin in human nature, not in prejudice, education or ignorance. They carry authority, and impress man with a sense of responsibility and obligation.

2nd, Every force in nature, to produce its own proper effect, must be furnished with a certain determinant suited to itself, holding it to a fixed line of action. But natural law is to the human will such a determinant. Ergo, natural law has place in man.

With Regard to the Major. The most holy will of God and His wisdom demand as much. God cannot be indifferent to the promotion of order in the universe; and, in any hypothesis but that set down in the Major, He would have been at too small pains to promote order.

With Regard to the Minor. Natural law alone exercises proper and becoming restraint over man. As a free agent no chain but law can bind him. Other agents are limited to this or that effect by a something implanted in their very nature. Man, therefore, should be held in check by a law bound up in his nature, born with him, and antecedent to all the declarations of divine and human positive law.

3rd, The whole world is willing witness to the reality of a natural law. The noblest among the minds of antiquity, poets, philosophers and statesmen, have left us their sentiments, couched in the choicest and sublimest language, e.g., Oedipus Rex, line 863–871; Antigone, lines 446–460. Plato, Apologia, par. 29, D. Ch. 17. Republic, Bk. 4, par. 427. Gorgias, par. 483, E; par. 488, b; par. 491, E; Cicero, pro Milone, Ch. 4, § 10. Philippics *XI*, C. 12, § 28. De Legibus, I, c. 6; II, c. 4. Lactantius, Institut *VI*, 8.

II. a, b, c. That is unchangeable, universal and eternal, which is necessarily connected with the essence of rational creatures, which is contained in God's wisdom. But the natural law fulfils this twofold condition. Ergo.

With Regard to the Major. ^{a,} Essences are unchangeable, i.e., that by which a thing is what it is, cannot change, as long as the thing remains what it is, for instance, a man. ^{b,} Essences are universal, i.e., wherever a man exists, there also a man's essence exists. N.B. The natural law is for this reason, at least in point of being or reality, universal. It is universally known, from the fact that no human being can be unequal to the task of acquainting himself with his own nature. Ignorance, therefore, of the natural law is the result of accident, not a necessity. Besides, no one is ignorant of a certain few very evident principles. ᶜ Essences are eternal metaphysically, not physically; in the sense that they have a being without beginning and without end in God's thoughts. Law can exist before its actual subjects exist, as happens when kings make laws with intent that they go into effect a year after their promulgation.

With Regard to the Minor. Natural law is reason's interpretation of the eternal law, and reason combined with animality is man's essence. The eternal law is God's wisdom, and the natural law is a reflection of the eternal. Objectively, natural law is eternal law, restricted to rational creatures, and in this sense it is eternal. Subjectively, natural law is reason's interpretation of eternal law, and in this sense it is temporal.

III. N.B. That some sanction is necessary, must be evident from elementary notions of justice, holiness, wisdom and providence. God could not consistently with His attributes impose on mankind so serious an obligation as the natural law, and then view with indifference its fulfilment and contempt. He would be unjust to men, if He failed to reward the doers of the law, and punish its violators. Men can merit de condigno with God because of the implicit promise in God's gift of free will. This supposed indifference, resulting from the absence of all sanction, would likewise be a blot on His sanctity. He would be decidedly unholy, if He treated alike sinner and saint, rebel and servant. His wisdom could be called into question, and His providence would be empty as a dream. Even human legislators are far-seeing enough, and zealous enough for law and order, to visit with punishment every infraction of their behests. When discussing Kant's autonomy of reason, we agreed that mere consciousness of duty done is not a sufficient reward for virtue, and that mere consciousness of a quarrel with ourselves is not an effective bar against crime. To prove, therefore, that complete and full sanction is reserved for the next life, we argue thus.

ᵃ· Virtue's complete and full reward cannot be contained in things, that must on occasions be sacrificed for virtue's preservation. But all the good things of this life, yea, life itself, must on occasions be sacrificed for virtue's preservation. Ergo, complete and full sanction is reserved for the next life.

N.B. Reward must be more attractive than the sacrifice. Cause cannot be inferior to effect. The sum of 499 dollars could never be full and complete return for 500 dollars.

b. Punishment must be such, that within reason no greater can be devised, because an infinite person is seriously offended. But present punishment falls short of this. Ergo, sanction is reserved for next life. N.B. The Major could read, Sanction, while not unduly severe, must be efficacious.

With Regard to the Minor. Defects of present punishment.

The just in this life suffer grievous ills, the wicked flourish.

The pangs of conscience are trivial compared with the advantages reaped from crime. The good always enjoy a preponderance of blessings over ills. This preponderance admits of degrees. It would be greater than it now is, if the prosperity of the wicked and the grievous ills of the just were interchanged.

An eternal hell is weak at times to stay the arm of sin; any threat of temporal punishment would on such occasions prove empty and worthless.

The wicked, who die in their sins, would be able to boast for all eternity of their superiority over God.

IV. 1st, *From the Very Meaning of God's Goodness.* Infinite goodness consists in a willingness to so far share itself with free beings as free beings desire union. But eternal punishment is not opposed to this willingness. Ergo, eternal punishment is not opposed to God's infinite goodness.

With Regard to the Minor. If free beings deliberately put themselves out of condition for union with God, the fault lies with themselves alone. God's goodness must not interfere with man's freedom. God stands ever ready to lavish His affections on the sons of men, and pour Himself out on them. He is not otherwise minded even towards sons who have forfeited their inheritance, and consort with the damned. But these sons are now unfortunately capable of hatred only, and utter strangers to emotions of love. They have rejected God, the universal good. Outside of universal good nothing but evil exists, and evil is the formal object of hatred. God's readiness, therefore, meets with an insuperable impediment, and is destined to remain forever void of effect. If the damned could love God, there would be no hell. *Confirmation*—God need not give to free creatures favors which they deliberately refuse. God wishes all to be saved with antecedent will.

2nd, *From the Absurdity Apparent in the Opposite Doctrine.* The denial of eternal punishment involves an absurdity. Ergo, eternal punishment is not opposed to God's goodness.

With Regard to the Antecedent. Union with God and perseverance in hatred of God are conflicting notions; and, were the punishment of sin anything short of eternal pain, sinners would after death, at some point of time or other, enjoy union with God and remain His enemies. Since man's period of probation closes with death, no power can avail him to change the relation he holds with God in his last moment. Any other view of probation would encourage crime in this life by unduly exalting God's mercy at the expense of His justice and holiness.

3rd, *From the Very Meaning of Sanction.* Complete and full sanction necessarily calls for eternal punishment. Ergo, eternal punishment is not opposed to God's goodness.

With Regard to Antecedent. Complete and full sanction calls for penalties, severe enough to ensure observance of the law. But, in the present order of things, nothing short of eternal pains can effect this result. Even with hell open before them, men daily commit crimes, and, driven by passion, take the dread risk.

4th, God's goodness suffers no loss, when He allows free beings to choose what they will. But free beings, when they spurn aside their true end, make deliberate choice of everlasting pains. Ergo, eternal punishment is not opposed to God's goodness.

With Regard to the Minor. They make choice of God's eternal hatred, without any chance of remedy; and hell is nothing more, nothing less, than God's eternal hatred.

V. Positive law derives from natural law its binding force, it is void of all effect when opposed to natural law, and is, in the main, only an application of natural law to particular places, times and persons. Ergo, natural law is the foundation and corner-stone of positive law.

With Regard to the Antecedent. God alone is vested with full and independent right to impose obligations on free-born men; and, if natural law contained no injunction regarding the duty of subjects to their superiors, positive law would be little better than an idle waste of words. The chief reason why most sensible men submit to the requirements of positive law, is found in the circumstance that they recognize divinity at its back. They know themselves smart enough to break the law without falling into the law's clutches, they regard it a too easy matter to cheat the law of imprisonment and chains; but they fear with a wholesome dread that eternal avenger of the law, whose eye never sleeps, whose prison-house never yields up its dead.

All human positive law, from whatsoever source its matter is derived, gets its form or binding force from natural law. Some positive laws urge matter already prescribed by the natural law, others urge matter in itself indifferent; and even in the latter case some natural law counsels the law-maker to legislate. We are talking in the main of positive laws belonging to the first class, though what we say is in a measure true of so-called purely positive laws. All authority is immediately from God; and, the gift once made, natural law prescribes obedience. Without this authority from God, no ruler has the right to make laws for free men against their consent, that is a prerogative of God alone; and God's connection with authority makes the presence of natural law imperative. As a matter of right, positive law without natural law for support, is not worth the paper it is written on. A king may have all the physical force needed to execute his rulings; but might is not right, and, unless natural law sustains him, he has no right whatever to impose his wishes on a free people. More men and better men are kept from theft and murder by fear of God than by fear of fine and imprisonment; and the few restrained by these lesser considerations alone are beneath our notice. They are not good citizens in the full sense of the word.

PRINCIPLES I, II, III, IV, V

I. A. God depends not on eternal law, and yet He owes it to His wisdom to work in harmony with order; and order is eternal law. Self-imposed dependence is no real dependence, and, therefore, no imperfection. Dependence implies two, and God is one. The lawmaker is superior to his law, but can elect to observe it. God must choose to observe His law, because He enjoys no freedom of contrariety regarding virtue and sin.

B. Reason is not the natural law. It makes the law manifest to men. The New York *Sun* is not the law, though it prints and publishes the law. Were reason the natural law, each individual would be a law to himself; and law is an obligation imposed by another.

C. The natural law leaves room for civil, because it omits details; and two sanctions are better than one. Some principles in the natural law are obscure, particularly in second and third classes.

D. The natural law depends not on the free will of God, but on His wisdom or essence.

E. First principles of the natural law are the same with all men. Men differ, when they come to apply these first principles. We instance the treatment some savages accord their parents and wives.

F. Before creation there was no actual subject for natural law. Possible subjects destined to become actual were enough. Distinguish between natural law objectively taken, and subjectively taken.

G. Natural law is against man's nature, because it destroys his freedom.

Answer: It destroys his moral freedom, not his physical freedom; the licere, not the posse.

H. Natural law would be inseparable from man's nature. And yet it is separate from infants and madmen.

Answer: It is separable from them in nearest first act, and in second act; not in farthest first act. Second act means actual judgment; nearest first act means readiness due to habits; farthest first act means intellect.

I. God is free; and, therefore, natural law is not necessary.

Answer: God is free to create, not free to impose law in the hypothesis of creation. Absolutely speaking, God is free;

hypothetically speaking, He is not free. No outside force compels Him, but His infinite perfection.

II. J. Principles of natural law. Three classes. First, evident; second, easily deducible from first; third, deducible from first and second with some difficulty. Examples are, Do good and avoid evil; worship God, honor your parents; fight no duel, tell no lie. Principles of first and second classes are called more general, and cannot be invincibly unknown to any man vested with the use of reason. Principles of first class are known per se and with evidence. Their matter is evident from study of terms; their obligation, from study of human nature, inasmuch as man is a being ab alio, not a being a se.

K. Whole nations went astray regarding theft, suicide, murder.

Answer: They knew the natural law, and went wrong in its application to particular cases. They killed their parents, to save them from greater evils. Parents asked children to slay them, not to be old and decrepit in next life. Theft was reputed skill; suicide, bravery; wives were sent ahead to be company for husbands.

L. God can change physical laws. Ergo, natural law.

Answer: No parity. Not against the nature of a physical force to refuse it cooperation, or oppose impediments, or use it for a contrary purpose, like fire for cooling. Physical forces are mere means, and can be howsoever employed. Man is more than a mere means. He is free, and has initiative of his own. To put an act intrinsically wrong, is against his nature, and God cannot hinder the thing. If God allowed it approvingly, He would be running counter to His wisdom and holiness.

M. In the cases of Abraham and Isaac, the midwives and Egyptian property, the patriarchs and polygamy, God changed the matter of the law. He did not dispense.

III. N. There would seem to be no sanction in this life, because pleasure attaches to vice, injustice is profitable, and virtue begets pain.

Answer: The pleasures of vice are not straight, but blended with manifold evils, that the wicked are little able to bear. Profit attaches to injustice, not essentially, but accidentally. Injustice on occasions proves most unprofitable. The pain virtue begets is easily borne, with the help of a good conscience and hope of future blessedness. One reward is essential to virtue, and can never be absent. It is a help to honorable conduct. Three rewards are connatural, supremacy of reason, resulting peace, and health of body. Rewards of a third class morally speaking accrue to virtue; and they are wealth, honor, esteem, and the like. Such rewards as naturally and morally speaking fall to the lot of virtue, can by accident fail, though not regularly. Virtue, besides, procures untold social advantages, touching family, state and Church. God sometimes visits His friends with adversity in the capacity of a Father, not a lawmaker. He sometimes rewards the wicked in this life, because the future life will admit of no recompense for the little good they do.

IV. O. Heaven and hell encourage men to work from an imperfect motive. But God recommends these motives not in an absolute way, but only in the supposition that other motives fail of influence with human imperfection. The process is negatively imperfect, or less perfect; not positively, or altogether imperfect.

P. There would seem to be no proportion between a momentary sin and an eternal hell.

Answer: No proportion of time, but of justice.

Q. The purpose of sanction is to correct the criminal, or restrain him from wrong. Eternal punishment defeats purpose.

Answer: Sanction can be viewed as a threat or an actuality. Its purpose as a threat is secondary; its purpose as an actuality is primary. Its complete or combined purpose is the preservation of order. Before order takes harm, it threatens; after order takes harm, it punishes, and so restores things to primitive condition of equity. The pendulum swings back. In this life sanction has for secondary purpose the correction of the criminal and restraint of others. Here we are in probation. In the next life probation is at an end, and sanction strikes a balance. Sinners, who refused God glory here, do unwilling homage to His holiness and justice hereafter.

R. Many atheists know nothing of hell. Ergo, no hell for them.

Answer: They doubt regarding hell, and by their own fault. They are not certain regarding its non-existence. It is enough for the criminal to put an act deserving the penalty. Murderers are hanged, whether they know the penalty or not.

S. Hell itself is not sufficient sanction. Ergo.

Answer: It furnishes motive enough for the law's observance, though it fails to coerce free men.

V. T. Every offense against positive law is against natural law, mediately not immediately. A fault against positive law is not necessarily against natural law, because natural law is the remote, not the near cause of positive law. In every such case no natural law would be broken, were it not for the positive law.

THESIS V

VARIOUS MORAL NOTIONS

The five causes of morality, final, material, formal, model and efficient. Generic and specific morality. Objective and subjective morality. Good, bad and indifferent acts. Morality's subjective measure is synderesis and conscience. Morality's efficient cause is intellect and will. Appetite, the passions, and will. Morality's root is freedom of will. Voluntary and involuntary acts. End and intention. Morality's obstacles, ignorance and error affect the intellect; the passions, notably fear, affect the will; violence affects executive not appetitive faculties, ordered not elicited acts. Jouin, 19–28; 48–56; Rickaby, 27–64.

Ethics is the science of putting order in man's free acts, with principles derived from reason for ultimate basis, the principles themselves being of the rock-bottom variety, last, farthest away, remotest from the student. Ethics is the study of morality in its last causes, compassed in the light of reason. Like everything else, morality has five causes, *final, material, formal, efficient* and *model. Its final cause,* its purpose, what the agent seeks in its prosecution, is happiness, complete and incomplete; and this phase of morality was discussed in our first three theses. Its end of deed is order in man's free acts, its end of doer is resulting happiness. Recall clock and clockmaker. *Its material cause,* its subject-matter, its content, the determinable element of which morality is made, like the body in a man, the bricks and mortar in a house, is distinctively human acts, acts proceeding from a free will and an intellect, adverting to the moral good or evil in a thing. And, though we gave these acts some notice in our first thesis, we delayed their full discussion to this present occasion, because persuaded that we can now under-

70

stand them better. *Its formal cause* is good and evil in the moral order; and these notions await fuller development. Good and evil in the moral order are regularly designated right and wrong. The second and third paragraphs of our third thesis deal with the formal cause of morality, inasmuch as they establish an essential, intrinsic difference between right and wrong acts, and supply us with a standard of measurement, enabling us to detect this essential, intrinsic difference. In other words, some acts are so right, that they get their rightness from nothing outside themselves; so right, that viewed in themselves they cannot be made wrong by Almighty God Himself; so right, that rightness is of their very essence and inamissible. Other acts are so wrong, that irregularity is in their very substance, irremovable therefrom by God Himself, and beyond being changed by law, custom, conscience or whatever else. Instances of the two classes are, love of God, worship, obedience to parents; and hatred of God, blasphemy, a lie. We distinguish between *generic morality, and specific*. *Generic* merely denominates an act moral; *specific* morality denominates it good or bad, virtue or vice. *The generic morality of an act*, making it moral, is settled by its origination in an intellect and a will. *The specific morality of an act*, making it good or bad, is gotten from its harmony in whole, or discord in part, with the objective order of things. *The determinants of an act's morality, specifically considered, are its object, its agent's end or intention, its circumstances.* If all three are in harmony with the objective order, the act in question is morally good; if any one of the three is at discord with the objective order, the act is morally bad. This last statement remains to be proved, and it will get our attention later. For the better understanding of generic and specific morality, it may prove a help to recall animal, man and brute, with their endless varieties. Animal is the genus; man and brute, the species; races of men and breeds of brutes are classes, not species. In much the same way, moral acts are the genus; good and bad acts, or virtues and vices, are the species; while virtues and vices, grouped under particular names, are classes, not species.

Moral acts, constituted by the fact that they proceed from

intellect and will, are a genus capable of division into the two species, good and bad acts. Harmony and discord with the objective order are their specific differences. Ethics is practical, and there is question always of an individual concrete act, and we want to know to what species it belongs. We say that object, end and circumstances are its specific determinants, and we are practically saying that the act is morally good or bad inasmuch as the whole individual moral act is in harmony, or part of it is at discord with the objective order. Whole individual moral act means object, end and circumstances. *Object means act, end means moral, circumstances mean individual.* Different virtues and different vices are not species properly so called. They are classes under species. Like man and brute in Porphyry's Tree virtues and vices are infimae or lowest species. They admit of different classes, but not of different species. An infima species cannot be conceived as a genus containing different species, but only as a species containing different individuals, and these in turn constitute different classes. There are no different species of men, though there are different races or classes of men; and so there are no different species of virtue or vice, but only different classes or kinds. Man and brute are different species of animal, because they differ in essence. Justice and charity are not different species of virtue, because they do not differ in essence, inasmuch as they are moral goods. Their essences, namely genus and specific difference, are the same, moral acts in harmony with objective order. Different species must have different essences, different classes have the same essence and different accidents. No one act can belong to two different species, but the same act can belong to two different classes. One act cannot be at the same time virtuous and vicious, though one act ordered by the will can be at the same time justice and charity, as when a man owes five dollars and gives ten. It is quite possible for a charitable man to become a just man, without ceasing to be charitable; it is quite impossible for a rational animal or a man to become an irrational animal or a brute. And what is true of man as a lowest species, is true of virtue as a lowest species. Though we are not now specially concerned with the classification of the different virtues and different vices, but with the specification of generically moral acts, it is quite true to say that object, end and circumstances classify virtues and vices as well as specify moral acts. Object, end and circumstances are not the specific differences of good and bad acts, but the specific determinants limited or determined by the specific differences, harmony and discord with the objective order. All three must be in harmony with the objective order to constitute a good act, discord in any one of the three with the objective order constitutes a bad act. In conjunction with harmony and discord they determine the specific morality of a generically moral act. They contribute jointly with harmony and discord to the whole essence of a morally good or a morally bad act. There are no different species of moral good and moral evil, though there are different species of morally good and morally evil acts. Justice is a species of morally good acts, it is not a species of moral good, because no moral good is contradictorily opposed to it. Man is a species of animal, because brute is contradictorily opposed to him. Justice and injustice are not species of virtue, because virtue is not common to the two. Justice and charity are not species of virtue, because, though virtue is common to the two, their specific differences are the same, and one is not contradictorily opposed to the other.

St. Thomas, S. T. 1, 2, q. 19, a. 1, contends that acts get their specific morality from object alone, to later share the prerogative with end and circumstances. Therefore object must admit of several meanings. In one sense or wide sense it includes end and circumstances, in the other it excludes them. In wide sense object of act means the whole term of the man's wish, the whole good thing known to the intellect and sought or chosen by the will, with every attendant circumstance. Like every whole the whole term or whole good has parts, and these parts are what we call the object in strict sense, end and circumstances. Object, therefore, in strict sense, is what the will on its own account and primarily wishes with a bearing on morality. Circumstances are accidents morally affecting the act, whether by way of object or by way of agent; and they are what the will wishes, not on their own account primarily, but on account of object or end and secondarily. They are answers to the questions, quis, quid, ubi, quibus auxiliis, cur, quomodo, quando; meaning who, what, where, with what helps, why, how, when. Some circumstances physically affect the act, and we are not talking of them. An instance would be to give an alms with the left hand or the right hand. Person is a circumstance, quis, or who, and it means here not the bare substance of a person, a mere man, a mere woman, a mere child, but a person as affected with modifications that base moral relations, like a father, a mother, a son, a layman, a priest. Some circumstances, like quantity, leave their acts in the same class of virtues or vices, as five or ten dollars in the case of theft; others, like place, put their acts in different classes, as theft in a church becomes theft and sacrilege. End is itself a circumstance, cur or why, and the same is true of object, quid or what; but just as quid or what, taken as a circumstance, is made to mean quantum, how much, or quale, of what sort, so cur or why taken as a circumstance is made to mean end of deed or finis operis, reducible itself to object. End as distinguished from circumstance means end of doer, finis operantis, an intrinsic accident of the agent, not an intrinsic accident of the deed; not the purpose nature attached to the work, but the purpose actuating the agent to perform it. Think of clock, time and money, with time for end of deed, or thing made, and money for end of doer or person making.

To constitute an act good all the determinants must be good, to constitute an act evil, only one of the three need be evil; and St. Thomas sees in this circumstance another proof of the difficulty attaching to virtue as compared with vice, declaring that the surpassing value of virtue makes the trouble worth while. This fact is gathered up in the terse saying, *"Bonum ex integra causa, malum ex quocunque defectu." Good results from a complete and total cause, evil from any defect in the cause.* What the agent chooses must be right, the reason why he chooses it must be right, and the circumstances attaching to what and why must be right. If any of the three happens to be wrong, the whole act is morally wrong.

Object is finis operis, end of deed; end is finis operantis, end of doer. The object of murder is the destruction of an innocent man's life, the object of theft is the seizure of another's property against his rational wishes, the object of a clock is the indication of time. The end of murder may be revenge, or plunder, or removal of an unfriendly witness, removal of a Church persecutor, kindness to a parent, and the like. The end of theft may be the purchase of an auto, alms to the poor, gift to a benefactor, payment of a debt and the like. Circumstances affect both object and end. Murder of a father by his son, in a church, to keep him from sin. Object can likewise mean the term of the act, terminus actionis; the person or thing the act touches or affects, God, self, the neighbor, creatures without reason. When God is object, because He is good, without any admixture of evil, no concrete act can be indifferent with regard to object, because turning towards complete good is necessarily good, turning away from complete good is necessarily evil. With self, neighbor and irrational creatures it is different; they are mixtures of good and evil, and turning towards them is not necessarily good, turning away from them is not necessarily evil. To turn towards the good in them, and to turn away from the evil in them are good acts; to turn away from the good in them, and to turn towards the evil in them are bad acts. Therefore, acts bearing on creatures, even in the concrete, are of indifferent morality on the part of object of the act. This is far from meaning that individual acts in the concrete are ever indifferent. They are always definitely good or evil, but they get their specific or definite morality not from object of act, but from end of agent, and no individual concrete act is without its definite and determined purpose. Hatred is all right, when aversion from evil involves tendency towards good; hate is all wrong, when aversion from evil involves aversion from good. To walk, to drink, to talk, are acts with self for object, and these acts are never put without a purpose or motive different from and prior to the acts themselves. Walking, drinking and talking cannot be motives for the wish to walk, drink or talk, because they do not exist before the wish is conceived, and cause must precede effect. Therefore, some motive prior to the wish inspires these several acts, and changes these morally indifferent acts on the part of object to specifically good or evil acts on the part of agent. Purposes like prayer, health, temperance, kindness, make these acts morally good; purposes like theft, gluttony, drunkenness, anger make these acts morally evil. And what is true of acts with self for object, is true of acts with the neighbor and irrational creatures for object.

Again, we distinguish between *objective morality and subjective morality*, much as we distinguish between objective certainty and subjective; and, just as purely subjective certainty, without objective for basis and foundation, is error rather than truth, so purely subjective morality, or subjective goodness without objective goodness for basis and foundation, is badness or vice rather than goodness or virtue. Hence, a man can be good, though he puts a bad act, he can be bad though he puts a good act, meaning always in the matter of conscience, or subjectively. He can tell a lie and think it a duty. His will is right, his mind is wrong. He can tell the truth and think it a sin. His mind and will are both wrong. One is morality of the man, conscience apart from act; the other is morality of his act, act apart from conscience. *Objective* morality is in the whole deed or act itself, without any reference whatever to the truth or falsehood of the doer's knowledge; and of this kind of morality there was question in the second and third paragraphs of our third thesis. The only kind of subjective morality, that regularly deserves notice, is the kind based on objective; and of this we speak when we say that the specific determinants of morality are the act's object, its doer's end or intention, and the circumstances affecting both. Conscience is the measure of pure subjective morality, and will get our attention later.

Certainty is entirely a matter of intellect, morality is a matter of intellect and will together. Certainty turns on truth, morality on conduct, and the will has more to do with conduct than the intellect. The intellect is true, objectively and subjectively certain, only when it grasps things as they are, only when it sees murder as murder, theft as theft. It is false, subjectively certain, objectively ignorant or wrong, when it grasps things otherwise than as they are, when it views murder as charity, theft as commendable skill. Intellect is only one factor in morality, will is the other and more important.

All three determinants, object, end and circumstances, have their own objective and subjective morality. Their objective morality is like a fact, and quite independent of the agent's thinking; their subjective morality is not a fact, but the view the agent's mind takes of them. Per se, and therefore regularly, man's mind hits the truth; per accidens, and therefore in rare and exceptional cases, the mind can miss the truth. In such exceptional cases subjective morality is at variance with objective, and ignorance is usually responsible for the mistake. This ignorance is either vincible or invincible, within the thinker's control or beyond it. Some degree of carelessness attaches to vincible ignorance, and carelessness is blameable and punishable. No such carelessness attaches to invincible, and it is therefore without blame and unpunishable.

Objective morality, as distinguished from subjective, is the morality of the object of the act in strict sense, and end, and circumstances, viewed as facts, as they are in themselves; subjective morality is morality of the same three determinants, as they are viewed by the mind of the agent. And this is what we mean when we say that subjective is the morality of the man, objective is the morality of his act. A man is not good, unless his purpose and its attendant circumstances are good, as well as the object of his act. Neither is he good, unless the object of his act is good, as well as his end and its attendant circumstances. Every act implies two things, a cause and an effect. A moral act implies a cause viewed morally, and an effect viewed morally. A cause viewed morally involves intellectual knowledge and free will with a bearing on moral right and wrong. An effect viewed morally is what results from the activity of a cause viewed morally; it is a physical act proceeding from a free agent, not considered merely in itself, but in its bearing on right and wrong. In every moral act the effect or term of the act fixes its objective morality; the cause, a composite of intellectual knowledge and free will, fixes its subjective morality.

Only free acts are matter for moral acts, choice is exercise of freedom, and choice is impossible without prior intellectual knowledge. Man's one free faculty is his will. His intellect, senses, appetite, locomotion are all necessary faculties, and they borrow whatever freedom we attribute to them from the will. Therefore, in strict sense only acts elicited by the will, only wishes as such, only internal acts of the will, begun and finished in the will, elicited and executed by the will, deserve and get the appellation, moral. Every act external to the will, whether it be a thought, or a sensation, or a passion, murder, or theft, viewed as proceeding from intellect, sense, appetite, or hands, is a necessary act, and therefore without its own proper morality; and every such act borrows morality from intimate connection with the will, from dependence in its first origin on the will, from the fact that, while it is finished or executed by another faculty, it is begun, elicited in the shape of a wish, ordered, commanded, prescribed by the will.

Hence our distinction between acts elicited by the will and acts ordered by the will. Elicited acts are internal acts, ordered acts are external. Both are moral acts, but after a different manner. Internal acts have their own independent morality, ordered acts have no morality of their own, but a morality derived from and dependent on the influence of the will, the part played by the will in their accomplishment. Murder and theft are always done in the will before they are done by the hands, and as outward or external acts their morality is exactly the same as that of the wish or internal act prompting them. In murder the outward act is in itself necessary, free by participation; the inward act is free in itself. The will makes the murderer kill, much as instinct makes the bird fly, with this difference, that while the will is free, instinct is a necessary agent.

In the concrete, and viewed as products of an individual man, all acts are either good or bad. In real life there is no such thing as an indifferent human act, a deliberate act neither good nor bad, but between both. In the abstract, and in the field of theory, walking, singing, and a thousand such acts are indifferent in themselves; but in practical every-day life all such acts are necessarily good or bad. Ethics has nothing to do with indifferent acts, because they fall outside its sphere. It is a practical, not a theoretical study. There never was an animal, without its being a man or a brute; and there never was a moral or distinctively human act, without its being definitely good or bad, from a moral point of view. Acts are morally good or bad, when they respectively help or hinder a man in his progress towards his last end, the possession of God in Heaven, the practice of virtue on earth. Man's destiny is the fulfilment of God's wishes in his regard, and we gather God's designs on man from a study of man's nature. Complete happiness is last factor in man's wishes; and, therefore his last end, because there is no good beyond. Because it leads to God or complete happiness, virtue constitutes incomplete happiness, the highest possible on earth. Virtue in turn means order in man's free acts, it means the performance of duty; duty springs from man's relations with the other moral units in the universe, God and neighbor; and these relations are based on the objective order of things, things as God made them, things as God views them.

And now to sum up, an act is first moral, then good or bad. All distinctively human acts are moral. Some are good, others bad; good, when they square with the objective order of things, as grasped by the intellect; bad, when they are at angles with this order. Objective order is embodied in the eternal law, made manifest to man in the natural law, and pushed to the limit of clearness in positive law; and for this reason, the natural law is morality's *model cause*. Eternal law is God's reason or will, commanding the preservation of natural order, forbidding its disturbance. Natural law is eternal law, become evident in rational nature; or, an inborn habit of mind enabling man to detect the harmony or discord in force between notions constituting morality's first principles. Positive law is an obligation founded on right reason, drawn up and promulgated for the common good by him who has charge of the community affected. Creatures inferior to man, from minerals to brutes, always keep the eternal law, the law set them by God, that aspect of eternal law applicable to irrational nature. A stone miraculously suspended in the air, is keeping the law of gravity as far as in it lies. Man is the only rebel in the universe, because man alone is free. Morality's *efficient cause* is man, viewed as an intelligent, free being. Morality is restricted to man, intellect and will are the two faculties in man directly concerned with morality, and of the two will is the more vitally important. It is the work of the intellect to know right and wrong, it is the work of the will to choose between them. *In the field of knowing synderesis and conscience are man's mentors,* they are functions of the intellect in its bearing on morality, they are reason restricted to the department of right and wrong. *Synderesis is the habit of morality's first principles;* and we saw in our fourth thesis that synderesis is unerring. The natural law is universally known, as well as universally existent. *Conscience is the application of synderesis to personal and concrete acts;* and conscience can be false as well as true, wrong as well as right. *Synderesis is intellect as it comes from the hand of God, conscience is intellect as modified by man;* and the whole truth is summed up in that statement from Major Logic, the intellect is per se infallible, and fallible per accidens. Synderesis elicits a speculative judgment only, conscience elicits a speculative and a practical judgment. One is Major; the other theoretically viewed is Minor in the Moral Syllogism, practically viewed it is the conclusion. One regulates our thinking, the other our doing. One is truth, the other is morality; and they are related like Logic and Ethics, inasmuch as Logic lays down rules for right thinking, Ethics lays down rules for right conduct. An example may make things clearer. Murder is wrong and a thing to be avoided. This particular killing I contemplate would be murder. Therefore I must avoid this particular killing.

Intellect, therefore, and will, or knowing and choosing, are what give being and essence to our moral acts, and they deserve most serious attention. They get full and complete treatment in Psychology; but, for present purposes, we must be pardoned introducing here certain truths, there proved beyond dispute. We begin with the consideration of man, as composed of body and soul. The two appetitive faculties in man are appetite and will; the passions are manifestations of appetite, and are nine in number. The will's freedom, the different classes of voluntary acts, the different kinds of intentions need to be explained. The parts ignorance and error, the passions and violence play in morality are questions to be settled.

Composition of Man. Man is a mystery. He is the microcosm; a mineral, a plant, a brute and an angel. He is a body and soul, matter and spirit. He is one complete substance and nature, made up of two incomplete substances and natures. Only live bodies are human bodies, and they alone are one incomplete substance. A dead body is no human body, it is an aggregate of many different complete substances.

The incompleteness of the body, as a substance, is situate in the circumstance, that it unites with the soul to form the complete substance, man. Its incompleteness, as a nature, is due to the fact that it derives its activity from the soul. The whole man is a complete substance, because he stands by himself, and enters into no combination with another. He is a complete nature, because he is the root and principle of all his operations. Body and soul are incomplete after different manners. The body is incomplete and non-subsistent. Without the soul it falls away and perishes. The soul is incomplete and subsistent. Without the body it goes on living and acting. And yet the soul is no angel, because its subsistence is incomplete; accompanied always by a connatural capacity for union with the body, to constitute one complete substance, man. An angel's subsistence is complete, and void of every such connatural capacity. Only as a composite of body and soul is man a complete substance and a complete nature. As such he is not a body, nor yet a soul; but a man. He is not a body-substance or nature, nor yet a soul-substance or nature; but a human substance and nature, with activities partaking of the two kingdoms of matter and spirit.

Hence, he has sense as well as intellect; he has appetite as well as will. In man's present condition his soul is root and principle of his thoughts and wishes, but with extrinsic dependence on his body, and this dependence is far from interfering with the soul's spirituality. This extrinsic dependence on the body, in a mediate way follows the soul to the next life, because in even its separated condition it thinks and wishes with the mediate help of species or images it carries, and these owe their first origin to phantasms, themselves products of the composite man.

Appetite and Will. But we are now concerned with man in this present life; and, because our topic is Ethics, his will

82 GENERAL ETHICS

demands most immediate attention. In this business of
morality the will is the thing, and a man's will is his heart.
*The will is best defined as a spiritual, inorganic faculty of the
soul, appetitive of good at the instigation of the intellect.*
It is a blind faculty, and gets light from the intellect. It
can act with or against the light. Good is its object, and
that is the quality intellect calls to its notice. Greater and
lesser have weight of course with the will, but no determining
or absolute weight. It is free, and can reject the greater
good to select the lesser, and all this with an abiding
knowledge of their relative worth. Experience is proof, and
facts are more stubborn than wrong principles, doped out to
strengthen the weak limbs of a lame theory. As soon as the
smallest conceivable particle of good sails into the mind's
vision, the will is ready to exert its energy. The will is free,
we say, and the world agrees with us. We mean the world
of common sense. There are a few restless spirits, who stand
for determination of will. But they are off the right track,
they purposely go wide of common-sense, they are chasing
rainbows in a wild search for novelty, no sober study of the
truth. The truth of the thing is that the will is free, and
Determinists are well acquainted with the fact. They feel
free to reject as attractive a good as the truth, and actions
are louder than words. When a man says one thing and
does another, we claim the privilege of gathering his real
sentiments from his deeds; and these idle philosophers talk
Determinism to do freedom. The will then is free, and it is
too late in the day to endeavor to correct the notion.

Omitting for the present the soul's executive energies, we
attribute to the soul *the power to know, and the power to
wish;* and this twofold power we denominate *its cognoscitive
and appetitive faculties.* Man wishes as he knows, and his
knowledge covers two kingdoms, that of sense and that of
intellect. His soul is the root of all his activity. Sight and
hearing are just as much rooted in his soul as understanding
or thought. But here again there is a difference. In operations of sense the soul is intrinsically dependent on matter,
in thought its dependence is merely extrinsic. Had man no
higher faculty than sense, his soul would be just as material
as the brute's. But he has a higher faculty, that of thought;

its operations are intrinsically independent of matter, spiritual, inorganic; and what is highest in a thing gives the thing its name. For present purposes we can call thought the soul's superior knowledge, sensation its inferior knowledge, with intellect and sense for corresponding faculties. *Because man wishes as he knows, we must recognize a double capacity for willing, a superior will and an inferior will, rational appetite and sensile appetite,* one intrinsically independent of organs, the other intrinsically dependent on same. Both are wills, both are appetites; but for the sake of clearness we call the first, will simply; the second, appetite. The passions are displays of the appetite, wishes are displays of the will.

The Passions. Our passions are as dependent on the body as our senses; our wishes are as clear of the body as our thoughts. The passions, like appetite their root, turn always on some particular good or its opposite; and, like sensation as compared with thought, are more manifest and closer to hand than wishes or acts of the will proper. The will has universal good for object, and it always embraces particular goods under the aspect of universals. Man wishes the office of president, not inasmuch as it is the office of president, but inasmuch as it is honor; he wishes the salary, not inasmuch as it is a set sum of money, but inasmuch as it is money. A hungry man wants food of any kind, food in general. A hungry horse wants this or that particular food, oats, or corn, or hay.

Passion, if we consult the word's origin, means suffering, a modification induced by impact from another. In oratory the passions are stimulations of pain or pleasure, meant to shape or color a man's opinions. In ethics passions are movements of the appetite, set on foot by the actual presence, or vivid representation, of an object wearing the appearance of good or evil. They are acts of the appetite, and have no part in angels or separate souls. And yet these passions have their counterparts in the thoughts and wishes of angels. Love, hate, desire are as native to angels as they are to brutes; but in angels they exist without any admixture of appetite; they are affairs of the soul, not affairs of the body. Man is capable of the love peculiar to angels, and of the love peculiar to brutes. His will is affected by the senses as well as by the intellect. Orators reach the hearts of their listeners by the passions as well as by arguments. And in his own case a man can be orator and audience. Passion always manifests itself in body-change, "the diffusive wave of emotion." All passion is emotion, but not all emotion is passion. Surprise, laughter, shame, are not passions, because they are impossible without intellect. Passions turn on good and evil affecting sense.

The ancients enumerated nine passions. They are all species of the generic passions, love and hate. Love has good for object; hate, evil. Hate is the negation of love, as evil is the negation of good.

Love; good is object, no limit
- *Desire* has absent good for object.
- *Delight* has present good for object.
- *Hope* has hard, but possible good for object.
- *Despair* has hard and impossible good for object.

Hate; evil is object, no limit
- *Abhorrence* has absent evil for object.
- *Displeasure* has present evil for object.
- *Fear* has hard and unavoidable evil for object.
- *Courage* has hard, but avoidable evil for object.

Anger is a mixture of desire, displeasure, hope.

Desires are physical and psychical. Both are from senses. Imagination has wider play in latter. Physical craves for quantity; psychical, for quality, e. g. A thirsty man craving water and champagne. Physical craves for limited objects; psychical, for unlimited, not in sense of universal, but in sense of colossal particulars, e. g. A thirsty man wants, not ocean, but enough; a miser wants all gold. Psychical desires are not intellectual desires. These last contemplate immaterial goods and material goods viewed in an immaterial way. Desire of perfect happiness is intellectual.

Delight, like desire, may be sensual or intellectual. The passion is sensual delight. Like desire, delight may be physical or psychical. Play of imagination makes difference, e. g. a wine-taster. Intellectual delights are superior to sensual, where minds and hearts are cultivated. Regarding the morality of an act done for pleasure, there is a difference between *acting for pleasure and living for pleasure*. The first is right,

Delight, like desire, may be sensual or intellectual. The second is wrong.

Anger is a mixed passion; it is desire of open vengeance for an open slight, attended with displeasure at slight. Hatred is usually chronic, anger is frequently acute. Hatred wishes evil as it is evil; anger, as it is just. Anger regularly wishes evil in sight of all; hatred is not seldom content with hidden evil. Anger stops, hatred continues.

The Will's Freedom. And now we leave the passions, these affections of appetite, to return to the will. Again, the will is a spiritual, inorganic faculty of the soul, appetitive of good at the instigation of the intellect. A voluntary act is such as proceeds from the will with a purpose in mind. Voluntary acts may be necessary or free; necessary, when the will is cut off from all choice; free, when choice is in its power. In Heaven love of God is a voluntary necessary act. In this life all our deliberate voluntary acts are free. *Every good in our acquaintance is a mixture of good and evil,* it falls short of the summum bonum or God, who is alone unmixed good. *The good in the object stirs desire; the evil in the object stirs aversion*. To desire is to select, to turn aside from is to reject. Therefore, whatever created good falls under our notice is, because of its mixed nature, capable material for selection or rejection, for desire or aversion; and when the will is able to wish or not wish, its act is free. *Freedom is an attribute of the will, enabling it, after equipment with every needed prerequisite, to still wish or not wish, to choose this or choose that*. This attribute follows the will all the way up to actual exertion of its energy. When it once makes choice, its freedom regarding this particular act is straightway at an end. It cannot wish a thing, and at the same time remain free to wish or not wish it. But up to the precise moment wherein it wishes, it certainly remains free to do one thing or the other. In perhaps plainer words, *it enjoys antecedent not consequent freedom*. When freedom turns on the power to will or not will, it is known as *freedom of contradiction*. When it turns on the power to positively wish or positively reject a certain thing, it is known as *freedom of contrariety*. When it turns on the power to wish this or wish that, it is known as *freedom of specification*. Thus, when I choose between reading and not reading, I am exercising my freedom of contradiction; when between loving and hating a person, my freedom of contrariety; when between reading and singing, my freedom of specification.

The most obvious meaning of freedom is separation or immunity from something. Freedom of will is immunity from determination, from necessary adhesion to some set line of conduct. The determining force can be conceived as intrinsic or extrinsic to the will. Immunity from a determining force intrinsic to the will is called *freedom from necessity*. The other is called *freedom from violence*. In our present condition, the will in all its deliberate acts enjoys freedom of the first sort. Things would be different, if we saw God face to face. The will in its elicited acts, in acts it begins and finishes, in acts the will itself executes, always enjoys freedom of the second kind. In ordered acts, in acts it begins, to leave to another to finish, in acts it commands another agent to execute, freedom of the second sort may be present or absent. When it is absent, the ordered act is not free. A prisoner in his cell is free to wish as he likes, and the law has no restraining influence over his will in the matter of its elicted acts. It can, however, with chains prevent him from walking, and so spoil him of freedom in ordered acts, dependent on his legs for execution. No elicited act of the will can be forced, because, in that case, the will would object and not object, a contradiction in terms. Freedom from necessity is the kind we vindicate to the will, and it is called *freedom of indifference, freedom of choice, free will, freedom simply*. A spontaneous act is opposed to a forced act, and force is extrinsic. All vital or immanent acts are of such sort. Acts proceeding from appetite, whether natural in minerals and plants, sensitive in brutes, or intellectual in man, are spontaneous. The highest spontaneity of man on earth is freedom, the highest spontaneity of inferior agents is necessity. Man's indeliberate acts are spontaneous with necessity. A voluntary and fully deliberate act proceeds from the will, with knowledge of end as such, and may be either necessary or free. A free act is an act of the will held to no set shape by anything in the will's nature or constitution. In this life, elicited acts of the will are free, not because they are elicited, but because their every object is a mixture of good and evil. Love of God in Heaven is an elicited act and necessary. Necessity is compatible with elicited acts of the will, as is plain from the case of the blessed in Heaven. *Freedom of indifference or choice, or free will, consists in passive and active capacity to wish or not wish in the presence of every needed prerequisite for wishing;* or it is a power of choice, enabling us in the event of several alternatives to freely choose one and neglect or reject the others. Freedom belongs formally and intrinsically to the will alone. The intellect is not free in the presence of immediately evident truth. Acts of other faculties are free in cause and extrinsically, inasmuch as the will orders or commands them. The will is superior to whatever preponderating influence or inclination urges, it can choose what we here and now know to be worse in preference to what we here and now know to be better, in spite of what Leibnitz says to the contrary.

Voluntary Acts. Whether free or necessary, all elicited acts of the will are voluntary. No elicited acts of the will are altogether involuntary. Ordered or commanded acts, viewed in their execution, may be altogether involuntary, e. g. imprisonment or upright position with arm extended. Elicited acts of the will begin and end in the will, ordered acts begin in the will and end in another faculty. Hence, we distinguish between acts altogether voluntary or involuntary, and acts partly voluntary or involuntary. When the act turns on an object desired in itself, and on its own account, it is wholly voluntary. When it turns on an object desired in no way whatever, it is wholly involuntary. When it turns on an object desired indeed, not however on its own account,

but on account of another closely connected object, it is
partly voluntary and partly involuntary. In a partly voluntary act the will embraces its object, but would never embrace it, if it could otherwise avoid some evil or compass
some good. Sailors, unloading their cargo into the sea during a storm, are the classical example. We likewise distinguish between a directly voluntary and an indirectly
voluntary act. The first turns on an object wished immediately and on its own account; the other, on an object wished
not on its own account, but because it follows necessarily in
the wake of the wisher's purpose. *An indirectly voluntary
act differs from a partially voluntary act in this, that the
former has for object a good consequent on the wisher's purpose, while the latter has for object a good antecedent to the
wisher's purpose, a means to his end.* Examples may serve
to make things clearer. Sailors in a storm lighten their
ship of its cargo as a means to securing their safety. Drunkenness is the indirect voluntary of excessive drinking. Indirect voluntary and voluntary in cause are of a kind. The
omission of an act likewise constitutes an indirect voluntary.

Intentions. Whatever influences the will is called an end
or purpose. This end or purpose, viewed as energizing the
will, is called the man's intention; and it may be formal and
actual or virtual, explicit or implicit, habitual or interpretative. It is formal and actual, when actually known and
wished, in a distinct way. Ordinarily our intentions are of
this sort. It is virtual, when, ceasing to be actual, it goes on
shaping our conduct with force borrowed from its original
impulse as an actual intention. In the course of a journey
our intention insensibly passes from actual to virtual. A
priest baptizing with distractions is another example. It is
explicit, when it keeps in view some distinct object; and our
intentions are regularly such at the first. It is implicit, when
it keeps in view some object not known with distinctness,
but involved in another. Thus, to explicitly purpose a journey is to implicitly purpose car-fare. It is habitual, when
once entertained it falls from memory, without being repudiated or knowingly withdrawn. The Morning Offering
influences after this manner all the day's acts. The intention perseveres not in act or in effect, but in habit; and it

influences subsequent acts. It is interpretative, when, of no
actual or virtual or explicit habitual force, it would influence
our conduct, if recognized with distinctness. Interpretative is same as implicit habitual, e.g., desire to be saved is
interpretative desire to be baptized. Such an intention suf-
fices for the valid reception of Baptism, when intention of a
superior kind is impossible. Virtual at least is always required in minister.

Ignorance and Error. Intellect and will combine to produce free acts. Choice pertains to the will, knowledge to the
intellect. Freedom, therefore, can be diminished by hindrance to choice and hindrance to knowledge. *Ignorance and
error can affect our minds, passion and fear can affect
our wills.* *Ignorance* is described as absence of knowledge.
It is that state of mind wherein no judgment or idea is had
of the thing unknown. If a man ought to have the knowledge in question, his ignorance is positive. If no such obligation exists, his ignorance is negative. Examples of negative are ignorance of medicine in a farmer and of philosophy in a Freshman. Examples of positive are ignorance of
medicine in a physician and of philosophy in a Senior. Ignorance is *vincible,* if, with the amount of study, to which a
man is held, it can be set aside; if such a measure of study
is of no avail to set it aside, the man's ignorance is *invincible.* Vincible ignorance is culpable; invincible, inculpable.
Antecedent ignorance has place before the man wakes up to
the duty of investigation, and it is invincible as well as inculpable. *Consequent ignorance* has place after the man
wakes up to the duty of investigation, and it may be vincible as well as culpable. Vincible ignorance is of three
kinds; *simple,* when some study is employed, but not enough;
stupid or lazy, when little or no study is employed; and
affected, when one purposely avoids every source of information to continue in his perverse ways. Acts are rendered
involuntary by invincible ignorance; not, of course, involuntary under every respect, but under such respect alone
as the ignorance affects or touches them; vincible ignorance
leaves them voluntary, but in a diminished degree. Invincible ignorance is wished in no way; neither in itself nor in
cause. Vincible ignorance is wished in cause. To strike a

priest, thinking him a layman, is no sacrilege. To eat meat on Friday, without taking means to clear up a suspicion, is sinful. When no such suspicion is present, no sin is committed. To studiously avoid enquiry about a fast-day, for the purpose of enjoying a full meal, is to incur guilt. Error is positive want of conformity between mind and object, it is that state of mind wherein a false judgment is had of something. It is material and formal. Material turns on wrong appearances of things. Formal confounds appearances with facts. Formal error is the acceptance of the false for the true, and admits of distinctions parallel with those of ignorance.

Examples of material and formal are, men seem trees, and men are trees.

Passion. Passion is sensile appetite, and we have already enumerated its different kinds. With consent of the will for point of departure, passion is antecedent or consequent. When passion turns on moral good, it is altogether honorable. When it turns on moral evil, antecedent passion is involuntary and without moral blame. Consent of the will changes antecedent to consequent passion, and such passion is voluntary; directly, when the will urges or commands it; indirectly, when disturbance ensues from will's vehemence. Motus primo primus is altogether antecedent passion. Motus secundo primus means incomplete consent; it is passion adverted to, and not resisted. Motus secundus means full consent and consequent passion.

Fear and Violence. We single out fear, because it is less a home-product than the other passions, and therefore more compelling.

Fear can be serious or light, intrinsic or extrinsic. Fear is dread of a threatening evil, apprehended as unavoidable. Serious dreads a great evil, certain or very probable, e. g. death, wounds, property, imprisonment.

Absolutely serious fear affects an ordinary person. Relatively serious fear affects a person of a certain age, sex or disposition. Absolutely light can be relatively serious.

Light dreads a lesser evil, or a great evil barely probable. Reverential awe can become relatively serious fear, especially in girls.

Fear is intrinsic when its cause is a necessary agent whether extrinsic or intrinsic to the person who fears, e. g. a contracted disease, meditation on hell, earthquake.

Fear is extrinsic, when its cause is outside the man and a free agent, e. g. enemy, highwayman, threats.

Free fear resembles extrinsic and is caused by the free act of a human being, e. g. highwayman. Free fear is just if the person causing it seeks to repel harm. Free fear is unjust, if the person causing it seeks to inflict harm. Necessary fear resembles intrinsic and is prompted by a necessary cause, e. g. earthquake, volcano, lightning.

Solutions: In case reason is not dethroned, fear, no matter how serious, leaves the act voluntary in a diminished degree, e. g. martyrs and apostates. Serious fear excuses from positive law, especially human. Unjust fear makes law-instruments invalid. Light fear is generally neglected before the law; in conscience it can have some weight in questions of compensation for loss. Violence cannot be done the will. Under violence the man makes free choice of escape from pain. An external act due entirely to violence is no crime in the unwilling agent.

THESIS VI

A human act gets its specific morality from the object of the act, from the agent's end or purpose, and from circumstances affecting both.—Jouin, 32–36; Rickaby, 31–41.

QUESTION

This present thesis fixes the specific determinants of morality. It answers the question, What makes a moral act good or bad, what makes a moral act the act of one particular virtue or vice rather than the act of another?

TERMS

Specific Morality. Specific morality is opposed to generic. Specific makes an act good or bad, an act of this or that particular virtue or vice. All virtuous acts are specifically the same in first sense, because harmony with objective order is the specific difference. All virtuous acts of different particular virtues are specifically different in second sense, because each particular virtue has its own specific difference; justice being specified by another's due; charity, by kindness to another; humility, by right esteem of self; and so of all the different virtues.

Object, End, Circumstances. All three, object, end and circumstances are specific determinants, and in both senses, fixing classes as well as species. *In the briefest language possible, objective morality arises from the object of the act, subjective morality from the agent's purpose, and circumstances modify object and purpose.* Circumstances are summed up in the Latin verse, Quis, quid, ubi, quibus auxiliis, cur, quomodo, quando? The verse means, Who, what, where, with what helps, why, how, when? Circumstances are objective, when they modify the matter or substance of the act; subjective when they modify the purpose of the agent. The

92

object contributes essential, intrinsic morality to the act; the end contributes accidental, extrinsic morality; circumstances, when limited to the object, contribute accidental, intrinsic morality; when limited to the agent, accidental, extrinsic morality. The end contributes essential intrinsic morality to the agent, circumstances contribute essential intrinsic morality to object and agent; and therefore end and circumstances are as much specific determinants as object, because a moral act is not object alone, but object, agent and circumstances taken together. To be a moral act, it must be an individual free act, voluntary and deliberate; and this quality implies end and circumstances.

Acts indifferent in themselves, because neither good nor bad from the viewpoint of object or matter, get all their morality from the agent's purpose and from circumstances. No deliberate act of the individual is indifferent. To walk and to write are in themselves indifferent; but no individual can deliberately walk or write without a purpose and circumstances, that commend or vitiate the act.

Object. When discussing the natural law in fourth thesis, we already described acts good or evil in themselves. They are opposed to morally indifferent acts, which, having no morality in themselves, get all their morality from purpose and circumstances. Acts are good in themselves, their object is good, when positive harmony with the objective order enters their constitution; they are bad in themselves, when discord with same attaches to them. We distinguish between inward acts and outward, or overt acts. The will is the moral faculty in man, the intellect is only its helper; and all a man's acts get their moral color from his will. Inward acts are acts elicited and executed by the will, they begin and end in that faculty; outward acts are acts elicited by the will and executed by another faculty; they begin in the will and finish in some other faculty. Elicited or inward acts have their own independent morality, gotten from object, end, and circumstances. Ordered or outward acts derive all their morality from their corresponding elicited or inward acts. Murder and theft are perpetrated in the heart, before they are accomplished by the hands. *In every moral act three distinct things are wished, the object of the act, the end or purpose*

*selected, and attendant circumstances, objective and sub-
jective.* Briefly, all three things are wished, object, end and
circumstances. All the three things wished must be morally
good, to constitute the act a morally good act. An act is
bad, when any one of the three is bad. Hence the axiom,
"Bonum ex integra causa, malum ex quocunque defectu."
*"Good results from a full and complete cause, evil results
from a defective cause."* In plain English, an act is good,
when all three constituents or determinants of morality are
good; it is bad, when any one of the three is bad. A moral
act is a chain made up of three links; it is good, when all
three links are good; it is bad, when any one of the three is
bad. A chain is no stronger than its weakest link, and this
moral chain is no better than its worst link. Therefore, the
fact that a deed is good in object, is far from settling its
morality. A wrong intention can make the best thing in the
world wicked. The fact that a deed is bad in object, quite
settles its morality, no intention in the world can save it from
blame. When discussing the natural law in our fourth thesis,
we described acts good or bad in themselves; and we were
talking about object, as distinct from end and circumstances.
Whatever good act gets its morality solely from end and
circumstances, is in itself morally indifferent. It is not morally good in itself, because in that case object would contribute
to its morality. It is not bad in itself, because in that case
it could never become good. Whatever act is good or bad
prior to end and circumstances, is good or bad in itself, because end and circumstances are the only other sources, the
only moral coefficients other than the act itself. Acts, therefore, are good or bad in themselves, when, abstracting from
end and subjective circumstances, they are in harmony or at
discord with the objective order; when, morally speaking,
they are or are not what they ought to be. Physical good is
divided into becoming, agreeable and useful, and moral good
admits of the same division. All three physical goods can be
basis for moral good, and they eventuate in moral good, only
when reason's controlling influence vests them with the quality of becoming good.

Viewing man as a moral being, his one true and real good
is virtue, because it alone appeals to the morally specific por-

tion of his being, the will as arbiter of good and evil. Even study, in itself becoming and real physical good, can by abuse readily become moral evil, and sink to the level of apparent good. Pleasure and wealth, in themselves apparent good, can, under the control of reason and an orderly will, rise to the dignity of true and real goods. Acts can be morally good or evil in themselves in a three-fold way. In themselves, on their own account, and absolutely; in themselves, on their own account, but not absolutely; in themselves, not on their own account, nor absolutely. Familiar examples of such goods are worship, charity and pious reading. Familiar examples of such evils are blasphemy, theft and dangerous reading. Good and evil of the first kind admit no change of matter. There is a something in the physical act of worship that makes its acceptance by the will a moral good, and this something cannot possibly be separated from the act. There is a something of the same kind in the physical act of blasphemy, and this something makes blasphemy irremediably and necessarily bad. Charity and pious reading become evil, when the money given as alms is stolen, when pious reading interferes with some higher duty. Theft and dangerous reading admit change of matter; and, this change supposed, they cease to be bad. What belonged to another may become mine, and its seizure by me is no theft. What would otherwise be dangerous reading and wrong, may become a necessary help to the acquisition of medicine or theology and entirely right.

And now to explain what we mean by in themselves, on their own account and absolutely. Blasphemy, theft and dangerous reading are wrong in themselves, because of wrongness involved in the three physical acts, because of native and inborn discord with the objective order of things. Blasphemy and theft are wrong on their own account, not on account of an outside cause, like the prohibition of a superior. Dangerous reading is wrong not on its own account, but on account of nature's decree against incurring danger without good and sufficient reason. Absolutely, implies no possibility of change in matter, and of the three blasphemy alone is absolutely wrong. In no hypothesis can the physical act of blasphemy fail of turpitude. The physical act of deliberately taking something in theft is wrong, only in the hypothesis that it is concerned with property belonging to another. The physical act of deliberate dangerous reading is wrong, only in the supposition that the risk is taken without due and sufficient reason. In the case of a child, play on the street against a parent's wishes, is not wrong in itself, or on its own account, or absolutely. The wrongness is not in the play, but in disobedience; the wrongness is due to the parent's prohibition, and with the parent's permission it would be entirely right.

End. In question of ends we hold discourse primarily of the end designated operantis, not operis; the end of doer, not the end of deed. The finis operis is independent of the doer, the finis operantis is wholly under his control. Recall the example of clock and clockmaker. The finis operis of a clock is to tell time, whether the clockmaker likes it or no. In fact, the end of deed cannot be entirely absent from the end of doer. The clockmaker can hardly make a clock without intending it to measure the flight of time. These two ends are like a combination of the object of the act and the agent's purpose, if the act's goodness in itself or badness in itself is conceived as the clock. The end of doer can be best called intention, or end energizing the agent. It gives morality to an act indifferent in the abstract, making it a morally good or evil act in the concrete. An evil intention vitiates an act morally good in point of object or circumstances. A good intention cannot change the evil nature of an act bad in point of object or circumstances. And all this is true of good and evil circumstances, with regard to good and evil objects and intentions. The agent's intention is his act inwardly taken, and our outward acts get their morality from their corresponding inward acts. Intention is an elicited act of the will, its execution is an ordered act of the will; and ordered acts of the will get their morality from corresponding elicited acts.

Circumstances. They are modifications of the act and agent due to person, quantity, place, helps, motives, manner and time. That circumstances alter the morality of an act, is evident from the following familiar examples. The execution of a condemned criminal by some private citizen, and by the proper public official. The circumstance of person makes the execution in one case an act of legal justice; in the other, an act of murder. To steal five cents, and to steal five dollars.

Quantity makes one sin venial; the other, mortal. To eat and drink in a hotel, and to eat and drink in a church. Place makes the difference between a meal and a sacrilege. To lie, and to confirm the lie with an oath. Manner adds perjury to falsehood. To drink, and to drink to excess. Quantity changes temperance to drunkenness or gluttony. Time makes eating meat on Friday a sin, likewise the omission of communion during the Paschal season. The circumstance, "in church," is as identical with "meal in church," as meal itself, circumstance is as identical with individual act as object.

Specific Morality. A moral act is an act making its agent good or bad, making its agent worthy of praise or of blame. *There are three elements in every moral act. It must be in the power of the agent, subject to his ownership, to make him worthy of praise or of blame. It must possess goodness or badness, to communicate the quality good or bad to the agent. It must be known for good or bad to the agent, to stir the agent's will.* Because of the first element, the agent must be able to do or not do the act, and the act itself must originate in free will. The second element is required, because nothing gives but what it first possesses, and the act must be in harmony or at discord with the objective order. The third element is needed, to stir the will, which is blind, and wishes only what the intellect first offers. A father's care of his child is a moral act, because it is in his power; a bird's care of its young is not a moral act, because it is a matter of instinct and beyond the bird's control. The man is physically free to care for or neglect his child; the bird is not free, it is physically necessitated by instinct to care for its young, or in certain contingencies to neglect its young. Instinct in man is subject to the control of his will.

Generic morality is the feature common to good and bad acts, like animality in man and horse; and origination in intellect and will is the one thing common to good and bad acts. Specific morality is one thing for good acts, another thing for bad acts, like reason in man, and sense in horse; harmony and discord with the objective order being the two differences. Higher species can be considered genera with regard to lower species; and the one thing common to all the virtues is harmony with the objective order of things; the one thing common to all the vices is discord with the same order. Charity, justice, humility are species of the genus, virtue; injury, injustice, pride are species of the genus, vice. Virtue and vice are themselves species of the genus, moral acts.

Object in our thesis means object in strict sense, term of the wish, finis operis. End means intention, and intention means the agent's apprehension and choice of the act in question. Circumstances mean modifications, whether of object or of end. These things premised, we are now ready to prove that a human act gets its specific morality, that a moral act gets its goodness or badness, that the act of a set virtue and the act of a set vice get their denomination from the object of the act, from the agent's end or purpose, and from circumstances affecting both.

PROOF

Acts are specified by their formal objects, and moral acts are no exception to the rule. But the formal object of a generically moral act is an object good or bad in substance, with all its objective circumstances; apprehended as such by the intellect, and chosen as such by the will, with all its subjective circumstances; not the object simply, nor yet the agent's apprehension or choice of it, but all three things together. Ergo, human acts get their specific morality from object, end and circumstances.

With Regard to the Major. The truth is clear in physical acts. Sight is sight because of color, hearing is hearing because of sound. To use the eyes on sweetness, or smoothness, or sound is not to see; to use the ears on color is not to hear. In moral acts good and evil play the parts of color and sound in vision and hearing. Freedom demands knowledge and choice, or purpose; individuality of act demands circumstances.

With Regard to the Minor. The object is the subject-matter, substance of the act; the agent's apprehension and choice of same are his end or intention; objective circumstances are identified with the object; subjective circumstances, with the agent's end or intention. When the eye sees green, a particular and present green is its formal object, and the eye makes the green object its own by entering into knowledge-relations with it. Its formal object is not red or an absent green, or a green with which it has no intimate relations. In a parallel way, when the will elicits a moral act, it chooses a particular good or evil object, represented to it as such by the intellect. Its formal object is not an object viewed as true, or one, or beautiful, but an object viewed as good or evil; not a good or evil object, that never through the intellect appealed to the will; not a good or evil object, that, after word from the intellect, the will never concerned itself with. When end vitiates a good object, the will puts a good thing to bad use, and the intellect is its accomplice. When circumstances vitiate an object good in substance and good in purpose, some accidental badness resided in object, or purpose, or both.

P.S. *Examples Wherein One or Several Elements are Present:* To collect money from a debtor, for the purpose of getting drunk; and to steal money from a neighbor for the same purpose. To deny self for the purpose of giving dinner to a beggar. To walk to church for purposes of prayer. To give alms to a poor man, with the design of making him an accomplice to murder. To give an alms, that a simple lie may be told. Firm will, purposing the lie, vitiates; not inefficax velleitas, mere advertence to wish, caring little whether the lie be told or not, ready to give the alms anyhow. Alms from pity and from vainglory; antecedent purpose vitiates, not concomitant or consequent. A person moved by vainglory to practise daily communion; intention disappears at the altar; non est in executione, sed fuit. To give an alms when forbidden, or though forbidden, or because forbidden; against poverty, against obedience.

N.B. No good end can justify a bad act; good end never justifies a bad means; murder of a Church persecutor, to help religion; defiance of Constitution, to promote Catholic education. Every bad end vitiates a good act. A good or bad end changes an indifferent act to a good or bad act respectively; and this is the one case where end justifies means. It is lawful at times to put a good act, though evil by accident results. The times are, when the good surpasses the evil, and the evil is neither directly nor indirectly intended. The evil is not even indirectly intended, when the good is equally immediate with the evil, and not accomplished with the evil for means. The good act is not lawful, if any of the above conditions fail of verification. A general in time of war is allowed to lay waste the enemy's territory to the harm of innocent citizens. A drunken man is guilty of the curses he utters, if he foresees them in some confused way when sober. Cursing is in this case an indirect voluntary, a voluntary in cause. A doctor is not allowed to kill the child to save the mother. He may remove a certainly dead fetus, not a probably dead fetus. He must never expose the child to danger of death without Baptism. He is allowed to administer medicine, that may by accident result in the child's death. His whole purpose must be to cure the mother, not to kill the child.

THESIS VII

Probabilism is a safe and correct system in matters of conscience. Jouin, 51–56; Rickaby, 152–159.

QUESTION

Rigorism or Absolute Tutiorism, Moderate Tutiorism, Probabiliorism, Æquiprobabilism, Probabilism and Laxism are systems in Ethics meant to help a man choose the right line of conduct, when doubt about right and wrong agitates his mind. As long as the doubt remains, he must do nothing, because it is highly immoral to even expose oneself to the danger of doing wrong. It would be in any case to sin, to act with this principle in mind, "I don't know, but I'll take the risk." *To act with a doubtful conscience is to sin, because it involves contempt of the law.* The man acting with a doubtful conscience cares not whether he keeps the law or breaks it. Among all the above systems, Laxism excepted, Probabilism apparently savors most of a risk; but, as we shall see, the Probabilist runs no risk, enters on no uncertainty, though he neglects the so-called safer course. He is certain that he is right, because a doubtful law certainly has no binding force. *Rigorism and Laxism* have been condemned by the Church in the persons of Alexander VII, in 1656, and Innocent XI, in 1679. Rigorism was taught by the Jansenists, and held that the opinion favoring the law must be followed as long as the opposing view is not certain. In doubt about Friday, you must abstain from meat, till certain it is not Friday. Laxism held that any opinion, with small or no sound reason in its favor, may be followed. In doubt about Friday, with no good reason for the doubt, you may eat meat. Tenuiter probabile non est probabile pro prudenti. In the case of a prudent man, what is only slightly probable is not probable at all. *Moderate Tutiorism and Probabilior-*

101

ism have no advocates to-day, and can be neglected. The first held that the opinion favoring the law must be followed, unless the opposing view is most probable; the second prescribes the same course, unless the opposite opinion is more probable. *Æquiprobabilism* allows departure from the law, if reasons for its non-existence are as strong, or nearly as strong, as reasons for its existence. Things are reversed, if doubt turns on the lapse or cessation of a law. Many Redemptorists profess to derive this last system from St. Alphonsus, though the saint is Probabilism's staunch defender. *Probabilism teaches that, in doubt whether an act is permissible or not, true and real probability in favor of the act or its omission makes one or other quite legitimate, though greater probability attaches to the contrary or so-called safer course.* If you have good and solid reasons for thinking that the day of the week is not Friday, you may eat meat, even if you have better and stronger reasons for thinking that it is Friday, provided only that you are not really and truly certain that it is Friday. If certain that it is Friday, of course you have no good and solid reason for thinking that it is not Friday. Your reasons must be good and solid, even if weaker than their opposites, because slight reasons are reckoned no reasons by the prudent, and Laxism is condemned by common sense as well as by the Church.

TERMS

Probabilism. Probabilism is as old as Christianity, and was in common use with the early Fathers and Doctors of the Church. Years ago it was called into question by decisions rendered against Laxism by Alexander VII and Innocent XI; but it always counted among its defenders the most celebrated theologians. More recently a wrong understanding of St. Alphonsus gave rise to Æquiprobabilism, and the Church has not directly settled the controversy between Æquiprobabilism and Probabilism. In Æquiprobabilism, if one of the two views is less probable than the other, it must not be followed; if the two views are equally probable, either may be chosen. In some few passages of St. Alphonsus, because of his zeal against Laxism, the less probable view is rated slightly probable and negligible in itself; and, therefore, its opposite becomes morally certain. Even with Probabilists, when moral certainty arises, only one course of conduct is open, because conscience is in that case certain and not doubtful. Moral certainty is firm assent of mind without dread of opposite, all based on laws governing human nature. Physical certainty is a parallel state of mind, based on laws governing physical nature. Metaphysical certainty is a parallel state of mind based on connection of identity between ideas in subject and predicate. Therefore, there are three kinds of certainty, metaphysical, physical and moral; and all three kinds imply firm assent of the mind, and exclude dread of the opposite, possibility of the opposite. In the abstract, physical and moral admit of the dread of possibility, due to a miracle, or to a departure from the laws governing human acts. In the concrete and in particular, even physical and moral as completely exclude this dread and possibility as metaphysical. Abstract possibility of the opposite is compatible with concrete impossibility of the same; and, unless circumstances rule out the concrete possibility of a miracle or of a departure from said laws, physical and moral certainty are out of the question. *Moral certainty is, therefore, just as tight and solid as metaphysical, in point of excluding dread of the opposite; and probability never rises to the dignity of moral certainty.* Probability always leaves the opposite a concrete possibility. Moral certainty, in strict sense, excludes possibility of opposite; in wide sense, it excludes positive probability of opposite, admitting its negative probability, based on slender reasons, accounted none at all by the prudent.

Conscience. Conscience is from cum and scientia, and means knowledge with a bearing on the good or evil of a particular human act. It is the subjective element in law's application, it is the immediate and proximate measure of a man's moral conduct. It is the work of the intellect in what we already established as the standard of morality, namely the objective order of things as grasped by the intellect. Consciousness is likewise from cum and scientia, and means knowledge with a bearing on the operations of the soul's other faculties. Conscience is not consciousness, nor is it synderesis, which is the habit of morality's first principles. Conscience is rather the application of synderesis to concrete and particular acts. Both are applications of law to moral acts, both measure man's conduct with law for standard; but, while synderesis in an academic way and out of court decides that murder, for instance, is wrong and must be avoided, conscience in a practical way and in court decides that this particular act, because murder, must be avoided. The object of the particular act, with end and circumstances, and their harmony or discord with the objective order of things embodied in the law, are the objective element in law's application; and this objective element is quite independent of morality's subjective element or conscience. *When the moral value of a man's act is under consideration, objective order measures conscience; when the moral value of the man himself is under consideration, things are reversed, and conscience measures objective order.* Morally speaking, a man's act has its matter and form from the act itself, without any reference to conscience; a man's conduct has its matter from his acts, its form from his conscience. A materially bad act is likewise a formally bad act; but materially bad conduct can easily be formally good conduct, and vice-versa. God can reward a wicked deed and punish an act of virtue, when conscience is invincibly false. He looks not to the act but to the heart of the agent; and material virtue, when accompanied by formal wickedness, is unspeakably worse than material sin accompanied by formal righteousness. Beyond doubt, the lay-brother, who drowned Chinese babies, after baptizing them, was rewarded for material and formal murder, and the ignorant fellow who lied, because invincibly persuaded that charity demanded it, was rewarded for a material and formal untruth. *Their acts were wrong, their conduct was right.* They were false to objective order, but true to conscience, and conscience measures objective order when a man's conduct is in question, not his acts. Conscience is *antecedent*, when it turns on present or future acts, and discharges the functions of a guide. It is *consequent*, when it turns on past acts, and plays the part of a judge. Conscience in strict sense is antecedent. Conscience is reason decreeing the lawfulness or unlawfulness of a particular act. Its decree always assumes the shape of a practical judgment, the conclusion of a moral syllogism, therefore I must do this or avoid that. Distinguish between conscience and its decree. Conscience is the mind exercising a particular function. Its decree is an act of the mind, a judgment. In strict sense, conscience has to do with acts on the eve of being accomplished here and now. The Major in a moral syllogism represents synderesis, the Minor represents conscience theoretically viewed, the conclusion represents conscience practically viewed; and therefore the conclusion best deserves the title, decree of conscience. The Major is remote principle or synderesis, the Minor is conscience in actu primo proximo, the conclusion is conscience in second act. With truth or harmony with objective order for viewpoint, conscience is *true or false, right or wrong*. If the premisses are true, or if they are invincibly false, conscience is right. If the premisses are vincibly false, conscience is wrong. With degree of certainty, or mind's acquiescence, for measure, conscience is *certain, probable or doubtful*. Recall the states of mind discussed in Logic, certainty, opinion, doubt. Doubt may be *positive or negative*. Positive has weighty reasons in its favor; negative has slight or no reasons in its favor. In matters of conscience negative doubt is neglected, because it is of no weight with the prudent. Doubt may be *juris or facti*. The first turns on a law's existence; the second, on some particular fact. Similar expressions are de jure and de facto in questions of property and authority; owner de jure and owner de facto; king de jure and king de facto. A doubtful conscience is in reality no conscience at all, because no actual decision is made. Darkness is the absence of light. In question of lawfulness or unlawfulness, not in question of validity or invalidity, in question of law not of fact, Probabilism with the help of a reflex principle changes a doubtful conscience to a certain conscience, and opens the way to action. A perplexed conscience sees sin in both alternatives, tender is severe with the slightest defects, lax unduly favors freedom.

Here is the whole truth about the bearing of conscience on morality. To be right, a man must act with at least a morally certain conscience in strict or wide sense, his final practical judgment regarding the lawfulness of an act must be at least

morally certain. His final practical judgment must admit
no sound or positive doubt, because to act otherwise would be
to expose oneself deliberately to the danger of doing wrong;
and moral certainty in wide sense is the highest we regularly
reach in daily life. Without detriment to the moral certainty
of his final practical judgment, his remote practical judgment
can be even positively doubtful or probable, because his conduct is not based on his remote practical judgment, but on his
final practical judgment; and with the help of a reflex principle he can transform his probable remote judgment into a
morally certain final practical judgment; and this in substance is Probabilism. By supposition, then, in Probabilism
a man's remote practical judgment is positively doubtful or
probable, the doubt is based on good and sound reasons in
the eyes of the wise, the doubt cannot be removed by study
or investigation; one or other course must be taken; he must
not even doubtfully go against the law; with the help of a
reflex principle he changes his conscience from doubtful to
certain, and neglects the doubtful law. As long as the law
remains doubtful, he is of course at liberty to keep it. He
is likewise at liberty to neglect it without wrong.

PROOFS

When conscience returns a clear and positive answer, it
must be followed. When conscience is perplexed, a man's
first duty is to enquire and seek information. If doubt remains after due enquiry, he is not held to the so-called safer
course, he is not held to suppose an obligation. Neither is he
allowed to act with a doubtful conscience. The Probabilist
runs no risk, enters on no uncertainty, though he neglects the
safer course so-called. Lacking available direct principles, he
calls a reflex principle to his aid. A direct principle lays
down the law, when conscience returns a clear and positive
answer. A direct principle is no help in this man's case.
He judges of his own act, taking into account his imperfect
knowledge and limited powers. He makes no attempt to
determine what another man with clear and positive knowledge ought to do. He calls to his aid this reflex principle,
"A doubtful law has no binding force." This is a reflex or

mind-principle, because objectively and outside of the mind nothing is doubtful. The question is, not the law absolutely, but the law as far as I can make it out. Liberty is prior to the law. Liberty is in possession. The law, to bind, must with certainty restrict liberty. Besides, no law binds, till promulgated. Promulgation connotes certain knowledge, not doubtful or probable merely; and, as long as doubt remains, the law is not promulgated for me, and the fault is not on my side. Authority is overwhelmingly on the side of Probabilism, and it would be long to quote authors. St. Alphonsus seems to favor Æquiprobabilism and Tutiorism, but he can be explained aright. With St. Alphonsus the safer course is alone morally certain; the safe course is not probable at all, and he is talking against Laxism.

PRINCIPLES

A. My doubt must be serious, and hold out against arguments for the existence of an obligation. No indulgence must be shown laxity of conscience, which leans on slender doubt. My doubt must persevere after due enquiry, and must be based on positive reasons against the obligation. My doubt must not be simple ignorance, it must be able to tell why. Some minds doubt without being able to give their reasons why. These minds must have recourse to others in moral questions. My reason for doubt can be an intrinsic or extrinsic argument. Hence another's opinion, when creative of solid probability, can suffice. The probability must be comparative, it must hold ground in face of opposing arguments. After all has been said, it must be not unlikely. It need not be more likely. That means more probable, not probable simply. My doubt must be practical, not speculative, because Ethics is a matter of conduct, not a matter of theorizing. Theoretically speaking, a man can be saved with confession once a year; practically speaking, and when easy opportunity offers, he must approach the sacrament oftener to be saved. All the difficulty turns on the varying amount of diligence necessary in enquiry to constitute it moral diligence. Deeper investigation is needed when matter in question is of vital interest, like confession, than when mere observance, like a fast-day. In question of rolling stones over a precipice, the doubt must be about the act itself, not about its consequences. It is certainly wrong to take any such risk, and Probabilism has no play.

B. *Probabilism is available only in cases involving the lawfulness or unlawfulness of an act, never in cases involving validity or invalidity; in cases of law, never in cases of fact;* because, while doubtful laws are a reality on account of needful knowledge and promulgation, facts are nothing unless sure and certain. *Lawfulness has an element of subjectivity, which is altogether absent from validity.* The phase of mind of the agent has no influence on the validity or invalidity of an act, or on the reality of a fact; it has a very perceptible influence on the binding force of a law. A law binds only when known, a fact is a fact whether it is known or not.

Examples of lawfulness are abstinence on Friday, Mass on Sunday, the Lenten fast. Examples of validity are marriage, ordination, baptism, real bread and real wine, wills, medicine. Examples of facts are utterance of a vow, seven years of age, baptism, priesthood, fast broken, debts paid. When a certainly valid sacrament is impossible, a dubiously valid sacrament is better than no sacrament at all, e.g., baptism with perfume, especially when necessity urges, and the sacrament can be afterwards repeated either conditionally or absolutely. Sometimes doubt regarding the lawfulness of an act arises from doubt regarding validity, and Probabilism is of no avail; because such conduct would betray contempt of virtue and too small fear of sin. To be husband and wife, a man and woman must be certainly married; and a doubtful marriage never makes a man and woman husband and wife; it leaves them single from the viewpoint of morality. Doubt regarding facts must be settled some other way, usually by an appeal to fixed principles, deriving their certainty from authority. Some principles of the kind follow. "Possession is nine-tenths of the law," for money in hand. "Apart from questions of justice, the probable fulfilment of a law is on a level with its certain fulfilment," for sins told or omitted at confession. "Facts must not be presumed, they must be proved," for fast before communion and for utterance of a vow. "In doubt stand to presumption," "Doubts must be settled with the help of what ordinarily happens," for a priest at Communion afraid that he has omitted the Pater Noster, for parts of Office.

THESIS VIII

VIRTUES AND VICES
Jouin, 56–70; *Rickaby,* 64–109.

Virtue is a habitus operativus bonus, vice is a habitus operativus malus. To translate, virtue and vice are good and bad habits with a bearing on work. The expression, with a bearing on work, serves to separate virtue from grace. Virtue in simple and strict sense belongs exclusively to the will; in qualified and wide sense it is applicable to whatsoever faculty in the man. Though prudence resides in the mind, it is directive of the will. A man is simply and in strict sense good, when his will is right. He is good in qualified and wide sense, when his legs are swift, when his eye and hand are ready to art, when his wit is quick; and we call him not good without any qualification, but a good runner, a good painter, a good scholar. Virtue is not said of irrational agents, because their conduct is fixed for them by instinct. Virtue postulates free will, because it helps to choose between good and evil. Silence is no virtue in a dumb person, temperance in food and drink is no virtue in an angel, because the dumb person and the angel are without any power to choose in these particulars. Silence in a talkative person, and temperance in a man are very decided virtues. Virtue, therefore, is a habit; *and Aristotle describes habit as a quality superadded to a faculty, rendering it well or ill disposed towards itself or something else.* Virtue, whether in strict or wide sense, dwells in some faculty of the soul, and favorably disposes that faculty towards itself or towards another.

The soul is remote principle of all the man's activities; *faculties are proximate connatural principles, superadded by nature to the soul; habits are proximate acquired principles, superadded not by nature but by personal endeavor to the faculties.* Therefore, the soul helps the man, faculties help the soul, and habits help the faculties. *Suarez offers this defi-nition of a faculty-habit, a quality hard to remove, super-added to the faculty, and meant of itself and primarily to assist the faculty.* This definition separates a faculty-habit from a soul-habit, from faculty, from act, from passing dis-positions, and assigns its purpose and efficiency. Habits re-side in faculties, that are vital and somehow intellectual. Infused or supernatural habits are communicated to the fac-ulty by God, and procure, not readiness in supernatural activity, but the very activity itself. Faith as a natural habit, and faith as a supernatural habit can serve for ex-planation. Natural or acquired habits result from reiterated acts of some one kind; they confer not the power to act, but the power to act with ease and readiness. *The faculty with-out the habit is simple power to act, the faculty with the habit is power to act with ease and facility.* Custom, because par-ent to habit, gets the name second nature. Faculty is first nature, habit is second nature. Habits of sense and habits of appetite explain themselves, likewise habits of mind and habits of will. Habits of will are moral habits, and are good or bad, virtues or vices. Physical habits are of indifferent moral worth, like study, talk, walk, thought. To include virtue in qualified and wide sense, as well as virtue in simple and strict sense, virtue is in general defined a habit perfect-ing, improving, rounding out a rational faculty and bend-ing it towards good. Good here means physical as well as moral good for the faculty, and good in the sense of con-duct; good for any faculty, and good for the will exclusively. Virtue in simple and strict sense perfects the will, and in-clines it to moral good. Virtue in qualified and wide sense perfects any other faculty, and inclines it to its own improve-ment. A habit that never betrays itself in acts is no virtue, because it falls away from its purpose. It is for facility, and facility without acts is impossible. Prudence, *recta ratio agibilium*, right order in conduct, is a practical, intellectual virtue; and for that reason, a moral virtue. It has a directive bearing on the will, and virtues concerned with the will are moral virtues. Here are four definitions of virtue, taken in simple and strict sense. *St. Thomas* defines virtue as, "habitus operativus bonus," a good faculty-habit, a good

habit bearing on activity; and good means moral good, not
physical. *Aristotle* defines virtue as a habit, that makes its
owner and his work good. *Aristotle* again defines virtue as
a habit, that chooses the middle course with respect to ourselves, said middle course being fixed by reason, as a man
of prudence would determine it; a habit of avoiding what
would be excess or defect in the esteem of a prudent man.
St. Augustine defines virtue as a good quality of will, a help
to right living, and no help to wrong. When St. Augustine
adds, "produced in us by God without our assistance," he
is talking of infused virtue. Like freedom, virtue resides in
the will as in subject, and in other faculties only inasmuch
as they work in connection with, under motion from, or under
control of the will. Prudence directs the will. Virtue is a
moral habit, moral habits result from moral acts, and moral
acts are one way or another acts of the will. Scattered acts
of virtue, no result of habit, never make a man simply and unqualifiedly good. They make him good with a qualification
and circumstances. The regularity and constancy secured by
habit, alone constitute a man simply and unqualifiedly good.
As St. Thomas says, regularity and constancy in good demand
that good acts be elicited with readiness, with unbroken uniformity, and with delight; and these requisites are verified
only when virtuous deeds become a habit, a species of second
nature.

*The moral virtues are divided into the four cardinal vir-
tues, prudence, justice, fortitude and temperance.* St. Thomas
offers these two reasons for the division. Objective order is
the standard of morality, reason must discover this order and
propose its commands to the will; the will in turn must execute these commands in its own field and in the field of the
passions, whether they tend towards good or away from evil,
whether concupiscible or irascible, desire or aversion. *Prudence*, the habit of doing the right thing at the right time, is
reason's helper; *justice*, the habit of giving everybody his due,
is helper to the will in its own operations; *temperance* helps
the will in its management of appetite's desires; *fortitude*
helps to manage appetite's aversions. Four faculties contribute to man's moral acts, intellect, will, appetite of desire

and appetite of aversion; and the four cardinal virtues in order keep these faculties right. *Circumspice, age, abstine, sustine.* Be sure you're right, then go ahead. These virtues are called cardinal, because they are to all the other virtues what the hinges are to the door; their support, basis of their utility, and surpassing them all in point of worth and necessity. All the other virtues can be referred to these four as parts to a whole. It is easy to see that no moral virtue is complete and perfect without these others. Obedience, for instance, is hard because of pride, sensuality, laziness, dread; and complete obedience is next to impossible without humility, temperance, diligence, courage. Want of temperance and avarice are often responsible for injustice, and there is no justice where these vices are in control.

Vice is virtue's contrary. It is *habitus operativus malus,* a habit helping a faculty to moral evil. We must distinguish in an evil habit or vice, as we distinguish in an evil act, a positive entity and a negative. The negative entity is its malice, and lies in its lack of moral goodness, its lack of harmony with the objective order. The formal object of a vice is some aspect of inferior good, at odds with the objective order, and inseparably connected with malice. Every virtue can count at least two opposite vices, one by way of excess, the other by way of defect. The seven capital or cardinal sins are rooted in the seven good things most calculated to excite the will to rebellion against reason or the objective order. They are vainglory, gluttony, lust, avarice, sloth, envy and anger. *The first four seek good in a disorderly way, the other three shun good because of some evil connected with it.* Goods of soul, like praise and honor, excite vainglory; goods of body with a bearing on the race's preservation, like unholy pleasure, are matter for lust; goods of body with a bearing on the individual's preservation, like food and drink, excite gluttony; outside goods like wealth provoke avarice. The good shunned may be one's own or another's. Sloth shuns one's own good to avoid labor; envy shuns another's good without thought of revenge, it is sadness at another's good because rated an obstacle to one's own. Anger shuns another's good with thought of revenge. Pride is queen of all the vices. In the order of intention pride is first of all the vices, in the order of execution avarice enjoys the prerogative.

Prudence. Aristotle defines prudence as recta ratio agibilium, right decision in things to do, habit of practical not speculative reason, helping to right decisions in question of moral conduct. Art is different, it is recta ratio factibilium, right decision in things to make. Art tends to make some outside work right in physical sense, prudence tends to make some act of the man morally good. Lessius defines prudence as a habit of intellect helping us to know in every emergency what is right and what is wrong. There are two kinds of prudence, personal and political or state prudence. The chief functions of prudence are euboulia, synesis, gnome, which mean habit of taking advice, habit of giving advice, habit of interpretation. The integral parts of prudence are memory, intellect, foresight, argumentation, skill, openness to instruction, caution, and wide range of vision.

Christ in the mystery of His loss in the temple is teaching a profound lesson in prudence. St. Luke tells the story in the ten last verses of his second chapter. "Did you not know that I must be about my Father's business?" Prudence in practice is the art of doing the right thing at the right time. Wisdom is her handmaid, her counsellor. She guides prudence in her choice of conduct. Wisdom is in the mind, prudence directs the will; and both together hath a perfect work. In the realm of conduct the will knows nothing, wishes everything; the mind knows everything, wishes nothing. The will stings the mind to industry and borrows in turn from its servant the light it needs. Prudence, then, with the help of wisdom, enables its owner to choose aright, when two lines of conduct are submitted to him for selection. Generally it manifests itself in a fixed phase of mind and will, perpetually ready to abandon the less for the greater. In the case under consideration Jesus had to choose between His Heavenly Father's business and His Mother's pleasure. His infinite prudence saw only one way open; and He tarried three days in the temple, in spite of the pang His stay inflicted on Mary's heart and Joseph's. A mere man, abandoned in the same predicament by prudence, would go terribly wrong and journey down to Nazareth with his parents. All our mistakes are due to want of prudence. Every duty we neglect betokens absence of the quality. Every law we break is a departure from its salutary promptings. We are abandoning the greater for the less; we are sacrificing the service of God for sloth, for selfishness, for personal comfort. It must have cost the Child Christ a heavy pang to inflict this pain on His Mother and St. Joseph. He was as desirous of their holy company as they were of His. His sorrow was an answering echo to theirs. But His Father's business beckoned Him from afar, and He had to follow. Everything must yield before God's service. Next to virtue, life is man's supremest good on earth, and the martyrs surrendered that. In the catalogue of present goods, parents, home and friends rank next to life; and religious surrender them, making every vocation to the monastery or convent a re-enactment of the sacred mystery we study.

Justice. *Justice is a constant and lasting readiness to render to everybody his due, it is a habit of will prompt and ready to render to everybody his due.* Constant and lasting are implied in the word, habit. One act of justice never makes a just man, because justice is a habit. Justice is divided into *commutative, distributive and legal.* St. Thomas calls legal justice general; he calls commutative and distributive, particular justice. St. Thomas treats this virtue of justice in his Summa 2.2. between Questions 57 and 122. Legal justice, he says, makes a good citizen, commutative and distributive make a good man. 2.2. Q.58. a.6. Justice is directive of a man's conduct towards others, under the aspect of what is due these others. Man can be taken as an individual or as a unit in the state. He has relations with the state as a whole, and legal justice helps him fulfil them. The state as a whole has relations with him, and distributive justice manages them. He has relations with individuals in the state as men, and not as citizens, and commutative justice is the virtue concerned. *Legal justice* is in the ruler effectively, in the subject executively. The ruler makes the laws, the subject keeps them. The ruler is rendering the state its due, when he makes laws; the subject, when he keeps them; both contributing to the common good. *Distributive justice* is di-

rective of the state or its head in the distribution of privileges and duties, dignities and burdens, rewards and penalties, influencing citizens to accept one and the other with
satisfied content. *Commutative justice* is directive of the
individual in transactions with his neighbor, involving sale
and purchase and kindred processes, designated in a general
way as exchange. Commutare means to exchange, as dis-
tribuere means to distribute.

Justice makes equality between two. In commutative the
transaction is between two individuals, buyer and seller, or
thief and his victim, as the case may be. One gives money
and gets wares, the other gives wares and gets money, and
there is equality or justice. One gets wares and gives nothing, the other gives wares and gets nothing; and there is inequality or injustice. The equality and inequality are
arithmetical, like 5 and 5, because such equality and inequality are possible in commutative. In distributive the transaction is between state and citizens. The citizens give service and get office, the state gets service and gives office. Distributive is less concerned with rewarding citizens than with
rewarding them in a proportionate way. If the state with-
holds reward, it is offending against legal and commutative
rather than against distributive justice. Distributive is hurt,
only when some citizen, as compared with another citizen,
gets a reward out of all proportion with his deserts. In distributive two citizens deserve well of the whole community
or state in different degrees. John is worth 4 degrees to the
state in point of meritorious service, and gets in return 8
degrees of reward in the shape of honor, dignity or office.
If James deserves well of the state to the extent of 2 degrees,
distributive justice demands that he get in return 4 degrees
of reward, not 6. John gets 4 more degrees than he gave,
James gets only 2 more than he gave. The citizens give of
their persons and get things, the state gets of their persons
and gives things; and, as between persons and things, the
only equality possible is geometrical or proportional, in this
case, 4:8::2:4. Arithmetical equality is possible between
things and things, and commutative justice is concerned exclusively with things. In legal justice the transaction is between citizen and state. The state gives law securing com-

mon good, and gets obedience. The citizen gives obedience,
and gets common good. Here there is question of things;
and, because of arithmetical equality, if the ruler makes 4
laws, every citizen has to keep all 4. The ruler as seat and
centre of authority is the state formally taken, citizens are
the state materially taken, and the ruler in his capacity of
citizen is part of it. In distributive the debt is owed the
citizen, and the state pays it. In legal the debt is due the
ruler or state, and the citizen pays it. Law is a debt the
ruler owes the community, obedience is a debt the community
owes the ruler. The ruler gets obedience, and gives common
good; the citizen gets common good, and gives obedience.

Of the three kinds of justice, distributive and legal are the
least definite; and, because restitution is practically impossible, they are of less importance than commutative in the
event of infringement. They are in the main observed, when
the ruler does his utmost to distribute favors and burdens
with a fair and even hand, when citizens abide by the law
in all its details. If worthy citizens fail of their due reward,
the ruler cannot make amends without doing injustice to
others already in possession of dignities; and to make restitution out of his own pocket would not be distributive justice,
which is concerned with the state's property, offices and
such, not with the ruler's private property. Favoritism and
nepotism are offenses against distributive, and they meet with
full treatment in the Summa, 2.2. Q.63. God plays no fa-
vorites, He is not a respecter of persons, A.A.10, 34. Penalties are restitution in the case of offended legal justice, and
the law never expects a criminal to bear witness against himself. Offenses against commutative justice are clear-cut and
well defined, the amount of restitution is a matter of arithmetic, and the obligation stands till the last penny is paid.

Commutative justice is a process of exchange, and all exchanges are voluntary or involuntary. Voluntary exchanges
constitute business, and base the virtue of justice; involuntary exchanges base the vice of injustice. With this twofold
fact in mind, St. Thomas in his Summa, 2.2. Q.61, a.3, furnishes us with a list of ordinary business transactions with a
bearing on justice, and a list of ordinary offenses against justice. Voluntary exchanges are involved in buying and sell-

ing, usufruct, lending and borrowing, renting and hiring, pawning, bailing. Involuntary exchanges are theft, robbery, murder, assault, imprisonment, blows, wounds, lies, detraction, false witness, insult, adultery with wife, seduction of slave. The whole of Question 62 deals with restitution in 8 articles. Between Questions 64 and 77, involuntary exchanges, or species of injustice, are discussed and explained. Between Questions 77 and 79, voluntary exchanges are treated, with special attention to buying, and selling, and interest. Question 79 deals with the integral parts of justice, do good and avoid evil, give everybody his due, and refuse nobody his due. From Question 80 to Question 123, virtues closely connected with justice are discussed, and they are nine in number; religion, filial piety, esteem, truthfulness, gratitude, defense, all enumerated by Cicero in his De Inventione, Book 2, along with friendship, generosity and equity. Connected virtues in part differ from, and in part resemble justice. Justice gives everybody his due according to equality. Equality is absent from religion, filial piety and esteem; due is wanting in the other six. Religion or duties to God cover QQ. 81–101; filial piety, 101; esteem, 101–106; gratitude, 106–108; defense, 108; truthfulness, 109–114; friendship or affability, 114–117; generosity, 117–120; equity, 120. He closes with a brief discussion of the Ten Commandments, or precepts of justice, 122. Equity or epikeia, supra justum, is a superior kind of legal justice, because it interprets law not according to words, but according to the mind of the lawmaker. No lawmaker can formulate a law able to touch every single occurrence. He legislates for ordinary contingencies, for what commonly happens; and circumstances can quite change cases.

Fortitude. Cicero defines fortitude as a judicious encounter with danger, and sufferance of trouble, or endurance of effort. It regulates the irascible passions embodying difficulty, just as temperance has to do with the concupiscible passions. Fear and courage are the two passions with which fortitude is especially concerned, keeping them both within the bounds of reason. Fear is dread of an evil conceived as unavoidable, courage is dread of an evil avoidable only at the expense of great effort. Fortitude is conspicuous in martyrdom, and naturally speaking fear of death is the greatest of all fears. Fortitude is more prominent in repressing fear than in exciting courage. It is harder to bear trouble than to attack it; because, in bearing trouble, the victim is weaker than trouble; in attacking trouble, the threatened victim is stronger than trouble. Besides, trouble in the case of fear is nearer being present, in courage trouble is future and farther in the distance. Fear is long, courage is short. Fear is a sin, when against order; when it flees evils that ought to be met in the performance of duty. Fear is no sin, when it flees evils that ought to be avoided, evils that can be avoided without detriment to duty. Timidity is excessive fear, rashness is excessive courage.

The four virtues connected with fortitude are spiritedness, grandeur, patience and perseverance. Inasmuch as it is a judicious encounter with danger, fortitude displays itself as spiritedness by way of preparation, and as grandeur by way of execution. Inasmuch as it is a judicious endurance of effort, fortitude displays itself as patience when trouble is short, and as perseverance when trouble is long. Magnanimity is grandeur in general, magnificence is grandeur in the department of expense. The latter moves men to make large outlays of money to ensure some grand project. Confidence and security are parts of spiritedness. Presumption is an excess of spiritedness. So is ambition, or inordinate greed of honor. Vainglory is likewise an excess of spiritedness. Desire of glory is not in itself wrong, when the glory sought is solid and true, when the seeker's purpose is right, and the means he uses are legitimate. Desire of vain or empty glory is wrong; and glory is vain or empty, when based on a thing that deserves no praise, when tribute from a man whose judgment is little worth, when turned to wrong account, not directed to the glory of God or the neighbor's salvation. Vainglory is one of the capital sins, and counts for daughters' disobedience, boastfulness, hypocrisy, novelty, stubbornness of opinion, contrariness of will, and disputatiousness. Want of spirit is opposed to spiritedness by way of defect; presumption, by way of excess. One attempts less than it ought to attempt; the other, more; while spiritedness attempts what it ought to attempt. Stinginess is opposed to magnificence.

One rates the cost and neglects results; the other rates results and neglects the cost. Extravagance is the opposite of stinginess. One makes man a spendthrift, the other makes him a miser. Patience is a remedy against sadness. All the moral virtues are helps to prevent the passions, in the presence of good or evil, from dragging reason to wrong. Patience, therefore, enables us to bear ills with an even mind, and not desert the right in an attempt to escape them. It is a virtue inferior to prudence, justice, fortitude and temperance, as well as to the theological virtues. Perseverance is part of fortitude, because it weakens fear and strengthens courage, always with a view to length of duration. Fortitude can be the work of a minute, perseverance is the work of years. Softness and stubbornness are opposed to perseverance by way of defect and excess respectively. St. Thomas deals with fortitude in his Summa, 2.2. QQ. 123–141.

Temperance. Fortitude controls the irascible passions in their retreat from evil, temperance controls the concupiscible passions in their pursuit of good. Pleasure is the one great good appealing to the concupiscible passions; and God, as a reward and incentive, attaches pleasure to conservation of the race and conservation of the individual. Pleasures of touch contribute to the conservation of the race, pleasures of taste to that of the individual. Therefore, temperance is most conspicuous in control of pleasures of the flesh, and pleasures of the table. Temperance restrains impurity and gluttony. Temperance is not abstinence. One uses pleasure within the bounds prescribed by reason, the other refrains from pleasure altogether. Naturally speaking, abstinence from all food and drink would be wrong, because use of some food and drink is a law of nature imposed on the individual. Abstinence from some certain food or drink would not be wrong, because no set food or drink is necessary to conservation of the individual. Abstinence from all the pleasures of the flesh would not be wrong in any individual, because conservation of the race is a law imposed on no individuals in particular, but on the race in general. If scattered individuals refuse to propagate, the race can still continue; if any individual refuses to eat, he will die. Others can propagate the race in our stead, nobody can eat for us. Therefore, while total abstinence from wine is quite right and highly commendable in any individual, the moderate use of wine is far from wrong. Total abstinence from pleasures of the flesh is the only line of conduct open to individuals outside the condition of marriage, because these pleasures of the flesh are for the conservation of the race, and marriage is the one process appointed by God and nature for the propagation of the race. Moderate use of these pleasures with a view to reproduction is temperance, and peculiarly a virtue of the married. No use of these pleasures, whether moderate or excessive, is alone legitimate with the unmarried. Temperance is abstinence from illegitimate pleasure, it is the moderate and sensible use of legitimate pleasure. Fasting in food, sobriety in drink, chastity in pleasures of the flesh are forms of temperance. Shame is a kind of chastity. Purity and decency are parts of temperance. Continence, humility, modesty, mildness, mercy, moderation, politeness have family-resemblances with temperance. *St. Thomas treats temperance in his Summa*, 2.2. QQ. 141–171.

THESIS IX

CHARACTER AND HABITS

MORALLY speaking, character is the man; every man's character is his own work; and our destiny for weal or woe is in our own hands. Character is no very profound mystery, it is the plainest of problems. All has been said, when we remark that *character is compounded of temperament and habits.* Our temperaments are common with other hereditary qualities we get from our parents; and, whether they are helps or hindrances to virtue and honesty, we must be content to employ them with thankfulness when they are helps, and supplement them with an abundant measure of good will when they are hindrances. No mortal can shift on temperament the blame for mediocrity. Parents are indeed responsible for tendencies and traits their children inherit, they are not responsible for their children's crimes. No man can allow temperament to bind him hand and foot and drag him to ruin, without proclaiming himself an abject slave, without trailing his dignity in the mire, without surrendering his birthright of liberty. Free will holds the key to the situation. Temperament is not omnipotent. It is a mighty factor for good or evil, but it is far from settling the question. Free will is mightier than temperament; the man born for conspiracy, treason and murder, can by dint of assiduous care become conspicuous for honorable valor, a red-hot patriot, a martyr in the cause of charity. The temperament of a degenerate, when free will is not yet submerged, is as much an instrument for good as the temperament of a saint. The degenerate has a harder road to travel; he has to walk with more care, more circumspection and more courage; but his feet are mercifully fitted for rough as well as smoother roads, and the precautions enumerated are within his power. Tendencies and traits he inherited from his progenitors can bend, without being able to break, his will; and with the iron in his nature he can stiffen his courage to meet whatever strain. Temperament is, therefore, no insuperable hindrance to the cultivation of character; and of the two elements making up character, temperament is less within our power than habit. Our temperament we never make, we receive it; but free will is its mistress, and, when the heart is alert, temperament never slips control.

Our habits we make for ourselves, they are the growth of scattered acts; and we form habits with our eyes wide open to the process and its consequences. Habits are even less a mystery than temperament. *They are facilities along certain lines due to the frequent repetition of separate and distinct acts.* Nobody knows with certainty the exact number of times an act has to be repeated to form a habit; but everybody is agreed that a habit of music, for instance, is out of the question without days, and weeks, and years of practice. And what is true of music is true of painting, oratory, honesty, veracity, all the arts and all the virtues, our moral as well as our physical activities. Even walking is a habit; and, though men and women pass from point to point in space with small reflection and less endeavor, it would pay the philosopher to know what mental exertion it costs baby to master this simple habit.

But what we would most of all insist on, is the circumstance that our habits are distinctively home-products. We make them, we never receive them; and we are entirely and utterly responsible for the part they play in our lives. Even when habits are once formed, our wills are free, and quite able to resist them; and, before they are formed, our wills are absolute, and supreme, and omnipotent lords of the separate and distinct acts that originate them. Hence, nobody can hide behind habit for excuse. The criminal who is such from habit, is even more blameworthy than the criminal such by surprise. Habitual crime is the growth of misspent years, and betokens an accumulation of shame. Wrong not rooted in habit may result from defective vigilance, want of experience, overwhelming temptation; and the law is more lenient with first offenders than with veterans in vice.

Though not omnipotent, habit is a mighty factor in the

formation of character and consequent conduct; and, therefore, our habits call for supremest care. Education is little
worth, unless it contributes to the formation of mental and
moral habits beyond reproach. Family is a wasted blessing,
unless boys and girls come out of it better prepared for the
battle of life. Government is a curse, unless its representatives are a perpetual incentive to the mental and moral uplift
of its citizens. Church itself and religion are of little use,
unless their professing members are bettered by contact with
their aspirations and ideals. An ideal father and an ideal
mother are mortals, whose behavior uniformly provokes children to the cultivation of every virtue, domestic, civic and
religious. The education that ministers merely to the mind,
with little or no concern for the heart, is as empty as a game
of hazard, and bound to work equal harm to family, state
and Church. Our years at school are the critical period in
our lives. Men and women are made and unmade during
this all-important season; and, if we leave school with wrong
habits, we are in imminent danger of ultimate loss, and
strenuous endeavor becomes the price of salvation.

Therefore, we ought to be supremely solicitous about the
quality of our habits, and we ought to take serious thought
of our equipment in habits. Measures must be taken to
break with undesirable habits, and precautions must be employed to strengthen and multiply right tendencies in our
character. We must encourage the good in us, keep down the
evil; and the whole process is summed up in the one word,
control. Nothing so develops character as self-control. Good
habits result from repeated acts of virtue, bad habits are
broken by repeated victories over temptation to wrong; and
control is fully equal to the double task. It is a two-edged
sword, it cuts both ways. Man, as now constituted, is inclined to evil from his youth; he leans towards vice and
away from virtue; he is swift to one, slow to the other; and
self-control, while it keeps him from slaving to base instincts,
urges him to develop the better side of his character. Without an abiding habit of self-control, success in life is absolutely out of the question. Without it, you cannot hope for
Heaven; without it, you cannot reasonably expect to escape
hell. Self-control is what makes men temperate, pure and

honest; want of this quality is responsible for the drunkards, the libertines and the thieves that infest our large and small cities. No one agency that I know is more conducive to the cultivation of self-restraint than family-discipline, school-discipline and the discipline of government or society. Every time a boy obeys his parents at home, he is adding a new asset to his worth as a man. Every time he breaks off play at the sound of the bell, he is laying deep and strong the broad foundation for the towering edifice of a splendid career. These instances of self-control are but the small and humble beginnings of future greatness; and, if the habit accompanies the boy into the world of industry, politics and business, he will as a rule be soon discovered, he will prove a winner, and the world will love him, the world will load him with the highest honors at its disposal.

Self-control, then, is the readiest measure of a man's character, and this sober truth deserves a large place in your thoughts. It is the one bit of advice I would impress on your hearts. Whatever books you read or study in after-life, read and study them with a view to growth in self-control. Cultivate a close acquaintance with the sturdy heroes of ancient and modern times, men of stout character, able to encounter and overcome hardships in their campaign for the right. Have nothing but contempt for the mean specimens of humanity, glorified in the modern novel and the morning newspaper, men and women that weak they cannot withstand temptation, men and women at the mercy of every vile desire that stirs in their bosoms. Have high ideals, live always a little superior to your environment, and never strike your colors to degraded public opinion. Know the right, and do it. Choose your friends with care, be citizens in the republic of saints, and keep company with heroes. To achieve greatness, is an arduous task, we need every little help; and the example of the illustrious is a tonic for activity in the upward process. Scorn to borrow your religion or morality from the world. The Church is their appointed teacher, and to look elsewhere for guidance is like drawing water in a sieve, or planting pumpkins for a harvest of roses. Be men of principle. Be the hero described by Horace. If the world falls in ruins at your feet, present a bold front to the crash.

Map out your lives along a line of conduct approved of by faith and reason, and then, whatever happens, keep your course undaunted. You may fail of success, as the term goes; you cannot fail of honor; and to go down to defeat with right, is better than to be crowned a winner with wrong.

THESIS X

RIGHTS AND DUTIES
Jouin, 71–75; Rickaby, 244–253.

RIGHTS are meant by nature to shield men from harm in their intercourse with others, and they accomplish this purpose by creating duties in others. They procure the same advantage for God, and prevent men from wronging their Creator. Right equips its owner with the moral power to do or exact something, duty compels its subject to render another his due. *Right has at least three meanings, justice, law, moral power.* Because right is opposed to wrong or injustice, right itself is justice or the just thing; and, because justice is a man's due, discharge of duty is the consummation of justice. Right is a man's due, duty is respect for another's rights; and, therefore, any refusal to fulfil a duty is an injustice or wrong. Because the essential purpose of all law is the establishment of justice, law itself has a claim to the title, right. In fact law, when couched in language, is but the concrete expression of a right; and this is true of every single law, of every collection of laws, and of whatever law borrows part of its compelling force from sources extraneous to the subject affected by the law. Civil law is largely a collection of rights the state undertakes to safeguard; canon law discharges the same function in matters ecclesiastical; and a law against burglary, with imprisonment for penalty, is concerned with a man's right to his property. Last of all, and in strict sense, right, viewed in its owner or possessor, is the moral and legitimate power to do something oneself, or exact its doing from another; the moral power to demand something, to hold something, or to use something as one's own. We have thus far taken three views of right. Viewed as justice or the right thing, it is a something to be

127

rendered by another. Viewed as law, it is a something outside the owner and compelling others. Viewed as a moral power, it is a something in the owner; and from this circumstance right has all its practical value and worth.

Right primarily means justice. Law is called right, because it is an expression of justice. The moral power to do or exact something is called right, because justice vindicates to everybody his due. *Suarez calls law preceptive right; the moral-power, dominion-right.* A right, therefore, is man's moral power over what is due him. Duty is not a power, but an obligation. Right means, I can; duty means, I ought. A right is called a moral power to distinguish it from might, which is physical power. Right touches only what is due the man, because justice is its foundation, and justice gives to everybody only his due, only what belongs to him. *A thing is said to belong to a person, when the objective order of things makes it his, when between him and it a necessary relationship of connection ensues.* This connection is physical and substantial in the case of a man and his life, a man and parts of his body; it is physical and accidental in the case of health, knowledge and the like; it is moral, when between the man and things external to him, like money, land, reputation, esteem, glory or fame.

A right would be little worth unless it created a duty in others. *A right is, therefore, a relation, with its subject, title and term. The subject is owner, the title is whatever fact creates connection between the owner and the thing he owns, and the term is the subject-matter of the right, as well as the person in whom the corresponding duty resides.* Holland distinguishes in every right *a person of inherence, a person of incidence, a thing and a fact.* He omits title, and makes fact mean the peculiar use of the thing or matter conferred on the owner by the right. God has no duties strictly so called, because duty taken that way, connotes a superior. Therefore, as between right and duty, right comes first. In the case of men, right in the person of inherence causes duty in the person of incidence; and, therefore, right precedes duty in the order of nature, though as regards the order of time both are simultaneous. Duty in the person of inherence always causes right in the same; and, therefore, restricting the question to the person of inherence, duty always precedes right in the order of nature.

Right is reducible to justice; and, because justice is threefold, commutative, legal, distributive, rights are of three kinds with distinctively peculiar purposes. In commutative justice, the purpose of right is liberty and independence in the disposal of one's goods. In legal justice, the purpose of right is the common welfare. In distributive justice, it is to safeguard the citizen against state-wrongs. A right in commutative justice can be surrendered, because no law forbids a man to submit to private wrong. Hence the axioms, "No harm is done a willing victim," and "Nobody is obliged to use his rights." In legal justice the ruler cannot legitimately cede his right, because laws are made and executed not for the ruler's advantage, but for the welfare of citizens. Hence the ruler is obliged to use his right.

Right connotes the moral power to employ physical force in its realization, because order demands that the inferior, or physical force be always at the call of the superior, or moral power. In society, to guard against abuses, the application of this physical force is reserved to the state, and is not left to the caprice of individuals. Physical compulsion, in potency or in act, is not of the essence of a right, it is a complementary property. Rights persevere in the absence of physical compulsion. No citizen is allowed to urge his rights against the state with the help of physical force, though the state enjoys this prerogative as against a citizen. Right order demands as much. In commutative justice, where help from the state is beyond reach, one citizen is allowed to use force against another, when his rights are endangered. Otherwise wrong would be without remedy.

When talking about good and bad acts, we contended and proved that some acts are intrinsically and essentially good or bad; that they get their goodness or badness from nothing outside of themselves, like law, or custom, or opinion; and that they are good or bad always, everywhere and in whatever circumstances. *Moral Positivism* is opposed to our doctrine, and maintains that nothing is good or bad in itself and unchangeably, but that good and bad acts are made such by something outside of, and extraneous to the acts themselves.

Hobbes ascribes all the difference to civil law; *Lambert*, to custom and public opinion; *Mandeville*, to the research of eminent scholars; *Nietzsche*, to pity for the weak; *Descartes and Puffendorf*, to the will of God; *Darwinists and Positivists in general*, to evolution.

Because rights are but prescriptions of justice, naturally enough they get the same treatment as good and bad acts, at the hands of these enemies to morality. Their sytsem is called *Juridical Positivism;* and, in a very few words, while refusing independent validity to natural rights, it vindicates validity to only whatever rights are declared such by vested authority. *All Moral Positivists belong to this school,* along with men like Hobbes, Bentley, Lasson, Hartmann, who make the state sole and single cause of all rights. *Rousseau* and his followers ascribe right to tacit or expressed agreement among men. *Savigny*, the founder of the historical school, refers everything to history, public law, and a people's customs. According to him natural rights are no rights at all, but only rules and standards for the establishment of rights. With him rights begin and grow in much the same way as a people's language.

Against all such false philosophers we contend for a definite collection of natural rights, vested with a validity independent of all positive law. Life, liberty and the pursuit of happiness are three such rights, enumerated and acknowledged by our Constitution. These rights and a multitude of others descend to man from his Creator, and positive law has nothing to do with their creation or production. Its whole business is to safeguard these rights, by hemming them round with the physical force at its abundant disposal. Right is reducible to justice, justice gives everybody his due, gives everybody what belongs to him; and life is ours not by favor of the state, but by the free gift of God. The state has its right to make laws and insist on their observance, not from consent, or agreement, or history; but from God, who gave being to the state, and equipped it with all the means it needs to fulfil its purpose. God never imposed a duty on anybody, without investing him with a right to all needed means. He has imposed a multitude of duties on men; and, just as these duties bind men without reference to positive law, so the rights attaching to them are quite independent of human legislation and authority. Positive law, without prior natural law, is a house without a foundation. Kings could make laws till doomsday without any appreciable effect, beyond physical force, unless natural law held subjects to reverence for authority, and obedience to legitimate rulers. Agreements and compacts would be empty scraps of paper, if fidelity to promises were not a prescription of the natural law. No international law would be possible, because there would be no competent legislator. Every civil law and every custom would be by the very fact just, law could make murder right, custom could make impurity a virtue.

And just as every positive law borrows all its efficacy from prior natural law, even so every positive right borrows all its strength and force from prior natural right. Positive law is an application of natural law, it makes natural law clearer, it adds to the moral sense of obligation and future sanction, attaching to natural law, the physical sense of present penalty in the shape of fine or imprisonment, attaching to every positive law enacted. When Kant distinguishes between juridical rights and ethical rights, when he separates the juridical order from the ethical order, he forgets that ethical rights, as compared with juridical rights, are the same as natural law, as compared with positive law. When he attributes greater efficacy and sacredness to juridical rights than he attributes to ethical rights, he is virtually declaring positive law superior to natural law, man superior to God; he is putting the cart before the horse, subordinating cause to effect, attaching more importance to the roof than to the foundation. Nature confers ethical, or natural rights; law confers juridical rights. Ethical or natural rights are unchangeable at the hands of men, they do allegiance to God alone, and God is their single executive. Juridical rights are open to change with change of legislators, and are in force only as long as the laws creating them remain on the statute-books. Law is law, only when based on justice; and juridical rights, opposed to ethical rights, are no rights at all. Juridical order is, therefore, only an integral part of moral or ethical order, and no more separable from the same than the head is from the man. The head cannot be separated from the man, without changing its entire complexion and substance. Juridical order, separated from ethical order, ceases altogether to be moral order; and rights conferred by law, in opposition to rights conferred by nature, are no rights at all.

God the author of nature seems destined to get small notice and smaller reverence from present-day writers on Ethics, thanks to the atheistic and irreligious trend of our times. And natural law, which has God for its maker, meets with the same full measure of contempt. *One writer on Jurisprudence, Holland by name, wants law in strict sense limited to human positive or civil law; barring from the title natural law, divine positive law in Scripture, and Church law.* He bars natural law, because it is formulated by an indeterminate authority; Scriptural law, because it is formulated by a superhuman authority; Church law, because it is formulated by a politically subordinate authority. All this is purely arbitrary, and betrays the man's atheistic tendencies. We grant that law in strict sense cannot be formulated by an indeterminate authority, but God in nature, God in Scripture, and Church, are no indeterminate authority, unless we want to turn atheists and infidels. Natural law and Scriptural law are divine law, divine law is as much law as civil law, God is its formulating authority, God is no indeterminate being, and only atheists and infidels can think the thing. Church law is as much law as civil law, the true Church is no indeterminate authority; and, whatever may be said of other churches, the true or Catholic Church is in its own sphere quite independent of the state, and it never presumes to legislate outside its own sphere. True, God is a superhuman authority; but even civil law, without superhuman authority at its back, is a dead letter and nothing worth. No mere man has a right to legislate for other men. All men are born free and equal, nobody is born a king; and the authority he gets immediately from God is what makes the ruler's pronouncements law. Without this authority, his pronouncements are empty words, and of no more worth than mine or yours. Therefore, God must not be denied the quality of lawmaker, simply because He is a superhuman authority. Therefore God's law, whether natural or Scriptural, is more law than civil law.

What Mr. Holland, perhaps, means is that God and the Church are less visible and less tangible than the state. But that is his own view of the thing. To the religious mind, and the man of faith, God and the Church are more solemn realities than the state. With Thomasius, Holland wants us to keep our sickles out of theology, forgetting that natural theology is as much philosophy as logic or psychology or Ethics, and that no part of philosophy, which is knowledge of things in their last cause, can be rightly understood without a fair knowledge of God, the first and last cause of all things. To doubt the propriety of conceiving God as a lawmaker, as Mr. Holland ventures to do, is not to keep one's sickle out of theology, but to assail all theology and all religion with an axe. God is more than a mere information-bureau, equally well satisfied whether His children accept His doctrine or not. He teaches with authority, and He wants His lessons learned; He is eminently a lawmaker, and sanctions His legislation with hell. He is a Father of too wise a kind to allow His sons to go what way they will. He wants their full obedience; and, if they refuse it, they know what to expect. And all this is clear from Natural Theology, without any appeal whatever to Supernatural Theology or revelation. Law in strict sense is an obligation or ruling founded on right reason, drawn up and promulgated for the common good by him who has charge of the community affected; and this definition is as fully verified in natural, Scriptural and Church law as it is in civil law. Natural law is from eternity; positive law, whether divine or human, is made or placed in time.

Holland is imitating Kant when he makes a difference between Ethics and Nomology. Ethics, he says, touches the will, the interior act, and it is a matter of conscience; Nomology touches the outward act, exterior conduct. Civil law belongs to Nomology, and it cannot fathom a man's thoughts or intentions with any degree of certainty, and very sensibly leaves them alone. It agrees to interpret them with the help of external acts. Divine law has God for author, and men's thoughts as well as their intentions are no mystery to God. Juridical legality is a different thing from Ethical morality. An act can be all right in the eyes of the law, and all wrong in the eyes of conscience. Civil law makes only indifferent acts good or bad, it leaves other acts where it finds them, and makes them merely legal. Ethics makes an act morally good or bad, prior to and independent of all civil law; and this is the big difference between natural law and positive law.

The ethical order must not be separated from the juridical order, because the latter is an integral part of the former. Ethical order is like the whole man, juridical order is like his head. Natural law prescribes civil law as a necessary requisite for the welfare of the state, and therefore all civil or positive law is but an emanation from natural law. The juridical order is right, taken as positive law; and all positive law is a derivation from natural law, which in turn is right in the ethical order. When Kant separates the juridical order from the ethical or moral order, when he ascribes all the force and efficacy of juridical rights to positive law, without any reference whatever to natural law, he virtually reduces all right to preceptive, and rejects dominion-right. Preceptive right is a prescription of positive law; and, without the support of natural law, positive law has no binding force. Dominion-right is a prescription of the natural law, and natural law binds, whether positive law supports it or not.

Kant denies all ethical or moral right, to admit only juridical right; and, therefore, he denies dominion-right to admit only preceptive right. It is wrong to say that laws urged by civil authority are not in themselves binding on conscience. Civil law looks to the external act, without a care for the motive; natural law looks to external act and motive both. No matter what his motive, civil law certainly binds the man in conscience to put the prescribed external act. Penal laws exert no strain on conscience beyond the acceptance of the penalty incurred; but that is due to the mercy of the lawmaker, and a matter of common understanding between ruler and subjects. Obligation to the law is no product of the man himself, it is imposed on him by another, and proceeds from the natural law and its author, God. Therefore, every illegal act is wrong; and yet not every legal act is right, because the juridical order is only a part of the ethical or moral order, and not the whole of it. A man's head can be sound, while the rest of his body is unhealthy.

Right as law is preceptive right, right as a moral power

is dominion-right; and the two admit of many divisions. *Law is private, public, international.* Law is *private*, when the two parties to the action are citizens, and the state is arbiter; *public*, when the state has action against the citizen or the citizen against the state, the state in both cases being arbiter; *international*, when the parties to the action are two independent states, and the world is arbiter. *Private law is substantive and adjective, normal and abnormal, antecedent and remedial, in rem and in personam.* Private law is between citizen and citizen. Substantive law defines the rights of individuals, adjective law indicates the process of their enforcement. Normal law is for persons of ordinary type, abnormal is for deviations from ordinary type. Antecedent law is for cases before wrong has been committed, remedial is for cases after wrong has been committed. Law in rem is against the world, law in personam is against some definite individual. The six normal antecedent rights in rem are, 1, right to personal safety and liberty; 2, right to society and control of family; 3, right to good name; 4, right to advantages of life in community and free exercise of profession; 5, right to property; 6, right against fraud and deceit. The first of the six secures owner against threats, assault, wounds, imprisonment, dangerous things and dangerous places. The second secures owner marital rights of husband over wife, parental rights of father over child, tutelary rights of guardian over ward, dominical rights of master over servant. The third secures owner against libel and such like injury. The fourth secures owner a livelihood, use of harbors and rivers, freedom from malicious prosecution. The fifth secures owner in his possessions. The sixth secures owner against damage accruing from fraud and deceit. *The two normal antecedent rights in personam are quasi-contract and contract.* Quasi-contract embraces these four headings, domestic, fiduciary, meritorious, officious. Domestic means one member of the family against another member. Fiduciary means trusts, matters of confidence, executors. Meritorious means right to indemnity for services rendered. Officious means use of public officials like postmen. Contracts are principal and accessory. Principal contracts imply no ulterior object, accessory imply security for another contract. Principal contracts are six, alienation, permissive use, marriage, service, negative service, aleatory gain. Accessory contracts are seven in number, suretyship, indemnity, pledge, warranty, ratification, account stated, for further assurance. Remedial law deals with offenses against rights in rem and in personam. Abnormal law is for deviations from ordinary type. Adjective law is opposed to substantive. Substantive creates rights, adjective enforces them. Adjective law is procedure.

THESIS XI

CONTRACTS
Jouin, 140–154; *Rickaby,* 253–255.

THE jurisprudence of contracts is a large question, and cannot obviously be treated here in detail. We are studying ethics, not law; and we necessarily restrict ourselves to what natural law has to say on the subject, leaving the question of positive or civil law in its bearing on contracts to the school of law. *A contract is an agreement and consent between several persons regarding some set object.* A one-sided or unilateral contract is in itself a mere promise; and, because of its nature it obliges or binds only one of the two parties to the transaction, hardly deserves the name. Its fulfilment is regularly a matter of fidelity to one's word, not a matter of justice. When, however, it raises the hopes of the promisee, and induces him to incur expense, it assumes the proportions of a two-sided contract, and involves strict justice. Justice likewise intervenes when the promiser means to bind himself in justice. Contract in strict sense creates a mutual obligation between two or more; and, therefore, only two-sided or bilateral contracts deserve the name in its completest significance. A contract creates rights and duties in both parties to the transaction. Take, for example, the commonest form of contract, that of buying and selling. The buyer assumes the duty of paying the price, and is invested with the right to receive the goods purchased. The seller assumes the duty of delivering the purchase, and is vested with the right to receive the price. The two persons are the efficient cause of the contract, the set object is its material cause, consent and agreement are its formal cause; and all three causes must fulfil certain conditions. The persons must be fit agents, they must enjoy the use of reason, and they must have full and free dominion over what they dispose of in the contract.

137

Natural law is sponsor for these two conditions. A contract means free consent, and that demands the use of reason. A contract is a function of ownership, and nobody gives but what he first possesses.

Civil law can for the common good prescribe other conditions, and their discussion belongs to the school of law. The matter of the contract must be possible, morally as well as physically; and, for obvious reasons, it must be legitimate. The consent given must be of such a nature that it really and truly creates an obligation. In other words, it must be true internal consent as well as external, and it must be entirely free. Natural law stands for the invalidity of feigned contracts, empty ceremonies without any intention to form a contract or assume an obligation, because natural law's avenger, or God, sees the heart as well as external facts. Civil law, because its maker's vision is restricted to external facts, counts valid every such feigned contract. It argues that the deceiver has violated another's rights, and must indemnify him even to the extent of putting true internal consent. Besides, the party deceived is never obliged to believe the deceiver, when he says that he made no true contract. A contract made with a full sense of obligation, and a determination to never fulfil it, is valid even in natural law.

Freedom is interfered with by want of knowledge or mistake, by fear and by violence. Substantial mistake invalidates a contract, e.g., wine and vinegar in a purchase. Accidental mistake, when responsible for the transaction, renders gratuitous contracts invalid, onerous contracts repudiable. External violence invalidates contracts. Internal fear, as long as it leaves freedom unimpaired, never invalidates. External fear, induced unjustly to effect contract, invalidates gratuitous, makes onerous repudiable.

Quasi-contracts get their validity from law, rather than from self-imposed obligation. Law imposes the obligation, not parties to the contract. No contract is made, law supplies, and deals with case in much the same way as if a contract had been made. Law casts duty on person of incidence without his agreement. Its four kinds are, family, trust, meritorious, officious.

Savigny defines a contract, as the union of several in accordant expression of will, to create an obligation between them. Hence his analysis of a contract into these four elements, several parties, agreement of wills, mutual communication of agreement, intention to create legal relations. About expression of agreement, Pollock says, "Courts hold men to fulfilment of intention, only when expressed in a manner that would convey to an indifferent person, reasonable and reasonably competent in the matter in hand, the sense in which the expression is relied on by the parties claiming satisfaction." Justice Blackburn, 1871, says, "Whatever a man's real intention, if he so conducts himself that a reasonable man would believe he was assenting to another's terms, and that the other party agrees, the man would be equally bound as if he had intended to agree." *Therefore, not what the man intended, not what the other party supposed him to intend, but what a reasonable man, i.e., judge or jury, would put upon such acts.* This is the objective theory of contracts. Holland sees these six elements in a contract, 1, several parties; 2, two-sided act expressing agreement; 3, matter agreed upon both possible and legal; 4, agreement of a nature to produce a legally binding result; 5, such a result as affects the relations of the parties to one another; 6, very generally a solemn form, or some fact affording a motive for the agreement. A formal contract observes formalities prescribed by law, usually writing. An informal contract is without prescribed formalities, but is based on some fact or consideration. The result of a contract is obligation between parties, conferring rights on one, imposing duties on other, partly stipulated in agreement, partly implied by law.

Holland divides contracts into principal and accessory, and we already enumerated them. Under permissive use he groups loan for consumption, loan for use, and loan for hire. In olden times loan of money ranked as loan of food, and it was a species of permissive use, the kind called loan for consumption, as opposed to the kind called loan for use. Interest then fell under the contract denominated permissive use for consumption. Such a contract calls for mere return of the food or money borrowed, or their equivalent; it is of its nature gratuitous, and the right to interest depends on special agreement. Hence the Church's condemnation of interest in olden times. All interest was considered usury or excessive interest, because increment, to which the lender was not entitled.

Cathrein divides contracts into gratuitous and onerous. Gratuitous are made in the interest of one party; onerous, in the interest of both. In gratuitous all the burden is on one party, in onerous both parties assume burdens. Gratuitous contracts are promise, gift, loan, deposit. Onerous contracts are buying and selling, letting for hire, partnership, interest. In a contract of buying and selling two mutually agree on merchandise to be received or given for a set price, and price usually means money. Between value received and price given there must be some equality, because people are not supposd to be making presents, when assuming onerous contracts. A thing's value is fixed in great measure by its perfection or usefulness in the eyes of men. We distinguish between use-value and exchange-value. Use-value is absolute, and depends on the thing's substantial usefulness. Exchange-value is relative, and depends on the thing's worth, as compared with other salable articles. Air, water, light have great use-value, small exchange-value. Price is exchange-value expressed in terms of money. To be fair and just, a thing's price and its value ought to be equal. Prices go into legal, natural and conventional. Law fixes the legal price, many circumstances fix the natural price, mutual agreement fixes the conventional price. Natural price, because dependent on circumstances, admits of a certain latitude; and can be high, medium or low. These circumstances are, the usefulness of an article, its scarcity, multitude of buyers, abundance of money. It is quite fair and proper to charge a price rated just by common opinion. Where law and opinion fail to fix prices, agreement must settle things.

Among other applications, the contract of letting for hire has place between employer and employee. This species of the contract is peculiar, inasmuch as the energies of a human being are involved in the transaction. Besides the payment of just and fair wages, the employer must impose on his workman no condition or burden derogatory to his dignity as a human being. The workman has no right to dispose of his energies in a way unsuited to his dignity as a man, and whatever employer compels him to do so is guilty of injustice. A just wage is a living wage, and that means money enough to enable the workman to live, and to live comfortably; to procure not only the necessaries of life, but a moderate share of its luxuries. The workman has no right to a fixed percentage of his employer's profits, because he is not precisely a partner; and yet, other things equal, the more an employer derives from a workman's labor, the higher are the wages due the workman, if price is to be regulated by the usefulness of the commodity purchased. It is extortion pure and simple, to coerce a workman into selling his labor at a price, altogether out of proportion with its value to the purchaser. And the immense fortunes, amassed by employers in short intervals of time, quite satisfy me that, whether awake to the fact or not, most employers are enriching themselves at the expense of their workmen, and actually stealing from the poor.

Law, public opinion, agreement, unaided by religion, will never be able to establish justice, as between employer and workman; because money can buy labor-leaders as well as lawmakers, capital can afford to laugh at public opinion, and free agreement is out of the question, when labor has to choose between low wages and starvation. The chiefest remedy for injustice is religion and dread of a future punishment. "All things obey money." Eccles. 10.19. God is the only judge industrial thieves need to be absolutely afraid of, because they can on occasions switch human judges with money, nearly everybody having his price; and the one way to escape fear of God and fear of hell, is to shake off all allegiance to religion. This labor-problem, because of its bearing on morality, is as much an affair of the Church as it is of the state. Till this problem is satisfactorily settled, it must remain a menace to the salvation of men's souls; and it is the Church's business to fight every such menace to a finish. All the world is her kingdom, workmen and employers alike belong to her jurisdiction; they are children in her house, and like a good mother she must keep down quarrels in the family.

And here is the plan our Church proposes. She counsels employers to cultivate with enthusiasm the two virtues of

justice and charity; she counsels workmen to cultivate with
no smaller enthusiasm the two virtues of honest content and
conscientious industry. In the matter of pay, justice means
a living wage for all, defectives out of the question, and for
workmen of superior ability a corresponding increase. *A
living wage means money enough to decently support the
workman and his family, without extraordinary labor on the
part of his wife and young children.* His wife must care for
his home, his young children must get an education, and
strengthen their weak bodies by play and exercise for the
years ahead.

The employer, who holds his workman to starvation wages,
is guilty of injustice; and the workman's consent to the
unholy transaction relieves the employer of no moral re-
sponsibilitiy. To take advantage of a poor man's needs, is
to rob him; and to force a hungry man to choose a half loaf,
when a whole loaf is his due, differs only a little from holding
up a traveler with a pistol. The traveler yields up his purse,
to escape with his life; and the oppressed workman yields up
his whole loaf, to escape from starvation. In the one case
it is the surrender of the purse or death; in the other it is
surrender of the whole loaf or no bread at all.

And charity is an altogether different virtue from justice.
Justice is close and tight, charity is a stranger to narrow
notions; it is as wide as the sea. Charity is more than mere
justice; to coin a word, it is superjustice. Justice gives
everybody his due, no more no less; and, if it leans at all, it
leans toward severity. Charity leans towards leniency, and
its donor glories in his dishonesty towards himself. It gives
to everybody more than his due, in the matter of wages as
well as of praise; less than his due, in the matter of penalties
as well as of blame. Charity, therefore, is a species of divine
superjustice, mercifully meant to correct the shortsighted justice of men.

*The employer is not absolute owner of his wealth, when God
is taken into account.* No man can, in the name of justice
or of charity, appropriate to himself a dollar of the employer's legitimate wealth; but God is first owner, God has prior
rights, and God can stipulate to what uses the employer must
put his wealth. The rich are God's almoners to the poor.

It is their sacred and solemn duty to relieve the wants of the needy with their superfluous wealth, and to give their workmen sometimes, not in the name of justice, but in the name of charity, a little more than they earn. When employers heed the demands of justice and charity, workmen will have no cause to complain, honest content and conscientious industry will be as easy as they are natural, differences between employers and workmen will disappear, and strife will be at an end.

THESIS XII

INTEREST
Jouin, 154–160; *Rickaby,* 255–263.

LOAN is regularly a gratuitous contract, whether loan for consumption or loan for use. Thus, when a person borrows a loaf of bread to eat it, he is obliged to return to the lender only another loaf of bread of the same quantity and quality. When a person borrows a book to read it, he is obliged to return only the book. *In olden times, because money was borrowed only for the purpose of purchasing food and the like, things consumed in their use, without producing new wealth, money-lending was a purely gratuitous contract, and all interest was rightly considered usury or extortion from the poor.* Hence, St. Thomas and all Church writers up to his time are violently opposed to the interest, considered perfectly legitimate in present economic circumstances.

All the difference is due to the different uses of money in their times and ours. *With them money was reckoned a good consumed in its use, a good productive of no new wealth. With us, money is a good not consumed in its use, a good decidedly productive of new and greater wealth, when combined with human endeavor.* Capital was of no practical use in olden times, to-day it is one of the chief factors in business of whatever sort. Money-lending has passed from loan to letting-for-hire in the catalogue of contracts, from gratuitous to onerous, and all because of different economic conditions. People now rent money to another, as they rent a house; and they have a perfect right to any just rate of interest they demand. And yet the frauds and thefts, perpetrated in modern times under cover of interest, almost persuade one to think that the world was certainly more honest, even if worse off materially, when all interest was condemned as usury, and

144

injustice and extortion; and, in the esteem of religious minds, growth in material prosperity is small recompense for moral degeneracy.

To make interest universally legitimate, there must be a something in money, that makes use of it by lender or borrower profitable, or productive of ulterior wealth. In other words, money must be fruitful, not barren; it must resemble a field ready for planting, not a loaf of bread ready for a hungry man. The money-lender must have a title to the interest he claims, and that title must somehow or other be intrinsic to the money itself. A title extrinsic to the money, might suffice to justify interest in the event of some agreement between lender and borrower; but nothing short of a title intrinsic in some way to the money, can justify interest in the event of no agreement whatever; and we contend that money loaned demands interest to-day of its very nature.

Four extrinsic titles justified interest, even when the Church was loudest in its condemnation of the practice; and they were, 1, loss of opportunity to make money incurred by the loan, or interruption of profit, lucrum cessans; 2, damnum emergens; unusual risk; 3, penalty for delay in payment; 4, legal reward meant for incentive to business. The Church always recognized the legitimacy of these several titles. Besides, people of great wealth could buy the right to farm revenues, and they could enter partnership, wherein without personal labor their money could earn an increment. It must be remarked that these several titles are extrinsic to the money loaned, and never created a right to compensation without prior agreement.

Hence, the Church regularly and consistently considered interest wrong, and branded all interest usury. *It defined usury as any attempt to draw profit and increment without labor, without cost, and without risk, out of the use of a thing that does not fructify.* It forbade a man to lend his horse to a neighbor as a gratuitous gift, and then without any warning charge him for the use of it, changing a purely gratuitous contract into an onerous contract. Men of early times saw only one value in money, its substantial value; and interest was something in excess of that value. They saw no fruitfulness in money, it was Shakespeare's "barren breed of metal";

and to charge extra for fruitfulness, it was on all sides conceded not to have, was robbery, injustice, extortion.

To-day all is changed. Commerce is so easy and extensive, remote regions are so close together because of steam and electricity, communication is so rapid because of telegraph and telephone, that for purposes of business the whole world is no larger than a single trading block in any city; and money has uses it never before enjoyed. Money is become a species of seed, a dollar judiciously planted can grow a thousand; and the seed-dealer is justified in charging one price and another for different varieties of seed, not precisely because of their substance, but because of the flowers or fruits they produce. And whereas in olden times the only legitimate titles to interest were extrinsic to the money itself, the four enumerated and explained awhile ago, *to-day the title to interest is intrinsic to the money itself; not, indeed, simply and without any qualification intrinsic, but after a manner and with a qualification, accruing to money from modern methods of business.* This kind of intrinsic title partakes of the nature of extrinsic and intrinsic titles. It is extrinsic, inasmuch as it is not rooted in the nature of money itself, independent of all circumstances. It is intrinsic, inasmuch as it attaches to money in fixed economic conditions like our own.

Therefore, the right to interest is not dependent on any civil law, but on the nature of things. For the common good, law can regulate rates of interest, it has no jurisdiction over the legitimacy or the illegitimacy of interest. Laws regulating interest may be just or unjust, and the state framing such laws must consult the objective order of things. In general, a fair rate of interest would be that portion of the profit, made by the borrower, left after deducting a fair recompense for his skill, labor and industry; and, in the main, that is the ratio just laws everywhere try to determine. Law cannot make wrong right, and plainly exorbitant rates, though sanctioned by law, continue offenses against justice. And yet, because, in the matter of justice, the presumption is always in favor of law, nobody need as a rule be disturbed, when he keeps within the limits of the law.

Money itself is only a medium of exchange, a standard or

measure of value. When business was small, all trade was simply an exchange of one article for another, and the transaction was called barter. As business grew, some set article was chosen as a general medium; and it became a standard, a unit for the measurement of value resident in other articles. A sheep could be made the standard; and horses, cows, houses, everything could be valued in terms of sheep. After centuries of experience the world seems to have settled on the precious metals, gold and silver, as money or media of exchange. Animals, shells, skins, wheat, tobacco, and a multitude of other objects have been employed in history as money; but all have yielded place to silver and gold, or to paper, entitling its owner to a definite quantity of silver and gold, when presented to proper authorities. Gold and silver were chosen because of becoming qualities they possess. They are durable, and wear well; their scarcity adds to their intrinsic value, and gives greater worth to small portions; they can be carried with ease from place to place; they are readily divided, measured and shaped; they are homogeneous throughout, and the same the world over. Coinage, reserved to the ruler, secures citizens, regarding the genuine quality of the realm's money.

Money, therefore, has a twofold value, material and formal, or moral. Its material value is its use in the arts and the trades. Gold and silver dollars can be turned into jewelery and the like. Its formal or moral value is its use as a medium of exchange, its purchasing power. In olden times money's purchasing power was restricted to things consumed in their use; when loaned, it was lent to purchase things of the kind; and so money never rose to the dignity of a fruitful good, productive of new wealth in its use. To-day money purchases things not consumed in their use, things productive of new wealth; and money, assuming the quality of what it can purchase, becomes by the very fact a fruitful good. In consequence, whoever lends money to another, has a right to the profit he might have earned with his money, while it remained with the borrower; and all this, not by virtue of any agreement, but in virtue of the change made in money by modern conditions. In other words, money is now an instrument of business and trade, and it demands a price, much as the store you rent to another, or the machine hired to manufacture some product. Money, therefore, is a fruitful good, because it stands for all purchasable commodities; and the loan of a fruitful good, in strict justice demands more than the mere return of the good, it demands a return of the fruit as well. Ballerini thinks that custom made interest illicit in olden times, because he reckoned it impossible to prove that anything in the nature of money forbids such recompense for its use. But St. Thomas and the others regularly appeal to the very nature of money, viewed as a thing consumed in its use. Others favor leaving everything to the intention of the borrower. They would consider interest wrong, in case the borrower meant to purchase food and the like; right, in case he meant to trade with it for purposes of profit. Charity might recognize a difference between the two cases, not justice. The two are onerous contracts.

THESIS XIII

MERIT AND DEMERIT
Jouin, 21–23; Rickaby, 152.

MERIT and demerit are fruits of morality. A man can merit with God and with other men. He can so behave towards God and men as to deserve in justice reward at their hands. Merit and demerit result from imputability, that quality which makes man the cause and proprietor of his acts. Only rational beings are capable of merit and demerit, because freedom is a requisite. Imputability implies ownership, and freedom alone vests man with ownership in his acts. Necessary agents are not owners. *Merit means right to payment for favor done another, it means reward. Demerit means right or liability to payment for harm done another, it means punishment or penalty.* Justice is the measure of merit and demerit. They even up justice, when the balance swings one side. Justice is the virtue that renders to everybody his due. It is of three kinds, commutative, man to man; distributive, state to citizen; legal, citizen to state, corporately and individually. Commutative demands strict or arithmetical equality between favor and reward. Distributive demands geometrical equality between favor and reward. Ordinarily a fair distribution of emoluments and burdens satisfies its claims. Legal regularly demands arithmetical equality, and is secured by law. *Equity is a merciful provision meant to be corrective of justice. It has application, where reward is due, not in strict justice, but from a viewpoint of fairness and honor.* It ministers to the incompleteness of legal justice. Commutative gets its name from the process of exchange, at the basis of business transactions, like trading, and buying, and selling. In this species of justice arithmetical equality, or that of 5 to 5, is possible, because

149

both favor and reward are things, money, for instance, and a horse. Distributive gets its name from the distribution in play, when offices in a government are parcelled out to deserving citizens. In this species, geometrical equality, or that of 6 and 4 to 3 and 2, is alone possible; because, while the favor is, as it were, a person, the reward is a thing. If a citizen doing 6 points of service gets an office worth 4, a citizen doing 3 points of service ought to get and office worth 2. Legal justice in point of equality resembles commutative, differing merely in origin. Physical violence does away with merit and demerit, because it destroys freedom of execution; but the moral violence duty or obligation exerts, because it leaves even the ordered act voluntary, has no destroying influence on merit or demerit. Duty or obligation removes the element of supererogation.

God can be said to owe things to Himself and creatures. He owes it to Himself to see to the fulfilment of His wisdom, will, and goodness in creatures. He owes creatures equipment with requisites to their nature. This second debt is rooted in the first, and so God is under obligation to nobody but Himself. God is just to the wicked, when He punishes the wicked, because it is what the wicked deserve. He is just to Himself, when He spares the wicked, because mercy is what He owes His own goodness.

Merit is of two kinds, de condigno and de congruo. One is based on strict justice, the other on equity. Harmony or discord with the objective order of things makes an act good or bad. Imputability has its origin in freedom of will, and makes an act blamable or praiseworthy. Justice measures an act's merit or demerit. To merit with men, the favor done must not be payment for antecedent debt, and it must be a favor asked or desired, or reasonably supposed such.

Man can merit with God and other men, because he can freely do them a favor. The favor changes the prior condition of justice, and calls for recompense to reestablish justice. Man's merit with God is not absolute, but conditional; and God has put the condition. Man owes everything to God, without right to any return. And yet, in making man free, God changes the aspect of things, and agrees to consider a favor, what is in reality a debt. This gift of free will is a virtual promise on the part of God to reward its right use, and punish its abuse.

God is incapable of intrinsic addition; but man can do God a kindness, by adding to His extrinsic glory; and virtue secures this addition. Man is at the same time a servant and a son of God. He merits with God as a son, and as a servant; supernatural reward as a son, natural reward as a servant. God is first cause of a man's free will, as He is first cause of every effect in the universe. But man is second cause of His free acts, in such manner that he contributes of his own to their reality, and exerts his own independent activity. Man in God's hands is no mere passive instrument, but active as well. God's promise makes man's merit de condigno. In the supernatural order this promise is writ in revelation; in the natural order, on the open page of creation. The discrepancy between man's acts and a supernatural reward, is atoned for by the addition of sanctifying grace. That quality renders them supernatural, and enables them to merit de condigno supernatural recompense, or Heaven.

THESIS XIV

*Utilitarianism is wrong, dangerous and absurd.   Jouin, 31;
Rickaby,* 177–191.

QUESTION

UTILITARIANISM is a standard of morality, set up by men
who want to keep God and a future life out of the question.
They ignore immortality, and with it the spiritual side of
man's nature.   They are not everywhere consistent in their
views; and, when trapped by their own words into some damaging admission, never hesitate to seek a refuge in self-contra-
diction.   William Paley, 1743–1805; Jeremy Bentham, 1748–
1832; James Mill, 1773–1836; John Stuart Mill, his son, 1806–
1873; John Austin, 1790–1859; and George Grote belong to
this school.

TERMS

Utilitarianism.   Its creed is formulated in two principles
and a law.   First Principle: Man's last end lies in this world,
and is the greatest happiness of the greatest number, meaning pleasure as well of the senses as of the understanding.
N.B.   Cudworth, Butler, Paley, and others, notably older
Utilitarians, mention God and a future life with respect.
John Stuart Mill and moderns in general resent all reference
to God and a future life.

Second Principle: Useful acts are right, hurtful acts are
wrong.   Acts are useful, when they result in pleasure; hurtful, when they result in pain.   Law: General results must
be taken into account, not particular; not the immediate result of this particular act, but what would result to society,
if this sort of act were generally allowed.

This last is what Paley calls the Law of General Consequences. It hits near our standard of morality, the objective order of things; and we have no quarrel with it. But we have a very serious quarrel with the *Principle of Greatest Happiness, and the Principle of Utility.* We have already proved that man's absolutely last end, his greatest happiness, lies outside of this world, and is God, intuitively possessed. We have besides proved that his greatest happiness on earth, his relatively last end, is the introduction of moral rectitude into his acts; and that moral right and wrong are constituted by harmony or discord with the objective order of things. Our three theses are a direct refutation of Utilitarianism.

If somebody wants to believe in the reality of a future life, the Utilitarians assure him that their doctrine menaces no harm to his aspirations. They are quite accommodating. "Take care of the things of earth," they say, "and the things of Heaven will take care of themselves." Christ taught the contrary, when He called the cares, and riches, and pleasures of life thorns that choke the seed and hinder it of fruit. Our friends meet this difficulty with a new distinction between Hedonism, pleasure for me, and Altruism, pleasure for the other fellow. These thorns of the gospel are the pleasures of Hedonism, not the pleasures of Altruism. Altruism then is their last end. To meet Utilitarianism on common ground, we must for the time being neglect the future life, and discuss with them man's highest good in this present life. We maintain that man's highest good in this life is the establishment of moral rectitude in his acts, calling the condition incomplete happiness, because, in life's sum of good and evil, moral rectitude procures the preponderance of good over evil. They maintain that man's highest good in life consists in the greatest happiness of the greatest number of mankind, and they seem to mean by happiness pleasure as well of the senses as of the understanding, physical as well as intellectual. It must be evident that we both agree in making happiness of some kind man's supremest good; and, if we contend for exactly the same kind of happiness, we are fools to quarrel. Our happiness is virtue, it is compatible with pain; it rates one unit of intellectual pleasure superior to many units of physical pleasure; it counts the intensest physical pain man can suffer, death amid the cruellest torments, martyrdom at the hands of Nero, less an evil than the slightest departure from the straight line of morality.

Of course, an ideal conception of incomplete happiness even in our theory would be a blessed aggregate of unvarying virtue, pleasure of body, and pleasure of soul, without the smallest trace of pain anywhere in the mixture. It would mean holiness fit for the altars, along with the money of a millionaire; the wisdom of the most consummate sage history knows; a mind free from business cares, a heart free from the aches of love; a body without the ills of disease, a soul without a sorrow; nights of refreshing sleep, days of uninterrupted ease, luxury and exhilarating enjoyment. But we are not the fools to think any such ideal condition possible since the fall. Apart even from the teachings of faith, we know that, ages before the parable of the seed and the sower, pagans like Diogenes and Zeno, Socrates and Plato, in the full light of reason, regarded the riches and pleasures of this life thorns in the field of virtue. Before the ominous words, "Go sell what thou hast, and give it to the poor," sounded on human ears, mere philosophers had buried their wealth in the sea, as a preliminary to the acquisition of virtue and wisdom. We must be content with the world as it is, we must be practical even in our Ethics, and write down man's highest good a species of happiness possible of attainment. This happiness is necessarily limited, it is incomplete, and we have reason to be thankful for the circumstance. It whets desire for the beyond, holds us to duty, and makes us stronger than unavoidable pain, that might otherwise overwhelm us with dread.

Happiness with Utilitarians would seem to be sometimes Hedonism, sometimes Altruism; pleasure for me, and pleasure for the other fellow. We repeat again, that if we misinterpret their writings, we honestly mean no wrong, and stand ready to make them due reparation for our mistake. If their greatest possible happiness of the greatest possible number is virtue, or moral rectitude in man's acts, the fight is over, and we are everlasting friends. If, on the contrary, it is either the Hedonism of Epicurus or the Altruism of modern atheists and materialists, the fight is on, and we are deadly enemies. Mill would seem to make it Hedonism, when he says that acts are right in proportion as they tend to promote happiness, meaning by happiness pleasure and the absence of pain. This doctrine makes good and pleasure identical, accounting the most pleasant pleasure the best pleasure. Paley very logically accepts this view of the thing, and maintains that pleasures differ only in duration or intensity, not in kind. With him pleasure of sense can surpass pleasure of mind. We maintain, on the contrary, that pleasures differ in quality as well as in quantity; that pleasure is not identical with good, but one of its three kinds or species; and that intellectual delight is a better pleasure than sensual, not because it is the more pleasant or lasting, but because it is nobler.

Good is of three sorts, becoming, agreeable and useful; honestum, dulce et utile. Becoming good appeals to what is specific in man's nature, his intellect; the agreeable is oftener than not a loud cry to what is generic in man, his animality; the useful is a mere help to the other two. The becoming is loved for itself singly; the agreeable, for the pleasure it creates; the useful, for an ulterior advantage altogether distinct from itself. Good itself is an analogical term; and, arguing from the word perfect, it means, in root, finish, completeness. That is man's good, which finishes, rounds out, completes his being. Primarily, therefore, good signifies the becoming; secondarily, and by analogy of attribution, the agreeable; secondarily still, but by analogy of proportion, the useful. Becoming good is loved on its own single account, not because of some third reality its possession secures. Agreeable good is not loved on its own single account, but on account of a third reality its possession secures, the satisfied feeling it induces. Useful good would never be missed, if only the advantage it helps to procure could be obtained without its assistance. Examples are knowledge, a banquet, and money. Real good is suited to the desires most in harmony with the nature that seeks it. Whatever good is opposed to real good is called apparent good. Man's real good is intellectual and spiritual, and, therefore, the becoming. When the agreeable and useful are directly opposed to the becoming, they are only apparent goods. Whatever real goodness they possess, is derived from the becoming, and dependent on the degree in which they meas-

ure up to the same. An apparent good is a real evil. Nearly
every good in nature is a mixture of the three, and it is one
or other according to the light in which it is viewed. Thus,
knowledge is in itself a becoming good. And yet, because of
the pleasure it ministers, and because of the opportunities it
affords for honor and wealth, it can readily enough descend
to the level of an agreeable or useful good. A banquet is a
becoming good, inasmuch as it is quite in harmony with
man's rational nature; it is an agreeable good, inasmuch as
it procures bodily pleasure; it is a useful good, inasmuch as
it wins for the host the favor of his guests. Between agreeable and useful good the distinction is clear and marked.
It is not so easy to discern between the becoming and the
agreeable. Pain can never be reckoned agreeable good; it can
be reckoned becoming good.

Pleasure and Pain. Therefore, these few words about
pleasure may help us to better understand things. Feeling
cuts so important a figure in modern Psychology that writers
assign it a faculty of its own, distinct from the faculties of
knowledge and desire, denominated cognoscitive and appetitive. Our English word feeling is fruitful in meaning.
Maher notes these four, *outer sensations, pain or pleasure,
excitement, certainty without motives.* Examples are, smooth
feeling of velvet, to feel hot or cold; to feel hurt, sad, joyful;
I have a feeling for you; to feel that it will rain. Emotion
occurs often in second and third senses. Passion is intense
excitement; affection turns on likes and dislikes with persons
for objects; sentiment is emotion in abstract and highly
wrought characters, as opposed to practical men. On this
question of pleasure and pain rare old Aristotle wrote the
final word centuries ago. St. Thomas in this particular makes
the Stagirite his model, and voices his sentiments with hardly
a word of correction. Modern writers are true, only when
they keep close to these master-minds; and the measure of
their departure from Aristotle is the measure of their folly.
Plato is responsible for the opinion that all pleasure is negative and relative. It is negative, inasmuch as it is mere absence of pain. It is relative, inasmuch as it is transition from
state of pain to opposite condition. And some pleasures of
sense lend color to his theory. Thus, the joy of eating and

drinking would seem to be dependent on antecedent hunger and thirst. Aristotle, however, calls attention to the fact that pleasures without number betray no such dependence on previous pain. He alleges for examples the delight attaching to mathematics, agreeable sounds and smells, the pleasures of memory, and hope, and imagination. *He makes all the reality of pleasure dependent on activity, calling it activity's efflorescence or bloom,*—''nil sine magno Vita labore dedit mortalibus.'' Each faculty in man has its own pleasure, derivable from judicious exercise. Count the antecedent exercise pain, and you have Plato's opinion of relativity. St. Thomas remarks that nobody enjoys uninterrupted pleasure, simply because the quality follows work. The faculty employed, and the object stimulating the faculty, gauge the intensity of a pleasure; and in point of duration it lasts as long as faculty and stimulus are in harmonious relations, one fresh and vigorous, the other fit and suitable. During early periods in the process, pleasure reacts to stimulate energy; but by degrees fatigue results, to first lessen the feeling and eventually close in pain. Hence the need of variety in this business of pleasure. The faculty is dulled by use, and a new stimulus must supplant the old, when fatigue ensues. As faculties are specifically different, pleasures of intellect and sense differ as much as the faculties themselves. Conflicting pleasures neutralize each other, and the faculty in question determines the moral rank of the pleasure. The nobler the faculty, the nobler the pleasure. Pain is pleasure's opposite, and eadem est ratio oppositorum. The nature of pain is manifest from our description of pleasure. It can have its origin in faculty or object. It accompanies excess or defect of energy or exercise, and is regularly due to pressure of an unfit or unsuited stimulus. These different characteristics of pleasure and pain have been gathered by Maher into two laws,—1, *Pleasure is healthy exercise or activity, pain is excess or defect of same.* 2, *Pleasure grows up to a certain limit, then it diminishes and becomes pain.* Variety contributes to pleasure, because the interval of change is a period of rest, and gives the dulled activity an opportunity to recover its sharpness. Accommodation can explain factitious pleasures as well as insensibility to pain. From long use the fac-

ulty of taste, for instance, loses its edge, and tobacco passes
from disagreeable to pleasant. Constant pain in much the
same way operates to diminish or quite destroy the discomfort.

*We maintain against modern writers that pleasure and pain
call for no third faculty, distinct from man's cognoscitive and
appetitive powers. They are but different aspects of cogni-
tion and desire.* Touch and taste call for new faculties, distinct and different among themselves; not feeling. Feeling
is best described as the tone of a function. The function is
exercise of a cognoscitive or appetitive faculty; the tone in case
of pleasure is spontaneous, healthy, harmonious exercise; in
case of pain, restrained, unhealthy, excessive exercise. The
theories about pleasure and pain are numerous, most of them
substantially the same as Aristotle's; and, as before remarked
regarding wrong theories, the measure of their departure from
Aristotle is the measure of their folly. Spinoza leans to
Plato's notion of transition from pain. Kant makes pleasure
the promotion of life-processes; pain, the hindrance of life-
processes. Schopenhauer and the pessimists view pleasure
as escape from pain by filling a want. Descartes and Leibnitz make it consciousness of perfection possessed. Hamilton
calls pleasure the reflex of conscious activity; pain, the reflex
of overstrained or repressed exertion. Bain describes them as
increase and abatement of vital functions. Physiologists in
general view pleasure and pain as integration or disintegra-
tion of neural elements. Grant Allen makes pain a destructive act, or insufficient nutrition in sentient tissue. Spen-
cer calls pleasure organic equilibrium, or harmonious func-
tioning, or struggle for life.

PROOFS

I. *Principle of Greatest Happiness.*
To return now to Utilitarianism. In its selection of man's
highest good, as already seen, *it veers between Hedonism and
Altruism,* pleasure for me, and pleasure for the other fellow.
Indeed some defenders of the theory try to combine the two.
But that is impossible. They are opposite poles. *Hedonism
is gross selfishness, Altruism rates selfishness the unforgiven*

sin. Hedonism certainly cannot be man's highest good, because it is pleasure; pleasure in turn is the effect, activity the cause; and the cause is always superior to the effect. Activity, therefore, is a higher good than the pleasure it produces; and no pleasure, whatever its kind, can be man's highest good. Becoming good is sought for itself, and for nothing beyond. Even knowledge, when sought for pleasure or gain, becomes an agreeable or useful good. *Man's highest good, therefore, cannot be pleasure of whatever sort, whether intellectual or sensual, because pleasure is at most an agreeable good, and man's highest good ought to be a becoming good.* Besides, pleasure is always an effect, and effects are inferior to their causes.

PRINCIPLE

A. The end is superior to the means. Pleasure is the end, activity is the means. *Answer:* This is in the order of intention, not in the order of being or reality. Redemption of mankind is the end; the tears and the blood of God are the means. Operis and operantis. Priority in order of being or reality settles dignity. Reversed in two orders of intention and being. End first in intention, last in being. Means last in intention, first in being. Ergo, activity is superior to pleasure, as cause is superior to effect.

Therefore, knowledge, clear of the pleasure it occasions, can alone be man's highest good. The pleasure may be inseparable from the knowledge, but this is far from constituting the pleasure knowledge itself. God known is man's absolutely highest good, and virtue is his relatively highest good, his highest good in this life. *Altruism cannot be man's highest good, because, as understood by the Utilitarians, it neglects two important factors in the makeup of virtue, self and God.* Again, if their Altruism means virtue, if it means measuring up to the objective order of things, the exact payment of all our debts to the neighbor, self and God, we have no quarrel with Utilitarianism, and we are Altruists as well as they. But, whatever their real sentiments, the writings of Utilitarians are proof conclusive that they ignore the interior life of the soul, the inner man of the heart, and give human society, the neighbor, the place that belongs to God. They mistake the political for the ethical end of life. They provide for a good citizen, a good husband, a good father; but not for a good man. They exaggerate a secondary concern, to minimize or altogether nullify what ought to be man's primary concern and first consideration. Therefore, the Altruism of the Utilitarians is no more man's highest good than the Hedonism of Epicureans. It wears a more decent appearance, but there is more logic or common sense in Hedonism than in Altruism. Both are vile errors, one from the viewpoint of gentility, the other from the viewpoint of philosophy; and only in the eyes of shallow thinkers are offenses against gentility viler than offenses against philosophy. Hedonism banishes God and the neighbor from morality, to set up self for idol. Altruism does the same unkindness to God and self, to fall down and worship the neighbor. And there you are.

II. *Principle of Utility.*

The Principle of Utility, which makes acts right or wrong, according as they are useful or hurtful to the greatest number, *stands condemned on these four counts:* 1, *It makes no difference between acts good and bad in themselves, confounding intrinsic value with extrinsic results;* 2, *affirms that the motive has nothing to do with the morality of the action;* 3, *levels all distinction between injury and harm;* 4, *and favors the theory confuted by Plato in his Republic, personal indulgence at expense of neighbor.* We already proved in Thesis III, that an essential, intrinsic difference exists between right and wrong in the moral order. We argued from example, alleging love and hatred of God as instances; and, for every believer in God, the argument is conclusive. Unfortunately for them, the Utilitarians prefer to keep God out of the question, and might logically take exception to our method. Love of parents and a lie might, perhaps, prove more acceptable examples; and they are equally well suited to our purpose. Therefore, according to us a lie is essentially and intrinsically bad, because of its very nature it is at odds with the objective order of things, imperatively demanding conformity of language with thought. A lie is radically wrong, because it is an abuse of language. It is wrong now, it was always wrong, and will forever continue to be wrong, even if God could wish otherwise, even if the whole world entered into a conspiracy to call it right. Love of parents is in precisely the same way an act intrinsically and essentially right. With Utilitarians a lie would be wrong, simply because of its consequences or effects; love of parents would be right for the same reason; and the Law of General Consequences, they think, makes their position impregnable. They would contend that lying and hatred of parents, if universally allowed, would work harm to society; and they are not far wrong in their contention. A bad act always breeds bad consequences, and in most cases this secondary norm of utility coincides with our own. As a rule, Utilitarians would scruple calling right whatever acts we call wrong, and theoretically their standard is not blameworthy. But in practice it is open to flagrant abuse, and it is responsible for much of the evil now prevalent in society. *Its advocates easily lose sight of the Law of General Consequences, and measure the quality of their acts by the advantage or disadvantage accruing to themselves personally.* If he is a Hedonist, the Utilitarian can see nothing but advantage in a lie, that procures him thousands of dollars to purchase the luxuries of life. If he is an Altruist and a diplomat, the Utilitarian can see nothing but advantage in a lie, that would save an entire community from the disasters of war. The temptation, then, is to think a lie right on occasions, and account so-called prudential departures from the truth no breach of morality. How often men yield to the temptation, every-day history is witness. *Individualism is the rich man's creed, Utilitarianism is the basis of his ethics; and the bad philosophy taught in our present day universities strengthens him in his position of greed and injustice.* Less conscientious Utilitarians teach, and avaricious misers among their followers ardently hold, that acts are morally right, when they tend to the doer's profit; and virtue comes to mean the accumulation of wealth by fair means and foul. If Utilitarianism were not wrong in itself, abuse of its principles is easy, and this abuse is most damaging in its consequences.

2. We have alsewhere shown motive to be one of morality's

determinants. Motive is the act in its subjective aspect, and its morality is quite as important as that of the object itself. We are agreed that no individual human act is indifferent, though in the abstract many such acts occur to mind, like walking, singing, study. Acts of the kind derive all their morality from the motive prompting their execution. To walk to the church for purposes of prayer, is right; to make the same journey for purposes of theft, is wrong; and all the difference is constituted by the walker's motive. Motive makes one man a worshipper, the other a thief. And we are not talking about the act of prayer or the theft; we are talking of the journey itself. The journey made by the prospective thief is as morally wrong as the theft he afterwards commits. This truth is even more evident in the case of a good act, done with an evil design. To give alms for the express purpose of making the beggar accomplice to a murder, is out and out bad. No matter how useful the gift may prove to the beggar, the act of the giver is thoroughly wicked; and what would be otherwise virtuous charity, is changed by mere motive to downright murder. This example slightly changed proves Utilitarianism immoral. Suppose the alms given without any wrong intention; later on, the beggar finds his benefactor engaged in murder, and out of gratitude goes to his assistance. The alms would have bad results and would therefore be wicked, an opinion altogether against common-sense. Our kindness would, then, depend on how people used it. I am aware that a man's motive, when once conceived and embraced, becomes part and parcel of his act, because the motive is the man. I am aware that honest Utilitarians would never reckon right, alms bestowed for so unholy a purpose; and all because conduct of the sort, if universally tolerated, would prove damaging in the extreme. And yet they are highly unphilosophical, when they brand such alms wrong, simply because of consequences or independently of motive. *The fact of the matter is that the act in question is damaging in its consequences, because it is morally wrong, and not vice-versa.* Causes never follow their effects; and the act is not, first damaging in its consequences, and then morally wrong; but it is first morally wrong, and then damaging in its consequences. The horse pulls the wagon; not the wagon, the horse. Scripture is of small weight with the average Utilitarian; and yet he may, in common with respectable unbelievers, have a measure of reverence for Christ's wisdom. Motive in His divine eyes makes a supreme difference between acts; and the first half of St. Matthew's sixth chapter contains His doctrine on the subject. We commend His words to the careful and reverent perusal of searchers for the truth. The acts discussed are alms, prayer and fasting.

3. If use and harm are the measures of morality, all difference between mere harm and injury disappears; and balanced minds are not ready to accept this view of things. *Injury adds wilfulness and malice to mere harm, which oftener than not is wholly without the stigma of moral blame.* The pedestrian, who tramples your watch to pieces on the dark street, works you a lot of harm, but no injury. The enemy, who deliberately and knowingly smashes the same with an axe, over and above the harm he works, does you a downright injury. In both cases the harm is practically the same; while injury is absent from one case, present to the other. Even if all men without a single exception were allowed to repeat the act of the innocent pedestrian, it could never become morally wrong, in spite of the harm consequent on its occurrence. And yet the harm done would prove as much a hardship to the watch's owner as the injury done him by his enemy. The effects of the harm and the injury are the same, the moral difference between the two is due to the agent's purpose, motive, intention.

4. Plato in his Republic confutes a theory of morals, that would seem to coincide in all respects with Utilitarianism. *Briefly, it stands for the contention that a man's highest good in this life is his own personal indulgence, at the expense of his neighbors.* Society, to keep down fighting and save the race from suicide, hampers this inclination, and blocks each individual citizen's aspirations for his own highest good. It forces him to forego the natural right he has to prosecute his own happiness, at the expense of his neighbors. In this way the interest of society is opposed to the interests of the individual, and life in a state is a real curse and only a makeshift blessing. Tyrants alone, in this theory, compass

highest good; their subjects, through no fault of their own, are hopelessly unable to realize their destiny in this life, that natural desire all men have to enjoy incomplete happiness, the preponderance of good things over evil things. And all because these shortsighted mortals, in common with the Utilitarians, establish man's highest good in pleasure or advantage, his supremest evil in pain or hurt.

Our theory makes moral rectitude or virtue man's highest good, and no tyrant can effectively keep his subjects from the attainment of this result in their lives. Again, it would be foully wrong to suppose that Christ or the early martyrs failed of man's highest good; and their entire lives were empty of what a Utilitarian world calls happiness or pleasure, and were crowded full of misery and pain. They compassed supremest good or incomplete happiness, simply because what the world calls happiness or pleasure cuts no figure whatever in the thing, and one unit of virtue outweighs units without number of mere physical pain or mental distress. Virtue is no artificial happiness, it is happiness of the solidest sort; and the pain endured for virtue's sake never loses its quality of bitterness. Saints never come to directly like self-denial, they like it only in an indirect way, inasmuch as it secures to them that virtue or holiness, which is the basis and foundation of man's supremest good on earth.

PRINCIPLES

A. *Stoic Formalism. Stoic Formalism is from Kant, and Kant's system of Ethics is a profound mistake.* The whole trouble with Kant would seem to be that he has hazy notions about God, and denies Him the quality of lawgiver. And all this in spite of an utterance on page 322, to this effect, ''Conscience must be conceived as the subjective principle of a responsibility for one's deeds before God.'' Abbott. *He recognizes only two lawmakers, self and the state.* Self is responsible for ethical law; the state, for juridical law. Hence his autonomy of reason in matter of ethical law. Reason is self, reason makes law, defines and imposes duty, sits in judgment, rewards virtue, punishes offenders in the domain of Ethics or internal morality. The state performs exactly the same functions in the domain of Nomology, Jurisprudence or external morality. *God occurs nowhere, no doubt because He is a noumenon.* Natural law with Kant is not divine law at all, it is as much human law as civil law itself, the only difference between the two being that the man makes natural law for himself, the state sets him civil law. In the field of internal morality, in the matter of acts not prescribed by positive law, in question of commands issued by what we persist in calling the natural law, man, according to Kant, is subject to no outside constraint; he has no Heaven to hope for, no hell to fear. In the field of external morality, in matters provided for by the statutes, in question of murder, ' eft and other penal offenses enumerated in the code, man is subject to constraint of the state, and enjoys the favor of possible fine or imprisonment as a deterrent from crime.

With Kant, natural law ought to fare worse at men's hands than positive law. When a man makes a law for himself, he can as easily neglect it; when a man is judge and jury in his own case, he is seldom convicted; when he executes law on himself, he gets off with a light sentence. When the state exercises these several prerogatives, the culprit is more likely to get his deserts; and this single thought would make positive law surer of fulfilment than natural law. God would neglect in the enforcement of His law a most efficacious help, employed by men in the enforcement of their laws. Ethical duty with Kant is self-imposed constraint; juridical duty is constraint imposed by positive law and its author, the state. Self-imposed constraint is no constraint at all; and ethical duty, to have any force, must be constraint imposed by the natural law and its author, God. Therefore, to act from a sense of ethical duty, is to act with an eye to God's attitude towards right and wrong, as well as with an eye to our own attitude towards the same; and Kant's autonomy of reason, and his principle about duty for duty's sake, are only half the truth; and, what is still worse, they are that half of the truth, which apppeals to only a select few in the republic of refined minds and critically exact moral tastes. The sanction of the natural law embodied in an eternal hell, is a much more appealing incentive to virtue than Stoic Formalism or subjective feelings of shame. *Remorse of conscience means more than shame, it means dread of hell; and the sinner is wide awake to the fact, that he has offended somebody distinct from and greater than himself.*

Utilitarians contend that happiness, or pleasure of mind and body, is man's destiny on earth, his supreme good, his last end; and many contend that it is folly to look higher. We already proved with irrefutable arguments that pleasure, whether of mind or of body, cannot be man's last end, either in this life or in the next. Stoic Formalism, a product of Kant's philosophy, is the opposite pole to Utilitarianism; and it contends that duty is man's destiny on earth, to such an extent that it is the single motive able to make his acts moral; and that pleasure, or whatsoever other motive, renders them unmoral. *Duty for duty's sake, is its slogan, and it accounts acts morally good, only when done from a sense of duty; unmoral, when done for pleasure or from any motive save sense of duty.* Kant is responsible for the system, and it is in line with his autonomy of reason, to be explained and refuted in our next thesis.

Against Utilitarianism and Stoic Formalism we contend that man's absolutely last end, his destiny in the next life, is complete happiness, the possession of God in the beatific vision; that his relatively last end, his destiny on earth, is incomplete happiness or virtue and resulting peace of conscience. The happiness we contend for is not the pleasure of Utilitarianism, nor is it the sense of duty advocated by Stoic Formalism. Happiness, whether complete or incomplete, is not pleasure of mind or body. Complete happiness is a heaped up measure of good with unending duration, a measure of good from which no particle of good is absent, altogether incompatible with pain and discomfort. Complete happiness is a natural desire, the one necessary wish of every man's heart, the hiding principle of every wish we conceive; and, therefore, our happiness in this sense cannot be excluded; and, if Kant were right, all our acts would necessarily be unmoral. Virtue is our destiny on earth, and therefore our duty; and the peace of conscience resulting from virtue cannot be excluded from our motive, and again all our acts would be unmoral. The consciousness of duty done is only another pleasure; and, before we do our duty, this pleasure in the order of intention can move us to act, without any detriment to morality. Whatever motive is compatible with virtue, be it pleasure, or wealth, or honor, health, wisdom or charity, can originate a morally good act; and there are virtuous as well as vicious pleasures.

Arguments against Stoic Formalism by Father Cronin, pp. 245–263.

1. It demands too much of human nature.
2. It is not contained in the idea of moral good.
3. It is disproved by works of supererogation.
4. All moral acts would be equally moral.
5. Eadem est ratio oppositorum. If acts were good solely on account of respect for law, acts would be bad solely on account of disrespect for the law. No criminal ever acts from disrespect for the law; but from motives of gain, revenge and the like. Ergo, no bad act.
6. There would be no room for merit. Every good act would be owed.
7. Happiness is inseparable from moral acts; and acts would be unmoral, when done from motives of happiness.
8. Motive would be respect for law as such. Bad legislation is law as such, and bad legislation never bases moral act.
9. Law is meant for common good, as means to end. To act not for common good, but for law, would be to make means superior to end.

Arguments in Favor of Stoic Formalism are Fallacious.

1. It is the creed of the crowd. Morality is in the will, not in the external act.

Answer: True, but the will gets its morality from object, end, and circumstances; pure selfishness does not of itself vitiate act; pleasure is good or bad according to object; duty is only one object of pleasure; love of duty is as much a moral principle as duty.

2. All outer objects are mere means to pleasure. Ergo, no proper motive.

Answer: The summum bonum is not a mere means to pleasure, it is happiness itself. It is man's end, not a means to his end. It is an affair of the intellect, not of the will. Law varies with the individual, the summum bonum or last principle of morality is the same for all.

B. *Hedonism. Father Cronin discusses Hedonism between pages 264 and 304.*

Hedonism of whatever kind is wrong, when it makes pleasure man's last end. Egoistic Hedonism is Hedonism proper: Universal Hedonism is Altruism or Utilitarianism. Pleasure for me, and pleasure for the other fellow. Some Hedonists: *Hobbes* says that any object of desire is man's last end, and this is Hedonism's most degraded type. *Aristippus* makes mental pleasure man's last end. *Mill* makes higher pleasures of mind man's last end; and this is a more refined type. *Cudworth* makes pleasures of virtue man's last end; and this is higher still. *Butler* makes pleasures awaiting men in Heaven man's last end; and this is the highest of all.

Answer: Pleasure is not our sole natural end, because it can be spurned aside. Happiness is our sole natural end, because it cannot be spurned aside. Pleasure is not man's last end, because it resides in the will, as the passion of delight resides in the appetite; and no act of the will can be man's last end.

Five Arguments from St. Thomas, C.G.3. 26.

1. Happiness is man's last end, and happiness is not delight or pleasure. Pleasure is an act of the will, object is prior to act, and will's object is prior to will's pleasure. Object is mover, pleasure is movement. Ergo, happiness cannot be an act of the will, it cannot be pleasure.

2. Happiness is no act of the will, it is not pleasure. *It would be either a, desire; b, love; or c, delight.* a, Not desire, which tends towards something not yet gotten. b, Not love, because love turns on absent as well as present good. c, Not delight, because delight is the effect; possession is the cause.

3. Happiness is not in act of the will, not in pleasure; because pleasure can be true or false, and ever the same with respect to rest or quiescence on part of the will, e.g., a drunken man and a philosopher. Real man and painted man differ by constituents of substance, and intellect makes pleasure true or false, not act of the will.

4. Delight is not desirable of itself, and, therefore, not

man's last end. Otherwise all delight would be desirable. Pleasure is of indifferent ethical value, sometimes good, sometimes bad; some delight is desirable, other delight is to be shunned.

5. Nature uses pleasure as means only. Ergo, not man's last end. Right order coincides with order of nature, nature orders things without mistake. Nature orders man as well as animals. *Delight is for activity, not the other way about*, e.g., use of food for preservation of individual. We eat to live; we do not live to eat. Without delight animals would not eat. Delight is the means, preservation the end. Pleasures of marriage are for preservation of race.

P.S. Title of last end is assigned to activity, whereby exterior thing is gained, e.g., act of getting the money is last end, not desire or love of money. God is last end, activity getting God is understanding. We cannot wish what we do not understand. Ergo, happiness is act of the intellect, not act of the will, not pleasure of whatever kind.

THESIS XV

Kant's autonomy of reason is wrong.   Russo, pp. 67–70.

THE greatest of all goods in the moral order, because true and absolute, is a good will.   All other faculties are good in the moral order, because of something they borrow from the will.   Morality is like freedom.   It belongs primarily to the will, and is passed along by the will to mind, senses, and all else in the man.   Mind in itself is a physical, not a moral good.   It is often an apparent good, and always a relative good.   It makes a good writer, a good philosopher, but not a good man.   *Nobody deserves Heaven for proficiency in mathematics pure and simple.*   Some of the greatest minds history knows are buried in hell.   No good will is buried there, because good will means virtue, and virtue is passport to the kingdom of God.   *Will is choice, and the best will, or the best good, is the best chooser.*   In morality choice lies between obedience to law and disobedience; and the motive prompting the choice has a decided bearing on its dignity and worth.   Respect for the law would seem to be the highest conceivable motive; and therefore two factors conspire to make a perfect will, obedience to law, with respect for the law for single motive or reason why.   Obedience and respect are paid to persons, not to things; and, therefore, we might better say, obedience to the lawmaker, and respect for the same.   Fear and hope are negatively imperfect motives as compared with love.

Up to this point we are a unit with Kant.   All the difference between us starts here, and it is rooted in the man's stupid conception of the law in question, and of the relative worth of motives urging to its observance.   *With him, the law to be obeyed is his categorical imperative, "So act that, if you had your way, your conduct would have to be made universal standard for the race."*   His categorical imperative emanates from his own reason, his practical reason, his will, without God or man at its back to urge its observance. It is his own private affair, a matter of business between himself and himself. If he follows orders, he does himself a kindness; if he breaks orders, he does himself an unkindness; and that is all. *No created thing is capable of uttering a categorical imperative, an absolute and necessary imperative, because no created thing is the absolute and necessary, and no effect can surpass its cause.* From relative and contingent beings like creatures, and practical reason is a creature, no higher than a relative and contingent imperative can issue.

And this is what we call Kant's autonomy or autocracy of reason, the enthronement of self as supreme arbiter of every man's destiny, the impudent usurpation by man of rights vested in the Creator, a virtual declaration of man's independence of everybody, God included, subservient to nobody but himself, subject to only such laws as he makes for himself, accountable for his conduct to nobody but himself, his own judge, his own jury, his own executioner. He gathers the purely subjective nature of his categorical imperative, the fact that all obligation in the man is due to a command he, and he alone, imposes on himself, from the circumstance that no other absolute and necessary command is conceivable. Everything falling under the experience of our senses is relative and contingent, the categorical imperative, as an absolute and necessary something, must have its origin in the practical reason, considered in action, the one phenomenon apart and distinct from sensile occurrences. *He sees the absurdity of attributing the qualities, absolute and necessary, to any product of the practical reason; and, therefore, acknowledging his inability to prove the absolute and necessary nature of his categorical imperative, he contends that these two qualities of his categorical imperative are a postulate of his system, and must be accepted without proof.*

He could have easily avoided all trouble by introducing God, the one absolute and necessary being in the universe, and ascribing his categorical imperative not to practical reason but to the natural law imposed on man by God, and brought to man's notice by reason. But the poor man is hounded everywhere by that ghost of his own making, nou-

mena, spirits, things in themselves, too far removed from the senses to base certain knowledge, matter for empty conjecture, sure in the event to propagate ignorance and superstition. God is a noumenon, a pure spirit, beyond the reach of eye, and ear, and all the senses, but quite within the reach of reason, arguing from the reality of patent effects in the universe to the reality of their cause. *Man's reason is for noumena, as his senses are for phenomena; and if our knowledge is restricted to phenomena, if we have no certain knowledge of noumena, we are little better than brutes, and in many respects their inferiors.*

With practical reason for single origin of the categorical imperative, reason is autonomous, its own lawmaker, and every man is his own standard of morality. More than this, every man manufactures his own moral obligations, imposes on himself whatever duties he sees fit to impose, selecting some, rejecting others, always with the proviso that he can reject to-morrow what he selects to-day. In other words, he is morally bound to the performance of this or that particular act, simply because he holds himself to its performance, not because any outside superior issues a command to that effect. *Kant stands for autonomy of will, as opposed to heteronomy. We stand for heteronomy of the will, maintaining that God is single author of moral obligation, that reason is the herald God employs to make His wishes known, that the true categorical imperative is the natural law, which is divine legislation, not human, which is found indeed in man's reason, without being derived from it.* We can all be found in the Woolworth Building Friday evening, but the Woolworth is no explanation of our origin. The laws of New York can be found in certain printed books, but the printer never made them. Kant wants us to think that we impose obligations on ourselves, simply because we wake up to the fact that we are under obligations. The objective order of things, as set forth in the natural law, arouses us to a sense of obligation, and this objective order of things is the handiwork of God, as well as the natural law embodying it. If man himself is altogether responsible for Kant's categorical imperative, man imposes this obligation on himself either with full freedom or with strict necessity. If with full freedom, it ceases to be real and true obligation; if with strict necessity, something distinct from the will forces its wishes on the will, and God alone, as maker of the will, enjoys this prerogative. Kant's imperative is a self-imposed command, one and the same person is ruler and subject; and a self-imposed command, because open always to revocation at the will of the subject, carries no binding authority. To save himself from open folly, Kant makes the reason ruler, the will subject; but reason and will belong to the same man, and no two persons are present. *When a man binds himself by agreement, or vow, the obligation arises not from the man himself, but from a precept of the natural law, an ordinance of God holding rational creatures to their promises.* The obligation is independent of man's will. He is free to make the agreement or not; but, once the agreement is made, he is not free to assume the obligation or not. He is free to put the condition or not; but, with the condition once placed, the obligation follows, no matter what he wishes.

Besides missing the true nature of the only categorical imperative worthy of the name, the natural law issuing as a command from God to do good and avoid evil, Kant beautifully mixes things in his discussion of motives and their relative dignity. The motive of obedience is the reason why the will obeys, and three possible motives for observance of the natural law at once suggest themselves, *respect for the lawmaker, fear of penalty and hope of reward.* All three motives are equally relative and contingent. The most perfect motive of the three is respect for the lawmaker; but this is far from rendering the other two positively imperfect or bad. They are at most negatively imperfect, or less good. They possess their own worth, they have their own goodness, though it happens to be inferior to the goodness attaching to respect for the lawmaker. The whole thing is like saying that imperfect love for God is inferior to perfect love for God, without ever becoming hatred. Only a bad motive is a positively imperfect motive. Negatively imperfect motives are good motives of varying degrees. *A five-dollar-bill is always money, though it is worth less than a hundred-dollar-bill. Only a counterfeit is no money at all.* And all three motives are compatible, not mutually destructive of one another. Nothing prevents a man from keeping the law out of respect for the lawmaker, from dread of penalty, and from hope of reward. *In fact, three motives are better than one, especially when the one chosen is the weakest of the three; and man's innate selfishness will always make penalty and reward more effective for good than respect for the lawmaker.*

PART II

SPECIAL ETHICS

INTRODUCTION

WE have thus far dealt in speculation of a general nature, without adverting much to individual emergencies in an individual life. We have rather laid down rules, sure to find application in every step taken with a bearing on morality. Now we proceed to examine the obligations arising from relations involved in certain conditions and contingencies of life. Man has dealings with God, with himself, and with his fellowmen. He occupies a well defined position in the universe, and his moral worth stands or falls with the attitude he adopts in his every day acts towards God, towards himself, and towards his neighbor. This threefold source of duty is common to every man born into the world, and independent of every later arrangement or added condition. It affects the individual as such. Nature, however, has besides constituted man a social being. It has ordained that at his very birth he belong to a family, and has made it quite impossible for him to continue in existence without entering into certain amicable relations with his fellows. Hence he finds himself by a very necessity of nature constituted at once a member of civil society or the state, as well as of domestic society or the family. Besides, God the author of nature has in the person of Jesus Christ established a third society, the Church, and has made membership in it an inevitable duty. These three societies, differing in scope and machinery, secure advantages and impose in return corresponding burdens. Fathers, mothers, brothers, sisters, children, rulers and subjects have set functions to discharge, and rectitude consists in strict compliance with their several duties. It therefore belongs to this part of Moral Philosophy to put in as clear a light as possible man's obligations as an individual to God, himself and his neighbor, and man's obligations as a social being to his family, to his government and its citizens, and to the Church appointed of God.

Religion is the one word expressive of man's duty towards God, and this religion includes worship of mind and body, and steadfast belief in revelation, or the utterances of God. Man is loyal to himself, when he makes good all the claims urged by reason in behalf of his own proper soul and body. Suicide, self-defense and duelling are topics of vital interest in this subject. Truthfulness in speech and the right to property are points particularly offended against in man's conduct towards his fellows. In the field of the family, or domestic society, marriage itself, celibacy, polygamy, divorce, education of child and the mutual relations between family and state, are questions of weighty importance. Man's natural instinct for political or civil society, society's end, its constituents, forms of government, state prerogatives, and sedition will occur for discussion in our consideration of civil society.

SECTION I. MAN AS AN INDIVIDUAL

THESIS I

Religion is man's first duty, a matter of essential necessity to the individual and the state. Worship, interior and exterior, private and public, is God's due. Man's duty towards revelation is to accept it, when known as such; to diligently seek and find it, when hidden, and when he has reason to suppose that it exists. Toleration in matter of dogma is absurd. Jouin, 71–96; Rickaby, 191–202.

QUESTION

We are by supposition dealing with men honest enough to admit God's existence and the fact of creation. We likewise take for granted the possibility and the fact of creation. For proofs of these several points we refer to Natural Theology and forward parts of Metaphysics. Man's duties towards others are based on relations in force between himself and these others; and the first condition that confronts him is, from the very fact of creation, that of utter dependence on God. Man is God's handiwork, and belongs to Him body and soul. In virtue of His supreme dominion God has an inalienable right to the completest service of His creature; and must, from the very nature of things, stand vested with a master's control over man's every faculty and energy. Worship, interior and exterior, submission of intellect and will, are the highest conceivable tributes of superiority one rational being can pay another, and religion embodies both. Faith and trust in God's messages, or the acceptance of revelation, is an element of religion on which champions of God's cause cannot with too much force insist in these days of irreligion and unbelief. Revelation is the channel through which men are advertised of the sort of service God wants, and ex-

177

perience is witness that worship weakens and falls dead, when the truths of revelation are once called into question and doubted.

TERMS

Religion. The word is of Latin origin, and authors are divided between three possible derivations. *Lactantius,* an eminent scholar and Church-writer, favors *religare* for root-word. Religion with him means a second bond or moral obligation, added to man's first or physical dependence on God for being, preservation, activity and care. *Cicero,* with whom *Lactantius* finds fault, ventures *relegere,* meaning to dwell on in thought, or meditate. His derivation gives large prominence to the theoretical side of religion. *St. Augustine,* seeing in the Redemption a second choice of God made by fallen man, traces the word to *religere,* to choose again. In classical Latinity religion is regularly identified with the feeling of respect and veneration entertained towards parents, relatives and friends.

But whatever may be said of ancient usage, it is quite certain that religion to-day, taken in a strict and technical sense, denotes a something referred to God alone. It is a duty, a moral attitude, or condition, or relation, based on man's physical dependence on God for existence, preservation, activity and control. It has for foundation the circumstance that God is man's first cause and last end. *Hence religion is generally defined, the duty to acknowledge and worship God as first cause and last end.* Acknowledgment denotes the free acceptance of a truth, and of whatever responsibilities attach to it. It supposes knowledge, and adds thereto an act of the will. Worship is testimony rendered to divine excellence, coupled with due submission. It is honor combined with submission.

Religion may be considered objectively or subjectively. *Objectively taken, it is a collection of truths expressive of the relations in force between God and man, and a catalogue of the duties hinging on these relations. Subjectively taken, it is the actual or habitual acknowledgment of these truths and performance of these duties.* Religion is a branch of justice, because it is God's due. It includes, among others, truths like the following, God created man, preserves him, exercises over him the controlling influence of a ruler and helper, rewards and punishes him in the next life as a most just judge. It includes the duties of adoration, sacrifice, prayer and faith in God's word. Religion is a branch of justice under the formality of God's due, not under other formalities. Religion is something more than mere good conduct and respectable behavior. Pagans and modern heretics in reducing the notion to limits so narrow forget that the will, the mainspring of conduct, depends for all its vigor on the mind or intellect. Luther's rule was, faith without good works; now the rule reads, good works without faith.

Viewed as a body of truths, religion is said to be theoretical, dogmatic, speculative. Viewed as a body of duties, it is said to be practical. Religion in both senses is essential. Theoretical religion without practical religion is imperfect. Practical religion without theoretical religion is often no better, no more sincere; and is always subject to decay and death. A religion may be false and wrong in one of two ways, either by paying homage to a false god, or by worshipping the true God in a way opposed to His wishes. Natural religion would be a thing no higher than human reason, with precepts possible of fulfilment to man's unaided resources. But we live in the blessed light of revelation, and the only religion now in vogue, and in vogue from the beginning, is revealed or supernatural. God has in His goodness deigned to stamp with the seal of His own word even such truths and such plain obligations as reason of itself can fathom.

Duty. Right and duty are correlative terms and inseparable. Right is one of the terms in our language, conveying notions at first sight whole seas different. Thus, the right is confounded with rectitude and conveys the notion of exact agreement with that straight line of conduct morality bids us walk. A right is something altogether other, and can be best perhaps described as, *the moral and inviolable power or strength to do or exact something.* The Romans had two words for our one. Right in the first sense, they expressed by rectum; right in the second sense, they expressed by jus. This jus is clearly connected with jubere, to order or legislate; and since all law is founded on rectitude, the choice

of the word was happy. A jus or right is an emphatic command, forbidding anybody to interfere with its enforcement.
It is creative of a duty in outside agencies, restraining them
from opposition to its peaceful fulfilment. Four elements of
a right are person of inherence, person of incidence, object,
and act.

Take for example ownership in a house and lot or parcel
of ground. The person of inherence is owner, the person of
incidence is the rest of the world, the object is the building
and piece of ground, the act is use for purposes of residence,
sale, changes, repairs, and against trespass. Right, therefore,
is an order issuing from the person of inherence or owner,
backed by the omnipotence of nature or God, and commanding the person of incidence, whether a set and definite individual or the world at large, to reverence the wishes of its
owner in at least one respect. God is the avenger of broken
rights, and nobody violates a right without disputing the
authority of God, and running counter to His wishes. Nature, and nature here means God, vests the owner of a right
with the authority of a king, and word from him in the matter of his right is word from God. Men on occasions lack
the physical strength needed to enforce their rights; but God
is their champion, strength never fails Him, and, whether in
this life or the next, God ultimately makes right prevail, by
actual accomplishment or, in event of its failure, by penalty.

Right and duty are therefore closely related, and a knowledge of one helps much to a knowledge of the other. A right
is a moral force, and depends by no means for its validity on
physical superiority. Rights are on this account often trampled and violated by might in a world of iniquity and wrong;
but nobody ever maintained that a right lapsed when borne
down by might. For the simple reason that they have no
intellect or will, and are therefore outside the category of
moral beings, animals have no rights. We owe it to ourselves
to treat them humanely; but, as far as they are themselves
concerned, cruelty to animals is no violation of a right. The
obligation engendered in others by the existence of a right is
sometimes negative, sometimes positive. There are in other
words rights of such a nature that they merely forbid outside
interference, without obliging others to help positively to their

realization. There are others, on the contrary, of such a
nature that they lay on others the responsibility of contributing by positive acts to their issue. Finally, right is founded
on law; and since law without God is a dead letter, any recognition of right is silent and sure testimony to the existence
of God.

Rights are personal or real. *A personal right immediately
affects the person of the possessor; a real right affects him
only through the medium of some second thing.* Instances
are, the right to life and the right to a piece of property.
Rights are likewise natural and inborn, or acquired. *They
are natural, if derived to man from his very nature. They
are acquired, if due to some free act, of which he acquits himself.* Thus, the rights to improve the mind, to defend life
when unjustly attacked, to acquire land, are all natural; and,
as such, beyond all possibility of loss or forfeiture. The right,
on the other hand, to ownership in this or that particular
strip of land, because largely dependent on some special activity freely exerted, is an acquired right, and admits, of loss
or change. Might can with justice and propriety be employed
to effect the enforcement of a right. Right, resident as it is
in the mind and the will, has claims on man's inferior faculties, and can call these forces that constitute physical strength
to its assistance. Neither is injustice done the party against
whom violence is used. If right primarily binds his mind
and will, small wonder if its influence extends to the members of his body.

A conflict or collision of rights is quite possible in certain
contingencies. In such an emergency only one of the two
rights is real. The other is no right at all, but only a shadow.
Right cannot in the nature of things be opposed to right.
When a clash of the kind occurs, the relative merit of the
two claims must be weighed, and the worthier must prevail.
Nature again furnishes us with the standard of measurement,
and the question must be decided in strict accordance with the
demands of nature's order. Thus, when some human enactment is in open contradiction with God's law, the human law
is no law at all. It must yield, and its framers are vested
with no prerogative of authority, as against the source and
author of all authority. In every well organized community

courts are established, and their word is supreme in the settlement of disputes turning on civil rights. No private citizen has the power to take the law into his own hands, and
decide quarrels with his neighbor. In this plan, justice may
on some rare occasions be defeated; but the order maintained,
and the bloodshed avoided, more than compensate for these
scattered wrongs. Rights have limits, beyond which they cannot be pushed. No right however valid can sanction the commission of sin. When pursuing a right, we must proceed
with caution, and avoid offending against the duties of others
and our own plain duty. Rights in many cases assume the
nature of privileges, and there is no law compelling a man
to everywhere make use of his privileges.

*Duty is the source of that inner consciousness of moral re-
straint which accompanies every dictate of the natural law.*
It invariably presents itself in the shape of a command,
ordering man to do or avoid something. It is a strict obligation, and man knows that, if he wants to remain true to himself and his nature, he must satisfy its demands. A duty, in
concrete terms, is this or that act urged or forbidden by law
and order. God's rights are the origin of men's duties; and
God, independent as He is of every superior, is a stranger
to duties properly so called. In figurative language we sometimes speak of God's duties to Himself and even to men.
But in strict usage duty always connotes a superior, a being
with full authority to impose the duty. Absolutely speaking,
then, right is first of the two in order of time. Confining
the question to man, duty always precedes right. All man's
rights are founded on the duty binding him to the accomplishment of the end designed for him by nature's Creator.
Whatever conduces to that end, without disturbing the reign
of justice, constitutes matter for a right. He is armed with
a right to repel whatever seriously and unjustly interferes
with his destiny's consummation.

N.B. Duty manifests the claims of moral rectitude, and
rectitude is the observance of relations, or conduct in harmony with the objective order of things. The order of excellence and importance prevalent in duties is, God, self, and the
neighbor. Compare Hedonism and Altruism. Ahrens and
Damiron would recognize rights in animals, because they are

called in Holy Writ sons of God, and because we are forbidden
to do them injury or cause them pain. We answer, Holy
Writ is on occasions poetic, and these scattered passages are
to be so interpreted. The Church is judge, not our opponents or ourselves. We slay animals for purposes of sus-
tenance, comfort and ornament. We must not be wanton in
our treatment of animals, because all such conduct is hostile
to the growth of mildness and meekness.

First Duty. In point of time and in point of excellence.
This duty of religion, to ensure good results in after life, ought
to be impressed on the child's thoughts from the earliest dawn
of reason, and all other duties, even towards his parents,
should be unfolded to his growing mind as corollaries flowing
from the first. He should be taught that parents, country
and friends, high as they stand in his esteem and love, occupy
only second place to God, and that at God's call all these and
much else besides must be abandoned.

Essential Necessity. Philosophy recognizes two kinds of
necessity, accidental and essential. The former hardly deserves the name. It represents a thing necessary only after
such a fashion that the effect can in certain circumstances
have place in its absence, and its functions can always be
discharged by some other object. Thus, for instance, brown
bread is said to be an accidental necessity of life. Essential
necessity truly deserves the name. It represents a thing so
necessary that in the event of its absence the effect is simply
out of the question. Thus, food of some sort is an essential
necessity for continuance in life. This essential necessity,
however, admits of degrees. It may be physical, or quasi-
physical, or moral. *A physical essential necessity forms part
of a thing's very being, body in man. A quasi-physical essential necessity contributes to a thing's well-being.* Want
of a necessity of this kind makes itself felt in a wholly different way from want of an accidental necessity. Sound health,
for instance, is a quasi-physical essential necessity for the
enjoyment of life. It cannot, like bread, be replaced by some
other commodity. *A moral essential necessity is an object,
thoroughly requisite for the rounding out of a man's moral
being.* It is an imperative call of conscience, a heavy and
unavoidable obligation. Failure to comply with its demands

disturbs that harmony with the objective order which constitutes man's last end or destiny in this life. We contend that religion, objective and subjective, dogmatic and practical, while not a physical essential necessity for individual and state, is for one and the other a quasi-physical and a moral essential necessity. We contend, in other words, that without religion man's physical life is beset with trials, troubles and dangers, that the state's welfare is seriously harmed, and that individual and state are out of harmony with rectitude.

Individual and State. Religion's bearing on the lives of individual citizens presents no difficulty whatever. Its bearing on the state becomes as clear, when we regard the state a moral person, affected with rights it can enforce, with duties it must discharge. With this view of the state we are acquainted from common every day experience. Our President and our Governors pay religious tribute to God, by proclaiming once a year the advent of Thanksgiving Day, by countenancing religious observance throughout the land, by prayer in our legislative assemblies, and at other functions of state. In distinctively Catholic countries the duty is accomplished with more solemn ceremony.

Worship. Testimony to divine excellence coupled with due submission. It is honor of a peculiar sort combined with submission. When the acts of homage are internal and unseen of men, the worship is interior. When these acts are external, and plain to the senses, the worship is exterior. Public worship, or social, is homage done God by the state in its representatives, not in private individuals. The observance paid God by citizens in their private capacity constitutes private worship. Only the godless deny the necessity of interior worship. But scores of writers endeavor to do away with the need of exterior worship, and public or social worship of whatever sort. Many are urged to take this step by hostility to the Catholic Church, so insistent on exterior worship. As a matter of fact, the vast majority of men to-day outside of the true faith, regard attendance at Sunday service a thing of minor importance, wholly beneath their notice, and no matter of conscience at all. Some, with a family resemblance to the traitor Judas, prate about the useless expenditure of money, wasted in the erection of edifices for purposes of worship. These proclaim with loud mouths that the green fields are God's temple, and that the birds of the air are His choristers. They declare external observances and ceremonies a hollow mockery, superstition; and never lose an opportunity to inveigh against them. But their own conduct is the weightiest argument against their words. They are monuments of decayed religious spirit, the unfailing growth of negligence in matters external.

Of the two kinds of worship, interior is, of course, the higher and more precious; but, constituted as he is, man depends for inner emotions on his outward behavior and deportment of body. When minded to pray, he needs to be surrounded with all the holy images, and with that atmosphere of quiet resident in our churches. He needs to go down on his knees, and fold his hands, and shut his eyes against the thousand distracting objects clamoring for his attention. Even with all the varied helps present in our houses of prayer, it is no easy task to check our senses, and address God with the profound respect, which is His due. Then too, the Creator made our hands, arms, eyes and the other members of the body, as well as the soul; and mind-worship to the exclusion of body-worship is paying only half our debt. Thomasius, Dunzi and Kemmerichius concede a measure of usefulness to exterior worship, but deny reason's ability to prove its necessity. Ahrens, infected with modern rationalism, frames up a definition of religion, from which he entirely excludes the necessity of exterior worship. "Religion," he says, "is a union of mind and heart with the supreme being." "Worship, therefore," with him, "is an intellectual and spiritual work only, which ought to refrain from representing God and His attributes by sensible signs." "One may," he continues, "call to his assistance some of the fine arts, such for instance as music and song, because these serve to more vividly express our notions of the infinite." He allows the sense of hearing to play a part in divine worship, he has no place for the eyes, and scents from afar Catholicity's veneration of images

Revelation. The word is a Latin derivative from re, back, and velum, a veil. It means therefore the removal of a veil, the lifting of some hidden truth into the light. In theology, revelation is defined as, *"A communication from God in language strictly so called, by which, on the authority of His testimony, He makes known to men truths in the order of salvation."* All creation is said to be a book, which sets forth with a great wealth of detail God's guiding presence, His attributes, and His wishes in our regard. But it conveys lessons through a medium different from language properly so called, and therefore falls short of being revelation. Revelation is the word of God, something once uttered by God for men's spiritual advantage. Its channels are direct speech, the written word, and tradition. He held immediate converse with Moses and the prophets, who afterwards at His express command committed His wishes to writing for the benefit of future ages. This body of revelation is contained in the Old Testament. Later on, He appeared among men, and in the person of Jesus Christ changed much of the old dispensation, and instituted the New Law, destined to govern His people without change or alteration till the end of time. He bade His apostles preach and teach His doctrine throughout the world. St. Matthew and St. John, with the disciples St. Mark and St. Luke, compiled the four Gospels, or narratives of Christ's life. St. Paul and others, under the influence of divine inspiration, wrote a series of letters or documents abounding with rules for the right ordering of Christian life.

God ordained that these writings should always remain in the custody of a living Church, which He solemnly founded and placed under the control of St. Peter and his successors forever. This Church is to be the arbiter of all religious disputes, and this Church is to decide beyond all appeal the amplitude of revelation. There is no higher court, empowered to review or reverse its decisions; and God has promised it immunity from error in matters of dogma. It is the guardian and authoritative interpreter of God's word, as contained in the Old and New Testaments; the witness to and the dispenser of tradition. For revelation is of wider extent than the mere written word, and embraces all the points of belief insisted on and taught by the Catholic and true Church of Christ, though not explicitly set forth in the pages of Holy Scripture.

Scripture itself bears us out in all these statements, but their further discussion belongs to the domain of theology. We have said enough to convince any honest mind that revelation is no empty dream. Scripture and tradition are its abundant sources, and he who diligently searches can easily recognize the contents of the Bible and the doctrines of the Catholic Church for the word of God. Miracles and prophecies are the most obvious of the seals divinity has stamped upon them; and the miracles and the prophecies we appeal to for the heavenly character of our religion, are beyond denial, and beyond serious dispute or doubt. God alone is equal to the infinite task of working real miracles, and uttering real prophecies; and when He invests a messenger with these dread prerogatives for credentials of his mission, that messenger is God's mouthpiece, and the tidings he brings are fresh from the lips of God.

Faith is the virtue called into play by revelation, and faith is not knowing, but believing. The truths of faith are not blessed with all the light, thrown round the axioms of algebra and geometry. They are obscure, hard to understand, and in some cases absolutely beyond human comprehension. More than any other act of the mind, faith makes large demands on free will; and this circumstance, constituting faith's merit, is responsible for faith's small influence with the ill-disposed. As an act of supremest homage, it is only just that it carry along with itself submission of will, the faculty whose surrender is a most pleasing sacrifice in God's sight.

Faith of the right kind, faith with the authority of God's word for root and motive, leaves a man no room for choice between dogmas that flatter and dogmas that pinch self. Every statement, whether it pictures forth the ravishing joys of Heaven, or the terrifying flames of hell, must be accepted with the same readiness and good-will. Of course, some of Scripture's utterances have a more important bearing on morality, a more intimate connection with eternal salvation than others; but all, all without a single exception, rest for credence on the self-same support, the knowledge and the truthfulness of God. If God could stoop to the meanness of deceiving man in the most trivial particular, man's trust and confidence in God would be at an end. Faith in any utterance of God, no matter how solemn and weighty, would then degenerate to stupidity. People outside our Church, people whose faith is measured by the canons of convenience, set apart certain far-reaching, general and palatable dogmas, and label them fundamental articles. They preach that these alone are to be believed under pain of eternal loss. Other articles of minor importance deserve no attention, though out of respect for God's word they ought not to be wantonly denied. With them, individuals are judge and jury in the selection; and confusion reigns supreme.

We too recognize a difference in importance between various parts of Holy Scripture; but no one sentence is so unimportant as not to demand our full faith and belief. We feel at liberty to deny nothing, we feel bound to believe at least implicitly the whole of Scripture's contents, and explicitly believe every dogma duly proposed to our consideration. And since every clause in the Bible descends to us from the same God who teaches the more important articles, our position is alone logical, our position alone approves itself to reason. To accept revelation as such means, therefore, a vast deal more than half-hearted and insincere believers to-day make it mean. To diligently seek and find revelation when hidden, implies a larger amount of labor than most strangers to the truth devote to this undeniable duty. Doubts daily cross their minds, and suspicions concerning the dangerous risks they are taking constantly arise within them. And yet these improvident philosophers, because the consequences of their mistake will become fully apparent only in the next life, prefer the ease of uncertainty, and the license their pretended ignorance lends to their low instincts.

Toleration. Nobody need be informed that the world is sadly full of different religious sects. A walk through our own city, with now and then a glance at the sign-boards conspicuously displayed at temple entrances, must effectually cure any doubt on the subject. Indifferentism is a rampant sin among us, so rampant that the early signers felt constrained to introduce into our Constitution a clause ensuring to every citizen immunity from persecution on the score of religion. Be it noted, however, that the toleration sanctioned by our government is merely political; and therefore not to be branded in virtue of our thesis absurd. Dogmatic toleration is as eminently absurd a notion as can well be conceived. Only a disordered mind could seriously entertain it. *Political toleration is mere permission, without the declaration of any absolute right, to practise false as well as true religions. Dogmatic toleration is permission along with the assertion of an absolute right to practise false as well as true religions.*

Political tolerance tolerates not mistakes, but people who make the mistakes. It can at heart abominate all false worship, and yet have a word of kindness for the victims of error. It takes men as it finds them, and merely permits all without distinction to practise whatever system of public worship they choose. It seals with its sanction no form of worship at all, but in the interests of peace allows the false and the true to grow up together till the harvest. And God allows that, in a permissive, though not in an approving way. Ardent lovers of the truth at first sight revolt against any such proceeding; but after calm consideration they settle down to the conviction, that in the present lamentable state of affairs it is the only feasible method. Christ once rebuked indignation of the kind in St. James and St. John. The Samaritans had shut their gates against His coming and these disciples said, "Lord, wilt thou that we command fire to come down from heaven and consume them? And turning He rebuked them, saying, You know not of what spirit you are. The Son of man came, not to destroy souls, but to save." St. Luke 9.54.

When authority permits a practice as abominable in the sight of God as heresy, it can still be justified on the double plea of inability to remedy the abuse, and refraining from the crime of formal cooperation. Were there no such escape from the difficulty, our rulers would be obliged in conscience to do one of two things. They would have either to expel all sectaries from the country, or whip them into submission to the true faith. But the one alternative is quite as impracticable and impossible as the other. Adherents to the true religion are not in the majority, and truth's victory would be uncertain. It is criminal to undertake any kind of a war without reasonable hope of winning. Catholics outnumber every single sect taken separately; but, in the event of force, error would unite against the truth, as against a common foe. Then, too, even were the triumph of truth an assured possibility, the land would have to be deluged with blood, and life would perish from the state. Submission procured by force is simply out of the question. Religion subjectively taken is largely a matter of free will. Liberty enters religion as an essential element, and religion embraced under stress of physical violence is hypocrisy.

Besides, the state by supposition lends no peculiar support or encouragement to false creeds, and in this particular escapes censure. Dogmatic toleration would be in effect, if our Constitution anywhere committed itself to the stupidity of declaring all forms of worship equally good. But you will look in vain throughout its pages for any such assertion. Well-meaning Catholics, to conciliate the esteem and friendship of separated brethren, sometimes stoop to the meanness of giving expression to sentiments of the kind. But their excuse lies in the fact that they are over-zealous for peace, and speak without due reflection. Rome recognises no compromise with error. She teaches her children to put on the feelings of charity and forbearance towards error's deluded victims, but denounces error as an unpardonable sin, and commends its slaves to the mercy and justice of God.

Absurd. The full force of this term implies something more than mere falsehood. It further conveys the notion of silliness and open war with reason's most evident dictates. A statement can well be false without being absurd. We are acquainted with many such statements. The falsehood they contain, lies deep beneath the surface, mixed with much that is true, and only diligent search can detect it. But dogmatic tolerance is so repugnant to common sense that we hesitate not to brand it absurd.

DIVISION

Four Parts—I, II, III, IV

I. Religion is (a) man's first duty, of essential necessity to (b) individual and (c) State.
II. Worship, interior and exterior, private and public is God's due.

III. Man's duty towards revelation is (a) to accept, or
    (b) seek it.

IV. Toleration in matter of dogma is absurd.

PROOFS

I. (a) The position and standing of relations fix the position and standing of duties. But of all man's relations
those with God are first in time and first in excellence. Ergo,
man's duty towards God, or religion, is man's first duty.

With Regard to the Major. Duties are the growth of relations in force between a man and God, himself and his neighbors. They are, as it were, an effect, with these several relations for cause; and effects partake of the nobility inherent in
necessary causes.

With Regard to the Minor. Existence and reality derived
from God and Creator are first requisites for whatever events
crowd into a man's after-life. To none therefore are we
more under obligation than to God. Nobody has more sacred
rights to our homage and service. No conceivable object is
worthier of our energies.

(b) A duty based on a relation arising from man's very
nature is a thing of moral essential necessity to the individual. But religion is a duty arising from just such a relation. Ergo, religion is a thing of moral essential necessity
to the individual.

With Regard to the Major. Duties are strict moral neces-
sities. Duties arising from man's nature are as close and
present to man as his very nature. They can no more be
absent from him, they can no more loosen their hold on his
allegiance than nature can abandon him, or reside somewhere
apart from him. That religion is a quasi-physical essential
necessity to the individual, favorable to his happiness, peace
and well-being must be evident from the line of reasoning
followed in proof of next clause.

(c) 1°. A moral person immediately dependent on God for
maker, helper, guide and rewarder lies under moral essential
necessity to acknowledge and worship God. But the state is
such a moral person, and religion is this acknowledgment and

worship. **Ergo, religion is a moral essential necessity to the state.**

2°. That without which duties of justice, honesty, and mutual harmony can in no wise stand is a quasi-physical essential necessity to the state as such. But religion is a thing of the kind. Ergo.

With Regard to the Major. Nobody will deny that the duties enumerated are of vital importance and large factors in the state's well being.

With Regard to the Minor. Remove God from the universe, destroy religion, and all moral obligation falls, sanction is idle, and states go down in ruin.

II. N.B. Worship offered to God, divine excellence itself, is called, latria. Worship offered the Blessed Virgin Mary, who borrows all her excellence from God, is called, hyperdulia. Worship offered the saints is called dulia.

The worship belonging to God is at least interior. In the case of individuals it must likewise be exterior or bodily, since man's dependence on God, extending as it does to body and soul, must be shown whole and entire. The worship rendered by the state must be social, and therefore visible or exterior. Public worship is worship rendered by the individuals composing a state, not in their private capacity, but as welded together by authority into one body politic.

III. Man's duty towards revelation is to (a) accept it, or (b) seek it.

(a) 1°. It is a rational creature's duty to accept for true every statement made by the God of truth and known for such. But man is a rational creature, and revelation is a body of statements made by the God of truth. Ergo, man's duty towards revelation is to accept it when known as such.

With Regard to the Major. Duties are the result of relations, and the relations in force between the Creator and His rational creatures make faith in the Creator's word an imperative necessity. God therefore has a right to man's mental submission when He speaks. That He invariably insists on this right, is evident from the circumstance that He is all-wise and all-true. He cannot, like limited and finite mortals, give expression to utterances, that owing to dearth of knowledge are tainted with falsehood. He cannot like fools talk for the mere sake of talking, without caring whether His listeners heed His words or not. Men can be guilty of folly of the sort; but God has too much reverence for language's end and purpose to so abuse it. When a man of ordinary common sense, blessed with a fair measure of seriousness, vouches for the truth of some fact, he can with reason feel offended at a refusal to abide by his declaration. God's attributes would make such a refusal a monstrous crime, and God's attributes make faith in His word an absolute duty.

With Regard to the Minor. That Scripture and tradition, or revelation, are a body of statements made by the God of truth is proved at great length in works on Theology. Philosophy left to itself can proceed no farther than demonstrate the necessity of accepting revelation in the event of its being made. It cannot, alone and single handed, conclusively prove that this or that set of truths constitutes revelation. History furnishes us with well attested facts, and philosophy can discover in these facts traces of God's presence.

Thus, the records of history are witness to the reality of Moses and the prophets, and to certain wonderful or miraculous events in their lives. They claimed for themselves the dignity of messengers from God to men, and left in writing to posterity facts, principles, and maxims, that God commissioned them to communicate. For credentials they appealed to miracles and prophecies, worked and uttered by them in the name of God. Philosophy is within its own province, when it undertakes to show that the writings of Moses and the prophets derive from these miracles and prophecies a divinity peculiarly their own. These two species of effects are beyond the reach of power inferior to God's, and God could never sanction lies by the performance of prodigies. When, therefore, He stamped with these seals of His omnipotence and wisdom the claims of Moses and the prophets, He signified as plainly as possible how He wished their statements to be regarded. He signified as plainly as possible that the words they committed to writing were His own words and had Him for author.

2°. From analogy. To God as the supreme being adoration is due; to God as the supreme good love is due. Ergo, to God as the highest truth faith is due.

(b) Contempt of revelation is contempt of God, and indifference to eternal salvation. But avoidance of contempt for God, and of indifference to salvation, is man's plain duty. Ergo, avoidance of contempt for revelation, diligent search for the truth, is man's duty.

With Regard to the Major. God wastes no words, and means His every message to be seriously taken. He is likewise anxious that all His children, without any exception, take full advantage of the instruction He proffers. He occupies the position of Lord and Father, and resents negligent attention on the part of such as He deigns to address. Revelation teems with documents designed for helps to attain to the Kingdom of Heaven, and the loss of these necessary helps through sloth is attended with damage and serious responsibility. It is quite impossible for me to think, that to-day's scoffers at religion and revelation are absolutely free from suspicion and anxiety, concerning the doubtful and preposterous position they occupy. And to let one single doubt in this matter of revelation remain unsettled, is to take sides with God's enemies, and to confide to chance eternal destiny for weal or woe. Plungers at a race-track, when placing money on horses, display more skill and prudence than the wiseacres, who, because of trivial difficulties, gamble in risks, and leave Heaven to a game of chance.

With Regard to the Minor. God has well founded claims on our reverence; and, apart from other considerations, we owe it to our souls and bodies to procure for them an abode of comfort, and happiness, and security against the endless ages of ages in store for them beyond the grave.

IV. 1°. Toleration in matter of dogma supposes that a system of religion false in itself, yea, immoral and unclean in its tendencies, can be an instrument in God's worship. But this supposition is eminently absurd. Ergo.

With Regard to the Minor. God is truth, God is purity; and falsehood, immorality, and uncleanness can have no part in His service. Any other notion would be unworthy of God's infinite majesty and degrading in the extreme.

2°. Toleration in matter of dogma supposes that religion can be manifold in such sort that a duty prescribed by one system can be neglected by another system, or totally condemned as dishonest by a third system. But this supposition is eminently absurd. Ergo.

With Regard to the Minor. The collection of truths and duties embraced in a religion, truly deserving of the name, ought to be one and the same for all mankind. Religion is the outcome of man's dependence on God; and, since the two terms of the relation, human nature and an unchangeable God, are the same the world over and for all time, religion the result of the relation ought to be the same, without shadow or suspicion of change or difference. Artificial changes, wrought in men's minds by education, prejudice, and other external agencies, are no excuse and no ground whatever for declaring that human nature in me is different from human nature in my neighbor.

PRINCIPLES

A. In every free act of the will, whether it be prayer or murder, man necessarily keeps his relations with God, manifesting and acknowledging his quality of dependence on God. Ergo, no religion needed.

Answer: Materially, I grant; formally, I deny. The dependence must not be in the free act, but in the very freedom of the act. The dependence manifest in the free act itself never bases religion. Otherwise brutes, plants and minerals would be capable of religion, and there would be no distinction between the service of brutes and the service of men. The difference would be merely on the part of the servant, not on the part of the service. Other creatures serve God, no matter what they do. Man in his free acts serves God only when he uses his will aright. The service God exacts from men is different from the service He exacts from brutes; and free will is index of His wishes.

B. God cannot be acted on. Ergo, He cannot be worshipped.

Answer: He cannot be acted on physically, I grant; morally, as in case of wrong or honor, I deny. Worship induces no intrinsic change in God. All the change is outside God. Worship changes us.

C. God is infinitely perfect.   Ergo, He has no need of worship.

Answer: He has no need of worship, as of a perfection antecedently absent from His being, I grant. He has no need of worship, as of homage which is His due, I deny. The millionaire may have no need of the five dollars you owe him, but the circumstance never excuses you from payment.

D. Reason would be the basis of moral obligation and the single origin of good and evil.

Answer: Reason manifests moral obligation, I grant. Reason makes or constitutes it, I deny.

E. Society owes worship. Ergo the family, and literary, scientific, athletic societies.

Answer: Complete society, I grant; incomplete, I deny. The family because complete and independent is a moral person and held to worship. Private societies of the kind mentioned, because incomplete and dependent on the state, are no moral persons, and under no such obligation.

F. The state has a temporal end or purpose. Ergo, no religion.

Answer: Its first and chief purpose is the temporal prosperity of its citizens. This purpose it must accomplish in a way befitting its nature, and by nature it is a moral person, under obligations to God. Ergo, while pursuing temporal good, it must not neglect the knowledge and worship of God.

G. Society is immediately dependent on the free will of man. Ergo, independent of God.

Answer: In its making, when not yet a person, I grant; when constituted and now a person, I deny.

H. In spirit and in truth, John 4.23. Ergo, no external worship needed.

Answer: The true meaning of the passage is a contrast between the Old Law and the New, between the letter or figure, and spirit or truth. Besides, insistence on internal worship is far from condemning external. Christ on no few occasions employed external worship.

I. The State can get along without religion. Ergo. Schiff, p. 511, n. 510.

Answer: We could transmit the antecedent and deny the

conclusion as inconsequent. Worship is a need to the state, not precisely because of advantage, but because of the nature of things. The state can get along somehow and imperfectly, I grant; as nature intended and perfectly, I deny.

J. Other incentives would hold men to honesty; a sense of honor, for instance. Ergo.

Answer: We could again transmit. Our argument is not based on advantage, but on the nature of things. These other incentives would be sufficient and efficacious, I deny; insufficient and inefficacious, I grant.

K. State and religion have two different ends, temporal good and spiritual. Ergo.

Answer: Different, when incompletely viewed, I grant; when viewed in their completeness, I deny. When viewed in their completeness, the ends of the two are one and the same, the glory of God. God is the absolutely last end of everything.

L. Church and state are distinct. Ergo.

Answer: Distinct and separate, I deny; distinct and not separate; I again distinguish. In the present order of things, with revelation, I grant; in the order of pure nature, without revelation, I again distinguish, completely distinct, I deny, incompletely distinct, I grant. In the order of pure nature, the state as supreme authority would determine religion; in the present order, revelation appoints the Church to that office.

M. "It would be easier, I think, to build a city without ground, than to establish or preserve a state without God and religion." Plutarch. "Time destroys extravagant opinions, it solidifies the judgments of nature." Cicero, de Nat. Deorum, 2.

N. No need to pray, because God knows everything. Kant.

Answer: S. Th. 2.2. q. 83, a. 2. "Men ought to do things, not for the purpose of changing the arrangements of Providence, but to accomplish results in accordance with these arrangements." We pray to change God's decrees, I deny; we pray to fulfil them, I grant. His decrees are conditioned. Gifts are made us, if we pray; withheld, if we neglect to do so. He knows from eternity whether He will relieve men

or not; but this knowledge is terminatively speaking consequent on our use of free will, on our choice or rejection of
prayer.

O. Truths above understanding would be a contradiction.
Ergo, no revelation.

Answer: Above all understanding both divine and human,
I grant; above merely human understanding, I deny.

P. No truth above human understanding, because its object
is all being. Ergo.

Answer: Its proportionate object is all being, I deny; all
material being is that; its adequate object is all being, I again
distinguish; inasmuch as the human intellect can understand
whatever being is duly presented or brought to its notice, I
grant; inasmuch as all being is as a matter of fact thus duly
presented or brought to its notice, I deny. There are more
things in Heaven and earth than are dreamt of in our philosophy.

Q. A truth above reason would be against reason, because
out of harmony with reason.

Answer: Out of harmony in a contradictory way, I grant;
in a contrary way, I deny. There is a difference between not
being a man's friend, not loving him; and being his enemy,
hating him. In much the same way to be on no terms of
intimacy with reason is not the same as to be opposed to
reason.

R. God has a right not only to worship, but to worship of
the kind He wants.

S. Religion is truth and justice. Truth is one, error is
manifold. Justice is one.

T. Christianity and Judaism are two opposite religions.
Ergo, if one was ever right, the other must always be wrong.

Answer: Opposite essentially, with regard to Christ, I
deny; opposite accidentally, with regard to circumstances of
time and form, with regard to Christ already come and Christ
yet to come, I grant. Christianity worships Christ already
come, Judaism worships Christ yet to come, the Messiah.

U. If an opponent admits Scripture. Christ wants one
Church, one fold, one Baptism. Christ wants His people to
guard against false prophets, and in the event of dogmatic
toleration false prophets must grow and multiply. Christ

wants His Church to endure forever. St. Luke, 11.17.
"Every kingdom divided against itself shall fall." "Now I
beseech you, brethren, to mark them who make dissensions
and offences contrary to the doctrine which you have learnt,
and to avoid them." Rom. 16.17. "But though we, or an
angel from Heaven, preach a gospel to you besides that which
we have preached to you, let him be anathema." Gal. 1.8.

V. Indifferentism and Liberalism are two theories based on
toleration.

Indifferentism { Absolute = No religion is necessary = Altogether wrong
is of two   and against whole thesis.
kinds   2   Relative = Some religion necessary, no one form before
                another, { Universal = All forms equally good.
                          { Particular = All Christianity equally
                            good.

Philosophy refutes universal; theology, particular, because
revelation enters question.

Toleration { Dogmatic = All religions equally good = Toleration of
is of two   error = Indifferentism.
kinds   Political = All public worship is allowed = Toleration of
               the erring = Liberalism.

Dogmatic is freedom of conscience, meaning immunity from
all restraint, moral as well as physical; from all law of nature
and all law of God. Political is freedom of worship, immunity from the moral restraint imposed by law of state and
Church, not from law of nature or of God. In a Catholic
country, Indifferentism of whatever kind and Liberalism are
regularly wrong, circumstances may condone Liberalism. In
a mixed country, absolute and relative universal Indifferent-
isms are wrong, and the aid of theology must be invoked to
prove relative particular Indifferentism wrong. In a mixed
country, that Liberalism is right, which for grave reasons
tolerates whatever false religions threaten no harm to the first
principles of morality; and every other species of Liberalism
is wrong. When a false religion threatens the first principles of morality, it must not be tolerated, because it is a
menace to not only the welfare but the very life of the state.
In the event of legitimate toleration, some grave reason, like
the violent disturbance of social order, must be present; be-

cause every false religion is an obstacle to the public good, and no risk of the kind can be legitimately taken without a serious and proportionate reason. The religion of the state ought to be one and true; but facts, over which we have no control, make this condition impossible in certain countries called mixed, and a sane Liberalism is the only alternative for them. By a Catholic country we mean a country, wherein morally speaking all the inhabitants profess the true religion. By a mixed country we mean a country, wherein men in sufficiently large numbers to destroy this moral unanimity profess false religions.

W. A Catholic country has no right to insist on the Catholic religion, (1) because God leaves men free; (2) because human reason is open to mistake in the matter of religion; (3) because the state has temporal good for end or purpose; (4) because a Protestant country would have the same right; (5) because the Catholic religion will prevail anyhow, as truth is stronger than falsehood; (6) because peace would be disturbed; (7) because such interference is everywhere regarded a species of tyranny.

Answers: (1) God leaves men free physically, I grant; morally, I deny; (2) Reason is fallible with regard to morality's first principles and immediate deductions from same, I deny; with regard to remoter conclusions, I again distinguish; if revelation lends reason no support, I grant; if revelation supplements reason, I deny. (3) The state has temporal good for immediate and incomplete end, I grant; for remote and complete end, I deny; that is the glory of God. (4) Objectively, I deny; subjectively, I again distinguish; if error has any right against the truth, I grant; if error has no such right, I deny. (5) Truth is stronger than falsehood objectively and intrinsically, I grant; subjectively and extrinsically, I deny. Men's passions commonly favor falsehood. (6) Peace would be disturbed in the very nature of things, I deny; by accident, I again distinguish; and for this very reason toleration is to be conditionally permitted, I grant; toleration is to be absolutely permitted, I deny. (7) Such interference is erroneously accounted tyranny, I grant; rightly accounted tyranny, I deny.

THESIS II

Suicide is a sin against nature. Death inflicted in self-defense is under certain conditions justifiable. Private duels are highly absurd, and contrary to the law of nature. Jouin, 96–118; Rickaby, 202–224.

QUESTION

Religion is the one word expressive of our duties towards God. It is a word of wide significance, and we were able in our first thesis to discuss only its most salient features. From among its varied contents we selected for study worship, revelation, and its concomitant question of religious toleration. Religion, of course, imposes on us the obligation of cultivating whatever virtues have a direct bearing on God. These virtues are in especial, faith, hope and charity; and they are for this reason called the theological virtues. There must, however, be a limit to our treatise, and we prefer to leave the fuller examination of these several topics to catechism and the Sunday-school.

These theological virtues as such would have no place in the natural order, because they have God as known from revelation for material and formal object. And yet corresponding virtues in the shape of love, hope, obedience, gratitude and fidelity would be serious obligations in even the natural order, and God as known by reason would be their object. Man is certainly bound to seek his end or purpose in life. We described it as proximately the introduction of moral order into his conduct, and ultimately the intellectual possession of God. Viewed one way or the other, this end is an arduous or difficult good, and tendency towards every such good is hope. Man is likewise bound to love God above everything, because right order demands that we make the dignity of love's object the measure of love's quality. God

201

is infinite good, the source and origin of all created good, and as such deserves to be loved above everything. Our duty of obedience flows from our relation of creature. We are the work of God's hands, and the artificer is absolute owner of the thing he makes. Gratitude and fidelity are obligations in view of the multitudinous favors conferred on us.

And now we pass from God to self. Man has duties towards his soul, he has duties towards his body. Obviously we cannot enter into all the questions suggested by these two component parts of man's being. We choose to busy ourselves in the main with his body, dismissing the soul with these few remarks. Man was created to the image and likeness of God, and this resemblance with the Creator is principally resident in the soul. His intellect and will must be therefore developed and made grow more and more like their divine prototype by steady improvement. With the Child Jesus he must grow in wisdom, age and grace. His mind must be stored with knowledge, human and divine; his will must strengthen itself in good. All the virtues with a bearing on the mind, all the virtues with a bearing on the will, must be sedulously cultivated; and passions, ready helps to wrong conduct, must be subdued and kept in tight check. Intellect and will must be shaped by diligent care into instruments calculated to procure their owner's welfare here and hereafter. Mind and heart must be trained along right lines; and this means education in its fullest and completest sense. This topic of education will get fuller attention when we come to discuss the duties of parents in particular. Suicide, with everything suggestive of suicide, is the chiefest offense man can do his own body; but this question is so closely connected with self-defense and duelling, that we choose to gather all three topics into one thesis. Suicide is destruction of life, self-defense is its preservation, and duelling partakes of the double malice of murder and suicide. We say nothing of murder, because it is too evident a violation of natural law to need notice.

Some philosophers, like Thomasius and Schopenhauer, object to the expression, man's duties towards himself. Regularly duties are between two different persons, and even in this case the relations establishing man's duty towards his own proper person are fundamentally between himself and God. His duties towards his neighbor rest ultimately on the same foundation; and merely to keep one set of duties apart from the other, we denominate them duties towards self and duties towards the neighbor. The whole man can be said to differ from his parts or faculties, and this circumstance would be basis enough for the expression, duty towards self.

TERMS

Suicide. Suicide is direct killing of self on one's own initiative. Life, because the root of all succeeding favors, is Heaven's first and highest gift; and, no matter how crowded with misfortunes, it never loses this quality of a gift. All things considered, its chief good lies in the circumstance that it is the one road leading to a happy eternity. Any other view of life's utility is a mistake, and sure to work sad havoc. Some enjoy a gilt-edged existence from the cradle to the grave. Others drag out a short or long period of disease, and want, and disappointment. But all, without a single exception, the poor as well as the rich, the unfortunate as well as the fortunate, can still count life a priceless jewel. When turned to good and proper uses, it can purchase a seat in the kingdom, a title to that supreme happiness, which constitutes man's last end.

And yet life is something more than a mere gift. It is a responsibility, and its giver attaches to it obligations, that its recipient is not free to abide by or shirk at will. When born into the world, a man, without being at all consulted beforehand, is set down in the midst of a multitude of relations, which produce unavoidable and stern duties. No man can escape them, no man can afford to trifle with them, without diminishing his dignity and suffering irreparable loss. Life is not given to mortals to be squandered on every chance attraction that happens along. It is not a toy meant by its gracious author to be used till it loses the power to please, and then be cast aside.

Everything in nature points to the fact that God created men as well as other beings to add their little measure to His glory. Everything in nature proclaims Him the author of life and death, and He is jealous of His prerogatives. Men, whether they will or not, have to procure the spread of His kingdom, and proclaim His sovereignty. In His all-wise plans every creature has its allotted time for life, and woe to the man who attempts to interfere with the plan. Men cannot call life out of nothing; men usurp a right belonging to God Himself, when without His sanction they put an end to their existence. They deny God service, they rob themselves of eternal glory, they plunge their families and friends into the depths of disgrace, they bequeath to their descendants a name of ignominy and shame, they curse their country with an example of craven-hearted cowardice and sottish impiety.

The crime of suicide is thoroughly wicked, and has nothing whatever to recommend it to the esteem of men born with high instincts. It is the mad act of a coward, and bravery is dishonored by being mentioned in the same breath with suicide. Fortitude impels the courageous to bear up under troubles that crush men of weaker mould. Fortitude is blessed with long vision, and in the very excess of pain looks forward to the hour when pain will be no more. It knows the weakness inherent in all the ills of this life, and is satisfied from experience that sufferance is their infallible remedy. With time they wear themselves out, and joy succeeds to sorrow. But the suicide, whose vision is as short as his patience, madly rushes through the first avenue open to escape. Instead of meeting an enemy to his happiness with a bold front, he turns his back and flees. The pit of hell-fire into which he falls has been robbed by his irreligion of all its dread reality. In the minds of the unfortunates, who trifle with thoughts of suicide, hell and Heaven are dreams, and never awaken serious consideration. They play the coward; and, choosing between a present and a distant evil, between a certain and an uncertain calamity, they avoid the one and fall headlong into the other.

Climate, heredity, racial characteristics, are not responsible for suicide. They may be occasions, but they are not causes. They may pave the way to self-destruction, but freedom of will always holds the balance of power; and, if freedom of will has been instructed along right lines of morality, virtue will always assert itself, and suicide will be hated with all the hate it deserves. Apart from their piety and religion, the people of Ireland, because of the misery attendant on hundreds of years of oppression, have small incentive indeed to continue a tiresome and from a worldly point of view hopeless existence. And yet consulting tables prepared for the World Almanac by Barker in 1894, Ireland and Spain contribute fewest to the army of suicides. Protestantism, with its impious principle of private interpretation, is the parent of unbelief, and countries cursed with its blight are rich in unnatural crimes of the sort. Here are a few interesting and instructive statistics culled from the table referred to.

Catholic	Rate per 100,000	Protestant	Rate per 100,000
Saxony,	31.1	Austria,	21.2
Denmark,	25.8	France,	15.7
Prussia,	13.3	Bavaria,	9.1
Sweden,	8.1	Ireland,	1.7
England,	6.9	Spain,	1.4

Common sense would lead us to expect no other result. Unbelief unsettles all the convictions implanted by faith, and faith is busiest with the reality of life beyond the grave. Faith is our soundest argument for the existence of Heaven and hell; and, when Heaven and hell become dim realities in men's minds, small wonder if they take all risks to avoid impending evils like disease, disgrace, poverty and disappointment.

Some ancient philosophers, like Seneca, Plato, Socrates and others, defended suicide, but on grounds far different from the silly pretenses set up by their modern imitators. It may be well to remark that the ancients never regarded suicide justifiable, when used as an exit from ills for which the suicide was himself responsible. Socrates thought self-murder ethically correct, only because he knew that after condemnation by the state authorities he had to die anyhow. Seneca and the rest thought it a laudable subterfuge only when cornered by adverse circumstances, over which they had no control. The old Romans considered these seven, justifiable causes for suicide. A disgust for life. The wish to be rid of a distressing disease. Regret for the decease of some dear companion. Shame at being an insolvent debtor. Ambition to

be spoken of after death, when there had been no honor in
this life. Dementia or insanity. Outrage to a woman's
chastity. But modern advocates of the revolting theory
preach its adaptability to every occasion. They draw no fine
distinctions between evils for which the victim of poison, pistol or the knife is himself responsible, and evils brought to his
door by friends or strangers. When life from whatever cause
grows disagreeably heavy, life, they say, should be pushed
aside. We have no excuse to offer for the mistakes made by
the wise of old, when defending the theory and practice of
suicide. It is explanation enough for us to know that faith
in God never had a tight or loose hold on their minds and
hearts, that their natural knowledge of God and a future life
was dim, obscure and imperfect, and that selfishness, with an
inborn tendency to comfort and ease, is as native to the sa-
pient philosopher as it is to the ignorant clod. But it is at
the same time worth noting, that the higher they climbed in
the scale of true wisdom, the less they conceded to this basest
of sins. See Cicero, De Senectute, c. 20; Somnium Scipionis,
c. 3; Virgil, Æneid, VI, 434.

No well balanced mind can for a moment doubt of the guilt
resident in suicide. In every well organized community any
attempt at self-murder is a crime punishable with short or
long terms of imprisonment. By measures of the sort the
state loudly proclaims its belief that suicide is not only a sin
against God and reason, but also a crime against a government's very existence. In general the state has small concern
for sins against God and reason. It rouses itself to persistent
activity against transgressors, mostly when its own life is
threatened. With the aid of a little reflection, we can readily understand that the encouragement of suicide in a republic would lead to annihilation. The godless among its
citizens, and they always constitute a large number, would
be apt at any moment to disappear from its ranks, and leave
to survivors an inheritance of untold shame and misery.

Suicide is so shocking a crime, an act so far beside the
promptings of nature, that men usually reckon its perpetrators
insane. Intense grief and overwhelmingly sharp pain can, of
course, unbalance the mind of a sufferer; and our Church,
with this fact in view, and because of the mystery that al-

ways attaches to a man's last moments, is extremely lenient in the application of its laws against suicide. The circumstance should not, however, lead us to conclude that every single act of self-murder is the freak of a lunatic. The careful preparations, the secrecy of proceeding, the efficacy of the means chosen, the schemes employed, often point to the criminal's full possession of his wits up to the latest breath. Besides, it is ill-directed charity to invariably excuse the folly of the dead by fastening on their posterity the hereditary taint of a reputation for insanity.

Thoughts of suicide cannot, of course, be seriously entertained by minds alive to religious instincts, to the true meaning of life and its attendant woes and joys. Minds dead to faith can easily fall a prey to the temptation, when their cup of sorrow overflows, and the future holds out no promise of respite. Incurable disease, disappointment in love or business, loss of motive, or purpose, or ambition, these several causes will operate to drag down to a suicide's grave the fool, who has cut loose from religion, and entertains only hazy and uncertain opinions concerning Heaven and hell. To the well instructed Christian these several misfortunes present no insuperable difficulty. He knows that disappointment here was the lot God's Son chose for Himself, when He condescended to put on our nature. He knows that every motive or purpose, his soul's salvation excepted, is beneath his contempt, unequal to the full dignity of his sublime calling, and worthy of only his waste energies. He reckons it a sin to allow any lesser aim to completely absorb his attention.

The Christian, therefore, goaded by despair, and urged in weaker moments to the crime of self-murder, must be compelled to refresh his memory of the lessons learned from a pious mother in childhood; and, if reason is at his call, he can pass through the temptation with safety. To the irreligious we can give no solid advice till they mend their ways, and get into the trend of mind God wants them to follow in His service. We might perhaps endeavor to convince them that no disease is absolutely incurable, that every cloud has a silver lining, that disappointment in love or business has often paved the way to life-long happiness and unprecedented prosperity, and that there is plenty of work in the world for

the energetic and industrious. But they will find it possible
to answer somehow every argument of the sort we have to
offer, and we shall find ourselves reduced to silence, or driven
in the end to the only true method, the only trustworthy
source of encouragement and comfort, religion and faith in
its principles. A sovereign remedy for suicide is Shakespeare's "dread of something after death, that undiscovered
country," that pit of fire, a sterner and more substantial
reality to men blessed with the instincts of faith than the
very ground they tread. Nor ever yet did man or woman
take the sad and unholy step of self-murder, until hell by
repeated insults to conscience had worn in his or her mind
to a thin shadow of itself.

Against Nature. We intend to prove our verdict against
suicide without once appealing to Scripture or the teachings
of the Church. And we emphatically condemn the conduct
of whatever sages, modern or ancient, from motives of moral
cowardice and selfishness ran counter in this respect to the
canons of right reason. No man is so wise but that free will,
influenced by mean and ungodly motives, can lead him into
the commission of horrible crimes. Socrates, Plato and others
were lying to their own hearts, when they endeavored to find
in philosophy an excuse for turpitude, into which want of
courage forced them.

Self-defense. This term is commonly used to denote *the
act of opposing force to violence when unjustly attacked.*
When it results in the death of the offender, no moral wrong
attaches to the slayer, if certain conditions have place. One
is at liberty to use this prerogative of self-defense, not only
when his life is in danger, but also when threatened with the
loss of some other great good, like wealth, virtue, bodily integrity. It likewise enables a friend to rescue a friend from
death or other heavy loss at the hands of an assassin or
thief. Self-defense is no legitimate plea for excuse, when
harm is threatened by one in a position to inflict just punishment. For instance, the criminal condemned to death by the
state has no right whatever to defend himself against the
executioner of the law's sentence. A child has no right to

resist a parent when chastised; a pupil has no right to quarrel with a punishment.

Philosophy further recognises these four conditions as necessary of fulfilment. First, the violence done the aggressor must be exerted only while the danger actually exists, not before, not after the attack. Besides, no other method of escape than a return of violence for violence must be in the innocent party's power. If flight is possible, flight must be had recourse to. No amount of dread concerning a reputation for cowardice will justify the killing of another. Secondly, no severer measures must be taken than are absolutely necessary. If a blow in the face will prove sufficient safeguard, a severe wound with a weapon is not justifiable. If a severe wound will serve to stay the aggressor, the party attacked must rest satisfied with inflicting the wound, and must not proceed to slay his assailant. Thirdly, there must exist between the good defended and the harm done the wrong-doer a well defined proportion. This provision is of special importance, when the protection of wealth or property is in question. Thus, a small sum of money is so little worth in comparison with a human life, that reason cries out against murdering a petty thief to save the contents of a pocketbook. Fourthly, revenge must have no part in the proceeding. No motive but that of self-defense pure and simple will justify an act so serious in its consequences as the destruction of a fellow-being. These four conditions combine to rid an act done in self defense of the moral wrong under other circumstances resident in it. They operate to bring about the state of things expressed by that phrase consecrated in the Latin tongue. "Servato moderamine inculpatae tutelae," "Observing always the due measure or moderation that frees self-defense from blame."

Of course, these precautions approve themselves to reason. It is, however, one thing to see their force and fairness, when coolly studying the subject; another, to apply them in the heat of action, when pressed into a tight corner, where a second's delay may mean death for the irresolute. Many a crime of murder, we are aware, is committed under the cloak of self-defense, and the Universal Reckoner alone can distinguish genuine from spurious cases. Civil law can hardly enter into men's motives. It decides, and generally has to decide, with the help of whatever light facts lend. It must of necessity exercise leniency towards the accused, who enters a plea of self-defense; and must give him the benefit of every little circumstance that favors his cause. We are ourselves disposed to be easy with the man brought face to face with death through no fault of his own, and forced by a mad adversary to make up his mind without much time for reflection. Theologians introduce into this question topics, that, without affecting the irreligious, have a practical bearing on the lives of religious people. They ask, for instance, if it is lawful to kill a drunken or mad assailant; if it is lawful to kill in defense of a neighbor; if it is lawful to kill when limbs are endangered, when chastity is assailed, or honor. They discuss what manner of threat constitutes an assault, and the relative weight of a blow in the face, when aimed at a man of dignity and an ordinary person.

Duels. Some regard the duel a species of self-defense. It is a means to which so-called gentlemen resort when their honor, not their life or material wealth, is in danger. The barbarous practice is now well nigh dead; but less than a hundred years ago it was conspicuously alive in our own country. Public opinion has finally succeeded in frowning it down, and, though preliminaries are even now arranged in the newspapers, the hostile meeting seldom or never has place. The custom has a long history. Traces of it are found in the earliest writings. It is, however, safe to say that the private duel is an invention of comparatively modern times. David and Goliath, the heroes of Homer, Livy's triplets, the Horatii and Curiatii, fought duels of a harmless and legitimate kind. The combatants in these several cases engaged in what for distinction's sake we style a public duel. They were representatives chosen by the leaders of two contending armies to defend by their prowess the fortunes of their respective sides, and no moral blame whatever attached to their act or its promoters. If reason sanctions war and allows whole armies of men to perish for the reestablishment of equity and peace, it is difficult to see how reason can enter a disclaimer against a species of combat, which settles the question of supremacy at the expense of one or a half dozen lives. Public duelling would on the contrary appear to be a humane substitute for the horrors of war. If the late rebellion or the recent World-Conflict could have been settled in some such way, a world of loss would have been saved the country.

Barbarians first gave to single combat a color of religion. They counted it an appeal to the God of right; and, when other testimony was wanting, called on Heaven in this crude way for a decision. The Trial by Ordeal had its origin in the same mistaken notion of Providence. Legislators of the Middle Ages had to consult these superstitions of their people, and enacted stringent measures to regulate loss of life. The Truce of God, established in 1041, forbidding duels, out of respect for the Saviour's Passion, between Wednesday and Monday, served as a check to frequency of duels. Every nation in history had its troubles with this abuse. As long as parties to a dispute agreed to submit their differences to the court of single combat, with the approval and under the direction of judicial authority, the evil was somewhat restricted, and wore a less repugnant appearance. But, when individuals, without any permission from the state, took justice into their own hands, and made skill in the use of weapons the sole arbiter of right and wrong, duelling lost its religious aspect, and degenerated to wholesale butchery. It was in any event a sad spectacle, and a growth of ignorance; but under these new conditions it was revolting in the extreme and attended with dreadful consequences.

Frenchmen have always kept well to the front in this particular branch of barbarity. Richelieu opposed the practice with all the strength of his legislative genius; and, to strike terror into its patrons, stopped not at beheading in 1627 one of the nobility, Count Francois de Montmorency. In Germany duelling is much in use at the universities; but, as swords are the weapons, and the bodies of the contestants are well protected, these encounters usually result in a few face-scratches, and seldom prove fatal. Among Irishmen Daniel O'Connell killed at least one adversary on the field of honor, D'Esterre, and his conduct in this particular filled the later years of his life with regret and sorrow. In America Hamilton and Burr fought a historic duel in 1804. Hamilton, the first treasurer of the United States, was killed, and Burr passed into obscurity and oblivion. Barron and Decatur, a man universally loved and one of our most celebrated commodores, fought soon after the War of 1812 at Bladensburg, a village about seven miles outside of Washington. Decatur was killed, Barron was severely wounded. The near neighborhood of Bladensburg to Washington, a rendezvous for all the political worthies of the country, made it a desirable location for battle-ground, and many a duel was negotiated there in the early days of the last century. Clay and Randolph fought in 1826. Andrew Jackson killed a Charles Dickinson, and participated in other affairs. Benton of Missouri killed a Mr. Lucas. Two members of Congress, Cilley of Maine and Graves of Kentucky, fought near Washington in 1838. Cilley was killed. Richard Somers had a record of three duels in one day. Debates on the floor of Congress often precipitated disputes, a challenge followed, and one or both of two fools died in the gray of the morning.

The custom may fairly be said to have taken its rise from the false notion that chance would favor the party in the right, and so manage matters that the wrong-doer would fall. But chance has no real existence, and God, who disposes of things in creation, has nowhere promised to turn the tide of victory this way or that. He has put at men's disposal other and more efficient remedies for wrongs done their honor, and these remedies are to be sought at the bar of duly constituted tribunals. If survival means vindication, that principal in a duel generally won it, who had the steadier arm, the truer aim, and the better education in the use of weapons. Duelling, therefore, defeats the very purpose for which it was instituted. Of course, a certain amount of bull-dog courage is displayed in the acceptance of a challenge, and this circumstance may help to commend the practice to some. They feel, no doubt, that, whether victor or victim, they have at least proved to the world that they are no cowards, and that friends will applaud their heroism in spite of the insult or insinuation that provoked the combat.

But common sense has at last begun to assert itself, and the civilization of to-day reserves its applause for valor of a sterner sort than the recklessness common to duellists and infuriated bulls. Public opinion frowns down exhibitions of the kind, and the makers of our literature have done much to bring about this happy result. Sheridan in his play, "The Rivals," mercilessly ridicules the custom. Writers poke fun at the abominable practice, and take advantage of every opportunity to show it up in its true colors. The consequence is that lucky rascals, who escaped the death they richly deserved, are no longer reckoned heroes. They are banished from good society, they are approached with horror, and their company is always productive of unease and discomfort. They are rated for what they in reality are, genteel murderers, with the blood of fellow-men on their guilty heads, and crying out to Heaven for vengeance. A prize fight would not seem to be a duel, with this for definition: *"A combat with deadly weapons, fought in a private cause, without the sanction of public authority, with prior agreement concerning weapons, seconds, place and time."*

DIVISION

THREE PARTS—I, II, III

I. Suicide.
II. Self-defense.
III. Duelling.

PROOFS

I. 1°. An act subversive of man's duty to God is a sin against nature. But suicide is an act of the sort. Ergo.

With Regard to the Major. Reason or nature insists on the observance of relations in force between God and rational creatures. These relations constitute duties, and violence done them is denominated a sin against nature.

With Regard to the Minor. We know from experience, from man's inability to produce life, that God alone is the author and preserver of life. We know, further, that God bestows life with a definite end in view. It is to be scrupulously used as a means towards establishing in ourselves and others moral order, and compassing eternal happiness. He gives man no absolute dominion over his life, but only what philosophers term use-ownership. Man is therefore obliged to apply life to the uses for which it is plainly intended, and keep to his post just as long as God sees fit to continue his existence. The fact that man is vested with the physical power to put a period to his life, is no sign that God has conferred on him absolute dominion over it. The same argument would hold good in the case of a thief unjustly possessed of another's property, or a murderer sending some weaker victim to death. Man's ability to inflict death on himself is only another effect of God's determination to leave His creature absolute freedom of will, and another proof that willingness or refusal to serve is a matter entirely within the domain of man's unrestrained choice.

2°. An act subversive of man's duty to himself is a sin against nature. But suicide is an act of the kind. Ergo.

With Regard to the Major. Man has duties towards his soul and body, and by deliberately cutting short his days he works irreparable injury to both.

With Regard to the Minor. Life, because of the chance to hope, is always and under whatever circumstances better even for the body than death. As far as the mind is concerned, no ills of life can rob it of opportunities to improve and enjoy itself. No matter what misfortunes overtake a man, no matter what pains and diseases distress him, he has it always in his power to compass his supremely last end, which we long ago agreed to call eternal happiness. He has it always in his power to add by repeated acts of virtue to the degree of glory awaiting him after death. Fortitude, patience, resignation to the Creator's will, all these meritorious acts put on new splendor, when exercised in the midst of trials and difficulties. Pagan poets and philosophers pause in their writings to contemplate and praise the heroism of suffering undergone in the cause of conscience, the sublimity of manly virtue struggling against odds that would overwhelm natures of a weaker sort. Seneca thinks no spectacle so worthy of Jove as that presented by a just man, engaged in a battle with adversity. Horace has these lines, "Justum et tenacem propositi virum—Si fractus illabatur orbis—Impavidum ferient ruinae." "If the world fell in ruins at his feet, the just and resolute man of principle would present a bold front to the crash.''

3°. An act subversive of man's duty to society is a sin against nature. But suicide is an act of the kind. Ergo.

With Regard to the Major. Man's birth into society gives rise to a kind of contract. Neighbors, banded together with him for the common good, tacitly agree to procure for him blessings absolutely out of reach in other contingencies. He, on his part, promises in effect to make due return to society for the advantages procured, and in cutting short his life he ignominiously falls away from his promise.

With Regard to the Minor. Every member of society is in justice bound to contribute his share towards advancing the interests of the community of which he forms part. He proves recreant to this solemn obligation when from shame, cowardice, or impatience he sneaks from the ranks and lays new burdens on other men's shoulders. I say nothing of the infinite harm a suicide does his family and intimate friends. It may happen that he leaves a wife and children to starve, or eke out a miserable existence on the charity of others. Certainly, he leaves as an inheritance to connections a blot of shame and a measure of disgrace, that no time or endeavor can wholly eradicate. Society has a right to expect from him an example of constancy, courage and magnanimity, and he slinks away conspicuous for weakness, cowardice, and a meanness of spirit without parallel.

II. A legitimate means to the effective preservation of a well founded right is justifiable. But death inflicted in self-defense is a legitimate means to the effective preservation of a well founded right. Ergo.

With Regard to the Major. A right vests its owner with the moral prerogative to enforce in others respect for its sacredness. It privileges the owner to use even physical violence, when men deaf to moral instincts attempt to assail it. A right would in any other supposition lose much of its efficacy, and would be of small practical utility. The world would be reduced to chaos, and injustice would everywhere prevail.

With Regard to the Minor. Life, liberty and the pursuit of happiness are in the words of our Constitution inalienable rights, and all three may be seriously interfered with by attempts from without. The death of the offender is at times the only effective bar against loss of life or property, and, as a consequence, desirable and morally correct. In such an event the transgressor, by deliberately putting himself in the wrong, forfeits his right to live, and, if killed, is done no injustice. Nobody can hesitate to regard the assailant's death an effective means to the preservation of rights involved. That it is a legitimate means, is evident from the circumstance that the innocent party would have to otherwise yield up his own life, or some possession a little less valuable, merely out of kindness to the offender. But kindness or charity of that sort is prescribed by no law of God or man. Love of neighbor sins by excess, when it moves a man to love his neighbor more than himself. To sacrifice one's life for a neighbor's salvation is not to love the neighbor more than self. That would be to sacrifice one's salvation for a neighbor's. The killing of an aggressor is not always obligatory.

III. A means founded on false principles, unsuited to the purpose intended, and wrong in itself, is highly absurd and contrary to the law of nature. But private duels are such a means. Ergo.

With Regard to the Major. Ethics can borrow no principles from falsehood, and wickedness shields itself behind excuses full of error, and easily detected. It is the mark of a fool to employ in the prosecution of some work agencies calculated to operate against and not in favor of the agent's aim. Foolishness degenerates to heinous crime, when the methods adopted, besides being unequal to the end proposed, are attended by consequences as serious as those that accompany private duels. A lavish waste of life is a direct insult to Almighty God, and as such deserves the severest condemnation on the score of morality.

With Regard to the Minor. The private duel had its origin among barbarians. The Lombards, with whom might always prevailed over right, introduced it throughout Europe. The Greeks and Romans, though acquainted with public duels, were strangers to the other custom. In its origin, therefore, this brutal practice rested on a notion subversive of all morality and truth, the sacredness of physical as compared with moral force. It was in a manner a necessary growth of early times, when law and order were subject to great upheavals, and tribunals of justice were little respected. The superstitious belief that God would interfere in an extraordinary way to save the innocent and destroy the guilty, was a new and grievous mistake added to the first blunder. In later times revenge was the element uppermost in the minds of combatants, and duels were tolerated on the plea that individuals have a right to seek on their own private account satisfaction for injury done their honor. But no principle can be falser. No community, no society or state could long subsist, if such a mode of procedure were once sanctioned and came into general use. For the settlement of disputes and reparation of assailed honor we have courts by law established, and death would result to authority, were any other process introduced. Were duels not prohibited by conscience, by reason proclaiming the truth, enemies in private life would fall to butchering one another, and the State would become a wilderness.

The absurdity of duelling is manifest from the fact that it shockingly fails to serve the purpose for which it was instituted. Whether it be viewed as a means of repairing the wrong done a man's honor and reputation, or considered a possible means of revenge, it has no one feature to recommend it. It is not an apt instrument for satisfaction, because the innocent party is just as likely to forfeit his life as the guilty. The event of the combat proves simply that the survivor managed his sword or pistol with more skill and dexterity than his victim. It certainly leaves the guilt or innocence of the survivor as much an open question as it was before the meeting. If the innocent party falls, where is the revenge? Certainly the man guilty of the wrong done by the injury or insult had no claims to revenge, and entered not into the struggle to vindicate himself. Honor is not man's highest good. And true honor is not praise in the mouths of men, but inward consciousness of right conduct and a virtuous life.

But the characteristic that emphatically condemns duelling is its own objective immorality. It involves a two-fold malice. The duellist commits a double crime with all the malice of attempted murder and attempted suicide; and on no few occasions the two attempts become accomplished realities.

The duellist, therefore, incurs whatever blame attaches to murder and suicide.   In morality, because will is the predominating factor, the difference between the attempt to do evil and the actual accomplishment of evil is accidental, and therefore negligible.

PRINCIPLES—SUICIDE

A. Distinguish between direct and indirect killing of self. Direct is suicide.   Indirect is death foreseen in some act put for a legitimate purpose.   Instances are, a fatal operation, jump from a high window in time of fire, nurse to plague-stricken.

B. Destruction is supreme act of ownership.   Man is vested with no such ownership in life, because its primary purpose is not man's advantage, but the greater glory of God.

C. Instinct of self-preservation is index of God's will in the matter, and of His disapproval of suicide.

D. God's permission can be presumed when serious spiritual dangers threaten, or life becomes oppressive.

Answer: Life's chief purpose, the greater glory of God, never becomes impossible; and only in this case can He be supposed to give permission.   With His grace, whatsoever spiritual danger can be met and overcome; and patience is a virtue.

E. Direct mutilation partakes of the malice of suicide.   And yet man is the steward of his life, if not its absolute owner. He is allowed to preserve his life at the expense of a limb. The part ranks lower than the whole.

F. Saints, who rushed to death, acted under inspiration, or through invincible ignorance, or committed indirect self-killing.

G. Our second and third arguments against suicide presuppose the first.   Thus, the drunkard committing suicide after a mission and a good confession would perhaps be consulting his own interests, but at the expense of God's rights as owner.   With St. Paul we can long to be dissolved and be with Christ, but always in a spirit of resignation to God's will.

H. We can reject a gift.   Life is a gift.   Ergo.

Answer: A gift meant primarily for our advantage and subject to absolute ownership, I grant; a gift meant primarily for the giver's advantage, and subject to only use-ownership, I deny.

N.B. Suicide is more than rejection, it is destruction of life.

I. Hume argues thuswise. If we cannot interfere with the course of nature to shorten life, we cannot interfere with the course of nature to prolong it. Eadem est contrariorum ratio. Ergo, it would be wrong to push aside a falling stone that threatened destruction.

Answer: Use-ownership empowers and obliges us to preserve or prolong our life. It vests us with no right to destroy same. That is the exclusive prerogative of absolute ownership. We are stewards, not proprietors.

J. It is lawful to choose a lesser evil for the purpose of escaping a greater.

Answer: The saying has some force in question of physical evil, none in question of moral evil. In the case of self, it can never become necessary to commit one sin to avoid others. It is always quite possible to avoid all sin. In the case of others, it would be highly wrong to commit one sin to prevent them from committing a thousand. Moral evil is never justified by good. The end never justifies the means. Suicide would be the lesser evil only in the supposition that it is not sinful. The smallest sin is a greater evil than physical evil of whatever magnitude.

K. Suicide is wrong because the man does himself an injustice. Nobody can do himself an injustice. Volenti nulla fit injuria.

Answer: Suicide is an injustice to God as well as to its perpetrator. Man has duties towards himself, and to fall away from them is injustice. The saying admits of exceptions, e.g., fraud in law.

L. Hunters dispose of birds and beasts without ownership in them. Ergo, a pari, a man ought to be able to dispose of his life without ownership in it.

Answer: Hunters have no particular or private ownership empowering them to exclude others. I grant. Hunters have no universal or general ownership as in things belonging to nobody in particular, I deny. Birds, beasts and all lower creation are by nature man's property to use them and destroy them as he sees fit.

M. A criminal condemned to death may lawfully execute himself at the bidding of authority. Ergo.

Answer: In suicide there is question not of public, but of private authority. Besides, some authors deny the legitimacy of every such proceeding, and they assign two reasons. The state is allowed to kill only as a measure of justice, and nobody can be expected to execute justice on himself. Nobody is a good judge in his own case, and therefore nobody is a fit executioner of himself. Every such arrangement is directly opposed to nature's instinct for self-preservation. Law must be possible.

N. One must take means to preserve his life and health; generally speaking he need not take extraordinary means, such as occasion serious inconvenience. Serious inconvenience excuses from affirmative law, and God is a prudent law-maker. The penances and fasts of the saints are opposed to no law of nature, even though they weaken the body and shorten life. Spiritual good is of a higher order than life and health. The harm done the body and life is indirect, not direct.

O. It is often lawful to expose oneself to death, when death is not directly intended, and a proportionate cause justifies the proceeding. Soldiers taken prisoners are not allowed to kill themselves to escape doing service to their captors. Sailors are allowed to jump from a burning vessel into the sea to escape death by fire. A soldier in time of war is allowed to set fire to a ship or tower, though it means instant death for himself, if the act causes heavy damage to the enemy.

PRINCIPLES—SELF-DEFENSE

A. This privilege of self-defense extends farther than life or property. A woman has a right to kill an assailant in defense of her chastity. Nobody has the right to kill another in defense of his honor or reputation.

B. An insane or drunken person is an unjust assailant, not formally but materially. The child in a mother's womb is in no sense of the word an unjust assailant. The mother causes the collision of rights, and must yield to the child. When violence is done her, neither she nor the child is to blame; and yet she comes closer to blame than the child for the condition of affairs, and must suffer accordingly.

C. Self-defense procures damnation of the assailant. Ergo, wrong. Self-defense sacrifices greater good to lesser. Ergo, wrong.

Answer: Essentially and of itself, I deny; accidentally and by way of occasion, I grant. Charity forbids us to procure another's damnation the first way, not the second way, unless the thing can be avoided without great inconvenience, and the neighbor is in extreme need. The thing can be avoided only at the expense of the innocent party's life, and that would be a rather serious inconvenience. The assailant is not in extreme need, because he can refrain from attack. Besides, the common good must be taken into account. Without this privilege life would be insecure.

D. In the case of a drunken or mad assailant damnation would be sure. Ergo, wrong.

Answer: No moral certainty on these three points, the exact spiritual condition of innocent party and assailant, and future salvation of party in the wrong, if spared for conversion.

E. It is wrong to kill another in defense of reputation or honor, not because reputation is a smaller good than life, property is that, but because the moderamen inculpatae tutelae is seldom or never verified. It is next to impossible to be sure of the serious harm attaching to slander, calumny and detraction before the harm is actually done, and then it is too late for defense; defense is out of the question, revenge alone is in order. Besides, escape from the harm is within easy reach of less radical measures. Opposite doctrine would be open to great abuse, and, though no doctrine is to be condemned because of extrinsic and accidental abuses, every doctrine, accompanied like this by intrinsic and essential abuses, deserves condemnation.

F. Reputation is a more precious possession than life. Ergo.

Answer: Fundamentally taken, inner virtue and honesty, I grant; formally taken, outer esteem and credit, I deny.

Reputation is the judgment passed by others on our conduct and affairs. Honor is outward manifestation of the good esteem we have of others. Fama from fando, to talk, the way men talk about us.

G. The end never justifies the means. Ergo.

Answer: Homicide is the means, and homicide is not intrinsically evil. Otherwise capital punishment would be wrong. It is a physical evil and in itself morally indifferent. While the end never justifies an intrinsically evil means, it often justifies a physically evil and a morally indifferent means.

H. God's right as Master of life and death is violated by the assailant, not by the innocent party.

I. We must love our enemies, but not more than we love ourselves. In all honesty we could account ourselves worthy of no better fate, were we the unjust assailant.

J. In this case, we should be in duty bound to kill our assailant.

Answer: Homicide is an extraordinary means, and we are held to only ordinary means. Circumstances like the support of a family can render self-defense a serious obligation.

K. Self-defense is not a morally bad act put to compass a good end. It is a morally good act, the preservation of one's life, and from this good act a physical evil follows, loss of life on the part of the unjust assailant. This death is not to be imputed to the innocent slayer, but to the unjust assailant.

PRINCIPLES—DUELLING

A. The duel is a species of defense against loss of property. To refuse a duel means dismissal from the army, reduction in rank, and consequent loss of livelihood. Ergo.

Answer: One must lose his livelihood rather than perpetrate an intrinsically evil deed. A duel contracts the malice of attempted murder and attempted suicide, and both deeds are intrinsically evil. A duel is no defense against an unjust assailant; and, therefore, the attempt on a rival's life has all the malice of murder. It is no mere exposure of life to a risk justified by a proportionate cause; and, therefore, it has all the malice of suicide. We are allowed to undergo danger to life with a proportionate reason. We are never allowed to seek danger to life with or without a proportionate reason. The duellist more than undergoes danger, he seeks it; because by the very seeking of danger he vindicates his reputation for bravery. A nurse in time of the plague merely exposes himself to danger, because his whole purpose is to minister to the sick, and danger contributes nothing to this purpose. In other words, the duellist makes risk to life a means to his end; the nurse employs other means like medicine, food, care and attention, and to these means danger is, much against his wishes, inseparably attached.

B. The state has no right to authorize a duel for the settlement of justice between two disputants. It is the state's duty to settle such disputes on their merits, punishing the guilty and freeing the innocent. If unable to arrive at a decision, it must give the benefit of the doubt to the accused. The state is not allowed to arbitrarily treat guilty and innocent alike by exposing them to the same risk. The state ought to put down duelling, and not encourage it. The Trial by Ordeal was all wrong and the Church consistently opposed it. God has nowhere promised to favor the innocent in tests of the kind.

C. Duels between students are sometimes against the law of nature, because they lead to serious wounds and mutilation.

D. Though a prize-fight is not a duel properly so called, on occasions it would seem to be against the law of nature.

E. It is lawful to use the one and fit means for defending honor. But the duel is such. Ergo.

Answer: If the one and fit means is at the same time legitimate, I grant; otherwise, I deny. A duel is the one and fit means not of itself and by nature, but by accident and the wrong views of men.

F. The duel is said to be wrong, because the good it effects is out of proportion with the evil. But the preservation of honor, rank and wealth is not out of proportion with risk to life. Ergo.

Answer: Because the immediate effect is out of proportion, I grant; because the remote effect is out of proportion, I deny. The immediate effect is to show courage, and that is out of proportion. Honor, rank, property are but the remote effects and even they are out of proportion. Honor is two-fold, honor in root, virtue and other good qualities provoking the esteem of others; and formal honor, the good esteem of others. Honor in first sense is intrinsic to the man and superior to life. Honor in the second sense is extrinsic to the man and far inferior to life. Honor in root is the man's own affair and cannot be touched by the neighbor. Formal honor, the kind duels mend, is beyond a man's own control and altogether dependent on the neighbor's whim and fancy.

G. A duel in no way resembles self-defense, because prior agreement is of its essence. This circumstance separates the duel from an ordinary fight or shooting-match.

H. The man who refuses to honor a challenge is a coward in the eyes of fools alone, and their opinion is no safe standard of morality. Moral courage is of a higher order than physical.

I. A woman is allowed to defend her honor to the extent of killing an assailant. Ergo.

Answer: Honor in this case means more than mere esteem; it means bodily integrity or chastity.

THESIS III

A lie is always and of its very nature wrong. To safeguard a proportionate right, the use of a broad mental reservation is allowed. Jouin, 106–109; Rickaby, 224–237.

QUESTION

In this matter of man's duty towards his neighbor, we single out the obligation of truthfulness and respect for the right of property in others. We treat these questions in separate theses, giving our first attention to the moral aspect of lying. Because truth is due the neighbor, and because men have an inviolable right to whatever they legitimately make their own, these two duties are branches or departments of the comprehensive virtue called justice, that habit of mind and will eternally ready to give to everybody his due. We shall see later that the lie is formally a sin against truth, not against justice.

DIVISION

Thesis has two parts—
I. The lie.
II. The reservation.

PART I. LIE—TERMS

I. *A Lie.* The Latin verb mentiri, meaning to lie, furnishes us with a true definition of the thing. It is supposed to be a shortened form of the expression, contra mentem ire, or menti ire, and signifies to go against the mind. Hence, a lie is best described as *locutio contra mentem, speech or language conveying the opposite of what we have in our mind.* It is want of harmony between what we say and what we think. It is opposed to moral truth. Truth is threefold: logical, ontological and moral; and harmony with something is the generic notion common to all three. Logical is harmony of mind with outside things, and affects our knowledge; ontological is harmony of things outside with the mind of their fashioner, and is said with reference to creatures and God; moral is harmony of language with thought, and is peculiar to intercourse of man with man. As we shall immediately see from St. Thomas, deception and intention to deceive play no part in the essential constitution of a lie. A material lie can be formal truth, and a formal lie can be material truth. No moral guilt, of course, attaches to a mere material lie, because moral blame attaches to the will alone, and in a material lie the will is right, the intellect is at fault.

St. Thomas is a safe guide in philosophy, as well as in theology, and it may, therefore, be useful to here note down what he has to say on the subject. I quote, therefore, at some length from his Summary of Theology. In the 2nd of the 2nd part, quest. 110, art. I, he has what follows:

"Truth and falsehood are the proper objects of speech. A disordered will can in this matter have one of two intentions or both, either to communicate a falsehood or, as an effect of the communication, to deceive some one. If therefore these three elements are present, viz.: falsehood of communication, a wish to communicate falseness and the desire to deceive, then is the lie a material one, because a falsehood is communicated; a formal one, because it is wilfully and knowingly communicated; and effective, because deception is wilfully and knowingly intended. Nevertheless, the lie derives its essence from the second element, i.e., the wish to communicate falseness, or a falsehood wilfully and knowingly communicated. Wherefore a lie receives its name in Latin from the fact that it is something said contrary to the mind's conviction. The circumstance that one designs to affect another's opinion with falseness belongs not to the nature or essence of a lie, but to a further perfection of the same. Even so with things in nature, an object, when once it assumes the form, attains to its allotted place in the universe of existences, even though the effect generally accompanying the form is for the time being absent, as is evident for instance, in a thing of weight when forcibly held aloft."

In the same part and question art. III in answer to the 4th difficulty he says:

"The sinfulness of a lie is derived not from the damage alone which it does our neighbor, but from its want of harmony with the order of reason."

The learned Doctor's words are quite plain. His idea seems to be this—A moral falsehood or a lie consists, as far as matter goes, in want of harmony between what is in the mind and the language used to express it. It, therefore, differs from logical falsehood, which means a want of harmony between some object in nature and the mind's conception of it. Hence a logical falsehood can readily enough be foundation for a moral truth; and a logical truth, foundation for a moral falsehood. Yet, such a factor is the will in all questions of morality, that the material moral falsehood is blameless until the intention of communicating as true matter known and understood to be false accrues to it and by union completes, perfects and finishes the lie properly so called. He insists very much on this point because the introduction of a third element, viz., the deception of our neighbor, is made too much account of by some authors.

The third element is a merely accidental circumstance, and contributes nothing to the naked essence of a lie. It is quite true that every lie will be accompanied by this third element or characteristic. For, it is difficult to conceive of a false communication known to be such, which will not at the same time procure, at least in intention, a neighbor's deception. But the lie is in full consummated, though this element be entirely wanting. As soon as the speaker attempts in his language to convey an untruth known to be such, so soon does he lie, whether he intends to deceive, or to amuse, or to help, or to injure his neighbor. The injury done his neighbor may be inseparably connected with the lie, and may have been uppermost in the liar's mind; but the injury derives its malice not from the circumstance that it is a lie, but from the fact that it is a wounding of charity, something quite distinct from the virtue of truth.

PROOF

I. The lie has its intrinsic malice from this, that it is a falling away from our duty, not precisely to our neighbor, but to God and to ourselves. He has wisely ordained, for the good of society, that words should communicate ideas, which would otherwise be so much dead lumber, for purposes of use to the neighbor. He has imbedded within us an instinct, as present as the nose on our face, influencing us to cherish truthfulness in our dealings one with another. The liar recklessly tramples this ordinance of God, and stifles within himself an instinct, which is among Heaven's purest and best gifts. Hence it is that God, who is avenger of broken ordinances and a jealous watcher of His gifts to man, punishes in a way known only to His victims the deliberate and downright liar. I should call for no more potent proof of God's interference in this matter than that furnished by the blush of shame and the self-condemning perturbation, visible all over the countenance of a liar in the beginning of his career, or of the ingenuous youth whose poorly ordered self-love has ensnared him into a cowardly untruth.

PRINCIPLES—LYING

A. Hugo Grote, a Hollander, for the seeming purpose of deducing principles subversive of society, though flattering the self-love of a dangerous few, offers this wrong definition of a lie: "A lie," he says, "is language or a manifestation in conflict with a right, which exists and belongs to him to whom the language or manifestation is addressed or directed."

Were this the proper notion of a lie, to say nothing of other absurdities painfully apparent in it, the liar's sin would inherit its essence from the injury done his neighbor. The conclusion, of course, would be that lies told by way of joke, helpful lies, and lies told by men in responsible positions to save a secret, are truths. We have already met this difficulty and shown conclusively enough that the idea of the injury done our neighbor by no means enters into the essential construction of a lie, and that it is an after and accidental effect, which may with the same influence on the act denominated a lie be present or absent. Besides, let the two latter species of a lie, countenanced by such false philosophers as Grote, come prevalent, and the intercourse of man with man will grow a scourge and a gift for which we should have small occasion to thank Heaven. Remember, however, that our decided and clearly expressed conviction with regard to the intrinsic evil of lying is based not on the injury done the neighbor, but on this one circumstance that it is an abuse of language, that God and nature intended to be used as a vehicle of thought. The inconvenience done the neighbor is a weighty argument to deter men from lying, and perhaps exerts a more universally dissuasive influence than our metaphysical argument. Still it is an extrinsic element and may lead to false, unfounded notions.

B. Milton, to prove that lying is at times admissible, asks this empty question: "If all killing be not murder; nor all taking from another, theft; why must all untruths be lies?" The answer at once suggests itself. Man must not kill another when innocent, he must not take from another unless necessity is extremely urgent; because in the one case and the other man has a right to his life and his property which he has nowise forfeited. It is not his nature to live forever but only as long as the body continues a fit tenement for the soul. Universal ownership is of nature and inamissible; but particular ownership is based on the man's own individual activity, open to loss, accidental in itself, and natural only inasmuch as it is rooted in the universal ownership which forever remains. But the sheriff commits no murder; the wretch dying of hunger, no theft; because the capital offender against society loses all prior claims to life, the former owner of the property is, in case of another's dire necessity, divested of his rights, nature depriving the property of any particular and specific owner. The obligation a man owes his rational nature in point of telling the truth can never change. In other words man's claims to life and property do not turn directly and wholly on his rational nature. His bounden duty to tell the truth flows directly from his rational nature.

C. One author insists very much on what he styles his metaphysical and absolute definition of a lie, viz., the privation of truth that is or ought to be due. The definition goes to greater lengths than is necessary, but its length does not lessen its correctness. It is emphatically correct. His explanation, however, of the word "due" is as emphatically incorrect, and evidently introduced to remove difficulties that were better removed otherwise. Of course, lying is the privation of truth that is due; but does it hence necessarily follow that lying is the privation of such truth only as is due the neighbor? Decidedly no! The truth in question may not perhaps be due my neighbor, but I owe it to the God who made me and to myself to use on all occasions language in exact accordance with the ideas in my mind.

D. If deceit entered into the essential constitution of a lie, the above author's remarks about primary and secondary intentions, or secrecy and deceit, would be to the point. St. Thomas a short while ago made it clear that the lie exists in a finished state before deception enters upon the scene at all. Deception may or may not be present. Its influence on the lie as such is the same. Like all accidents it can, indeed, modify the evil done. It can make it greater by adding a sin of unkindness to that of cheating God's intent, but it cannot make a bit of language truth or falsehood. Like all things intrinsically or of their very nature evil, no conceivable intention can make a lie good and praiseworthy. Who can blaspheme without sinning, who can hate God without sinning? But this impossibility arises from the mere circumstance that blasphemy and hatred of God are intrinsically evil. In the same way the second, third, fourth and all the intentions possible in a lie are swallowed up in the first, viz., the wilful and deliberate communication of falseness as truth. This intention comes first, this intention is the life and being of a lie, and not even the gaining of Heaven can justify it.

E. A lie is wrong because it is an abuse of speech. But other abuses are not wrong. Ergo, neither is a lie for this single reason wrong. To walk on the hands is an abuse of the hands, but not therefore wrong.

Answer: To walk on the hands is abuse of the hands in strict sense, I deny; in wide sense, I grant. Abuse in strict sense is use that destroys or hinders the purpose intended by nature. Walking on the hands leaves them wholly capable of the functions for which nature intended them. But a lie aims at the destruction of speech's natural purpose, the communication of our ideas or of truth.

F. The purpose of speech is the good of society and the lie far from being a hindrance or a damage to society, is on no few occasions a positive help and advantage to same. Ergo. A lie can at times happen to be the readiest means to avert a war or a murder.

Answer: Material advantage is not the criterion of morality, but the objective order of things. A lie is not primarily wrong because it works evil to society, nor is the truth primarily good because it is of advantage to society. Harmony with the purpose of speech and discord with same constitute the goodness of truth and the malice of lying respectively. Even material advantage can never in the long run result from an intrinsic evil like lying, and this is evident from the Law of General Consequences discussed in the matter of Utilitarianism. But this is not the root-reason for the immorality of lying. If a lie were allowed, to avert some particular evil like war, or procure some particular good like a livelihood, its approbation would work to the complete destruction of credit among men, and that evil would be worse than a hundred wars.

G. A lie might be permitted for very grave reasons, and within these limits all danger would be removed. Ergo.

Answer: The danger would still stand, because in that case every individual would be absolute judge of the weight of his reasons; and credit would be universally shaken. Besides, the lie is intrinsically and of its very nature wrong, deriving its malice from no such accidental and extrinsic circumstances as harm and advantage.

H. Homicide in self-defense is right. Ergo, a pari, a lie in self-defense is right.

Answer: Homicide is not an intrinsic evil, as is evident from war, hanging and self-defense. Homicide is changed to murder by the injustice done the person slain, and by the usurpation of God's rights as the Lord and Master of life and death. A lie is intrinsically wrong, and God Himself cannot make it right. God cannot bestow on others a right, in which He is not Himself vested.

I. To lie is to talk otherwise than as you think. But the objector on a circle talks otherwise than as he thinks. Ergo.

Answer: The objector talks as he thinks, but he is at the same time playing the part of another. Actor on stage.

J. Communication of thought to another, whether by speech

or other arbitrary signs, is of the essence of a lie. It takes two to converse, and in strict language nobody ever talks to or addresses himself. Therefore, a false statement shouted to vacancy or the wind is not in strict sense a lie.

K. Lies are usually divided into jocose, officious, official and injurious. Not all jokes are jocose lies. Equivocation and mental reservation save many jokes from the malice of sin. Others, while plain misstatements, are so openly absurd that they can be rated mere material falsehoods, free from the guilt of a formal lie. Instances are, Washington is not dead. Miss Liberty is walking the harbor. And yet many jokes are lies, and their perpetrators incur all the blame of sin. Officious lies are meant to be helpful, injurious are meant to harm. Outside of injurious lies, which wound charity as well as truth, the sin is never more than venial. Official lies are sinful subterfuges employed by men in authority to keep state secrets, and are no less blameworthy than the rest.

L. The mouth that lies kills the soul. Wisdom 1–11. Ergo.
Answer: Formally, I deny; preparatively, I grant.

PART II—RESERVATION

II. We now take up a few difficulties, which to some appeared so formidable, that only a wide departure from philosophy's common notion regarding a lie seemed capable of solving them.

TERMS

Reservation. Everybody grants that there are secrets without end, which must under no consideration be delivered over to unauthorized enquirers. Philosophers are a unit on this point. But how to perform this nice and difficult duty without at the same time wounding truth, is a task nowise easy. Deep silence will not, it is quite certain, always extricate the honest man from his straits. His secret may be natural, or a secret of promise, or a secret of trust. We may suppose, too, that matters are come to such a head that a direct answer alone will satisfy the questioner. An innocent mental reservation seems to be on such an occasion the only means of escape. It can be reconciled, too, with our rigorous doctrine on lying, and needs no such laxity of principle as is advocated by some authors. In mental reservation several very important items must be carefully attended to, not precisely because a lie is told, but because even though the truth is told, such manner of telling the truth is full of danger to mutual converse, to the union of families, and to the well-being of the state. Observe, therefore, that the notion uppermost with us in thus hedging about mental reservation with cautious conditions is not at all to make lies less frequent, for on no occasion do we consider a lie lawful, but only to shield man in his dealings with his fellows.

There are, then, two sorts of mental reservation, one always to be abominated, the other to be sometimes commended. They are the pure and the broad. He uses a mental reservation, who, when conveying information, so manipulates his words, that the listener will in all probability derive from them only false notions. The pure mental reservation furnishes the listener with no external clew to the truth, and renders it absolutely impossible for him to escape the mistake; and is in simple language a lie, under no circumstance excusable.

Pure means language of itself, and from present circumstances, restricted to one meaning, out of harmony with mind of speaker, in harmony with same when something retained in the mind is added, e.g., "Have you eaten anything?" "Nothing at all," *understanding* meat.

Broad means language externally conveying the speaker's true mind, intelligible from circumstances, in spite of a certain ambiguity and obscurity. Listener is cause per se of deception, not talker. Proximate end is to convey mind. Remote is to hide truth. Remote end must be legitimate. Hence no broad in contracts, *questions of justice,* courts of law. Only proportionate cause justifies.

Protestants are fond of reproaching us with the laxity of our moral theologians in this matter of mental reservations. But, whereas our moralists utterly condemn the pure, to admit the broad mental reservation only for the safeguarding of a proportionate right, Cranmer, Henry VIII's archbishop of London, when taking his oath of fealty to the Pope, contrived a pure mental reservation, a lie, and so stained his immortal soul with a perjury unexampled.

PROOF

The broad mental reservation, available only when great interests are at stake, not in every trifling affair, leaves it possible though difficult for the listener to still detect, if he proceeds with prudence, the speaker's meaning. In other words, the speaker returns to the questioner a double answer, a jumble of what is in his mind and what is outside of it. That part of his answer, which is language in harmony with his mind, he considers, and every fair-minded man must consider, a sufficiently truthful answer to the question; that which is wide of the mark may be considered something superadded, not intended indeed to form part of the answer to the enquiry made, but to some enquiry that might have been made. If the imprudent listener confounds one part with the other, he has himself to blame; and no great unkindness is done him. But the lie is absent, not because no injury is directly done the neighbor, but because the group of words can be construed into a meaning in perfect harmony with the speaker's mind.

This I recognize as the limit to which mental reservation can be pushed, when it is borne in mind that only motives as serious and grave as the saving of an innocent life, the retention of a close secret, liable if revealed to undo somebody, the life of a state, can counterbalance, the baneful effects not of a lie; for, I repeat it, no lie is told; but of the apparent unkindness contained in the very act of giving to the person addressed an opportunity to go astray, and fervently wishing that he may do so. The preservation of a cigarette is not motive enough for a broad mental reservation. For a pure mental reservation, between which and a lie I can see no difference, even the preservation of the innocent is not motive enough. Remark, however, that, when an innocent life is at stake, common charity obliges you to take all legitimate means to its defense; and, therefore, common charity imperatively demands a broad mental reservation, that namely which through the agency of some external sign leaves it possible for the person deceived to avoid deception.

PRINCIPLES—RESERVATION

A. About the prisoner at the bar in the civil court of justice, this solution appears most praiseworthy and is wholly satisfactory. Words are but arbitrary signs. When, therefore, the expression, "Not guilty," has come by the common consent of mankind to mean, "Not proved guilty," a man, though actually guilty, says nothing contrary to what he has in his mind when he answers, "Not guilty." For, even in his own mind he is not proved guilty, and according to common usage or agreement, which alone imparts meaning to words, he has made no other statement.

B. The priest is bound by his duty to an authority far higher than that attached to any civil court of justice to preserve inviolate a confessional secret. No sane, unprejudiced judge will require at his hands the communication of such a secret. But there are on record instances of bigoted and unscrupulous ministers of the law, who endeavored to wrest from the priest's bosom truths more sacred than fall to the lot of physicians, lawyers or friends. In such cases it is a sacred duty imposed upon the priest to maintain even unto death his seal of secrecy. He is not, however, in any sense of the word permitted to lie. He is at liberty to profess that he knows nothing whatever of the matter in question, but must contrive to give his hearers an opportunity to understand, if they will, that he represents a twofold character, that of the priest or representative of Christ, and that of the citizen or subject of the law. He must, without at all compromising his penitent or endangering the seal of the confessional, advertise the questioner of his determination and right to answer all enquiries put to him as a citizen or witness in his capacity of man or of individual of the community, not in his capacity of representative and vice-gerent of God. His answer, therefore, which intimates entire ignorance of the subject under discussion, is not language out of harmony with what he has in his mind, and therefore not a lie. As citizen, he has no knowledge whatever of the point in question; and he has signified his determination and right to speak in that capacity only. As far as in him lies, his language should also convey to the minds of his hearers an exact representation of what he wishes to communicate. If they foolishly imagine that his denial extends also to knowledge acquired in the confessional, they have to· blame only themselves for their ignorance. In fact, if, after taking the ground that he is by right divine entitled to assume these two characters of man or citizen and vice-gerent of Christ, he should affirm as a witness on the stand acquaintance with the secrets of Confession, he would be guilty of speech out of harmony with what he has in his mind, i.e., of a lie.

C. In point of sacredness the secrets of lawyers, physicians and friends come next to those of the priest. Professional men, and men whose faith is plighted to friends, have duties in this regard to which they must nowise prove delinquent. Nevertheless, such men, though they be lawyers, must cherish truth in their everyday dealings with themselves and others; and, therefore, they are not allowed to save a secret at the expense of truth. But no such unlawful proceeding is necessary. The secret can be saved without any harm to truth. For, apart from professional knowledge which he is by no means supposed to reveal to an unauthoritative enquirer, the mind of the lawyer, physician or friend is a perfect blank regarding the information desired. An imprudent man may misunderstand and may so misconstrue the reply made by the physician, lawyer or friend as to fancy that, when he professes only partial ignorance or ignorance under one capacity, he confesses to ignorance under every capacity. But even in this case the deception, which in itself would not make the assertion a lie, is the fruit of imprudence on the part of the interpreter, and can with justice be imputed to the witness as to an occasion only, not a cause or at most a cause by accident.

D. Evasions, or answers that simply stand off the questioner, and merely betoken by the communication of irrelevant knowledge an unwillingness to satisfy morbid curiosity are, of course, at all times and on all occasions licit in themselves. They need never be united with falsehood, though they can readily enough become faults against common charity,

pretty much as the withholding from a neighbor any good
in itself harmless and easily parted with by the possessor.

E. Equivocations are not necessarily out of harmony with
the speaker's mind, because, as usage itself gives to words
of this stamp a multiplied meaning, the speaker is, of course,
at liberty to attach to them whatever one of the several meanings he chooses. Charity imposes upon him the duty of fur-
nishing the person addressed with hints sufficient to put him
on his guard against deception. Continual and unwarranted
equivocation would be a sin; not, indeed, against truth, but
against the love of neighbor which nature exacts of us. When
a just cause is present, certain sorts of verbal misleading
are not sinful. The presence of any cause whatever exerts
no such potent influence as will change a lie to a good deed.
By no manner of means can a lie be made commendable. But
this verbal misleading is a denial of straightforward charity,
which a fellow-man can of right exact at our hands, only in
certain contingencies.

To deprive him, therefore, of this right, it must first have
come into collision with some right of a higher order, and so,
in virtue of a solid ethical principle, lose for the present its
force and efficacy. In other words, some higher good than
the performance of an act of kindness to a neighbor, little
deserving of it, may be lawfully aimed at, not by a lie, but
by a legitimate verbal misleading. A lie is also a misleading,
but it is altogether illegitimate, so much so that were Heaven
itself or the conversion of the whole world to be had for a
lie, the liar would not be justified. It would, however, be an
act deserving of all praise to compass the conversion of one
single soul by the use of an evasion, a legitimate equivocation, or a broad mental reservation, hedged about by all the
conditions above set down.

F. St. Alphonsus Liguori, among the foremost of our moral
theologians and a man noted for his leniency towards sinners,
adopts in his works principles and logic which pushed to their
furthest possible limits verge on looseness, without, however,
incurring the reproach. The Church, too, has approved of
his writings. But it must be remarked, by the way, that her
approval in such cases is rather negative than positive. She
simply says in the Brief issued, "Nothing in his works has

been found worthy of censure." This by no means prevents
you or me from adopting opinions at variance with his, or to
quote again, "This is said, however, without on that account
judging that they are reprehended who follow opinions
handed down by other approved authors."

G. To sum up, and so bring our remarks to a close, this is
in short our view of the matter. A lie or a wilful and deliberate speaking against what is in the mind has a decidedly
twofold malice: one, primary, specific and all important; the
other, secondary, accidental and of less importance. The
primary malice of a lie is bound up in the fact that it is an
abuse of the Heaven-sent faculty of speech. Its secondary
malice is derived from the circumstance that every lie is an
injury done the neighbor. The lie, therefore, can never be
justified. Silence, evasions, equivocations, broad mental reservations are not lies; and can, therefore, be tolerated when
some just cause, some good of more vital concern than the
kindness of straightforward truth is the motive that prompts
the speaker. Instances—not guilty—not at home; priest, lawyer, friend; state officials, "What news, my lord?" "I don't
know; I haven't read the papers." "Do Christians believe
in a Trinity?" "They believe in only one God."

H. Mental reservation and lie have the same evil results.
Ergo.

Answer: A lie is wholly misleading; a reservation is partially misleading. A lie deceives per se, a reservation deceives
per accidens. This accidental deception makes the indiscrim-
inate and universal use of reservation wrong. The legitimate use is restricted to safeguarding a proportionate right.
A lie is the cause of deception; a reservation is mere occasion
of the same.

I. Mental reservation is flagrant abuse of language. Ergo.

Answer: A reservation fills a double function. It conveys
our thought and conceals our thought. Inasmuch as it conveys our thought, it is the truth; inasmuch as it conceals
our thought, it is at times a species of unkindness. The deed
itself is morally right, our purpose would in other circumstances be unkind; but the charity due an imprudent, meddle-
some and unauthorized questioner yields in importance to
the right we safeguard. Manifestation of our mind is the

finis operis or proximate end in reservation; concealment is the finis operantis, or remote end. Manifestation comes first in order of execution; concealment comes first in order of intention.

J. A pure mental reservation is a lie, because the words, as they stand, convey the opposite of what the speaker has in his mind, and no accompanying circumstance helps the listener to a knowledge of what the speaker has in his mind. Here is an instance: "Have you eaten anything?" "Not a thing." The party interrogated has eaten a Friday dinner, and he means that he has eaten nothing in the line of meat. A broad mental reservation conveys what the speaker has in his mind in so concealed a way that the listener, if at all imprudent, will gather the opposite of what the speaker has in his mind, in spite of helps against deception derivable from such attendant circumstances as tone of voice, common usage, gesture, official capacity and the like. Usage after all fixes the value and meaning of words, and usage can alone determine whether any given expression is a pure mental reservation or a broad mental reservation.

K. *Ethics of Secrets:* There are three kinds of secrets: 1. Natural. 2. Secret of promise. 3. Secret of contract.

A secret is natural, if the obligation to keep it hidden has its origin in nature. Whatever private knowledge we have of others able, if revealed, to work them harm in point of reputation, property and such, constitutes a natural secret. A natural secret becomes a secret of promise, when, after coming into possession of the secret, we promise the party in question not to reveal the same. If such promise is exacted from us before we come to knowledge of the secret; in other words, if the secret is confided to us only after a promise on our part to keep it hidden, the secret of promise becomes a secret of contract. All three kinds impose the obligation of secrecy, but the binding force of the obligation varies with the kind of secret. The order of importance in ascending scale is: Natural, Secret of Promise, and Secret of Contract. To reveal any secret, to whatever class it belongs, some proportionate reason must be present. A weightier reason is needed when a secret of contract is in question than when there is question of the other two. Nature forbids us to harm another without good and sufficient reason. A promise binding by way of a man's word or by way of justice, according to the intent of the person making the promise, calls for even a better and a weightier reason. The contract involved in a secret of the third kind renders its violation a more serious matter, and only the gravest of reasons can justify the violation of such a secret. The contract in question may be either express or tacit, and it regularly accompanies professional secrets. If serious harm threatens the state, or an innocent person, or either of the two parties to the contract, even a secret of contract can without wrong be revealed. If there is question of harm already done, a natural secret, or a secret of promise must be revealed to a judge or superior making lawful enquiry. In this last case a secret of contract is privileged, and must not be revealed even to a judge or superior. In no emergency must the secrecy of the confessional be violated.

L. St. Alphonsus Liguori—Second Commandment. Dubium 4; 151–172.

151. Not wrong to swear to equivocal statement, when one has good reason, and the equivocation itself is lawful; to do so without good reason, not perjury, but mortal sin against religion; oath abused.

Three kinds of equivocation:

1. Word has two meanings, e.g., volo, from velle and volare.

2. Word has two senses equally common, e.g., Peter's book whether owner or author.

3. Word has two senses, common and unusual, e.g., literal and spiritual.

The Baptist is Elias. St. Matt. 2–14; I am not Elias. St. John 1–21.

I say no, whether affirmation or negation.

152. A pure mental reservation is never lawful; a broad is right when good reason is present, e.g., I go not up to this festival day. St. John 7–8; He also went up, not openly 7–8; openly, from context.

Of that day and hour no one knoweth, meaning end of world. St. Matt. 24–36. No one knows to tell, from context.

Reason for broad, the one legitimate way to hide a secret.

153. If asked to testify as God's minister, priest can deny.

THESIS IV.

Man's right to ownership, whether temporary or lasting, is derived to him, not from any formal compact, nor from any civil law, but from nature. Jouin, 118-140; Rickaby, 278-297.

QUESTION

Socialism is the economic error we combat in this thesis. Man's right to property in capital is the precise point attacked by Socialism, and we meet the enemy by setting this right to property in whatever good on a basis that cannot be shaken or overthrown If nature equips man with equal right to exclusive ownership in the capital he invests and in the food he eats, no legislation can in ordinary contingencies with justice separate him against his will from his capital or his food. That ownership in capital is a natural right, independent of compact and civil law, is with us a basic principle; and, once this point is settled, Socialism and its philanthropic but wild contentions in behalf of oppressed labor, fall to the ground. There are other arguments against Socialism, and we mean to call attention to them in due process of time. But in basing man's right to ownership on nature, our present thesis is a sweeping condemnation of Socialism and kindred theories. Socialism and Communism are systems at first sight identical, but very distinct when more closely studied. As long as men possess minds and use them for purposes of study, the two systems stand about equal chances for universal sway. As long as man's wickedness remains what it is, to encourage oppression of labor and contempt of the poor, so long shall their advocates harangue crowds of listeners intellectually too feeble to see beyond appearances, or reason to remote conclusions.

Socialism assumes the hue of whatever mind falls under its sway, and is therefore as varied in its outlines as the physiognomies of men. But there are some broad features, and on these we now insist. He therefore would seem to be a Socialist, who holds it proper and exclusively proper for man to turn over to the Socialistic commonwealth whatever property can in good faith be styled capital. He prescribes under pain of sin community of goods not strictly necessary for the consumer's use. He would allow the railroad magnate to earn his annual salary as president of a corporation, but would forbid him to lock up in his private safe more of that salary than would furnish himself and his family with the necessaries or even the luxuries of life. In fact he would make the railroad magnate a paid servant of the commonwealth after confiscating or buying his railroad, and would strip him of his capital and all chance to accumulate capital, reducing him to a level with the operatives he now robs of the fruit of their labors. Millionaires would become extinct specimens, and the state treasury would distribute to the poor a surplus, in comparison with which any prior surplus would be mere pocket-money. The condition of God's poor would be so far bettered that Heaven would become a reward out of all proportion with the small price paid for it. Leisure, and ease, and retirement on a competency, would be worn out notions. The whole world would put on the busy appearance of a beehive. After one year all the drones would die, and this gap in nature would remain forever empty. With no fund for a rainy day, work would be eagerly sought and as zealously performed. Industry would be life, idleness would be death. What a picture! Nobody can immoderately chide the generous but shallow-brained enthusiasts, who see in this wonderful transformation the dawn of millennium. But it costs no great effort to set aside poetry, and view this theory, as all philosophical theories must be viewed, in the even and full light of reason. Socialism, whatever may be said of its possibilities as a system for men with other hearts and other passions than ours, is certainly doomed to remain idle as long as time lasts. Its refutation is clearly and satisfactorily set forth in the arguments to be advanced in support of our thesis.

The Communist, recognizing no difference between capital and other possessions, cries out for a share in every man's goods; and in return lays open, as well he may, to every chance-comer his own meagre store. Communism is insanity or gross depravity. Communism has no redeeming feature. We are bad enough, when at our best, but make us Communists, and we should in a twinkling degenerate to cutthroats, thieves, devils incarnate. There would be no security at home or abroad. Our very friends would mix our cup with poison. Our lot would be incomparably less endurable than that of lions and tigers roaming the jungle. No doubt a chosen few can so discipline their greed, and so develop their esteem of eternal riches, as to work even more strenuously than otherwise without any pecuniary reward in view. But to assert that the whole race is morally capable of such perfection, and that the whole race is ready and eager to put off selfishness, and sap its strength to feed and clothe the worthless and idle, is the empty vaunt of ignorance, and worthy of only the man who knows neither himself nor other men. Communism maintains that everybody is to own everything, and that the common vagrant and the man who tries to do his duty, the outcast of society and the man high in his neighbors' esteem, are in some unexplained way to have an equal share in the enjoyment of this world's goods.

Our thesis, we flatter ourselves, strikes at the very root of Socialism and Communism. We are far from contending that the natural law imposes on individuals the duty of owning goods in severalty, nor yet that natural law absolutely forbids and discountenances community of possessions in any and every possible combination of circumstances. But we do maintain that natural law unequivocally and unmistakably imposes on mankind the duty of refraining from all undue meddling with the neighbour's private property. We do maintain that a man's right to his field and to his capital has all its strength, not from formal compact or civil agreement, with which indeed man can so far tamper as to change or even repeal them; but from nature, which lies outside of man's dominion, and acknowledges obedience to God alone. We do maintain that neither Communism nor Socialism is prescribed by the law of nature or by the obligations of man to man; that they are not expressly, immediately and universally forbidden by the law of nature. We do maintain nevertheless that they are implicitly, mediately and in particular circumstances, which now obtain throughout the universe, absolutely condemned by the voice of nature, with intent that the condemnation endure until this world of ours is peopled with a race strangers to the passions that agitate our bosoms. We are ready to grant that no peculiar offense is committed, if a body of men come together in harmony and agree among themselves to convey to some common treasury all their wealth, with the understanding that it is to belong to no individual precisely, but to be used by all in common as events fall out. We are ready to further grant that he would be a benefactor of the race, who could so work on the minds and wills of capitalists and landowners as to induce them of their own free-will to divest themselves of their superfluous moneys, and confide the same to the state or to some equally responsible corporation for distribution among the poor. But we reprobate as firebrands to the republic the hot-headed fanatics, who open wide their mouths and cry out that capital is sin, and that ownership of land is a crime against nature. We are not afraid to give utterance to the opinion that all such intemperate zealots should be deprived of the power they wield for harm among the desperate mob and placed with convenient despatch between the four walls of the city-jail. The millionaire may legally be induced to part with his money-bags for the weal of the populace. He is, however, undeniably free to close his ears to all such extravagant pleadings of misapplied humanity, and in ordinary contingencies law cannot forcibly extort from him a penny in the name of justice. What has once fairly slipped into his coffers is his in spite of the universe, and this one circumstance imposes on the world at large the solemn duty of respecting that right, and allowing him to possess his own in peace. His acquisition of the wealth is no necessity of nature, neither is his close retention of the same; but, once acquired, his will about the disposition of his dollars is law, and with all the grim necessity of nature's ordinances debars others from approach, and imperatively demands non-interference. Of course, I speak of wealth legitimately come by, and nowise forfeited by debts afterwards contracted, or at the competent command of higher rights.

TERMS

Right. The moral power or force, in itself inviolate, to do or exact something.

Ownership. The right to claim some external and material thing as one's own, subject always to restrictions imposed by higher rights.

Ownership is one species of dominion or lordship, jurisdiction is the other. Dominion or lordship is the right to claim a thing as one's own. Ownership is lordship turning on external and material things like money, land and kindred articles. Jurisdiction is lordship turning on spiritual objects like the minds and wills of men, and it is a prerogative of rulers. The clearest title to lordship is production, and God alone is true Lord, true owner, true ruler, because God alone in true and strict sense makes or produces things. Men make nothing, they merely change things. Men, therefore, are owners and rulers not by essence, not in an independent way, but only by participation, and with utter dependence on God's good pleasure. Ownership enables them to dispose of external and material things that really and truly belong to God. Jurisdiction enables them to control minds and wills that really and truly owe allegiance to God alone.

Ownership, then, is the right to keep and to use external material things as one's own, subject always to restrictions imposed by rights of a higher order. Three elements deserve notice. To keep and to use, imply a bond of union between property and owner. As one's own, excludes others from possession and use. Restrictions, remove all danger of Exaggerated Individualism, which would make individual ownership in man entirely independent of God and law. The bond of union is commonly called the title, and is whatever fact stamps and seals the material good in question as property belonging to the owner. In origin it is not civil law, it is not compact, it is not labor alone or work on the object of ownership. It is what we call occupancy, and occupancy is best described as the actual appropriation of a thing along with the avowed intention of holding on to it; or more fully, as seizure of material goods belonging to nobody in particular, with the intention of retaining them as one's own, accomplished with the help of clear and manifest signs, whether physical or moral. These signs are different in different cases. Crops are harvested, animals are killed or captured, fields are fenced, money and deeds are passed, verbal agreements are made. This is effective occupancy, other kinds are legal and political, from civil law and international. The restrictions we impose are fruitful in consequences. Individual ownership can collide with rights in God, and rights in the state; and in every such collision individual ownership must yield. God alone is absolute owner of everything. He owns the man as well as the man's property, and can dispose of both according to His good pleasure. God never abdicates His dominion in men or things, and He makes men gifts without ceasing to be their owner. The landlord remains owner when he rents his house to the tenant. As against God, man never rises higher than relative or use-ownership, and he must use whatever gifts God makes him with a view to the promotion of God's greater glory. Hence, the right to individual ownership in the rich never excuses them from the obligation of charity towards the poor; and denial of charity on their part is a species of robbery against God. As against the state and individuals composing it, man's right to individual ownership is absolute. Neither state nor individuals give the right, and, therefore, neither state nor individuals can take it away. And yet in virtue of the adage that the part is servant to the whole, the state has rights in this matter of ownership that the individual owner must acknowledge and respect. The state cannot take away the right to individual ownership, but it can in emergencies divert private property to public uses. It can call citizens to service in time of war, and virtually deprive them of ownership in their own lives. It can impose taxes and customs, it can institute condemnation proceedings, and exercise all the various functions implied in Eminent Domain.

Eminent Domain is no proof that individual ownership originates in the state or civil law. Quite the contrary, it is open acknowledgment that the state and law have no such efficacy. In condemnation cases the state when possible makes compensation to the owner, and the prerogative is exercised only in serious public need. If individual ownership had its origin in state or law, compensation would be no requisite, and the will of the state in whatever trivial emergency would justify the proceeding. When courts of law settle cases in property, they virtually acknowledge that the right of ownership has a validity all its own, independent of their rulings. They never create or confer ownership, they determine where it exists. They hear testimony, examine documents, and take every means to discover in what party the right resides and decide accordingly, all which would be needless waste of time, if the court could of itself vest either party to the suit with the disputed right.

This ownership is of many different kinds, absolute and relative; perfect and imperfect; direct and indirect; transient and permanent; public and private; collective and individual; abstract and concrete. Absolute ownership is independent ownership, and in strict sense accrues to God alone. It means the right to dispose of and use a thing at pleasure, without restrictions imposed by another. *Relative ownership* is dependent ownership, and strictly speaking all human ownership is such. It means the right to dispose of and use things, not at pleasure, but within limits prescribed by God or nature. Men have the physical power or freedom to abuse things, but they are without the moral power or right to do so; and all their ownership is by very nature subservient to the good pleasure of God. As between individuals human ownership can be said to be absolute as well as relative. As between state and citizen Eminent Domain is only a seeming denial of absolute ownership. The right to ownership is not taken away by the state, it ceases because of collision with a higher right. *Perfect ownership* extends to substance and use of a thing, while *imperfect* extends to only one or other of the two. Imperfect ownership is direct, when it touches the thing's substance; indirect, when it touches the thing's use. Landlord and tenant are examples.

Ownership is transient or temporary, when it turns on goods consumed or destroyed in their use, on goods that cannot of their very nature successively belong to two or more owners. Food is an example. *Ownership is permanent,* stable, lasting, when it turns on goods practically indestructible, and open to successive possession by several. Money, a field, a house, capital are examples. Capital is practically indestructible property, that tends to the production of new wealth, and is opposed to what constitutes transient ownership. Money invested in a business or deposited in a bank can be called capital. The same object can be basis for both transient and permanent ownership. Wine and bread, for instance, can be regarded as food or as articles of trade and commerce. We maintain against Socialism that man, when he acquires dominion over property of either denomination, transient or permanent, food or capital, is only applying a right, with which nature at his birth vested him. We maintain that his right to land and capital is just as sacred as his right to the food he eats, and that he can, therefore, be no more deprived of one than of the other. Food is a more immediate need to existence than land or capital; but transient ownership without permanent is precarious, insecure, well nigh impossible; and the owner's title or occupancy is equally valid in the two cases.

Public ownership is ownership vested in a perfect society, like the Church or the state; *private ownership* is ownership vested in an individual or in an imperfect society, like a business partnership, or the whole human race. Private ownership, therefore, can be individual or collective. *Individual* attaches to a definite physical person, and it implies exclusion of other owners; *collective* attaches to a moral person, or to several physical persons taken collectively not distributively. This collective ownership is common ownership, and it can be positively common or negatively common ownership. In collective ownership goods are common to several in such a way that none of the several can exclude the others from their possession or use. Obviously, such collective ownership is barren and of no practical utility to individuals. Collective ownership is an advantage, only when reducible to individual ownership. Individual ownership is part and parcel of the very word, property or proprium.

Collective ownership of this practical kind is positively common ownership and negatively common ownership. *Positively common ownership* is reducible to individual ownership only by favor of all the individuals in the community, or by favor of a head or person in authority substituting for all the individuals, never by virtue of independent activity on the part of an ordinary individual in the community. As far as individuals in the community are concerned, positively common ownership remains forever common in potency as well as actually. All power to change positively common ownership to individual ownership resides in the members of the community as a whole, or in a head substituting for these members. *Negatively common ownership* is reducible to individual ownership, not by favor of community's members or a head, but by virtue of independent activity like occupancy on the part of any single member, without reference to the other members or their representative. Negatively common ownership is in itself actually common, but potentially individual, reducible to individual by virtue of independent activity on the part of any single member in the community. This example from Costa-Rossetti, page 363, may serve to elucidate things. Some forest is government property either in such a way that no citizen is able to cut down and appropriate trees in the forest without permission from all the other citizens or from the head of the government, or in such a way that any citizen is at liberty to cut down and appropriate trees, not already appropriated by others, without any permission whatever from his fellow-citizens or the government's head. In the first case individual citizens enjoy positively common ownership in the forest, in the other case citizens enjoy negatively common ownership.

Of their very nature, and apart from every other consideration, the material goods of earth belong to nobody by way of actual individual ownership; they belong to everybody, not by way of positively common ownership, but by way of negatively common ownership. In other words, actual individual ownership is not from nature, potential individual ownership is from nature. Positively common ownership is neither actual nor potential individual ownership; negatively common ownership, though not actual individual ownership, is potential individual ownership. Actual individual ownership is not natural, in the sense of inborn, because otherwise everybody at his birth would have a definite supply of material goods set apart for his own exclusive use. Positively common ownership is not natural in the same sense, because otherwise persons born into the world could never on their own initiative become individual owners, but only by favor of every single individual of the race, or by favor of some person in authority substituting for every individual. Negatively common ownership of everything is natural in the sense of inborn, because it is the only species of common ownership able to eventuate, with the help of occupancy or personal endeavor, in actual individual ownership, the one kind of ownership universally prescribed or counselled by nature in present circumstances.

If God wants individual ownership, no right of jurisdiction in a ruler can impose collective ownership, because jurisdiction in a ruler is subservient to the will of God; and no sane ruler, as a matter of fact, ever attempted the usurpation. That God in present circumstances wants individual ownership, is clear from the constitution of man, and from evils inseparably attaching to collective ownership. Had man continued in primitive innocence, or had the race never amounted to more than a few families, collective ownership would have in its favor arguments now altogether wanting. The passions of men and the numerical vastness of the race plainly declare against universal collective ownership. In the present system of individual ownership disputes are all too common, in collective ownership quarrels would be multiplied a millionfold. Therefore, individual ownership is not from nature in such a way that collective ownership is in every conceivable case against nature. Positively common ownership is not from nature at all, but from agreement sanctioned by nature in particular instances, as in religious communities or associations. Negatively common ownership is from nature in such a way that denial of it in any particular instance is against nature.

Nobody is born an actual individual owner by virtue of very birth, nobody is born neither an actual nor a potential individual owner. Everybody is born a potential individual owner by virtue of very birth. Therefore actual individual ownership is a prescription of nature in much the same way as marriage; and, though Church and state may make laws regulating marriage, they must not absolutely forbid members or citizens to marry. Positively common ownership is no more a prescription of nature than membership in a business firm; negatively common ownership is a prescription of nature in much the same way as desire of complete happiness. Negatively common ownership is everybody's natural right, absolutely inamissible, inalienable and beyond the reach of human legislation, whether ecclesiastical or civil. Negatively common ownership is practical potential individual ownership, every practical potency involves future reduction to actuality, and to unduly interfere with actual individual ownership is to violate and attack nature.

Abstract ownership is another term for negatively common ownership, *concrete ownership* is another term for individual ownership. Abstract ownership, then, is that natural right inherent in all new-born babes, whether they be of noble or plebeian origin, to get and to hold as their own whatever material goods of the earth they may in after-life legitimately acquire. This abstract ownership becomes concrete at whatever particular moment the child or the man assumes towards a material object some relation which justifies his claim to its exclusive possession. It is a fact readily granted by all that God presented to our race in the person of Adam the territory of the universe with all its splendid blessings. The earth with all its contents was made for Adam and his descendants to the end of time. This gift was made to Adam as to an individual, it was made to the rest of the race as it then existed, viz., as to an abstraction, or to some actual non-being. Adam was created not an individual or exclusive owner of the earth and all its goods, but only a negatively common owner. This abstract ownership he converted into concrete ownership with the help of occupancy, and by his own personal endeavor he became individual and exclusive owner of such portions of the earth and its goods as he made exclusively his own. Adam certainly began as an individual owner, because there was nobody to share ownership with him. God never settled unconditionally and unexceptionally whether the descendants of Adam should be positively common or individual owners. He vested them with negatively common ownership, left the future to natural reason, and virtually decreed individual or exclusive ownership as the system best suited to ordinary mortals after the fall and a sufficiently widespread growth of the race.

Eve and her children by virtue of negatively common ownership, their natural right, had full power to become in the nature of things individual owners; but the union between husband, wife and children demanded by the family persuaded them to be content with positively common ownership, dependent on Adam's good pleasure. Even nowadays nature counsels collective ownership in the family. When husband and wife keep separate purses, peace in the family is menaced, and mutual union is not what it ought to be. Even nowadays nature counsels positively common ownership in religious communities, in comparatively small gatherings of spiritually minded men, banded together for purposes of perfection along the lines of the gospel. And yet collective ownership is not their natural inheritance in the same sense as negatively common ownership; and, while surrendering the use of the right, they cannot alienate or surrender the right itself to become individual and exclusive owners. Adam, Eve and their children were, therefore, to all intents and purposes religious in the matter of ownership, with Adam for superior or substitute for the others.

Had primitive innocence continued, had man's passion or appetite for worldly goods remained forever subservient to reason, the system might have persevered without change and threatened small or no harm to moral order. But the fall of man and consequent loss of primitive innocence made individual ownership the one safe form of ownership for the bulk of mankind. Adam, therefore, and all his descendants began as negatively common owners. Adam changed this negatively common to individual ownership with the help of occupancy. Eve and her children changed it to positively common ownership. When men grew numerous enough to make individual ownership advisable, men changed negatively common ownership to individual with the help of occupancy and kindred titles, like accession or increment, contracts and inheritance. Abraham and Lot possessed land in common till a quarrel between their shepherds urged them to divide their common holdings and live as individual owners or proprietors. Abraham on at least two occasions purchased land from the Egyptians, showing that he respected the right to individual ownership in his neighbors. History everywhere bears witness to this ruling of nature in favor of individual ownership, and at the present time no considerable body of men, outside of religious orders, lives according to the tenets of Communism or Socialism. Men like Fourier, 1772–1837, Owen, 1771–1858, and Cabet, 1788–1856, have tried the thing, and egregiously failed. Owen's New Harmony colony in Indiana lasted two years; Cabet's Icaria Community in Illinois, after repeated reverses between 1849 and 1895, entirely disappeared in the latter year. Nature enters no protest against collective ownership in the family, it enters no protest against collective ownership in religion; but it very decidedly protests against collective ownership for the bulk of mankind as constituted since the fall.

Formal Compact. Civil Law. Nature. The Socialists and Communists, who despair of ever being able to prove that their systems would be more replete with blessings for mankind than the system of individual ownership, now so universal, attack the justice of man's plea for the right to individual ownership. For, be it remembered, we maintain that no man can divest himself of his natural right to individual ownership any more than he can divest himself of rationality. He can so abuse his faculties as to lose the use of his reason, but the use of reason and rationality or reason itself are two things quite as distinct among themselves as the builder and the house he builds, or the mind and the thought it thinks. Even so, the religious who binds himself by solemn vow to poverty, or to life without individual ownership of anything, forever retains that right to individual ownership. He goes down to the grave without ever enforcing the right, but the right itself is as present and live in him as it is in the richest landlord or capitalist. He cannot surrender his right to individual ownership. He can and does surrender all desire to enforce that right. Man's right to individual ownership is, therefore, so just that he cannot even himself legitimately or otherwise deprive himself of it. It is therefore an indispensable requisite of his nature and our all-wise Maker did not so constitute us that an element of injustice should be absolutely and unavoidably inseparable from our nature. If man's right to individual ownership could fall back for foundation on only a formal compact, as Heyne and Grote opine; or on civil laws, as Montesquieu, Bentham and Hobbes groundlessly imagine, then indeed Henry George and men of his stamp could question the justice or injustice of that right, could examine the terms, and the legality, and the reasonableness of that compact and those civil laws. But, as we mean to show in our proofs, no such supposition is tenable.

DIVISION

Three Parts—I, II, III.   Not Compact, Not Law, But Nature

PROOFS

I. Whatever is asserted without proof, can likewise be denied without proof. But this first theory advances no proof of the fact that an agreement or covenant respecting individual ownership was once entered into. Therefore, this first theory is simply denied.

With Regard to the Minor: 1°. History, that is most ancient and authoritative, bears witness to the contrary fact, viz., that, before any agreement was ever entered into, man recognized within himself and applied the right to individual ownership with which he was born. History, both ancient and modern, is authority for the fact that bodies of men and women, like the primitive Christians and the religious orders, have by a formal compact agreed to relinquish the use of this right, without of course being in the least degree capable of shaking off the right itself. Unlike the propounders of the false theory here refuted, we have ancient historical remains, such as monuments and tablets, to which we can refer. The book of Genesis, written by Moses, the most ancient and best authenticated history written, no matter what scoffers say to the contrary, carries the question back twenty centuries before Christ and plainly indicates that in the time of Abraham the right to individual ownership was enforced and respected. On two separate occasions at least Abraham buys pieces of land: once for a family burial-plot, again for a camping ground. Gen. 23–6, 8, 9, 11, 14, 18, 20; 33–19.

With the Egyptians, whose history is among the earliest recorded, Joseph is said to have purchased in time of famine all the land of the people. Monuments have been discovered and are now visible in the museums of Europe, on which are traced distinct and unequivocal records of business transactions in property, which would be wholly meaningless if individual ownership were not recognized. One of these monuments, that of King Senefra, dates its origin from a period ten or twelve centuries in advance of that of Abraham.

2°. Another argument might be drawn from the fact that community of goods, as our opponents themselves confess, would never have been necessary if men had not been born with the same dispositions for virtue and innocence, and that exclusive individual ownership necessarily resulted from differences of disposition in this matter. But it is a fact witnessed to by the wise and the ignorant alike that man was created on a plan of perfectibility, and that, even if Adam had prolonged to his descendants the reign of primitive innocence, there would still have prevailed among them degrees of virtue and perfection. 3°. Besides, if community of goods were natural, and exclusive ownership unnatural, the savages roaming the plains and living from hand to mouth would be men more according to God's mind than the inhabitants of cities with all their wisdom and knowledge. 4°. The philosophers opposed to us would deplore communism as a machine of the devil. But communism is the legitimate outcome of any system that makes man's right to individual ownership depend on human agreement or civil law. For human agreement and civil law admit of change, even when the change is actually from better to worse.

II. No effect can be ascribed to any cause of a perfection inferior to its own. But individual ownership is a universal custom of universal duration among men. It cannot, therefore, be referred, as to a cause, to so inconstant and so restricted a factor as civil law. Besides, individuals in society, to create exclusive ownership by civil law, must have had before such a proceeding exclusive rights to the goods and parcels of land deeded over. Otherwise, the whole proceeding was illegal and unjust, as the parties engaged in it disposed of that which did not belong to them. Right of jurisdiction could never create the right, because jurisdiction touches the obedience of subjects, not their property. Even nowadays when through some legal scheming a rightful owner is ousted from his property, do fair-minded people for a moment imagine that the schemer assumes or puts on a right to the ill-gotten goods? Does the schemer himself fancy that before God and conscience the theft is justified? By no means. But were civil law the cause of man's right to exclusive ownership, the opinions of the fair-minded in the supposed instance would be empty imaginings without any foundation in fact, the stings of conscience would be unnecessary pain, self-inflicted, without any assignable cause or reason. If law could once change positive common to exclusive ownership, law can now change exclusive ownership to positive common.

III. Man is born to live an allotted time and work out an allotted destiny, and his Maker has furnished him with natural rights to whatever is needful for that existence and for the attainment of that destiny. But individual ownership is a means necessary to that existence. Therefore man's Maker has furnished him with a natural right to individual ownership, and this individual ownership extends itself to temporary and lasting objects.

With Regard to the Major: Every-day experience is proof of the first member, conclusive enough to convince the most sceptical. The absurdity of conceiving man alone, creation's noblest work, placed here to no intended purpose, while everything around him works unto an end, is indeed overwhelming. The prudence and justice of his Maker would render it absolutely impossible to fancy man bereft of means necessary to the attainment of his end.

With Regard to the Minor: To foster existence, it is a requisite that man be solicitous about procuring what beseems life. But by very nature man's solicitude is but feebly or not at all aroused save in the search for things that belong to himself alone, that cannot be claimed or appropriated by others. Life without peace would be without joy and would be even impossible. But deprive men of the right to individual ownership, and life would be a warfare, a struggle for existence in the truest and strictest sense of the word, peace would flee the earth. There are innumerable other arguments applicable here, but all will suggest themselves to the enquiring mind. I would only note the following. Use or transient dominion is certainly a natural right. It must be plain to all that this right is little worth, unless, for instance, the farmer can raise his crop without fear that a stranger may come in the harvest-time and appropriate his sowing. The sculptor will be little tempted to ply his art, unless secure in the possession of the block of marble on which he works. Laziness, and hunger, and death, are in sure prospect when any chance-comer may with impunity lay hands on the products of the industrious. There will be nothing in store to tide the laborer over the darksome days of sickness and old age. His young family will perish before it reaches maturity. Charity and bigness of heart in the dispensation of goods will be utter strangers to earth. Add to all this the fact that the lie would be given to the sentiments and opinions of our fathers and forefathers, who all strenuously maintained that the right to exclusive ownership of property is inherent in man, and as much a part of man as his nature.

PRINCIPLES

A. In case of extreme need the baker loses his right to individual ownership of part of the bread in his shop. This circumstance is due to a phenomenon in question of rights, which has its parallel in that of physical forces. In the matter of physical forces the weaker by a kind of inherent necessity yields to a stronger force. Even so, in rights, which are moral forces, the stronger always takes precedence of the weaker right. But one sort of force never intrenches on the domain of the other. Thus, the strongest imaginable physical force can never obtain legal mastery over the weakest imaginable moral force or right. Necessity or indispensableness of the means involved is always the measure of dignity attached to a right. Four kinds of necessity are recognized in the order following: absolute, extreme, serious, commonplace. A divine right demands the sacrifice of a human right. The right of a natural society or state, when all the conditions are the same, demands the sacrifice of a right belonging to an individual of that natural society or state.

B. The acknowledgment of right to individual ownership is the innocent and accidental occasion of many quarrels and disputes. But such quarrels or disputes are rather the outcome of perverse natures, and with a small amount of common sense can be avoided. But in community of goods quarrels and disputes would constitute the essential and unavoidable order of the day.

C. The community of goods in use with the apostles, primitive Christians, and religious orders is no denial of the right to individual ownership, but a voluntary and meritorious cession of the practical advantages ordinarily attendant on the application of that right.

D. Civil law surrounds with all possible safeguards the citizen's privileges accruing to him from the natural right to individual ownership, and takes all possible means to ensure harmony and order among claimants; but civil law by no means creates the right to individual ownership. In all its enactments it supposes the right itself already possessed.

E. Absolutely speaking, it would of course be quite possible for an individual to come into the possession of a whole continent; but relatively speaking, i.e., taking all circumstances into account, such possession would be utterly impossible. In Moral Philosophy, as elsewhere remarked, because it is an eminently practical science, circumstances cannot in justice be neglected. Therefore, it is enough to remark, as answer to this seemingly formidable objection, that individual ownership of a whole continent is entirely out of the question. God's ownership forbids that the race be pushed into the sea.

F. Abstract ownership is a natural right emanating from God, and independent of all civil law. Concrete ownership is natural in foundation, strictly human because of occupancy, and dependent on civil law in its application. Law cannot in general forbid concrete ownership; but it can prescribe methods and limits, to safeguard the common good. Occupancy is more than a mere condition in question of concrete ownership; it is proximate cause or title. The expression, this is mine because I made it my own, is proof of occupancy's causality. No danger from Socialism attaches to this concession, because the natural right, or abstract right of ownership, always stands; and this bases concrete ownership. Law will enforce right when formalities are observed, not otherwise. Right may be present, State will refuse to recognize; and all that to further the interests of peace and prosperity. Law never creates or causes the right unless the state is prior owner; it safeguards right already present. It assists the obedient, refuses to assist the disobedient; and these latter must prosecute their right without help from the law.

G. In spite of individual ownership the use of things remains always in a measure common. Concrete ownership is a human right. Divine law ordains that the goods of earth contribute to the support of all mankind. In extreme need human right must yield to divine law, and in this emergency all goods become common, to rescue the needy from destruction. In the same way the rich are obliged in charity, though not in justice, to relieve the needy poor with their superfluous wealth. The poor cannot appeal to this principle as to an excuse for lawlessly plundering the rich. The duty of the rich has its origin in charity, not in justice. Rights and duties in question of justice turn on determined persons and definite matter, not in question of charity. All the needy cannot be relieved; and, therefore, the rich are at liberty to make a judicious selection. Besides, superfluous goods cannot be determined by any hard and fast rule, and everything is left to the prudent charity of the wealthy owner.

H. Religious never divest themselves of the right to ownership, but of its exercise.

I. The right to use is basis of the right to own, and yet individual ownership seems to destroy the right to use. It destroys in others the right to use, and that is no contradiction.

J. By nature all things are common in negative, not in positive sense.

THESIS V

Socialism is false in its principles, morally impossible in itself, and quite absurd. Cathrein, 283–303.

QUESTION

Karl Marx (1818–1883), is the acknowledged founder of present-day Socialism, the species called democratic; and his work on Capital can be taken for a fair exposition of its tenets. It condemns the present condition of society as deplorable and unjust. It is deplorable, because in business everybody does as he likes, trusts capture the wealth of the world, capital practically destroys competition, and mankind goes into two armies, the classes and the masses, captains of industry and the proletariat, or capitalists and slaves to capitalists. It is unjust, because capital enriches itself by taking unfair advantage of labor, monopolizing such channels of wealth as land, factories, mines, railways, and seizing every opportunity to rob the masses of the fruit of their labor.

Marx sees in every product of labor a twofold value: *its use value,* and *its exchange value.* A coat's use value is fixed by its physical and chemical properties, which determine its usefulness as an article of wearing apparel. Its exchange value depends on the amount of money it is worth in the market, and is always in excess of its use value. This excess it gets from the workman's labor, which is represented by the difference between the cost of raw material and the selling price. In much the same way, the tailor's labor has a twofold value; one, use value; the other, exchange value. Its exchange value is the wages he gets from his employer, its use value is its exchange value along with the profit accruing from such labor to his employer. Suppose a tailor makes a suit of clothes a day. Suppose the suit worth twenty dollars, the raw material five, and the tailor's wages five. The cloth's use value will be five. In this way the use value of

260

the tailor's labor, added to the use value of the cloth, gives the market price of the suit, and the excess of use value over exchange value in the tailor's labor represents the employer's profit. This excess of ten dollars the Socialist styles capital, and in his eyes the whole process of commercial profit is a species of robbery. But he is blind to the fact that the employer has a sacred right to wages as well as the tailor, and it is not at all exorbitant to rate what he contributes to the suit of clothes in the way of skill, management, rent and what not, twice as valuable as what the tailor contributes. And this continues true, if the employer be an out and out capitalist, contributing nothing to the industry but his money. For great mental effort was expended somewhere in the accumulation of this money, and such effort deserves a reward or wages. The capital invested stands for the work expended in its accumulation. Certainly the employer ought not be allowed to oppress his workmen, or keep their pay down to starvation limits. But that is an affair labor itself must regulate by organization and by appeals to the state when necessary. And all appearance of dishonesty must be avoided, no crime against the natural right of property must be committed in the process, and the wrongs of the poor must be righted without despoiling the rich of that capital, which is as much theirs as the dinner the workman eats is his.

In spite of what Socialists preach to the contrary, society is not going to right itself by the commission of another colossal wrong. Religion is the God-appointed remedy for this evil, and for whatever other evils afflict mankind. The evolution to which Socialism looks for relief is progress backwards, and would, if realized, land labor in infinitely worse conditions than it now knows. Socialists see in the gradual diminution of conspicuous capitalists a hasty advance towards the time when the poor, far outnumbering the rich, will in sheer disgust confiscate the goods of the wealthy, and inaugurate a new era of universal prosperity. The world, they think, will undergo a complete revolution in the matter of morality, religion and civil government. God will be dethroned in the universe, religion will be beaten down, individuals will be kings, every man will be his own law, passion will usurp the place of reason, and the world will go its own way to perdition. By a most pernicious and offensive propaganda they are getting men's minds and hearts ready for the change. They are preaching atheism everywhere. Fear of God is a check to their iniquitous progress, and this fear must be proved a fiction. The old doctrine of Heaven and hell teaches patience, and impatience with their lot can alone goad the poor to excesses. Conscience, with its antiquated standard of morality, bars spoliation of the wealthy; and conscience must be taught that self-advantage is the first law of nature. The Church is in league with capital to enslave the masses, it is the paid agent of capital, advocating for a pecuniary reward the need of obedience to authority, and encouraging laziness in its ministers, fattening on the credulity of the poor. The State, as at present constituted, is a foe to labor, and capital's most steadfast ally. Government, therefore, must be overthrown, and on its ruins the socialistic commonwealth of pure democracy must arise. Free love, community of wives, and all their attendant abominations must not only be tolerated, but encouraged; family life must be forever obliterated; children must be reared by the state, much as ranchmen raise their cattle on the plains. These are some of the flattering inducements they hold out to their followers, and the wonder is that their ranks are not more crowded than they are.

Socialists regularly and persistently deny that their system contends for any of the degenerate practices just enumerated; but the writings of their leaders give the lie to every such protestation of innocence. They are shrewd dissemblers; and, where the truth about their theory would hurt the cause, policy urges them to hide its base consequences, and clamor aloud that their one holy purpose is to raise up prostrate labor, and better the condition of the working classes. But accurate quotations from recognized authorities on socialism bear honest witness to their true purpose; and we mean, before we finish, to gather a short but startling array of such quotations. Fortunately for the truth, socialism is its own worst accuser, and its own propagators voice its severest condemnation. These are necessary, logical consequences. Fanatics among them are alone logical. Moderate socialists are not true socialists.

The central feature of the whole system is the abolition of individual ownership in capital. Collective ownership vested in the Socialistic Commonwealth will constitute the new order of things. This commonwealth will be radically democratic, a return to the days of Demosthenes, when Athens met in the agora to frame laws, elect officials, and settle weighty affairs of state. It will assume complete control and ownership of such sources of revenue as land, houses, machinery, manufactures, mines and railways. Municipal ownership is only a step towards the realization of their plans, and advanced socialists are far from satisfied with this settlement of the question. They complain that municipal ownership merely shifts the trouble without removing it root and branch, because government in this event turns capitalist; and it makes small difference to labor whether public officials or private citizens prey upon its profits. In this commonwealth all magistrates, without a single exception, will be immediately elected by the people, directly responsible to the people, and subject to the sharpest kind of scrutiny at the hands of the people. They will be labor's paid servants, not its lords and masters. Privileges will be dead, all will be on a level, every citizen will be on an equal footing with his neighbor. Suffrage will be universal, officials will be closely watched, the common people will frame laws, sentence offenders, and execute judgment; and government will resolve itself into a vast trading concern, with every individual citizen an active partner in the business. Men of special parts will be selected to regulate the manufacture and distribution of products. The proceeds of labor down to the last penny will find their way into the laborer's pocket, and overproduction as well as scarcity will be a thing of the past. Officials will assign to each member of the commonwealth his own proper share and his own fixed kind of labor. Nobody will be allowed to cultivate idleness or enjoy superfluous ease. Rights and duties will be distributed with an even hand. There will be no merchants, no buyers and sellers. Goods will be stored in public depots to be distributed among the people in shares determined by individual industry. In lieu of money, pay-checks will be issued, entitling holders to fixed portions of the common products. Transient ownership will stand inviolate, and nobody will have a right to interfere with the neighbor's use and management of whatever articles of consumption he justly makes his own. Then follow in funereal order a long line of logical and fatal consequences.

There will be no God, no religion, no Church, no priests. There will be no family. Instead of marrying, men and women will mate for a short or long season, like the beasts of the field and birds of the air. Children will not know their fathers, and soon after their birth will be handed over to the commonwealth by their mothers, to be reared and educated at the government's expense. Divorce will disappear from the statute-books, when free love is made the uniform practice. Women will be on a footing with men, and work side by side with them in every department of industry. The time mothers hitherto wasted raising a family will be mercifully saved to labor by the establishment of state-farms for the upbringing of the young.

DIVISION

Two Parts—I, II

I. False in principles.
II. Impossible and absurd.

PROOFS

Its three chief principles are, [a.] *the theory of values;* [b.] *the equality of men;* [c.] *materialistic evolution.*

a. Socialists contend that labor gives whatever article of trade its true worth. In other words, they exaggerate labor's exchange value at the expense of the article's use value. In other words, the higher the price of a thing, the higher the wages for making it. But it can readily be shown that merchandise is quite as dependent for worth on its use value as on labor's exchange value. A thing's physical and chemical properties have quite as much to do with its price as the labor expended in its manufacture. The labor being the same, wine from one vineyard can be worth a hundred times as much as wine from another vineyard. Labor need have nothing to do with the difference of value in two fields. Wood, wheat, precious stones, in many cases derive their value from natural causes, antecedent to all human endeavor. Labor, of course, contributes to a thing's worth; but oftener than not its use value, its substance, is the weightier factor in determining price. The exchange value of a workman's labor is not measured by what it takes to support him, but by his strength, skill, energy and experience as well. The operative and the manager can equally well live on five dollars a day, but while the operative ought to be in justice content with five, the manager has a perfect right to demand ten. And in the adjustment of wages, the world of sensible labor will never be led astray by the senseless theories of socialists.

b. All this socialistic talk about man's equality with man is noxious nonsense; and to nobody is the folly of the thing better known than to socialist orators themselves. As a matter of fact, they reckon themselves leaders, and are not slow to insist on their superiority. They are prophets among the people, and dumb compliance with their wishes is first requisite for initiation into their company. Men are equal in the abstract, in the possession of human nature with its constituent elements; in the concrete, in accidental accomplishments, men are as far removed from equality as the remotest star from our earth. Fathers and mothers are above their children, rulers are above their subjects, where money counts the rich are vastly superior to the poor, and in the realms of art a consummate painter or sculptor is hardly on a level with a practical farmer or a man of toil. And socialism can try till doomsday, it will never succeed in eliminating these accidental differences among men. They would persevere in the impossible event of Socialism's establishment, because God wants them, and God's wishes cannot be frustrated.

c. The materialistic evolution of socialism is but a conceited aping of what is going on in the scientific world, and what one must expect when ill-trained minds of Shakespeare's mechanicals dabble in philosophy and theology. The pantheism of Hegel, the materialism of Darwin, now occupy the middle of the stage, and the attention they are getting is a necessary evil. They will die eventually, as all previous errors died; but in the process of their killing they cannot but be prominent. On the day of his hanging the condemned criminal gets a whole page in the newspaper, while an honored President meets with the scantest notice. Socialism, to be abreast of the times, casts its lot with modern thinkers, and sees in its establishment the consummation of evolution. Unable to see in man anything higher than mere matter, socialists profess to think him hopelessly subject to material forces and economic environment. To know the political economy of an age in history, is to know its religion, its trend of thought, and its civilization. Christianity was accordingly due to the economic notions prevalent in Christ's time; Protestantism started up in obedience to economic changes in human affairs; and Socialism, without any effort on its part, is bound to be the reigning style in the immediate future. Everything points to its swift inauguration. Religion is fast losing its hold on the minds of men, morality is making unto itself other standards, trusts are crushing competition, absorbing the wealth of the world, centralizing resources, and cutting down the number of enormously rich men to wonderfully small limits. Machinery is crowding labor out of the market, obliterating the middle class of thrifty workmen, and making wider the line of division between the rich and the poor. Discontent is growing among the masses, and the hour is not far distant when this discontent will make itself felt, when the people will rise in revolt, and the commonwealth will complete the work of centralization begun by the trusts, and vest all ownership of capital in the people.

But man is not the weather, to be determined by physical and material forces. He has an intelligent mind and a free will, both spiritual, immortal, and in last analysis quite independent of matter. He is his own master, maps out his own conduct; and, though subject to temporary aberrations from mental and moral straightness, he generally hits the truth, and at least approves of what is right. He is the creature of his environment, but never its unwilling slave. The prejudices current in this or that age of the world deeply affected successive generations of men, but there were always enough honest men in the world to keep the heritage of truth safe from lasting harm, and help it to ultimate victory. Man's mind was made for the truth, and, though its native imperfection lays it open to the danger of going wrong at scattered intervals, in the main it steers a straight course, and, accidents aside, it invariably finishes where God would have it finish in moral knowledge. If all rivers ran upward, if stones in the air continued to ascend instead of falling to the ground, it would be less a miracle than the altogether unnatural enslavement of any large collection of minds to moral error. What is in a measure true of even scientific judgments, where passion, prejudice and education play so conspicuous a part, becomes absolutely true in question of ethical judgments, based as they are on human nature, and making mute appeal to the God of nature for a share in His own infallibility. Mind is spiritual energy, it does only partial allegiance to matter, and under ordinary circumstances its testimony is unerring in religion, morality and topics with a bearing on these momentous questions. Political economy had little or nothing to do with the growth of Christianity. Christianity swept the world because its principles are true and stand for the right. It grows, and it must grow till the end of time, because its tenets are as indestructible as the truth, on which they are based. Protestantism is wrong; and, not political economy, but the perverseness of men's hearts is its explanation. Its baneful influence was most severely felt in sections of the world where morality was lowest and men's aspirations were grossest. Its first recruits were degenerate priests and nuns, men and women impatient of virtue's restraint; and while its gospel of self-indulgence attracts meaner characters of the sort, its inborn wickedness urges honest and heroic souls to supreme disgust. It is gradually disappearing from the face of the earth, and it is to-day but a mocking shadow of what it was in its origin. In this twentieth century the line of division between Protestantism and paganism is hardly discernible, and it threatens before the century is over to altogether vanish. Individual ownership, rooted in nature, is championed by Christianity, and stands or falls with its supremacy in the world. Collective ownership is as false as Protestantism, and must share its fate. It may hold men's attention for a long or short period of time, it may make conquests in this or that corner of the world; but it can never hope to prove lasting or compass universality. To become socialistic, the world must repudiate nature, God, religion, morality; and that catastrophe can never befall the race.

II. *False in principles, socialism is morally impossible in itself and quite absurd.* Bare mention of the insoluble problems attaching to the scheme, must satisfy the most incredulous about socialism's impossibility as a system. Hard and fast lines would have to be drawn between articles of consumption and articles of production; and the wisdom of Solomon would scarcely suffice for the task. To avoid waste, the quantity and quality of needed products would have to be fixed with some degree of exactness; and the world would hardly contain paper enough for lists. To make wise appointments, the commonwealth would have to get into the closest kind of touch with the inclinations and abilities of its citizens. Change of residence or employment would be out of the question, and men would be as much permanent fixtures as houses or fences. And yet men are not going to lose their love for travel. Some climates, some situations, some skies will always be more appealing than others. Home will be without meaning when house and land are property of the state. Distribution of duties will be a ridiculously wide field for discontent. If everything is left to the free choice of the citizens, there will be a rush for easy and pleasant places. Nobody will want employment of a hard, humble, unhealthy nature. If citizens have no choice in the matter, no more degraded form of slavery can well be conceived. In any event it will be a colossal undertaking to single out the milkmen and miners, factory-hands and farmers, cooks and streetsweepers, nurses and doctors, lawyers and policemen. Incentive to industry will be wanting. Inventive genius will not be cultivated, when the profit accruing from new machinery goes, not to the inventor, but to the people at large. There will be no equality of rights, if some certain men pursue the professions like law, medicine, education; and there will be no professions, unless some certain men pursue them. Professions and trades call for years of training, study and patient exercise; and, if no corresponding reward attaches to this excess of labor, men devoting themselves to the trades and professions will be models of unselfishness. If such rewards are meted out, class distinctions will be inevitable, and the commonwealth will be divided into rich and poor, educated and uneducated, gentle and plebeian, men of brains and men of toil. According to whatever standard products are distributed, innumerable difficulties will arise. If number of heads is the standard, it will be unfair to make no difference between the industrious and lazy, skilled and unskilled, the strong and the weak. If hours of work are the standard, an active workman will produce in a given time twice as much as a lazy workman, and can well be dissatisfied if his reward is the same. If excellence of work is the standard, it will be practically impossible to measure the different degrees in occupations like medicine, law, education, agriculture. If activity is the standard, every workman will have to be under the constant supervision of a dozen or more watchers and measurers. If need is the standard, a whole army of judges will scarcely suffice to determine the peculiar needs of each individual in the commonwealth. With no motive for energetic endeavor, men would discharge their duties in the most perfunctory manner. There would be no family to care for, no provision to make for rainy days. While young and strong, the necessaries of life would be men's daily wages. When old and infirm, their existence would be, to say the least, precarious. Socialists must, besides, have unlimited faith in human nature, when they suppose that officials will measure up to requirements in the matter of prudence, wisdom and honesty; that they will be immune from selfishness, satisfied with their pay, wholly intent on the common good. They credit the common people with no smaller virtue, when they suppose that subjects will dutifully hang on the nod of superiors, experience no pang of greed, and contentedly pass their lives in hard and humble avocations with a view to furthering common prosperity. In Christian communities, where such virtue is promised a surpassing reward, where the opposite vices are threatened with dire disaster, saints of the sort are few and far between, rare enough spectacles to excite comment and wonder.

Absurd, because unworkable—To be a system, it must be workable. Ergo workable and unworkable.

Scholion—Agrarian or Land Socialism.

Henry George, who died in 1897, advocated a modified form of socialism. He wants the state to become owner of such immovable property as land, fields, forests, mines and houses. His followers are styled Land Socialists or Single Taxers. The arguments they employ are nothing worth. In the main they rest their case on these six.

1. History is witness that collective ownership of land originally prevailed everywhere, till violence and fraud substituted the present system of individual ownership.

2. Labor is the single title to individual ownership, and labor cannot produce land.

3. Without collective ownership of land nobody can appropriate to his own use the produce of his labor.

4. Equal right to live postulates equal right to land.

5. The first to enter a theatre has no right to debar later arrivals from sittings.

6. Land owners absorb an undue proportion of the world's wealth—unearned increment.

Answers: 1. History bears opposite witness; and we can appeal to the Hebrews, Assyrians, Egyptians and Chinese, in whose early records no trace of collective ownership in land can be found. Whatever may be the truth regarding early ages, it is certain that civilization stands for individual ownership.

2. This second argument proves too much, and applies as well to movable as to immovable goods. The labor being the same, statues of gold, marble and wood, are of different values. The sculptor's trade would be worthless, unless he owned the material, in which he worked.

3. A man has no right to the produce of a farm, unless the farm belongs to him; but he has a right to wages for the labor exerted in cultivating another's farm.

4. Ownership of land is no requisite for support. Merchants traffic in crops, and make a comfortable living without owning a square inch of ground.

5. The first to enter has a right to debar others from his seat, without preventing others from taking such seats as are empty.

6. These are the equations he uses to prove the undue in-

crease of rent, the unearned increment: Crop = rent plus wages plus interest. Ergo, crop minus rent = wages plus interest. The higher the rent goes, the lower wages and interest fall; and the lower the interest, the smaller becomes the crop's value. He seems to forget that if the crop grows in value as the rent rises, the wages and interest will remain the same, and that a lower rate of interest on a larger principal is equivalent to a high rate of interest on a smaller principal. Five loaves distributed among five men are better than ten loaves distributed among twenty. Similarly, five per cent. of five hundred is greater than ten per cent. of one hundred.

Finally, Land Socialism is morally impossible. All land cannot become the state's exclusive property. Three possible methods of public ownership in land suggest themselves.

1. The state can hold all land as proprietor, and hire men to work it.

2. The state can hold all land, and rent it to tenants.

3. The state can leave individual owners in possession, and exact the equivalent of rent as taxes.

Answer: 1. The first method is condemned by George himself. It would destroy agriculture, encourage idleness in workmen, spoil the land and do away with the whole class of honest farmers, who cling to homesteads and their clustering traditions.

2. The second method would prove no less destructive. Nobody would improve the land on account of uncertain tenure, the soil would be worked to death for large profits within limited periods. No ditches would be dug, no marshes would be drained, rotation of crops would be neglected, no foresight would be used, no expense with an eye to the future would be undergone, and in short order the land would become a barren waste.

3. The third method commends itself to George. He would leave the farmers in possession, and exact from them as taxes that portion of the crop equivalent to rent, making some small allowance from same as incentive to make improvements, better the condition of the land and erect necessary buildings. He thinks that this one source of revenue would meet all the necessary expenses of the government, and would impose no other tribute. Hence his system gets the name of Single

Tax. First of all, it would be difficult to say what proportion of the crop would equal rent; what, wages; and what, interest. If a small bonus were offered farmers, they would grow lazy; if a large bonus were offered, it is hard to see how other taxes could be dispensed with. What has been said of farms can with some unimportant changes be said of real estate in the shape of city sites and residences.

PRINCIPLES

A. *Some Quotations:* "Archbishop Corrigan and Bishop Quigley alike charge Socialism with hostility to religion. These charges are unqualifiedly false, and we challenge their authors to quote one phrase from our party platform, that would in any way tend to support their accusations. They cannot do it, for Socialism has no concern with religion."

—*The Worker*, Mar. 16, 1902.

Answer: Socialism is not to be gotten from the platform of a party in New York; but from the writings of its recognized leaders and exponents. Socialism is international and was never meant to be sectional. Therefore it ought to be the same all over the world; and, if the New Yorkers above quoted want to be considered good Socialists, they must change their manner of talk.

"There is no such thing as European Socialism or American Socialism. There is only one kind of Socialism the world over, International Socialism."

—Haverhill, *Social Democrat*, July 20, 1901.

Now let us hear how Socialists the world over talk about religion:

"The possession of the means of livelihood gives to the capitalists the control of the government, the press, the pulpit, and the schools, and enables them to reduce the workingmen to a state of intellectual, physical and social inferiority, political subservience and virtual slavery."—Socialist Platform.

" Christianity to-day stands for what is lowest and basest in life. Official religion and militarism are the two guardians of capitalism, and the subtle methods of the church in destroying the manhood of the soul and keeping it servile are infinitely more to be dreaded by the socialist movement than the world's standing armies." George D. Herron, in *Advance*.

"How has the ruling class established this control over its members and its slaves? In three ways, through religion, through public opinion, and through the law, with its judges and soldiers. Religion is perhaps the most powerful of these means of maintaining class society, by inducing the members of the subject class to act contrary to their interests and in accordance with that of their masters. Christianity is the most effective of all. It has operated primarily by the offer of rewards in Heaven and the threat of punishment in hell."
—*The People*, New York, Feb. 18, 1900.

"Christianity is a huge and ghastly parasite, consuming billions of treasure out of the labor and the patience of the people, and is supremely interested in keeping the people in economic and spiritual subjection to capitalism. The spiritual deliverance of the race depends on its escape from this parasite. The world must be saved from its salvations."—George D. Herron, in *Worker*, New York, Nov. 10, 1901.

"The truth is, as all thinking men are aware, we have no such thing as intellectual honesty in the sphere of religion. The deity men pray to and exhibit in theology is not a moral being. If ever in the history of the world any human institution was completely and finally discredited, it is the religious institution, whose putrid and decaying carcass here at the beginning of the twentieth century menaces the life of men."—William Thurston Brown of Rochester, in *Socialistic Spirit*, June, 1902.

"The Church is one of the pillars of capitalism, and the true function of the clergy is to chloroform the workers, to make docile wage-slaves of them, patient and contented with their lot in this world while expecting a glorious reward in the next.—Henry Quelch, in the *Social Democrat*, March 15, 1903.

"Christianity is an enemy of liberty and of civilization. It has kept mankind in slavery and oppression. The Church and State have always fraternally united to exploit the people. Christianity and Socialism are like fire and water."—Bebel, 1901.

No Christianity:

"One word on that singular hybrid, the Christian Social-ist. The association of Christianity with any form of So-cialism is a mystery, rivaling the mysterious combination of ethical and other contradictions in the Christian divinity Him-self."—Bax, in "Ethics of Socialism."

"The terrible condition of our poor is due to the two curses of our country and time. These two curses are Capitalism and Christianity."—Dr. Averling, in *To-day*. Free-love hus-band of Karl Marx's daughter. Suicide.

"That familiar fallacy, the ethics of Christianity and So-cialism are identical. It is not true; we do not ourselves in most cases believe it. We repeat it, because it appeals to the slave-mind of the world. There is no wrong, however ter-rible, which has not been justified by Christianity, no move-ment for human liberty which has not been opposed by it.—The *Comrade*, N. Y., May, 1903.

Atheism:

"And while all of us are thus indifferent to the Church, many of us are frankly hostile to her. Marx, Lassalle and Engels, among earlier socialists; Morris, Bax, Hyndman, Guesde, and Bebel, among present-day Socialists, all are more or less avowed atheists; and what is true of the more notable men of the party is almost equally true of the rank and file the world over."—James Leatham, in "Socialism and Char-acter."

"Marx was an avowed atheist."—Dr. Averling, in "Charles Darwin and Karl Marx."

"Religion is a fantastic degradation of human nature."—Karl Marx.

"In politics, the republic; in economy socialism; in reli-gion, atheism."—Bebel.

"As the religion of slave industry was Paganism; as the religion of serfage was Catholic Christianity or Sacerdotal-ism; as the religion of Capitalism is Protestant Christianity or Biblical Dogma; so the religion of collective and coopera-tive industry is Humanism, which is only another name for Socialism."—Bax, in the "Modern Revolution," p. 81.

"The idea of God is the keystone of perverted civilization; the true root of civilization, the true root of liberty, of equality, of culture, is atheism."—Karl Marx, in "Secret Society in Switzerland."

No divinity of Christ:

"Can we keep a picture of Christ in our Socialist headquarters? It can stay, but the picture should be without a halo, and should have the words beneath it: To Christ, who was a man and a martyr to the principle of brotherhood among men."—Oddino Morgari, Turin.

Science and Religion:

"Science and religion are in inverse ratio to each other; the one diminishes and grows weaker in the same proportion that the other increases and grows stronger in its struggle against the unknown." "Under the influence of scientific culture religious convictions will perish by atrophy."—Enrico Ferri.

Free-will and Determinism:

"It is not the conscious mind of man that determines the form of his being, but, vice versa, the social form of his being determines the conscious actions of his mind."—Karl Marx, in "Critique of Political Economy."

Morality without religion:

"We bring back ethics from the clouds. Morals being purely secular in origin and purpose should be kept free from all contact with religion."—Spargo, in "Where we Stand," p. 19.

"Morality and ethics have nothing to do with religion. Fools or hypocrites assert the contrary. They regulate the actions of men towards each other; religion regulates the actions of men towards supernatural beings."—Bebel, in "Woman Past, Present and Future," p. 147.

Free-love:

"Three great obstacles block the path of Social reform: private property, religion, and the present form of marriage."—Frederick Engels.

"Thanks to the wrong conditions of society and the state, woman is to-day without rights and in countless cases is condemned to wedded or unwedded prostitution. The intercourse of the sexes is unnatural and immoral,—socialism will bring the emancipation of woman as well as of man. It will destroy prostitution, whether it walk ashamed under the mantle of marriage for wealth or convenience, or whether it run shameless painted and naked upon the street."—Liebnecht, in "Socialism, What it is." Chicago, Aug. 1, 1901.

"Legalized monogamic marriage and prostitution are based essentially on commercial considerations. The one is purchase, the other is hire."—Bax, in "Outlooks from a New Standpoint."

"The reverence of the bourgeoisie for the monogamic principle now rests almost entirely on the fact, that he objects to being exposed to the danger of having to put his hand in his pocket for the maintenance of his neighbor's children."—Bax, in "Outlooks," p. 151.

P.S. Herron was deposed from the ministry for abandoning his wife and taking a soul-mate. Dr. Averling, already married, lived as a husband with Eleanor Marx, Karl's daughter. When his love grew cold, she drank poison. Averling sex-crazed soon after died.

B. *Encyclical of Pope Leo XIII.* *"The Condition of Labor."* May 15, 1891.

Exordium—Elements of conflict between capital and labor are:

1. Growth of industry
2. Discoveries of science
3. Changed relations of masters and workmen
4. Millionaires and paupers
5. Trusts and labor-unions
6. Irreligion.

Hard to find a remedy because:

1. Guilds are gone
2. Religion is repudiated
3. Usury-sharks are common
4. Monopoly prevails in trade
5. Consolidation of interests fosters giant corporations
6. Contract-labor.

A. *Wrong Remedy*—Socialism—collective ownership of capital in land and money.

1. Socialism hurts labor, because capital is as much a need to workman as it is to his employer. He ought to invest his savings in land and business. Capital is his wages in another shape.

2. Socialism is unjust, because man has natural right to exclusive ownership on account of reason and knowledge of future. Man differs from brute in this that he sees beyond the present, and makes provision for the future.

3. The state has no right to interfere with exclusive ownership, because the individual and his natural right are prior to state.

4. Man has a natural right to whatever he honestly makes his own. By work of body and work of mind he makes land and capital his own. By care and improvements the farmer as truly makes the land as the crop he raises.

5. Mankind approves and has always approved of exclusive ownership, the civil law recognizes and safeguards the right.

6. God in the seventh and tenth commandments forbids interference with the same.

7. Man is free to marry, and exclusive ownership of land and capital is more a need when children put in an appearance.

8. The state must respect family rights because of their precedence in point of time and importance.

9. Socialism cannot legitimately do parents the injustice of robbing them of their children.

10. In short, socialism would prove a heavy curse. It would introduce disturbance, slavery, envy, evil speech, quarrels, poverty, neglect of talent, misery and dishonesty, to say nothing of atheism, anarchy and free-love.

B. *Right Remedy*—Religion—I, Church, aided by II, State.
I. a. The Church is equal to the task.

1. It can do all that its founder accomplished.

2. To attempt to do away with classes in society, would be to quarrel with God and court defeat.

3. To suffer is the lot of humanity, and the poor will be always with us.

4. Hostility between the classes is not a necessity of nature.

b. The Church has efficacious means to destroy hostility, if rich and poor heed her advice.

1. She counsels duty and justice to each class.

2. The workman must scrupulously keep agreements; do no injury to the employer or his property; earn his wages; resort to no violence, riot or disorder; and avoid evil men.

3. The employer must not count his workmen slaves; he must respect them as men and Christians; he must bear in mind that labor is no shame, that it is inhuman to treat men like mere chattels for purposes of gain.

4. Workmen must be allotted time for duties of piety, safeguarded from dangerous occasions. They must not be taxed beyond their strength, and due regard must be had for age and sex in the allotment of tasks. They must not be defrauded of adequate wages, no advantage must be taken of their helplessness. No fraud, or force, or usurious dealings, must be practised by the employer against his workmen.

5. She reminds both classes of the future life awaiting them and of its paramount importance.

6. The rich must use their money with a view to salvation. They are almoners to the poor, and exclusive ownership never excuses them from the duty of sharing their goods with the needy in the name of charity.

7. The poor must be content with the lot of Jesus, Mary and Joseph. They are walking in God's footsteps. Finally, rich and poor alike are sons of God, and in this respect equal.

c. The Church applies the remedies at her disposal with an unerring hand.

1. She educates the world with all the authority of her founder; and while most intent on men's spiritual good, she neglects not their temporal welfare.

2. Deacons were appointed in the early Church to serve at table.

3. The patrimony of the Church was a mammoth poor-fund.

4. Her religious congregations have charity in every form for purpose.

II. The State must cooperate with the Church.

1. Law must consult the moral well-being of subjects, and must be just to all classes. It must safeguard the whole community and its individual parts, rich and poor alike.

2. Law must not unduly interfere with liberty, and undertake only what is required for remedy or removal of danger.

3. Though the rights of all must be religiously respected, the poor are entitled to special consideration. The rich are more able to protect themselves.

4. In behalf of capital, private property must be guaranteed; strikes must on occasions be taken in hand by the law.

5. With regard to workmen, their spiritual and mental interests must be ensured. Man cannot give up his soul to servitude. The law must insist on Sunday as a day of rest, and protect the poor from grasping speculators. Hours, child-labor, woman-labor, are within the province of the law. It must take into account that in all contracts rest for soul and body is a condition expressed or understood.

6. Though wages are largely a matter of free agreement, the law must not allow greedy employers to impose on the poor. Personally, the workman is free to accept or reject terms, but poverty at times reduces him to a state of necessity in the matter of agreement, and the law must keep the employer from forcing unreasonable terms on his workmen. The victim of low wages is oftener than not forced and far from free.

7. The law must encourage economy and ownership among the poor by inculcating thrift. Ownership among the poor has these five excellent results. It brings rich and poor together, it weakens monopoly, it procures abundance and prosperity in state, it fosters love of country and lowers taxation.

8. To cooperate with the State, employers and their workmen must get together. Labor must organize for mutual help. Scripture is warrant for organization. The state must recognize lesser societies, and encourage rather than hamper them. It should interfere only when such societies threaten the common good. It has no rights regarding societies responsible to the Church.

9. Unfortunately for labor, workmen's societies are in the hands of the wicked, and spirited Catholic champions ought to take a strong hand in their affairs.

10. In labor unions piety should not be neglected, officers ought to be prudent and honest. One great need is a committee to settle grievances between workmen and employers.

Peroration:

Early Christians can be incentive to courage. They were poor, but winners. Prejudice and money are in the way of success. Workmen, formerly cowards, will be reclaimed to religion and labor. Religion and her ministers must help.

THESIS VI

The right remedy for labor troubles is union between employers and workmen, based on inequality; consulting the interests of both in such a way, that they enjoy life and its comforts along with freedom and peace. Russo, 178–191.

QUESTION

The labor-question is the social question of the hour. This labor problem, because of its bearing on morality, is as much an affair of the Church as it is of the state. Till this problem is satisfactorily settled, it must remain a menace to the salvation of men's souls; and it is the Church's business to fight every such menace to a finish. All the world is her kingdom, workmen and employers alike belong to her jurisdiction, they are children in her house; and, like a good mother, she must keep down quarrels in the family. Hence her prayer that workmen and employers may come to a swift understanding, settle their mutual differences, and work together in harmony towards salvation. The Church herself cannot settle the problem, the state itself cannot settle the problem. The Church can help, the state can help; but, unless honest cooperation on the part of workmen and employers seconds their efforts, Church and state are practically powerless. The Church can preach, the state can legislate; but their subjects have free wills, and free will is too strong an agency to be overpowered by either a sermon or an army. The man himself holds the single key to the situation. Only the owner of a free will can reduce it to terms, and make it walk right ways with content. When the owner's mind is right, when his will is strong for the good, mistake is a remote possibility; and the grace of God is the one lamp to flood the mind with unerring light, the grace of God is vested with some of God's own omnipotence. This grace can be purchased by prayer. When once workmen do their whole

280

duty by employers, when employers do their whole duty by
workmen, there will be no labor-problem; the industrial world
will be at peace; the time, energy and brains hitherto wasted
in quarrels, wrangles and disputes, will be saved and made
subserve the interests of virtue.

TERMS

Union. The labor-trouble manifests itself in moral unrest,
in mutual hostility between workmen and employers and in
wide fluctuations of wealth. Relations between workmen and
employers constitute a separate branch of rights and duties,
and therefore a distinct branch of Ethics. The workman has
a right to wages from his employer, the employer has a right
to his workman's labor. It is the workman's duty to give
his employer stipulated labor, it is the employer's duty to
give his workman stipulated wages. The relations between
workman and employer have their origin in an onerous or
bilateral contract, creating obligations in the two parties to
the contract.

*This contract is the root of all the trouble in labor-ques-
tions, and modern notions regarding it are at times absurd
and opposed to the natural law.* They restrict the contract
to the workman singly, without taking into account his wife
and children. They reduce the whole question to an effort on
the part of the employer to get the greatest amount of labor
for the smallest possible wages; on the part of the workman,
to get the greatest possible wages for the smallest amount of
labor. They forbid every other consideration to workman
and employer. Every such view of the wage-contract is
wrong on these several counts. It oppresses the poor, and
against all justice forces them to the acceptance of iniquitous
conditions and starvation wages. It promotes strife and
hatred, goading the poor to desperate measures against the
rich. It encourages violence and disorder, inciting the poor
to steal, to wantonly destroy property and to defy the law.
It hurts wife and children. They must work, to supplement
the husband's low wages. No woman can work abroad, and
at the same time properly care for her children. The right
to an education is sacred in boy and girl, and education calls

for years of constant and absorbing toil. It tends to utterly
destroy the family, keeping its members far enough apart to
kill love, and trust, and deep esteem; provoking carelessness
and want of interest in domestic concerns, and leading to
illicit attachments and unnumbered abuses. The Egoism it
encourages threatens the state with disaster, responsible as it
is for the luxury, hardness of heart, absence of charity, wide-
spread corruption, waste of wealth and consequent dishonesty, conspicuous in the rich; and in the poor, hate, desire
of revenge and plunder, ending in theft, robbery and murder.

*Other Reasons for Labor-Troubles, Because Provocative of
Disunion.* Disappearance of guilds, for which labor-unions,
because of irreligion, are no suitable substitute. Every man
for himself, on the pretext of liberty and equality. Wide-
spread use of machinery takes workmen from their homes to
the factory. Speculation, stocks, get-rich-quick concerns, fortunes made and lost in a day. Civil laws dictated by Liberalism; no duties; might over right; opinion of the majority.
Laws of succession, and small holdings. Militarism makes
young men lazy and morally corrupt.

Wrong Remedies

Socialists clamor for equal distribution of profits; workmen and employers on an equality; proportional shares; fixed
wages along with part of profits, cooperative plan; state control, set wages, hours, work for all, right to employment.

Conservative Liberals want books open to state for settlement of wages and share in profits; officials to regulate relations between workmen and employers; alms to the poor out
of taxes, hence progressive taxes. Scientific Liberals or Malthusians advocate limiting number of children in family.

Socialists and Malthusians need no refutation. Conservative Liberals are wrong, their remedies are useless and harmful, because opposed to peace of mind, love and mutual trust,
common prosperity and secure possession of property. The
poor resent favors from the law; favors would be legal obligation, not displays of kindness; distribution would be uniform,
and blind to concrete circumstances; officials would seek their
own advantage; inspectors without number to guard against
graft. Ergo, useless agencies for the promotion of peace and

good will. Harmful because of tendency to Socialism and baneful centralization.

Right Remedy

In the words of our thesis, union between workmen and employers, based on inequality; consulting the interests of both in such a way that they enjoy life and its comforts along with freedom and peace. The remedy we advocate is a restoration of the guilds of the Middle Ages, with what changes present conditions demand. In this union the employer must be superior; the workman, inferior. The workman, however, must in no sense of the word be a mere machine in the hands of his employer for the accumulation of wealth. The employer must in kindness provide for the workingman's needs, and help him in various ways to meet his wants and discharge his different duties. He must not be wholly intent on his own advantage, but consult also the good of his workmen. Workmen must be content with their lot, harboring no desire to better their condition by unfair methods or by taking what belongs to others, all intent on using their own rights, caring for their families, and giving the best in them to their employers.

PROOF

Along with contract regarding labor and wages, by very force of natural law, workmen and employers have respective rights and duties, looking to their mutual peace and advantage. But the union we advocate would secure these rights and duties. Ergo.

With Regard to the Major: Exaggerated individualism is wrong in employers. They are not absolute lords of their own property. God alone enjoys absolute ownership in things. Man's ownership is limited by moral obligations, with a bearing on less fortunate neighbors. One of the means God employs to procure the advantage and comfort of all, is the unequal distribution of wealth prevalent in the world, enabling the wealthy to cooperate with Providence in alleviating the distresses of the poor. Nobody has the right to turn all his wealth to his own exclusive advantage and comfort. Charity never loses its claims on the wealthy, and whatever contracts are made always presuppose in the makers a willingness to discharge their duties and respect the rights of others.

Workmen must avoid whatever savors of socialism, communism or injustice. They have families to support and children to educate. Their wives must not neglect domestic concerns or the duties of motherhood. Their children cannot, before they are sufficiently grown, be subjected to long hours of labor without detriment to their health and education. Workmen must be given abundant opportunity to save their souls by prayer and other practices of piety; and time must be allowed them to discharge this duty. They must be enabled to put by a penny for a rainy day, and so escape starvation when disabled by disease, weakness, or old age. Whatever contract the workman makes presupposes in him the wish to comply with his duties, and means to their fulfilment; and nothing short of force or violence can hinder or impede him in this important matter.

With Regard to the Minor. The union we advocate between workman and employer, far from promoting unfriendliness, would contribute much to peace and prosperity. It would, of course, militate against the accumulation of abnormal fortunes, and so rid the world of whatever sudden reverses and financial upheavals minister to men's sorrow and foment hatred. Employers, therefore, must not unduly tax their workmen's strength, or impose long hours. They must employ women in lighter work, as far as possible in their own homes. They must allow children to work in their factories only when sufficiently grown and sufficiently educated. They must give their workmen a living wage, enabling fathers to support their families without need of hard work on the part of their wives and children. They must keep their hands at work even in business crises and periods of depression, to free them from dread and anxiety when times are busy. They must devise some way of insuring their workmen against accidents like sickness, broken health and old age.

PRINCIPLES

A. *Wages.* Workmen have a right to fair wages, employers must not be plundered. In this labor-question two extremes must be avoided. Socialism exaggerates the workman's rights; wrong political economy, the employer's. Salary is wages agreed upon by contract. This contract between workman and employer is onerous and bilateral, creating in both parties definite rights and obligations. Like all contracts, to be valid, it must be free from deceit, mistake and violence. The employer purchases not only the workman's labor, but all its fruits. Proudhon distinguishes between the workman's labor individually taken, and in gross; giving the employer the first, refusing him the last. Proudhon is wrong for two reasons, 1°. The employer is responsible for his workmen's labor in gross, because he assembles them, he portions out their work, he equips the factory, selects the material, buys machinery, chooses efficient hands, sells the product in season. 2°. The workman's efficiency is limited to his labor individually taken; his labor in gross is due to the employer's industry, and therefore belongs to him. Besides, in time of business depression the loss falls on the employer, not on the workmen. Contraries call for kindred treatment; and, if the loss due to business depression is the employer's burden, the profit due to business prosperity ought to be the employer's reward.

Socialists like to view the contract between workman and employer in the light of a partnership. It is nothing of the kind. It is a pure and simple contract of buying and selling. In partnership profit and loss are shared, in buying and selling no such division has place. In this matter of wages, the mere fact that workman and employer agree on a definite sum of money, is far from settling the whole question. Of course, the workman owns his labor, and can dispose of it as he chooses. Law perhaps never looks beyond, but conscience may still take offense; and conscience has claims on employer and workman alike. Fraud, mistake, violence may influence the terms, and so vitiate the whole transaction. A traveller freely yields up his purse to the highwayman, but he surrenders his money to save his life. In much the same way, the workman may freely contract with his employer for starvation-wages; but, in the event of refusal, death from want may stare himself and his family in the face. He chooses a lesser evil to escape a greater; and employers, who, to strike unfair bargains, take undue advantage of their workmen's helpless-ness, are nothing short of highwaymen. The law protects them, but God has a heavy punishment in store for oppressors of the poor, and for such scoundrels as defraud the laborer of his just wages. In the eyes of the law, if a man wishes to submit to injustice, he may do so. The contract is not void, but voidable. But in the eyes of God the employer, who forces his workman to submit to starvation-wages, is a crim-inal and deserves to be punished.

This other view may help to a clearer understanding of things. In contracts of buying and selling equality, as far as possible, between the thing purchased and its price must be kept. The employer buys his workman's labor, monopolizes his time and strength, cuts him off from other revenues of sup-port, and reduces him to the condition of wearing out his life in his service. In all fairness the workman must get from his employer in return the means needed to sustain his strength, to minister to his declining years, to repair the waste of his own life by the upbringing of children. And this is practically what we mean by a living wage, a minimum wage, a salary enabling the workman, no matter what the nature of his labor, to comfortably support and educate him-self, his wife and several children. Causes without number operate to raise and lower wages, but no reason can per se justify wages less than this minimum or living wage. Jus-tice is hurt by every departure from this rule, and the em-ployer is ordinarily a thief, because he is enriching himself with the goods of others. If workmen and employers could be once gotten to heed these demands of justice, labor trou-bles would be at an end; and, since no outside agency, like the state or law, seems able to bring about this happy con-summation, the solution lies with the workmen and employers themselves; and union between the two for mutual help and support, a deeper reverence for justice and charity in their mutual dealings, are necessary steps in the process.

B. *Unions and Trusts.* Sometimes the workman is to blame for strained relations; at other times, the employer; and in-stead of getting together to settle their differences, they stand farther apart with the help of labor-unions on the one hand, and trusts or monopolies in trade on the other. Labor-unions are meant to save workmen from the rapacity of employers, and they accomplish their purpose by regulating wages and the hours of work a day. Their members are enjoined from giving their services to such employers as refuse to abide by the laws of the union; and thus they hope to put employers of the kind out of business. Employers hit back by a counter combination, refusing to hire union-labor, or maintaining what is called the open shop, where union and non-union labor are indiscriminately employed; and thus they hope to subject the workmen to their own wishes, and nullify the hampering influence of labor-unions. Labor-unions, when no violence or injustice intervenes, are quite legitimate, and ought to be countenanced by the state. What is true of labor-unions is true of trusts and monopolies in trade. What is allowed one workman or one employer is allowed a multitude of either. But certainly one workman is allowed to refuse his services to whatsoever employer, and one employer is allowed to refuse employment to whatsoever workman. Ergo, unions and trusts are quite legitimate. The whole process is the common exercise of a common right. Neither combination hurts the rights of individuals in the other. The purpose of the two is praiseworthy, disposal of their property to best advantage. Besides, men have an inborn leaning towards organization and consolidation of interests. It belongs to the state to safeguard the rights of its citizens, and control of these unions is within the province of government. Labor is the weaker party, as compared with capital, and deserves fuller protection at the hands of the state. Capital has few opponents among writers on political economy. Opponents to labor complain that the methods it employs are inefficacious and productive of evils. Individual workmen, they think, ought to yield to the good of the community at large. Hence, with them, labor-unions ought to be abolished. They ought perhaps to be restrained, but not abolished. Facts prove the efficacy of labor's methods. Times without number employers have yielded to the just demands of their workmen, when threatened by the loss attendant on a walk-out. It is no argument to say that with higher wages prices will be raised to offset the advantage. The raising of prices is no necessary consequence. The employers will simply have to be satisfied

with smaller profits, and enough dealers will always be found
to maintain lower prices.

C. *Strikes.* The loss sustained by workmen in course of a
strike is their own private affair, and no concern of the state.
The state must not unduly meddle with the private affairs of
its citizens, the common good is its whole purpose. Strikes,
no doubt, work harm to employers and others besides the
workmen; but they are not on this account necessarily wrong.
When harm accrues to another from a neighbor's act, no
blame attaches to the neighbor, when he has a perfect right
to put the act in question. The injured party must have a
clear right to restrain the neighbor from said act. A mer-
chant is certainly allowed to divert trade from his rival in
business, so long as he restricts himself to honorable methods.
The workman is clearly within his right, when he refuses to
barter his labor for unsatisfactory wages; and a strike in itself means nothing more. It makes small difference from a
moral point of view whether one man strikes or a whole
union.

When strikers resort to wrong methods, the whole face of
the question is changed; and they ought to be restrained,
without being robbed of their plain right. Their demands
must not be unjust, they must not induce others by force or
violence to quit work, they must have recourse to no lawless
procedure, they must not with violence prevent others from
taking their places. These evils are not of the essence of a
strike, which is mere refusal to work. Strikes must not be
forbidden because they are sometimes attended with evil consequences. That would be poor logic. Abuses in the prosecution of a right must be checked by the state, but the right
itself must be respected. Boards of arbitration appointed by
the state might prove a great help to the solution of this
question. But the one effective remedy for things is a wider
and wider diffusion of religion, and the enthusiastic cultivation of virtue.

SECTION II—DOMESTIC SOCIETY OR THE FAMILY

THESIS VII

*Marriage is honorable and in harmony with man's dignity.
Jouin,* 160–172; *Rickaby,* 263–270.

QUESTION

Society in General. We pass now from man as an individual in his private capacity to man as an individual unit in society. We recognize three kinds of complete societies. They are domestic, civil and ecclesiastical, known as family, state and Church. Society itself in the general acceptation of the word means a union of two or more persons with a common aim or purpose. Such a union necessarily supposes in parties to it an intellect capable of grasping a general good, and a free will able to direct the agent's energies. Society is, therefore, a something proper and limited to rational creatures. Instinct guides brute creation in the performance of works that imitate the unity of design apparent in human society. The characteristic difference between man and brute is thus tersely and beautifully hit off by Lytton in "My Novel"—"The herd of deer shuns the stag that is marked by the gunner, the flock heedeth not the sheep that creeps into the shade to die; but man has joy and sorrow not in himself alone, but in the joy and sorrow of those around him."

Society is made up of two elements. Multitude constitutes only its material or less important factor; its formal being arises from that unity of purpose or harmony of action derived to it from authority. Another item of consequence in the nature of a society is its completeness or incompleteness. The only valid excuse for any society's existence is the definite end or scope it proposes to itself to compass; and this

289

end, whatever it may be, furnishes us with a clew to the rank it can with justice claim in the order of societies. Much, too, depends on the solution of the question of a society's completeness or incompleteness. If complete, it can vindicate to itself a species of independence in its own sphere of activity, and can warn off all intruders. If incomplete, it is essentially dependent on the complete society of which it forms a branch, and cannot with any show of right object to outside interference. A society is complete, if the end it aims at bears a universal aspect, or at least claims some influence over every single energy exerted by members of the society, or is of such a nature that it cannot be classified under any of the purposes for which other complete societies exist. It is incomplete, if the good aimed at is restricted to certain lines, appeals not to all a man's energies but only to one or several, and readily ranges itself under the comprehensive object of some known and complete society. Instances of incomplete societies are a Literary Club, a Reading Circle, a Lyceum, a Business Partnership, Knights of Labor. These several bodies are all intended solely to promote the intellectual, financial and social interests of their members; and, as such, fall under the jurisdiction of that complete society denominated the State.

Only three societies are recognized as complete, the Family, the State and the Church. All three are man's natural guardians from the cradle to the grave in different spheres of activity. The State is a centre, and procures for a man goods pertaining to this life, and apt to suffer loss in his intercourse with his fellows. The family is the doorway to the state, it is the state in germ, and secures to a man the splendid gifts of existence and an education, enabling him to cope with neighbors in the state. The Church, besides promoting peace and civilization in the state, busies itself with concerns of vaster importance, the business of souls with God, the consummation of a happy eternity. The family can be best described as a union of husband, wife and children for mutual assistance, the procreation and education of offspring. It is an institution designed first and foremost for the perpetuation of the species and for the bestowal of that home-training, which rounds out a man's development, without which in spite of State and Church future citizens will necessarily be unfinished and imperfect. Its second scope is the mutual help, assistance and comfort afforded the man and woman thus united; a help, assistance and comfort they cannot legitimately enjoy in any other condition of life. The State is a complete collection of men banded together for the purpose of safeguarding their rights and securing their common good. It secures to men material advantages they could never hope to enjoy in their individual capacities, advantages altogether distinct from such as Church and family confer. The Church is a collection of men banded together for purposes of eternal salvation by profession of one and the same faith, and by participation in the same sacraments, under the rule of duly accredited superiors, especially the Pope of Rome. This is an exact description of the Roman Catholic, the only true Church, as propounded by Cardinal Bellarmine. We strenuously maintain that no other body of men is truly deserving of the name, Church, and regard all the sects as associations far from divine, human institutions subject to the jurisdiction of the several states that countenance their establishment. Every society is, morally speaking and in the eyes of the law, a moral person. Community or singleness of aim makes one the minds and the wills of the individuals, and in the language of philosophy a person is a being possessed of mind and will. Every society is, therefore, from this point of view really and truly vested with rights and amenable to definite duties. The whole difference between an individual and a society is expressed when we say that the individual is a physical person, the society is a moral person.

TERMS

Marriage. The family is compounded of at least two elements, conjugal society and paternal. The first results from union of man and wife, and takes its rise from marriage. The second supposes the advent of children, and regulates the relations between parents and offspring. Marriage may be considered as an act or a state. Taken as an act, marriage is a contract by which a man and woman mutually surrender each to the other the use of their bodies for generative purposes, and bind themselves to live together in unity. Taken as a state, marriage is a union between man and wife with all the characteristics of a life-partnership, a condition of affairs in which two minds have but a single thought, two hearts do beat as one.

Marriage is the plan divine wisdom hit upon for the propagation of the human race, and the traits of the human species are so admirably adapted to the plan that extinction is a very remote possibility. The Creator has fitted the two sexes with physical and moral qualities such that one sex is the complement of the other, one fills the other's needs, and the two united in matrimony come near the perfection of an ideal human being. To secure the preservation of the race, God has implanted in men and women a passionate leaning towards wedlock. He has at the same time denied man characteristic virtues that can be borrowed only from woman. A woman in the same way is something incomplete, unless a man's companionship contributes new perfections to her life. Man has arms and limbs stored with strength, woman is of a more delicate mould. Man's physical force makes him impetuous and brave even to rashness. A woman's bodily weakness renders her slow to violence and timid. Woman's influence curbs man's fiery spirit, man's influence raises woman's courage and allays her fears. Man is quick to think, and rushes to conclusions; woman is slower, and by her deliberateness checks man's mistakes. Man is rough and ungentle, woman is smooth and mild-mannered; and the blending of these opposite qualities results in commendable hardihood and strength of character. Man is impatient in the face of obstacles and difficulties, and if left to himself would dash out his life against them; but woman is patient and longsuffering, and her example is a perpetual incentive to that perseverance, which, combined with energy, is sure to win. Man is something of a stranger to pity and only extreme misery appeals to his attention; woman is all sympathy and awake to every cry of pain or wretchedness. Man is easily dejected and cast down by adversity, woman never parts company with hope, and is a past grand master in the art of comforting and encouraging. We might thus go on indefinitely marking off the traits peculiar to one sex and the other; but from the few hints set down it must be evident that man and woman were meant by Heaven for mutual help and assistance. When they combine forces, they make of what would be two imperfect lives one single power for happiness, good and blessedness. Of course, this desirable turn of events is had only when man and woman in marriage honestly co-operate with God's designs. If His plans are disregarded, marriage can become a positive curse and a heavy misfortune. The worst evil this earth knows is the abuse of a good thing; and marriage is so good a thing that Christ Himself went out of His way to grace a wedding with His presence, and bless it with His first miracle.

Intellectual acumen of very ordinary quality can readily understand what a hell on earth married life can become when accursed of God. The indissolubility of the marriage-tie makes escape impossible. Enforced singleness is the only alternative; and, if offspring has blessed the union, this lone remedy is almost out of the question. A hundred causes are at work after marriage to steal away the allurements, that before the event seemed destined to last forever. Its joys become humdrum and tiresome. The monotony of one person's perpetual company is killing. The partners to the contract, like all mortals, have their faults; and these faults show head with amazing rapidity. Unforeseen difficulties arise, and nothing short of God's grace can keep man and wife to their duties of love, affection and mutual support. If religious need grace to persevere in their heroic purpose, their brothers and sisters in the world need it none the less to live up to their obligations without blame and without reproach.

Marriage is said to be a lottery. Of course, the risks deter very few from choosing the state, and to be unduly influenced by the dangers inseparably connected with it, would be rank cowardice. To adopt the profession of bachelor from baser motives, would be a crime. About celibacy we shall have more to say later. With God's blessing and a fair measure of good will these dangers can be reduced to mere shadows, and everyday experience is standing proof that they need frighten no man of trust and courage.

Neglecting for the present details that belong rather to the province of spiritual advice, common sense vouches for the supreme need of friendliness and love in the man and woman contemplating marriage. Friendliness is the entrance court to love's shrine, and without love marriage must prove a wretched failure. Kindred tastes, kindred studies, kindred pursuits, may indeed produce friendship and agreeable companionship; but without genuine love they cannot serve as solid supports for marriage. The reason is evident. Tastes, studies, pursuits are concerns of the head and hands, they never reach the heart. It is a union that must endure in spite of the senses, in spite of crooked reason, in spite of every conceivable adversary. It is an amalgamation of wills, and a man's will is under control of his heart largely, and love is only another term for the heart's activity.

This love is an elusive thing and hard to analyze. That love lives of beauty seems certain, and beauty is of all degrees and phases. To begin with, there is beauty of body and beauty of soul, and the two are independent possessions. Very few of God's creatures own the combination. Beauty of body most frequently turns the head of its possessor, and makes the soul hideous with pride, unkindness and a host of other vices. Lack of bodily charms concentrates the unfortunate's attention on the cultivation of inner good qualities, with a view to covering outward deficiencies. Since, therefore, this twofold beauty is of rare occurrence in one and the same person, men and women who rush into love must fasten their hearts on one or the other. In choice of an anchor, endurance and strength are deciding characteristics; and as between beauty of body and beauty of soul there can be no quarrel. Growth in years is a condition of our existence, and age develops wrinkles, prime destroyers of fair features. Age bends the body and works sad havoc in its shape. The soul is beyond the reach of time's ravages, and improves like wine with age. Its beauty lasts forever, and hopes tied to it will never slip their moorings. Of course facial attractions are seldom altogether wanting, and lovers have a knack of discovering lines and curves that escape the untutored and uninterested eye.

It is no mistake to look for some attractiveness of form and figure in a future partner. The blunder consists in being blind to everything else, and foolishly expecting love to last after its sole motive has disappeared with the progress of years. Lacordaire has some very striking language on the topic. "Love," he says, "has but one cause, and that cause is beauty. Whenever man is in presence of a nature in which that terrible gift shines, if he be not sheltered by a divine shield, he will feel its power. However stubborn, however proud he may be, he will come like a child to bend at the feet of that something which he has seen and which has subdued him by a look, by a hair of its neck—'in uno crine colli sui'—according to the admirable language of Scripture. Beauty which is the source of love is also the source of the greatest desolation here below, as if Providence and nature repented of having endowed some of us with so rich and rare a gift." Later on, adverting to the beauty rooted in virtue and holiness of life, he says, "Man is invested with a beauty he had not before. But what beauty? If I look upon you, I see no change. Your face is the face I knew yesterday, and you have even lost something in the correctness of the lines of your physiognomy. What new beauty have you then received? Ah, a beauty which leaves you man and is nevertheless divine. Jesus Christ has put upon you His own image; He has touched your soul with His own; He has made of you and Himself one single moral being. It is no longer you; it is He who lives in you. That beauty which the world sees not, we Christians perceive. It pierces through dishonored humanity. We feel it, we seek it. It attracts us, not for a day, like human beauty; but with the indelible charm of eternity. One day, and perhaps soon, that speech which announces doctrine to you will grow dull. Decline draws near to man with rapidity, and brings with itself solitude and oblivion. When that time comes, there will remain to me in your souls only the recollection of an echo. But to me, as to you, in life as in death, the beauty which comes from Christ will remain; His visage which is upon us and the love which springs from it, to gladden us while living and to embalm us in the tomb." Conf. 25.

Honorable means in harmony with man's dignity. Because it is an article of faith with us, and, therefore, a truth contained in revelation, that virginity and celibacy are preferable to wedlock, and that single blessedness is better and hap-

pier than marriage, we Catholics are accused by our enemies
of belittling matrimony, a great sacrament in God's Church.
But the charge is wholly unfounded. In fact, matrimony is
nowhere done so much reverence as in our Church. True,
our priests, in virtue of their calling, are debarred from all
the comforts and solaces of the wedded state. But they make
free choice of the sacrifice with their eyes wide open, and are
by no means forced into the difficulty. Long before ordination they are made acquainted with the sternness of their
vocation, and before they take the final step are unrestrain-
edly free to follow any easier path of duty. Far from dis-
countenancing marriage, priests are the first to urge its advantages on young men and young women so inclined. They
certainly maintain with the Council of Trent that celibacy
or virginity is a more desirable state; but prudently warn
away from these higher fields of virtue souls not manifestly
invited by Heaven. They can appeal to the following facts,
when challenged for proof that Catholicity entertains a higher
and more sacred esteem for matrimony than sects outside of
the true Church. First of all, Catholicity ranks matrimony
one of the seven sacraments. It counts entrance into this
holy state without confession and a clean heart a sacrilege.
It so vindicates matrimony from everything profane, that it
forbids the civil power to touch it. It employs the magnificence of its ritual to deck with all possible grandeur the solemn ceremony. It sets apart a special Mass, special prayers,
special blessings for the occasion. It abominates and anathe-
matizes that plague-sore of modern civilization, that foul
wrong to Christ and His Church, that menace to peace of
families and the life of the state, absolute divorce. The
Church has fought many a battle in history to defend marriage against the attacks of mad fanatics and rebellious heretics. The Manichees were among the first to attack its sacredness. They condemned it as the immediate means of propagating and multiplying original sin. They appealed to passages in St. Paul like the following:

"It is good for a man not to touch a woman." 1 Cor. 7. 1.
"That they also who have wives be as if they had none." 1
Cor. 7. 29. "And they who are in the flesh cannot please
God." Rom. 8. 8.

But the Church for the insults thus offered Christ's doctrine branded them heretics, and the Church's Doctors rid the faithful of uneasiness and doubt by interpreting aright the texts called into question. In reference to the above arguments we say that, regarding the first, God permits the propagation of original sin to avoid extinction of the human race. Regarding the second argument, St. Paul refers to women who are not the wives of the men in question. In reference to the third, St. Paul refers to the married state as being short, and that the end of the world for each individual man is when he dies. Regarding the last, St. Paul is talking about the spirit and the flesh.

PROOFS

1. That is honorable and in harmony with man's dignity, which tallies with the divine decrees and with an inborn inclination rooted in the senses and in reason. But marriage is such. Ergo.

With Regard to the Major. Man's true honor and man's true dignity consist in perfect harmony with his Creator's wishes, and in obedience to legitimate instincts implanted in his bosom. These wishes of the Creator are distinctly legible in His works, these legitimate instincts are keen, and always commend themselves to conscience.

With Regard to the Minor. We gather God's wishes and designs on human nature from arrangements made by His wisdom and plain to the senses. Difference of sex, the whole physiological structure of man and woman, the moral characteristics of the one and the other, are evident signs that God wants them to marry. Man's instinctive inclination to wedlock, approved and encouraged by reason, is another overwhelming motive. The desire is not confined to the lower or sensile faculties of man's nature. Marriage with men is a higher and more ennobling act than intercourse between beasts, than union for mere purposes of pleasure. It is a want which, left unfilled, affects a whole life, and makes that nice balance of qualities already referred to either an absolute impossibility or a tremendous difficulty. Young men and young women, who with the approval of God and religion

do violence to the inclination, and sacrifice on the altar of
God's love the joys, and the comforts, and the hopes, resident
in marriage, are nothing short of heroes and deserve monuments. They have at the hands of Catholics, able to appreciate the motive and the measure of unselfishness displayed, a
reverence, a respect and an affection denied every other acquaintance. His vow of chastity is the secret of the priest's
success with men. The nun's influence on the street, in our
homes, on the battle-field, everywhere, is due to the same
cause. And the day of judgment will reveal the magnanimity of many a man and woman outside of religion, who
from regard for parents or equally high incentives underwent
the martyrdom of distasteful singleness. Many an old maid
would challenge our admiration, if only the secrets of her
heart were laid bare.

2°. Whatever is necessary to the right increase and preservation of the human race, is honorable and in harmony with
man's dignity.

But marriage is such. Ergo.

With Regard to the Major: Man is the pinnacle of creation and the end or wherefore of the whole visible universe.
God, therefore, wishes His most perfect work to prosper and
continue till the consummation of time.

With Regard to the Minor. Marriage is the method by
divine law appointed for the propagation and continuance of
the human species. Man's offspring, because of peculiar conditions, needs during the first period of existence and childhood the fostering care of a mother and the directive energy
of a father. If deprived of this twofold help, children would
grow up too weak and too unable to perform the functions
of moral and physical life. The race would go to ruin and
disappear in a single generation. God has so ordained that
the young of other animals either have no need at all of
parents after birth, or need their assistance for only a limited period. But the child's helplessness makes the presence
of a father and a mother imperatively necessary for years.
It is a remarkable fact, too, that the progeny of the nobler
animals in brute creation imitate more or less in this particular the offspring of men.

Other proofs for believers:

Hebr. 13.4. Marriage honorable in all.
Gen. 2.24. Mark 10.7. A divine institution.
John 2. Christ at Cana.
Eph. 5.25. Dignity of sacrament.
Multiplication of souls for Heaven.

Rickaby, p. 264. If one refuses to eat, nobody can eat for him. If one refuses to propagate race, others can supply. Remote obligation, proximate obligation. If race threatened to become extinct, law against bachelors. Some excused; entirely free; unable to find or to win. Foregoing marriage for purposes of travel, study or devotion can be a good thing. Self-preservation; old without young; winter without spring. The two ways of propagating the race are, marriage and promiscuity of love.

Promiscuity of love is rejected because eventually it would be suicidal, and would lead to infertility, disease; it has been pronounced physiologically impossible because of resulting barrenness.

Furthermore, promiscuity of love is against the two ends of marriage—fides, rational; proles, animal.

The mother imparts love. The father imparts wisdom and firmness. Both manifest interest in the child. There is mutual faith. Plato and Aristotle insist on both, on account of opposite characteristics already noted.

THESIS VIII

Celibacy, when love of virtue is its motive, is more excellent than matrimony. Jouin, 172–174.

TERMS

Celibacy. Word-meaning: Coelibatus or coelebs is from κοιτη, λειπω); or from (coelum, βαινω); or from κοιλιβος = orbatus = orphaned. The two first derivations mean respectively to forego marriage and to journey towards Heaven.

Celibacy and virginity compared. Virginity means integrity, or immunity from pleasures of the flesh. It is twofold, physical and moral.

Moral, or integrity of mind, is purity, chastity, continency, or a habitual state of opposition to thoughts, desires and deeds connected with suggestions of the flesh. Physical virginity is a corresponding condition of body. Celibacy is life outside of the married state, and its patrons are commonly entitled bachelors and maids. God's law and nature's express prohibition against the indulgence of pleasures connected with wedlock, when perpetrated outside of the holy state of marriage, make virginity the only approved course compatible with celibacy. Any departure from this stern law constitutes sin, and any other view of celibacy would be wicked. Hence, though celibacy and virginity are distinct ideas, and of very different objective value, they practically coincide, if men and women want to lead upright lives, in strict conformity with God's wishes and the laws of morality.

Outside of the priesthood and religion, or dedication to God's service by vows, celibacy is always unstable, and remains a matter of choice up to the latest breath of the man or woman preferring the condition. But aspirants to the priesthood, or to the perfection of the religious state, must make up their minds once for all, and abide forever after by the decision. Hope of relief, after the step has been once

300

taken, would rob the sacrifice of half its heroism. The irrevocable nature of the obligations assumed by priests and persons consecrated to God renders their conduct to people outside of the Church, and unacquainted with the workings of God's grace, a mystery offering to their shallow ignorance one only solution, that of broken vows and damnable hypocrisy. Indeed, without supernatural assistance, without the strictest kind of compliance with the rigorous precautions prescribed by the Church, there would in many instances be no other avenue of escape from the difficulties encountered.

Celibacy in the Church of Christ is an assured institution. Since that memorable day the Master said to His puzzled apostles, "He that can take, let him take it," St. Matt. 19.12, multitudes of men and women have heeded the hard counsel, and persevered till death in a life more befitting angelic spirits than bodies of flesh. St. Peter is the only one of the twelve mentioned in the Gospel as married, and tradition is witness that after his call to the ministry he lived apart from his wife. Certainly the custom of clerical celibacy, now and for the past 1500 years universal in the Western Church, dates its origin back to the times of the apostles. The only legislation on this point, explicitly laid down in St. Paul's letters, is a rule to the effect that bishops be men of one wife, i.e., men who never married a second time. But hints about the discipline in use are manifest in Christ's exhortation, Matt. 19.12, in St. Paul's letter, 1 Cor. 7.32, in the Apocalypse, 14.4, "There are eunuchs who have made themselves eunuchs for the kingdom of God." "He that is without a wife is solicitous for the things that belong to the Lord." "These are they who were not defiled with women, for they are virgins."

The primitive Church knew well the secret of strength hidden in the celibacy of the clergy. It appreciated the value of that apostolic freedom, which cannot be hampered by the cares of a family, and took it for granted that God expects from His ambassadors and representatives the service of an undivided heart. The early Christians, with the words of Christ still ringing in their ears, must have regarded continence a diviner gift than marriage, and would not be insensible to the desirableness of this ornament in their priests.

Writers tell us that a marked difference on the score of celibacy existed in the Eastern and Western Churches from the beginning. The Latins always betrayed a decided leaning towards strict celibacy as a profession. We have records to prove that in the fourth century celibacy was of obligation for clerics in the three highest orders of subdeacon, deacon and priest. In the year 305 a council of Spanish and African bishops held at Elvira insisted on the rule, and emphasized its enforcement by new enactments. About the same time, 325, in a council at Nice an attempt to introduce the same law into the Eastern Church was defeated by the efforts of a holy abbot named Paphnucius. There always, however, existed in the East a tradition to the effect that no cleric should marry after admission to orders, and this law is in force with the Greeks to-day. Pope Siricius in the 4th century under pain of excommunication forbade priests of the Latin communion to have intercourse with their wives, and declared the children of such intercourse illegitimate. At Tours in 567 married monks and nuns were visited with excommunication, and their marriages were declared null and void. Among the Greeks the ordinary or secular clergy are not by rule celibates. They must, however, marry before elevation to the priesthood, and on the death of his wife the priest must become a monk. Their bishops are chosen, not from the ranks of the secular clergy, but from among the monks or religious. To obviate the difficulty, students in Greek seminaries leave the house of studies before taking deacon's orders, and return married. They are then ready for ordination to the priesthood, and are free to live with their wives after the ceremony.

Celibacy, as is evident from this circumstance, is a matter of Church discipline, not a restriction imposed on the ministers of the altar by Christ or the Gospel. As such, the law of celibacy could for sufficient reasons be revoked by the Pope to-morrow. But no such calamity is in near prospect. The so-called reformers in 1520 agreed among themselves to preach down celibacy by word and example, as a thing contrary to the natural law; and, like all advocates of theories grateful to human nature and luxury of sense, soon attracted a crowd to their standard. Level headed students of the impious movement, set on foot by these rebels against Church authority, are of opinion that Luther's sensuality had more to do with the revolt than his ambition. It would be sacrilegious and contrary to common sense to imagine that zeal for God's glory had anything to do with the scheme. Monks, and nuns, and priests, who fretted under the discipline of their vows, were only too glad to find an excuse for passion in reform's convenient doctrine. They were only too eager to enroll themselves with these slaves to passion. Why, even in old Greece and old Rome, the priests of the nation were exempt from the penalties inflicted on celibates in every other walk of life. Vestal virgins, recreant to their vow, were burnt to death. No sacrifice, no act of religious worship was considered complete, unless supplemented with a virgin's prayers. Celibacy with Greeks and Romans was invariably accounted the privilege and the duty of the priesthood. The consecration of this condition to persons immediately connected with the service of the gods, is a living index of the sacredness of celibacy, and of its superiority from a religious and moral standpoint over matrimony. It is likewise a tribute from antiquity to the good sense displayed by the Church, in imposing the obligation on her clergy, a sweeping denial of Protestantism's pretensions to piety, and an emphatic proof that the reformers of the sixteenth century were sunk lower in the depths of sensual degradation than the very pagans.

Virtuous Motives. Celibacy, in the words of our thesis, is more excellent than matrimony, only when adopted from virtuous motives. When adopted from sinister designs, to enjoy luxury and dissipation with more freedom, to wallow in unclean pleasure without the care attendant on the raising of a family, it is a crime in the eyes of God and men, deserving of eternal chastisement and the scorn of time. This reflection, no doubt, induced the ancients to enforce against celibacy, outside of the priesthood, the severe penalties in evidence on their statute-books. In Sparta bachelors were reckoned infamous. The law permitted women to seize and torture them in the temple. In Rome they were denied the rights of witnesses, their last wills and testaments were not respected, and they were threatened with horrible torments in the future life. Plato saw fit to insert in the code of law,

304 SPECIAL ETHICS

framed to regulate his imaginary republic, a clause to the effect that citizens not married before 35 years of age should ever after remain ineligible to offices of whatever sort. Writers remark, however, that, with progress in Greece and Rome, celibacy became daily more common. Athletes, scholars and men of various professions were accorded the privilege of enjoying single blessedness unmolested, and were put on a footing with the priesthood in this particular. Philosophers, like the disciples of Pythagoras and Diogenes, always claimed the right to forego marriage for purposes of study, and had their claim allowed.

And now a word about modern celibacy, which threatens to become so serious an evil that some legislators have debated the advisability of imposing a yearly tax on bachelors. Without wishing to range ourselves with Horace's "laudatores temporis acti," we feel prone to acknowledge that marriage has lost on the affections of men and women that hold it had a hundred years ago. In the higher walks of life it is infrequent and oftener unhappy than of yore. In the lower levels of society, barring the setbacks consequent on extreme poverty, marriage holds its own; and, because of the strength locked up in union, will forever retain its charms and attractiveness for the poor. But marriage's losses are perhaps most noticeable in the middle ranks. Men and women comfortably well off and able with ease to live on the products of their own labor, are daily becoming more and more content with themselves, more and more loath to enter into relations of close affinity with others.

The "new woman" is much to blame for the sorry pass to which things are come. She aspires to be in some respects a man. She joins the army of workers, invades the professions, and intrudes herself into employment once considered her brother's peculiar property. Timid man shudders at her energy, and is conscious of a lurking suspicion that marriage would mean for him enthrallment. He knows, and knows instinctively, that God mercifully meant him to be head of the family and his partner's superior in matters domestic. In the good old times women found it pleasant and easy to acknowledge the supremacy of men, and trusted to their native art and sweetness to cajole husbands into a slavery, blissful, because gilded with ignorance. But now the women ambition and fill with more or less success the parts of men, and even if they never resort in matrimony to open handed revolt, are always in a position to unfurl the standard.

One writer contends that solicitude for the support of a family makes marriage particularly injurious to the professions. Lawyers, ministers, judges, statesmen, will be in continual search for the dollar. They will in a mercenary spirit pursue methods, preach sermons, hand down decisions and frame laws, all with a view to coin. They will on occasions yield to the temptation to work along dishonest lines, to do violence to the gospel in reducing Christianity to a minimum of hardship, to accept bribes, and open the palm for lobbyists' money. Their work will certainly not be disinterested; and, when a spirit of self-interest dominates, true work and good results are next to impossible. Domestic felicity is necessarily selfish, celibacy is in the nature of things more open to generous impulses. Men wedded to their profession solely, are capable of larger and better work than men wedded to their profession and a wife. Married men must, if true to their obligations, devote no inconsiderable part of their time and attention to the mistresses of their homes. These suggest themselves as a few of the motives calculated to nowadays frighten men away from matrimony.

Women on their part can afford to be more exacting than formerly in their choice. The new movement in their favor, this modern emancipation of the sex, has thrown open to them many and various avenues for a livelihood. They are in consequence more independent, and less liable to be disappointed, when trusting to their own resources. A woman is, besides, never at a loss to make her habitation put on all the appearance of a home. She is easily man's superior in this respect. A bachelor's apartments never wear anything but the semblance of a den. The newspapers, too, make the proceedings of the divorce court public property; and in nearly every case the woman's wrongs fill a large part of the story. From the sad experience of her sisters every woman knows pretty thoroughly the risks she takes when sealing herself over for better or worse to the amiable tyrant, man.

Thus, the two parties to the contract are thoroughly well advertised of the evils attendant on matrimony, and their dread of the relation rises. The thought robs of some of its humor that title of an old book, "How to be Happy, though Married," and vindicates to Fenelon's description of marriage more common sense than was first granted it, "un etat de tribulation tres penible, auquel il faut se preparer en esprit de penitence, quand on s'y croit appelé." "A state of tribulation, painful in the extreme, for which he who thinks himself called to it must prepare himself in a spirit of penance." But marriage, after all, is an institution of God; and religion can throw round it a halo able to make it a thing of surpassing beauty. All the evils hitherto mentioned are but accidents. They are not inseparably interwoven with marriage. They all take their rise from a mistaken notion of things, and first put in an appearance when the grace of God has abandoned the hearts of man and wife. The sacrament, when worthily received and approached with the proper dispositions, can store two souls with a measure of heavenly strength abundantly able to tide them over all the troubles and trials attached to their station in life. The husband, if docile to the inspirations of grace, will continue to his latest breath what God wants him to be; the wife will prove forever a real helpmate, not a stumbling block; and marriage will assume all the proportions of a magnificent blessing.

There are two kinds of celibacy, virtuous and vicious. Motives make difference. Virtuous has for motive the honor of God, salvation of souls, prayer, study, charity, chastity. Vicious has for motive opportunity to sin with freedom; no watchful eye of wife, wrong company possible, excessive ease and leisure.

More Excellent. The excellence of celibacy is a settled question with Catholics. The Council of Trent defined it against the reformers, and our thesis is a dogma of faith. Here are the exact words of the definition: "If any one presumes to say that the state of marriage is to be preferred before the state of celibacy and virginity, and that to remain in celibacy or virginity is not better and happier than to be joined in wedlock, let him be anathema." Sess. 24. Can. 10.

Theologians remark that the goodness and happiness here

vindicated to celibacy are spiritual, not material, not the result of sensual pleasure. They describe this sort of goodness as union of the soul with God in love, this sort of happiness as the joy resulting to the soul from this union.

The reformers of the sixteenth century were not the first heretics to attack celibacy. One Jovinian, a writer of St. Jerome's time, and condemned by Pope Siricius in 363, waged incessant war against the holy custom. Strange to say, he never himself led a wife to the altar, and lived in open contradiction with his theories. St. Jerome was so vehement in fighting down the influence of Jovinian's pernicious doctrine that his zeal sometimes got the better of his prudence, and he seems to inveigh against matrimony. Luther was pleased to denominate virginity, "unholy superstition, because a manner of worship nowhere countenanced by God." He likewise called it "folly," imagining, no doubt, that every man was as incontinent as himself. The rationalists style virginity, "A horrid monster, destructive of nature."

We must as mere philosophers endeavor to make good our position without reference to the Scriptures as inspired writings. Passages will, however, be cited from their pages, because we must never forget that we are merely assuming the rôle of philosophers, without ever ceasing to be in reality children of Christ's Church and Catholics. The perfection and the blessedness of union with God are not notions beyond the reach of any mind acquainted with our earlier statements concerning man's last end.

PROOFS

1°. In comparison with matrimony, that state is more excellent which has fewer hindrances to union with God and fewer disquieting desires. But celibacy, when love of virtue is its motive, is just such a state. Ergo.

With Regard to the Major: The excellence we vindicate to celibacy in this present proof is made up of moral rectitude and resulting happiness. Union with God is the acme of morality; and desire is the root of unrighteousness, as it is the destruction of union.

With Regard to the Minor: St. Paul urges this advantage—''He that is without a wife is solicitous for the things that belong to the Lord, how he may please God. But he that is with a wife is solicitous for the things of the world, how he may please his wife, and he is divided.'' 1 Cor. 7.32.

Another writer, the author of ''Natural Law in the Spiritual World,'' beautifully shows how attachments of whatever sort are obstacles to the soul's progress towards God. Taking a tree or plant for instance, he derives lessons from the advantages of an environment free from neighboring trees and plants. He finds that the sole excuse for pruning is the circumstance that profitable growth is developed by lopping off superfluous branches, and confining energy to as few centres as possible. Centralization and unity of endeavor are the secret of success in every department of the universe. Attachments are hindrances in the matter of spiritual development. Even harmless friendships are a drain on the soul's vitality, and great saints succeeded where others failed, only because their days knew many a sweet hour hidden with God alone.

2°. A good in the order of virtue is more excellent than a good in the order of nature. But celibacy is a good in the order of virtue; marriage is a good in the order of nature. Ergo.

With Regard to the Major: Virtue is, after all, the only true standard of man's excellence. Exercise of mind and will puts him on a plane outside of and above brute creation, to which he is half-brother.

With Regard to the Minor: Even naturally speaking, celibacy, when prompted by virtue, is heroic; and heroism is the badge of manhood. It is the crowning effort of a mind carried to the highest degree of cultivation, of a will schooled to the limit in mastery of self. The ancients in honoring the Vestals, and setting so much store by the prayer of virgin-maidens, paid homage to the excellence resident in celibacy. Celibacy is altogether an affair of the soul, marriage is largely an affair of the body.

3°. Marriage is largely a process common in effect to man and brute, it is prompted by the animal within us. Celibacy is life in harmony with what is highest and best in us. It is a reminder of the angels. In the words of our Lord, ''in the resurrection they shall neither marry, nor be married; but shall be as the angels of God in Heaven.'' Mt. 22.30.

4°. Pleasures and cares detract from higher interests. Constant endeavor to please one another. Worry and hustle to maintain rank. Education of children. Eagerness for fat inheritances.

PRINCIPLES

A. *St. Thomas. C.G.*

1. Matrimony for good of race, celibacy for good of individual. Ergo.

Answer: What is for good of race need not be executed by each individual. Race will be preserved, even if some refrain from marriage and adopt celibacy, to better pursue other purposes that make for the good of mankind.

2. Organs fashioned, inclinations implanted by God. Ergo.

Answer: This provision was made for the race in general. All have likewise the power to become carpenters and soldiers. Only a certain few follow these employments. Enough will always get married. Self-denial quite as important as enjoyment. Abstine et sustine.

3. Good for one, better for many, best for all. Ergo.

Answer: The eye is better than the foot and yet man is not perfect without the foot. Some must marry, some must remain single.

4. Virtue in moderation, celibacy an extreme. Ergo.

Answer: Extreme all right when it accords with reason. Celibacy accords with reason, though angelic, and above the common measure of men.

5. Concupiscence inflamed, perpetual struggle. Ergo.

Answer: Struggle not so perpetual as family cares. Temptation comes and goes. Every victory weakens passion. Self-denial and practice deaden desire. Marriage encourages the animal and unfits the mind for contemplation. Marriage may be better for this or that individual. Hence, ''he that can take, let him take it.''

6. ''Increase and multiply.'' Gen. 1.28. Ergo.

Answer: Obligation for race in general, I grant. Obligation for individuals, I deny.

N.B. Christ and St. John with many a saint would have

broken the law. The saying can mean a benediction, not an order. Marriage more necessary at the beginning. Hence virginity reserved for Christians. St. Jerome: Matrimony instituted to people the earth; virginity, to people Heaven.

B. 1. Tim. 4.2. Doctrine of devils, forbidding to marry.

Answer: Church never forbids to marry. Men make free choice of celibacy. Church encourages to marry. Men must abide by condition of society they enter.

1 Cor. 7.2. Let every man have his own wife.

Answer: Habeat not ducat, keep not take. Question about men already married; 27. Seek not a wife, no contradiction.

1. Cor. 7.26. For the present necessity, virginity good.

Answer: Necessity means family cares, not end of world. St. Paul is an inspired writer.

1 Cor. 9.5. Power to carry about a woman ($\alpha\delta\epsilon\lambda\phi\eta\nu$ $\gamma\upsilon\nu\alpha\iota\kappa\alpha$ $\pi\epsilon\rho\iota\alpha\gamma\epsilon\iota\nu$).

Answer: St. Paul carried none. Not a wife, but a Christian woman. Holy women in Christ's company. All right among Jews, scandal among Gentiles. Hence St. Paul omitted it. Douay = a woman, a sister; like viri fratres.

THESIS IX

Polygamy, though not against strict natural law, little accords with the same. Jouin, 174–177; Rickaby, 270–274.

QUESTION

The wickedness of an act or state is measured by its departure from right reason. When marriage defeats the purpose for which God instituted the condition, marriage becomes harmful and morally wrong. In the light of our knowledge, God could have had but two chief ends in view in the institution of marriage, the propagation of the race, and the mutual advantage of husband and wife. The first of these motives, far and away the more important, constitutes the primary end of marriage; the other, quite important too, constitutes its secondary motive. Were polygamy opposed to the proper increase of the human family, we should not hesitate to brand the practice a crime against strict natural law. It would seem, however, to fall short of heinousness so grievous, inasmuch as it nowise operates against the due begetting of offspring. The children of such a union have no uncertain father, and the responsibility of support in polygamy, as well as the responsibility of education, attaches to some definite individual. The absence of this feature in polyandry, or life led in common by a woman with several men, renders it peculiarly iniquitous, an open violation of strict natural law. Another particularly obnoxious circumstance inseparable from polyandry, is the consequent barrenness of the woman. Such a state of affairs is nothing short of prostitution; and, while it would be the inevitable outcome, if polygamy once became universal, it would be the logical consequence of that equality, supposed to be in force between man and wife. The sexes are so evenly divided, that in the case of universal polygamy there would not be enough women, and sin would be the only recourse for men strangers to restraint. Besides,

women in this matter of marriage ought to be on an equal
footing with men. If the husband in virtue of marriage has
exclusive rights over the body of the woman, the wife must
be understood to have no less exclusive rights over the body
of the man. Polygamy, however, is an open declaration of
the contrary. It concedes to woman no right of the kind,
and at the same time positively forbids her the measure of
liberty granted the man. She is bound to give him her undivided affection. He is free to parcel out his love as he
sees fit. Only women lost to all sense of decency and self-
respect could for a moment contemplate such degradation;
and polygamy, as a matter of fact, recruits its ranks by
yearly inportations of fallen women from large centres. But
we are anticipating our proofs. We said, when discussing
the natural law, that polygamy was one of the vexed questions in that department of ethics. We then chose that explanation of the natural law, which distinguishes three classes
of sins against the natural law. To refresh the memory, recall what was then said.

TERMS

Polygamy. It is a pretty well settled fact in theology that
monogamy was matrimony's primitive form. An explicit law
restricting a man to one wife occurs nowhere in the early
pages of Holy Scripture. Pope Innocent III, and all Catholics with him, find an implicit declaration of such a law in
Gen. 2.24. Adam is addressing Eve, and he says, "Wherefore a man shall leave father and mother, and shall cleave to
his wife; and they shall be two in one flesh." Pope Innocent sees in this passage a condemnation of polygamy, saying,
"Adam did not say three or more, but two. He did not say,
'shall cleave to his wives, but to his wife,' nor was it ever
lawful for a man to have more than one wife at a time, unless God by express revelation allowed him the privilege."
Many are of opinion that polygamy before the deluge was
neither practised nor lawful. The almost fabulous ages
reached by men of that period rendered the practice quite
unnecessary. God withheld the permission, because fearful
that men would easily come to regard polygamy the natural,

not the exceptional form of marriage. Besides, any wide-spread increase of the human race would have been to little purpose, as nearly all mankind was to perish in the deluge.

Against Calvin, who agreed to regard the patriarchs of the Old Law common sinners, all Catholics maintain that after the deluge, in virtue of a private revelation communicated to Noah and his sons, polygamy became legitimate, and flourished among the chosen people with God's full sanction. The reason assigned by St. Chrysostom and St. Augustine for God's departure from the old rule, was a wish to have the race multiply more rapidly. Some find an objection to Catholic doctrine on this score, in the circumstance that with the patriarchs one woman was called wife, the others were called concubines. But our answer is, that the woman styled wife was singled out from the others for the care and government of the house. Her children were the father's heirs. The others were employed altogether for purposes of generation. Their children were never regarded heirs. This distinction is evident from Gen. 25.6, where Abraham gives all his possessions to Isaac; and to the children of the concubines, gifts. Another objection arises from the rebuke administered to Solomon in 3 Kings 11. for surrounding himself with a multitude of wives. But he sinned by excess in having a thousand. He likewise allowed them to call away his heart from God, and had intercourse with strangers and idolaters, against God's express command to the contrary. About the legitimacy of polygamy among the gentiles, or nations outside of the Hebrew people, writers are divided. Some are of opinion that the practice in their regard never had God's sanction before or after the deluge. Others incline to the theory that God's wishes were communicated to them through the Jews, and polygamy became their privilege after the deluge.

Children of the Catholic Church need not be told that Christ instituted a thorough reform in the marriage laws of the Old Dispensation. Whatever may have been the view entertained of polygamy before His coming, He not only declared sinful, but likewise stamped all unions of the sort null and of no force as marriage-contracts. In the New Law women added to the first and lawful wife deserve only one name, and submit to a life of shame, condemned by the Gos-

pel and common decency. The Anabaptists in the time of
Luther openly defended polygamy as a divine institution.
Luther himself encouraged Philip of Hesse, one of his spiritual children, to keep a second wife in his house for the
fuller satisfaction of his passions. Indeed, Protestantism of
whatever brand, in sanctioning divorce, lends support to a
species of polygamy infinitely more damnable and revolting
than Mormonism or the beastly rites of Zululand. Mormo,
the mythical founder of Mormonism, during his lifetime
strenuously forbade polygamy. One Joseph Smith, a suc-
cessor and real founder, introduced the doctrine after a
dream, which he dignified with the title of a revelation.
There are in our statute-books laws against polygamy; but
they are defeated in Utah by the difficulty of procuring unprejudiced juries, and by the unwillingness of witnesses to
testify against offenders. In countries like Turkey, where
polygamy is the rule and monogamy supposed to be the exception, men with more wives than one are far from numerous.
Only the very rich are able to support a multitude of women;
and poverty, mercifully coming to the assistance of morality,
checks the growth of this shocking crime.

It may be well to pause here for a moment, and set down
some of the reasons usually alleged in favor of the statement,
that monogamy was marriage's primitive form. God furnished Adam with only one Eve; He employed only one rib,
not several. Gen. 2.21. Adam himself, as remarked by Pope
Innocent, voiced God's wishes in the rule, "He shall cleave
to his wife—they shall be two in one flesh." Gen. 2.24. The
Jews themselves always reckoned polygamy a thing out of
harmony, not in accordance, with the law. Noah and his sons
had each a single wife when entering the ark. Job was a
man of one wife. St. Peter, to follow Jesus, left his wife,
not his wives. Nature declares for monogamy, inasmuch as
the ratio of the sexes universally and invariably keeps close
to equality. The small excess of male births observable preserves a balance against the dangers of death by war and
accident, to which men are almost exclusively exposed. Cardinal Bellarmine finds an argument in favor of monogamy
in the Scripture-narrative of Eve's production from the side
of Adam. She had her origin not in his head, to denote her

subjection; not in his feet, to free her from the suspicion of servitude; but in his side, to constitute her man's peer and companion.

The two leading texts of Scripture advanced by the Catholic Church to prove polygamy not only a sin, but also a vain pretense of marriage, a species of adultery, are contained in St. Luke 16.18, and St. Mark, 10.11. The passages are as follows, "Every one that putteth away his wife and marries another committeth adultery against her." The condition of the man who retains his wife and marries another should be no better than that of the man Scripture declares guilty of adultery; because in the one case and the other the foundation for the crime is the same. The first wife, whether put away or retained, remains his lawful wife; and adultery is unchastity between one married and a person not his or her lawful spouse. If, therefore, Christ is authority for the statement that absolute divorce is adultery, He none the less positively declares that polygamy is adultery. He calls things by their right names, He emphatically condemns the one abuse and the other, and He robs of all veneer the revolting crime peculiar to modern fanatics, who seek an excuse for their beastliness in the pages of Holy Writ, and the equally revolting crime of to-day's society, countenanced by the corrupt civil law, encouraged by greedy and unprincipled lawyers, and winked at by creatures of money and fashion, who like to look forward to the time when their own turn to apply for a divorce will come.

PROOFS

That little accords with natural law, which violates the secondary ends of marriage. But polygamy is a thing of the sort. Ergo.

With Regard to the Major: Natural law is the manifestation of God's eternal law, reason is its herald. Nature, or reason, the voice of God, wants us to apply things to their appointed purposes; and marriage is no exception to the rule. Marriage, therefore, when used at all, must be a help to the accomplishment of whatever designs God had in instituting the condition. Reason acquaints us with these designs, and draws marked lines between their relative importance. It recognizes two distinct intrinsic and inborn purposes inseparable from marriage, because essential to its existence. They are the contract and the resulting bond or obligation. It recognizes two other intrinsic or inborn purposes, separable, however, from marriage, because accidental additions to the contract and the resulting bond, marriage's constituent elements. These latter purposes are children and mutual companionship. The extrinsic, accidental purposes of marriage are too numerous to mention. A few of the most important are the help, the comfort, the pleasure derivable from another's labors, consolation, and willingness. These extrinsic purposes are generally entitled the secondary ends of marriage, and it must be plain that any wrong done marriage on their score is little in harmony with natural law. For natural law intends agencies or institutions not only to promote the primary and principal purposes for which they are designed, but also to refrain from putting hindrances in the way of their secondary or less necessary purposes.

With Regard to the Minor: Polygamy certainly offends against these two secondary ends of marriage, the mutual comfort and assistance of husband and wife, and the sensual gratifications, that act as a remedy for the stings of concupiscence. Friendship and love must serve as the foundation for whatever offices of kindness have place between the man and woman, and a friendship embracing equally all the wives is an utter impossibility. In the nature of things, one woman will always be conspicuous in the eyes of the husband, she will be more loved than the others, her children will be more petted than those of the others. The first will surely grow old; and, when ugly and cross, will be transplanted by another. The patriarchs, no doubt, were able to avoid this mistake. But nature in them was helped by the abundant grace of God. They were saints, and stood constant guard against surprises by nature. Their love for their wives leaned on supernatural motives for support, and, as these motives underwent no change with growth in years and loss of physical beauty, their love persevered till death. Besides, God to prosper His own institution was after a manner obliged to see to it that polygamy among the patriarchs worked no such evil results. Now, however, things are different. Polygamy, far from inheriting the blessing of God, rests under the shadow of God's most solemn curse. Small wonder, if it is attended with a thousand inconveniences; small wonder, if corrupt nature wreaks its utmost power for harm on the men and women who embrace the condition in defiance of Heaven. Who will attempt to picture forth the quarrels, hates and complaints sure to occur among the women in polygamy? Why, envy and jealousy at the present time, under the saving rule of monogamy, are the root and cause of family disorders without number. Peace and quiet can hardly take up a permanent abode under a roof that shelters even two jealous women. Durandus urges against our argument the old objection derived from use and abuse. Polygamy, he says, is nowise to blame for the evils, because they are no necessary result of the system, but only an accident. Bellarmine makes apt answer when he says that the non-occurrence of these annoyances in polygamy would be a most miraculous accident. Polygamy, besides, reduces woman to the level of a servant or slave. The inferiority it of necessity imposes upon her contributes largely to the disappearance of true love. When a man is blessed with but one wife, he is eminently careful to keep in her good graces. His wife is as independent as himself, and she can threaten him with punishment, if he persistently misbehaves or refuses point blank to conduct himself properly.

THESIS X

Incomplete divorce, or separation without any attempt to contract a new marriage is sometimes allowable. Complete divorce, or separation affecting the marriage tie, though not evidently opposed to strict natural law in every conceivable case, is nevertheless out of harmony with that secondary law of nature which counsels the proper. Jouin, 177–185; Rickaby, 274–278.

QUESTION

When we deny that absolute divorce is evidently and in every case opposed to strict natural law, we are far from lending favor to this abomination of modern crime and godlessness. We merely acknowledge that emergencies can occur, in which reason, unaided by special light from Heaven, can discover in absolute divorce no open and destructive war with marriage's primary purpose, the due propagation of the species. When we supplement that statement with the other, that it is out of harmony with a secondary law of nature, we at the same time vindicate to God sufficient cause for Gospel legislation against it, and prove human lawmakers, who dare spread its sanction on their statute-books, enemies to the human race and defiant destroyers of morality. For it is God's business, and the business of human lawmakers, to elucidate points just like the present, not evidently contained in strict natural law, but clearly enough prescribed by reason to rob of all excuse legislators who neglect its warnings. Any attempt on the part of civil authority to run counter to such counsels of nature, is open rebellion against God and conscience, and is sure to have for result the anger of morality's avenger and political ruin; disaster here, and hell hereafter. Human law cannot make a wrong of this sort right, and statesmen may legislate till doomsday, courts may forever continue rendering decisions in accordance with empty stat-

318

utes, without ridding of responsibility before God the sly scoundrels, who take advantage of corrupt and vile laws to escape marital obligations; without removing from the hearts of these slaves to passion a lingering dread of future punishment for violation of God's most sacred, most holy institution. Laws conniving at thievery and murder would be hardly more hostile to reason, more ruinous to morality, than the divorce laws at present in use everywhere. These iniquitous devices for the encouragement of evil countenance a polygamy more horrid and revolting than the system in favor with Mormonism. They foster the commission of crimes unfit even for chaste ears, and promote the reign of injustice, cruelty and hardness of heart among men and women alike. Their very existence is a convincing proof, that the sacred condition of marriage will never enjoy the security it ought to possess, until placed entirely and utterly under control of Church jurisdiction. God meant it to be subject only to the touch of His Church, and society is now reaping the harvest of ills sown, when misguided zealots first taught that marriage was a department into which the state could intrude itself. The sons of these fathers may cry out as loud as they will against the dire lengths to which civil authority seems willing to go in the destruction of the marriage bond. But their cries will prove of little avail. The only true remedy for the disorder lies in the full restoration of the rights of the Church over all the details of this great sacrament. Politicians and lawyers are not yet grown the honest and God-fearing men, privileged to handle and regulate so holy a concern as this great sacrament; and their sacrilegious interference leaves spots like the smudge of hell-brands.

TERMS

Divorce. Divortium, the derivative of our English word, is plainly from divertere or divortere, to turn aside; and means journey in a different direction. Divorce is therefore a parting of the ways. The husband and wife break company. He goes to the right, she to the left; and there is an end. Divorce is of two kinds: incomplete and complete. The former, oftener called in Church and law language separation or divorce a mensa et toro, from bed and board, is freedom from the obligation of support and cohabitation. The party, favored with such a decree, while not at liberty to contract a new marriage, is relieved from the burden of expense and disagreeable company. Such a condition has, of course, its drawbacks. It condemns husband and wife to all the unpleasantness of enforced singleness; and often influences them to patch up their differences, and agree to forget the past. It is, when cause is sufficient, entirely legitimate, and the only species of divorce sanctioned by the Gospel and the true Church of Christ. Complete divorce pretends to declare null and void, what God himself by the mouth of Jesus Christ declared forever inviolate. It pretends to loosen a bond or knot that God Himself declared forever in force. It pretends to vest a man or woman, in virtue of a decree made by an irresponsible judge, a usurper, in whom no proper jurisdiction resides, with leave and license to marry two, three, four, twenty times, every single marriage bond remaining intact. It pretends to entrench polygamy, successive if not simultaneous, behind the law; and would make of society, if the instincts of decency were not on occasions stronger than temptation, a veritable pest-house of moral lepers. Briefly, the law of divorce authorizes husband, or wife, or both, for causes listed with a mock gravity in the code, some serious, others trivial, all different in different countries and states, to take new partners, when old grow tiresome, or offensive, or injurious.

History's earliest reference to divorce is contained in Deuteronomy 24.1. Moses enumerates among the laws appointed to govern God's people the following: "If a man take a wife and have her, and she find not favor in his eyes for some uncleanness: he shall write a bill of divorce and shall give it in her hand, and send her out of his house. And when she is departed and marrieth another husband," etc. This law admits of two interpretations, and the doctors of Israel at the time of our Lord's coming were divided into two camps. Some, identifying themselves with the school of Schamai contended that adultery was the only valid excuse for a divorce. Others, belonging to the school of Hillel, maintained that trivial difficulties and disagreements operated to justify a wife's dismissal. If a woman let the broth burn, if the husband found a woman fairer or more to his liking, he was at liberty to send away his first wife, and make room for the second. But the world was 2500 years old when Moses, by reason of their hardness of heart, permitted the Hebrews to put away their wives; and Christ in St. Matthew 19.8 is authority for the statement, that "from the beginning it was not so." We have already seen that God sanctioned polygamy among the patriarchs without at all doing violence to the natural law. He surrounded the exceptional condition with safeguards that effectively hindered the abuses otherwise inseparable from it. God was certainly at liberty to grant the further privilege of divorce to His chosen people, and He was certainly powerful enough, and had enough expedients at His service to render the favor innocuous. In fact, divorce is not far removed from polygamy, and it would be quite natural to expect one permission to follow fast on the heels of the other.

An old historian, Valentinian, dates the first decree of divorce in Roman annals 520 years after the foundation of the city. All through the time of the Empire the abuse steadily grew with the decline of morals, that eventually hastened the downfall of imperial Rome. Cæsar and Pompey availed themselves twice of the right conferred by law. Cicero put aside his first wife, to marry a woman of great wealth, and speedily got rid of her also. The advent of Christianity changed the whole face of things. The Mosaic Law was abolished, and with it polygamy and divorce disappeared from among the people of God. Christ condemned the two practices in no uncertain terms. Christian princes naturally experienced great difficulty in rooting out of the minds of their people prejudices in favor of the old order. They had necessarily to proceed with slow caution, and gradually introduce into the laws of their kingdoms laws subversive of paganism and in full harmony with Gospel morality. But, whatever the nature of their enactments, no argument can be borrowed from them against the assertion, that absolute divorce from the very foundation of the Church became a matter of ancient history and fell into disuse. Certainly, no one could for any cause whatever, in the face of Christ's declaration against divorce, appeal to its protection and retain the name of Christian.

And so, down to our own times Catholicity has unflinchingly kept its arm raised against this relic of Judaism's perverseness, this taint on the escutcheon of pagan Rome's grandeur. One of her Popes could have saved an empire to the faith by weak concession in the matter; but, like Horace's hero, he preferred rather to have the world at his feet in ruins than join hands with iniquity. Surely, the grace of God, and that grand promise made him in the person of St. Peter, could alone carry Pope Clement VII safe through the temptation. The difficulty between Napoleon and Pius VII might also be here discussed. Luther, the head and front of the so-called Reformation, had no such support, and no wonder attaches to his indorsement of the abuse. He had to appeal, in common with the other Reformers, to the Gospels for arguments that gave dubious color to his theories; and, like all false philosophers in a similar position, was not long finding them. He condoned polygamy in Philip of Hesse, "to provide for the welfare of this monster's body and soul, and to bring greater glory to God." He quieted the scruples of priests, monks and nuns, who tired of their vows and sought in matrimony release from their self-imposed bondage. Small wonder, then, if he granted the ordinary faithful, who clamored for recognition in the general distribution of favors, the freedom and license native to absolute divorce.

Protestantism, because without a supreme spiritual head, logically handed over the management of marriage to the tender mercies of the state. Kings, and statesmen, and politicians of every degree of depravity conspired to rob this divine institution of its sacredness; and in Protestant countries marriage is a mockery of the beautiful thing God made it. It is become with them a bare business contract, removed from the jurisdiction of God's visible representative on earth, and subject, like other commercial transactions, to the passions and prejudices of the uninitiated and the profane. The result is that marriage is become an affair of no stability whatever, a companionship, altogether dependent on the shifting whims of men and women. In Prussia, for instance, as late as 1870, drunkenness, extravagance, and, where no children blessed the union, mutual consent, were some among the trivial causes justifying absolute divorce. Till 1857 England acknowledged no absolute divorce. In that year adultery and certain other crimes of great enormity were decreed lawful grounds for action. The Civil Code of France exacted no more serious condition than mutual consent of husband and wife. The legislation was changed in May, 1815, and up to 1870 no absolute divorce was recognized in France.

America is a veritable paradise for discontented couples. Each State has its own catalogue of excuses for the sin of divorce, and the Federal government allows each to go its own chosen way. As matters stand, we are the laughing stock of the nations. Some enthusiasts are of opinion that improvement would result from limiting divorce-legislation to Congress at Washington. Of course, such a procedure would procure uniformity in our marriage-laws; but if this uniformity were based, for instance, on the loose morality that now obtains in Maine, Connecticut, Montana and Illinois, it would prove more of a curse than a blessing. Besides, the individual States are too jealous of their rights to yield without reluctance the advantages pecuniary and otherwise, accruing to them from this traffic in sin. In Maine a divorce may be granted, "when the judge deems it reasonable, and proper, and consistent with peace and morality." In Connecticut, from 1849 to 1878, divorce-law included "general misconduct." In the latter year the rather vague and uncertain term was removed from the list of causes. In Montana divorce may be granted, if the party "leaves the petitioner and the Territory without intention of returning." Utah grants divorce, "when it is proved that parties cannot live together amicably and separation is desired." In Illinois the whole question is left to the discretion of the Court. Indiana follows in her footsteps. New Hampshire decrees divorce, when petitioner proves three years' absence, not heard from. New Jersey, adultery and desertion for three years. New York, adultery alone. South Carolina is the only State in the Union that recognizes no absolute divorce. A law to this effect was enacted in 1878. After a glance at divorce legislation in the different States, one is impressed with the fact that New England and the Northern States are most lax in this regard, while the South leans towards severity. But in virtue of the principle, generally adopted in courts throughout the country, that divorces decreed in one State hold good in every other State, the strictness displayed by this or that State is of very little effect as a hindrance to the spread of divorce and its attendant evils. A bona-fide residence in any State empowers a person to sue for divorce in the name of its particular laws, no matter where the crime charged was committed, no matter where the party against whom proceedings are taken chances to be. The majority of States, New York among others, insist on a residence of one year before filing petition. Some few prescribe two years. Others, like New Jersey in the case of desertion, require three. In other cases New Jersey is satisfied with residence at the time of application. Six months suffice in Arizona, California, Idaho, Nebraska and Wyoming. When other notification of defendant is impossible, publication in the newspapers is, as a rule, valid in law.

The blighting influence of the system on our families and society is bound to grow under the fostering care of greedy lawyers and unprincipled politicians. It is already become a veritable scourge, and honest-minded men of every shade of belief recognize that a halt must soon be called. A writer in the *Princeton Review* 10.39 brands the practice as New England polygamy; and, much to the disadvantage of divorce, draws a striking contrast between it and the polygamy of Utah. Divorce is, in sooth, nothing short of a species of polygamy. The polygamy of Utah is continuous or simultaneous, that of New England is successive or interrupted. But the one as well as the other is nothing short of sinful intercourse with a plurality of wives. In Utah the mode of life is banned by law, and men convicted of adopting it are liable to fine and imprisonment. In New England it is not only lawful, but courts of law devote much of their time to rendering decisions in its favor. Citizens of Utah contract alliances of the kind in secret, behind doors locked and barred against officials and unfriendly witnesses. Divorced men and women wed in the public eye, with a solemnity surpassing in grandeur that which surrounds the weddings of common folk. Church and State lend their august presence to the mock ceremony. The minister is there in robes of office to bless what God in the same instant curses. The court, the highest judicial authority in the land, lends its seal and signature to grace the occasion, and arms the principals with a lengthy document setting forth their emancipation from marital disabilities. In Utah the polygamist considers himself bound in conscience to display some little affection towards deposed rivals for his love, to keep them under his roof, care for their children, and decently inter them when dead. But polygamy in New England imposes no such burdens. It vests the man with full prerogative to heartily hate the spurned and abandoned wife, to cast her into the street, and make what disposition he likes, or is able to make, of the children. Of course, the women in Utah are constant sufferers from the pangs of jealousy; but their pain is lessened, because spread out over a long stretch of time. New England would seem to behave in a tenderer and more merciful way towards the poor victims. The blow is inflicted in a moment, and all is over. If despair and dejection succeed to the hope and prospective cheerfulness that never abandon the Mormon woman, New England is not to blame. That misfortune lies with the deluded fool, who ought to sprinkle her woes with patience and cultivate stoutness of heart. She can, besides, derive comfort from the thought that New England is far more impartial than Utah. The Mormons concede to men alone the right to marry often. Their women are as much bound to rest satisfied with one marriage venture as women in monogamy. Mormonism advocates polygamy; it tolerates no polyandry. But the Puritans distribute their favors with a more even and more open hand. Their sense of fairness and justice, no doubt, influences them to include woman in the general amnesty. Women, therefore, are in New England as free to exchange husbands as men are to exchange wives; and polyandry is the crumbling foundation of tottering Puritanism. Polygamy is, besides, a cheap market-commodity in New England. In Turkey the privilege is so much a luxury that very few are able to avail themselves of it. In Utah it is surrounded with almost the same disadvantages. No inconsiderable sum of money is needed to defray the expenses of a large household of wives and children. But in New England ten dollars or even fewer will tide a man over each new matrimonial venture. A license, a ring and the auspicious presence of a minister or magistrate can be procured for even five dollars.

Another very objectionable feature of divorce-law is the encouragement it offers to crime. Where adultery is the only admissible plea for separation, the man or woman is not long committing the crime. After the necessary sin is committed, he or she rises in open court and unblushingly acknowledges the deed. Witnesses are summoned to narrate all the revolting details of shame, and the court, instead of throwing the self-confessed criminal into jail, makes out for him or her a bill of divorce. Where cruelty must be proved to have the bonds loosed, the dissatisfied party straightway proceeds to make things hot for the other; and, instead of being punished according to deserts, is rewarded with a release. Thus, by a strange perversion, law becomes the aider and abettor of crime, adultery and cruelty go unpunished in courts of justice, and a reward is put on things sinful in the eyes of God and in the eyes of men.

The children of divorced parents start on the journey through life, equipped with grand ideas of human nature. The two beings by God appointed to introduce them into life, and store their minds by maxim and example with principles calculated to guide their future years, teach them from the very outset the doctrine of devils and iniquity. From them these tender and confiding children learn that quarrels, strife and bitterness are the normal condition of human nature. They learn that marriage is a contract of convenience, of binding force only as long as it subserves the ends of luxury and sensuality. The result oftentimes is, that these children, following in the footsteps of their parents, rush into hasty marriages, satisfied that matters can be mended when the emergency arises. And so the evil is propagated; and so the foundations of the family and of society are being gradually loosened. Parental affection is losing its hold on the youth of the land. Mothers are inculcating as a first duty on their daughters hatred of their father. Fathers are impressing their sons with the supreme importance of despising their mother. Parental authority is fast becoming a by-word. Children can hardly learn obedience from masters, whose example is a continual incentive to unease and rebelliousness.

The Catholic Church, the pillar and ground of truth, recognizes no ground for absolute divorce. Its authorities have sometimes decreed the dissolution of apparent marriages, and allowed the parties to the false contract to enter new alliances. But its decisions are always based on reasons antecedent to the marriage in question, not consequent on the same. With God for guide and with the immediate assistance of the Holy Spirit, it counts no marriage at all a union vitiated by any one of the fifteen impediments reckoned invalidating. They are:

1. *Mistake.* $\begin{cases} \text{substantial—person} \\ \text{accidental—qualities} \end{cases}$

natural law.

2. *Condition*—slave and free—ecclesiastical law.

3. *Orders*—priest, deacon, subdeacon—ecclesiastical law.

4. *Relationship.* $\begin{cases} \text{Natural—same blood—direct line, indefinitely—collateral line, to 4th degree.} \\ \text{Spiritual—Baptism and Confirmation—minister and sponsors with child.} \\ \text{Legal—perfect adoption.} \end{cases}$

5. *Crime.* $\begin{cases} \text{Adultery only—real, formal, consummated—promise—during life of both.} \\ \text{Homicide only—conspiracy, intention, death.} \\ \text{Both together.} \end{cases}$

6. *Different worship*—baptized and unbaptized. Mixed marriage, hindering, not invalidating.

7. *Violence*—serious, not light—external and free—unjust, intention.

8. *Bond*—no mere rumor—moral certainty.

9. *Decency*—betrothed to 1st deg.—ratified marriage to 4th.

10. *Age*—12 and 14.

11. *Affinity*—sexual relation with relative. Licit to 4th; illicit to 2nd.

12. *Clandestinity*—Trent—priest and two witnesses.
13. *Impotence*.
14. *Abduction*.
15. *Vow*—solemn.

Four lesser impediments, hindering, not invalidating:

1. *Church law:*
   - particular—priest or bishop—betrothed with another—suspicion—quarrels.
   - general—consent of parents—banns—mixed.
2. *Time*—open and closed—solemnities—Advent to Christmas—Ash Wednesday to Easter.
3. *Betrothal.*
4. *Vow*—simple, not solemn—vow of no marriage, chastity, entering religion, priesthood.

Dispensations:

Four of fifteen from natural law and divine prohibition—no dispensation.

They are:

Relationship, 1st degree in direct line, father, mother, brother, sister; marriage-bond; impotence; mistake.

Other eleven admit of dispensation—difficulties of procuring innumerable.

Many Protestants, lost to all sense of shame, consider marriage an affair of the State exclusively, and pretend to regard divorce granted on whatever plea a legitimate proceeding, that frees the two married persons in the sight of God from all mutual obligations, and empowers them to form new alliances. Dean Mansel, p. 102, says: "The Church of England has never authoritatively sanctioned any other separation than that a mensa et toro; and this with an express prohibition of remarriage (Canon 107)." "In practice this legislation is neglected." Knabenbauer, in Matthaeum, 229. Others among them recognize only one legitimate excuse for divorce, and that is adultery. They profess to found their doctrine on words contained in St. Matthew 5.32 and 19.9. "Whosoever shall put away his wife, excepting the cause of fornication, maketh her to commit adultery." "Whosoever shall put away his wife, except it be for fornication, and shall marry another, committeth adultery.'' Before discussing these two passages, it may be well to set down St. Mark's and St. Luke's renderings of the same doctrine and St. Paul's references to the same. ''Whosoever shall put away his wife and marry another, committeth adultery against her.'' St. Mark 10.11. ''Every one that putteth away his wife and marrieth another, committeth adultery; and he that marrieth her that is put away from her husband, committeth adultery.'' St. Luke 16.18. ''Therefore, while her husband liveth she shall be called an adulteress, if she be with another man.'' Rom. 7.3. ''Not I, but the Lord commandeth that the wife depart not from her husband. And if she depart, that she remain unmarried or be reconciled to her husband.'' 1 Cor. 7.10. The words of St. Mark and St. Luke certainly make no allusion to adultery or anything else as motive for absolute divorce. They are nevertheless as reliable witnesses to the truth as St. Matthew; and could not possibly have omitted so important a point in Christ's doctrine. St. Paul is likewise no authority for absolute divorce. He is plainly for the perpetual indissolubility of marriage, and hints at only one species of lawful separation, imperfect, or partial divorce, without any attempt to contract new alliances. Whatever difficulty, therefore, attaches to the words of St. Matthew ought to be settled without injury to the expressions contained in the other Evangelists and in St. Paul's Epistles. A reconciliation of the various texts is quite possible, and that reconciliation is had in the doctrine propounded by the Catholic Church. According to this doctrine, St. Matthew introduces adultery as a seeming exception to the indissolubility of marriage, but only as a legitimate plea for partial divorce, or separation a mensa et toro. In this sense, the man who lives apart from his wife for any reason save that of adultery or its equivalent, is responsible before God for the sins she will almost surely commit because of the violent temptations to which in consequence of past habits she will necessarily be exposed. He will be the indirect cause of her crimes, and will, therefore, be guilty of her adultery in cause or indirectly. Whoever attempts to marry a wife thus put away commits adultery formally. Whoever after dismissing his wife, even for adultery, attempts to marry another, commits adultery formally.

All tradition is with Catholicity in this interpretation of the text, and absolute divorce properly so called was an abuse introduced into the Scriptures by the so-called reformers. The different stands taken by Catholicity and Protestantism in this matter of divorce, due entirely to the sense laid on a sentence in St. Matthew's Gospel, are only another proof of how necessary a requisite for religion is the establishment of a final court, beyond which in the settlement of Scriptural disputes there can be no appeal. The large part that tradition must likewise play in the formation of belief is also brought into conspicuous notice. The text in question, besides the interpretation forced upon it by Protestanism, admits of at least seven others, all decidedly opposed to the theory of absolute divorce. Of these, the first four can be with difficulty defended. We prefer to reject them. Two others we admit, without adopting. The last or seventh we prefer, as most in accordance with the context, and the surroundings in which Christ gave utterance to the words.

The first opinion maintains that Christ busied Himself on this occasion in explaining the Old Law for the benefit of the Jews present. The New Law was not yet in full force, and He availed Himself of chances to explain it in private. According to the Old Law, when adultery intervened, no difficulty presented itself, because the woman was sentenced to immediate death by stoning, and death of course dissolves the marriage bond.

The second opinion holds that Christ wished the old permission concerning absolute divorce to continue during the short period of transition from Judaism to Christianity.

Dix and Dollinger are authority for the third opinion, that Christ called attention to an impediment, considered invalidating among the Jews, viz., sins of impurity committed before marriage.

The fourth opinion, adopted by no less learned a person than Pope Innocent III, has more weight in its favor. It makes Christ's declaration a withdrawal of the ancient privilege enjoyed by the Jews, that, namely, of issuing to their adulterous wives a bill of divorce. This opinion, therefore, makes the words of Christ as recorded by St. Matthew read as follows, "Whosoever shall put away his wife, excepting even the cause of fornication, and shall marry another, committeth adultery," etc.

The fifth opinion is ascribed to a pupil of Cardinal Patrizi, himself an eminent exponent of Holy Scripture. This pupil communicated his lights to the cardinal, who at once adopted the explanation offered, and made it his own. It makes the seeming exception introduced by Christ turn on the concubinage of Herod and Herodias. This Herod had taken to wife Herodias, the spouse of his brother; and St. John the Baptist, the Lord's precursor, had met his death for upbraiding the prince with his incestuous marriage. Christ was at the time of the discourse in Herod's dominion, and took advantage, according to the opinion, to administer another rebuke to his sinfulness. He says, therefore, in as many words, "I except the case of Herod and Herodias. They ought to be separated, because they are living in open concubinage."

St. Augustine (de adult. conj. lib. 1, cc. 9.11) adopts and strenuously advocates the sixth opinion, and his authority is of the utmost weight in matters Scriptural. He takes the exceptional clause for an intimation that Christ wishes to altogether prescind from the question of an adulterous woman's dismissal. He knew the Jewish prejudices in favor of the Mosaic bill of divorce, He knew the determination of His questioners, the Pharisees, to entrap Him, if possible, in a statement at open variance with the Mosaic Law, and to avoid danger He answers that divorce is nowise permissible outside of adultery. The case of adultery, for reasons of prudence, He declines to discuss. In this opinion, He was asked if divorce was at all permissible. He makes direct answer with regard to every conceivable plea, adultery alone excepted. About adultery He preserves silence. Protestantism can derive no comfort from this interpretation. It would be highly wrong to argue thus, "Outside of adultery divorce is unlawful. Ergo in case of adultery divorce is lawful."

Our interpretation, in most general use nowadays, supposes Christ to distinguish between perfect and imperfect divorce, and to lay down the whole Catholic law concerning each species. With regard to imperfect divorce, He allows separation from bed and board only in the event of adultery or its equivalent, and burdens with the woman's consequent sin the conscience of whatever man sends his wife away for any lesser cause. With regard to perfect divorce, or absolute dissolution of the marriage tie, He denies its existence, and proclaims every union founded on such divorce sheer adultery. The words contained in St. Matthew 5.32, hardly admit of doubt, "Whosoever shall put away his wife, excepting the cause of fornication, maketh her to commit adultery, and he that shall marry her that is put away committeth adultery." The words contained in St. Matthew 19.9 are a little less obvious, and the dispute generally centres round them. "Whosoever shall put away his wife, except it be for fornication, and shall marry another, committeth adultery; and he that shall marry her that is put away committeth adultery." Protestants want the exceptive clause to be repeated, so that the text may read thuswise, "Whosoever shall put away his wife, except it be for fornication, committeth adultery; and whoever shall marry another, unless she has been put away for fornication, committeth adultery." Protestants have for this arbitrary repetition of the exceptive clause no conceivable authority in grammar, or logic, or context. In a proposition of the kind, when a double subject enters, the exception does not necessarily affect the second of the two members. Instances without number could be cited in proof of the exact contrary. "Whoever kills another, except in case of self-defense, and whoever robs his victim is guilty of sin." "Whoever strikes another, unless unjustly attacked, and whoever blasphemes his assailant is guilty of sin." "The executioners of Jesus, unless excused by ignorance, and His blasphemers were guilty of sin." The whole context bearing on the passage under consideration, the circumstances of time and place and the characteristics of the listeners, are emphatically in favor of our interpretation. Christ expressly revokes the Mosaic privilege, conferred on the woman by the bill of divorce. The bill of divorce was granted solely with a view to rendering her eligible for future marriage. In declaring that the man who marries a woman put away commits adultery, He clearly maintains that she still remains the lawful wife of her first husband. Adultery can have no other meaning. If the marriage were dissolved by her sin of adultery, and Christ wished to deprive her, by way of punishment, of the freedom granted her wronged husband, He would call her second attempt at marriage by some other name than that of adultery. Adultery means impurity in married persons.

Returning again to theology's views on the indissolubility of marriage, we can enunciate everything in this short thesis, "By divine law matrimony, whether between believers or unbelievers, whether consummated or not, is in every case intrinsically indissoluble, i.e., dissolution or divorce is absolutely outside the power of the contracting parties. Matrimony between believers, if consummated, and between unbelievers as long as neither husband nor wife receives Baptism, is besides extrinsically indissoluble, i.e., dissolution or divorce is outside the power of any being or authority under Heaven, and adultery makes no change in the law." Matrimony's intrinsic indissolubility is evident from St. Mark 10.11—St. Luke 16.18—Rom. 7.3—1 Cor. 7.11. St. Matthew is likewise a witness to the same truth in 5.32 and 19.9; but his testimony is somewhat obscure. Church writers say that he introduced the exceptive clause, permitting partial or incomplete separation, i.e., from bed and board, out of deference to the Hebrews for whom he composed his Gospel. These Hebrews, accustomed as they were to the bill of divorce, naturally looked for some loophole of escape from matrimony's iron-bound indissolubility in the New Law. St. Matthew with Christ's sanction offered them the alleviation of partial or incomplete divorce. The other two Evangelists, St. Mark and St. Luke, writing for the Gentiles, men without Jewish prejudices, thought the concession of too small moment to mention it. If Christ had in mind absolute divorce, St. Mark and St. Luke would have done the Gentiles a heavy wrong in hiding from them so sweeping and so all important a permission.

From the passages cited it must be plain that matrimony is so indissoluble that new nuptials cannot be contracted without adultery, and union with a second partner during the lifetime of the first is adultery, only in the supposition that the first partner forever remains husband or wife, as the case may be. Nothing short of the clearest evidence, gathered from the context or some different Scripture, or the nature of things, will justify the establishment of an exception to this universal law. The entire context of the three Evangelists is plainly against any such exception. Christ in every neighboring line is talking of the unity of marriage, its obligation of inseparability, e.g., St. Mark 10.9—10.8—10.6—10.7—10.5. The murmur of discontent or disapproval is a remarkable indication in St. Matthew 19.10. It is a well known fact that there were two schools among the Hebrews, each entertaining its own views with regard to reasons justifying the issuance of a bill of divorce. One school, that of Schamai, rated adultery alone or its equivalent justifiable excuse. The other, that of Hillel, rated any trivial cause of discontent ground sufficient. It is more than probable that the apostles belonged to the school of strict rigidity, and would have had little fault to find with Christ's new legislation, unless it decreed adultery itself no valid pretext for divorce.

In the opinion current among Protestants Christ left the indissolubility of marriage just where He found it, and did nothing to provoke a murmur among the followers of Schamai. About different Scriptures, it would be absurd to think that St. Mark and St. Luke composed their Gospels in such a way that their readers to understand would have to consult St. Matthew. In matters less important they might of course have omitted here and there points that seemed to them superfluous; but this privilege of absolute divorce could hardly appear to them too insignificant a thing to be neglected. Besides, all the verses preceding and following the disputed verse in St. Matthew leave no room for the exception in favor of adultery read into Scripture by Protestantism. Such an exception is justifiable only when the passage in question admits of no other possible meaning. We have already seen seven different meanings, each of which admirably fits the words and admits of defense. Last of all, everybody admits that St. Matthew in these particular passages is obscure and hard to understand. St. Mark and St. Luke are on the contrary clear as crystal, and impress the mind with their simplicity. It is against all rules of interpretation to endeavor to fix the meaning of simple and straightforward statements by reference to statements that are intricate and involved. St. Matthew should, therefore, be elucidated with light borrowed from St. Mark and St. Luke; and any contrary method merits the contempt of scholars.

In the nature of things, or viewing the matter in the light of common sense, the weight of argument is with Catholicity and overwhelmingly against Protestantism's flimsy pretext for divorce. Reason rebels against any enactment liable to promote the spread of adultery. And Christ would be promulgating just such an enactment, if He sanctioned absolute divorce in the case of even so detestable an evil as marital unfaithfulness. The divorced woman, often the guilty partner, would be free to marry again, and would thus enjoy a privilege denied some pious sister, deserted by a worthless husband. The result of such legislation could inevitably be nothing short of the multiplication of unlawful attachments and sinful intercourse. Divorce would be a reward reserved exclusively for adulterous women. Dissatisfied mates would, and dissatisfied mates do, commit adultery with the openly avowed purpose of rendering the law of divorce operative. The law of Christ would be more favorable to the growth of adultery than the Mosaic Law. Moses visited the adulteress with death by choking or stoning. Were Christ's law what Protestantism makes it, she would be at liberty after her crime to seek comfort in new nuptials.

St. Paul, in 1 Cor. 7, treats in detail and explicitly the subject of marriage, and therefore, we can trust, delivers himself of the whole truth. In verse 10 he says, "the Lord commandeth that the wife depart not from her husband. And if she depart, that she remain unmarried or be reconciled to her husband." Plainly, there is question here of separation founded on a solid title, on the adultery of the husband. Were the woman's departure justified by no such reason, St. Paul would be the first to urge her immediate return. When, therefore, he counsels her to remain unmarried, and solemnly declares that singleness or reconciliation is the only course sanctioned by God's law, he necessarily understood adultery to be no ground at all for absolute divorce. If the husband's adultery destroyed the marriage bond, the

wife could with perfect freedom contract a new alliance.
Again, in Rom. 7.3, St. Paul gives advice wholly incompatible
with modern notions of divorce. ''Whilst her husband liveth, she shall be called an adulteress, if she be with another
man.'' This rule is absolute, hedged round about with no
conditions or exceptions; and is only another index of how
Christ wants the exceptive clause in St. Matthew to be interpreted. Death, and death alone, can invest the surviving
partner with the right to enter a second marriage.

The Catholic Church, therefore, can never recognize the
validity of an absolute divorce, decreed by the civil court.
It forever considers divorced men and women as truly married, as much husband and wife as they were before the State
interfered; and never reckons them capable of receiving this
sacrament anew. The customs and laws of our country make
it more or less necessary for Catholic judges and Catholic
lawyers to conduct business on lines opposed to the spirit and
principles of their Church.

About judges, obliged by their office to decree absolute divorce, there can be no great difficulty. They are chosen or
appointed to decide according to evidence and the law of the
land, and if unfaithful to their duty would have to relinquish
their position. They can without scruple of conscience issue
such decrees, though they inwardly know that before God
their decision is far from annulling the marriage contract.
All this is true, even if the judge knows to a certainty that
the parties concerned are determined to avail themselves of
all the privileges allowed by the law. Such a judge lends no
formal cooperation to the sinful acts liable to result from
his judicial action. He brings no influence to bear on the
iniquitous intentions of the divorced parties. On the contrary, he deprecates their conduct, and sincerely hopes that
they will consider the divorce mere separation from bed and
board, and act accordingly. Even Catholics are at liberty to
take advantage of whatever temporal benefits may accrue
from what the State calls an absolute bill of divorce a vinculo;
but this must be done always with the understanding that before God the marriage remains intact till death, and precludes
all possibility of wedding another during the lifetime of
either.

Catholic lawyers are more open to blame in this matter of divorce than Catholic judges. The lawyer enters more actively into the designs of his client than the judge; and is, therefore, permitted only what the client himself can with a safe conscience attempt. He can without sin push a divorce case, when aware that the marriage attacked was never, on account of some invalidity, a marriage at all, or when the person he aids intends to seek only the temporal redress derivable from incomplete divorce. If he knows for certain that his client is set on marrying anew, after the decree is secured, he cannot with a safe conscience handle the case. Only certain and sure knowledge of the client's unholy intention can create in the lawyer this serious obligation of non-interference. Mere rumors, guesses, suspicions are of no weight.

No one can, of course, deny that our Church's refusal to acknowledge absolute divorce is attended with many evils for unhappy couples. It is a law opposed apparently to human liberty, to the principal end of marriage, and to the happiness of many a man and many a woman. And yet all laws are framed with a view to that principle held holy and sacred in legislation, ''Law has for primary object the good of the whole community or multitude, not the particular good of this or that individual.'' Whilst peremptory denial of the legality of absolute divorce hurts few or many individuals, it nevertheless operates as a salutary check on evils innumerable in the community. Husbands and wives are bound to swallow their griefs in silence and make little of ordinary difficulties, when they know that they are hopelessly debarred from relief, offered by the State's loose enactments concerning divorce. Besides, law of its very nature restricts human liberty, and keeps it within the bounds that separate it from license. Whatever injury Church legislation does marriage's principal end, the propagation of children or human happiness, is merely accidental, indirect and confined to a small number of individuals. Its beneficial effects, on the contrary, are inestimable, and far in excess of the inconveniences it occasions; and in the field of legislation general or public good is the thing of importance.

DIVISION

THREE PARTS—I, II, III

I.   Incomplete divorce, allowable.
II. Complete divorce, not evidently and in every conceivable case against strict natural law.
III. Complete divorce, always against secondary law of nature.

PROOFS

I. In marriage that is allowable, which, resulting in no permanent or undeserved evil, procures peace for the innocent, punishes the guilty, and promotes contentment. But incomplete divorce, or temporary separation, is sometimes a thing of the sort. Ergo.

With Regard to the Major: A lasting and unbroken union is of course very desirable in marriage; but disagreements are likely to arise in married life, and render such a union quite out of the question. One party to the contract may behave so scandalously that the severest sort of punishment must be employed against him. In such circumstances every legitimate channel of relief must be available, and every penalty short of dissolution must be put at the disposal of the innocent. Dissolution itself, were it not for higher reasons condemned by God Himself, would not be too severe a measure in certain emergencies.

With Regard to the Minor: Love may grow cold and fall to intensest hate. Husband and wife cannot in this sad turn of events safely live together under the same roof. Temporary separation may work a change in their dispositions, and, when out of one another's sight for a while, the old love may be renewed and former relations may be resumed with pleasure and content. Reconciliations and lifelong happiness are often the consequences of temporary separation. Adultery, continued abandonment and persecution are grievous crimes against the innocent partner, and no penalty short of temporary separation is commensurable with the wrong done.

II. Complete divorce, not evidently against strict natural law.

Evils forbidden by strict natural law are threefold:

(a) things wrong in themselves, and on their own account.

(b) things wrong in themselves, not on their own account, but on account of some violated right.

(c) things wrong in themselves, not on their own account, but on account of danger connected with them.

But complete divorce is not evidently and in every conceivable case evil in any of these three ways. Ergo.

(a) No one contends that divorce is as much an evil as blasphemy. We have historical evidence of the fact that God once sanctioned absolute divorce. His approval of blasphemy, if such a thing were possible, would not relieve the act of its inherent sinfulness.

(b) The right violated by divorce would belong to God, or husband and wife, or children of the marriage, or society. God's right in the premises would be made manifest by revelation, and natural philosophy is a stranger to revelation. Husband and wife could agree to forego whatever rights divorce would jeopardize. Some unions are never blessed with children, and divorce would not act against children already grown up and freed from parental authority. Society could likewise surrender all rights endangered by the practice, and to-day society practically surrenders these rights. Therefore, the wickedness of divorce is not evidently and in every case derivable from a violated right.

(c) Dangers, likely to arise from abuse of the privilege, could be reduced to mere shadows, by restricting its use to such exceptionally rare accidents as, for instance, barrenness, leprosy, impotence. Danger, then, is not an element everywhere and evidently apparent in the institution of divorce.

III. Complete divorce is out of harmony with that secondary law of nature, which counsels the proper. Everything opposed to the best interests of marriage and a hindrance to the easy accomplishment of marriage's purpose is out of harmony with that secondary law of nature which counsels the proper. But absolute divorce is a thing of the sort. Ergo.

With Regard to the Major: Nature is a jealous guardian

of the right; and reason, her herald, is loud against not only open violations of her plainest laws, but also those lesser evils that threaten harm to her beneficent plans. Absolute divorce hurts marriage in four very vital particulars, and, apart even from the heavy condemnation of God, has nothing to recommend it to the mind of the philosopher.

With Regard to the Minor: These four vital particulars are:

    a. Mutual friendliness between husband and wife.

    b. Education of their offspring.

    c. Woman's happiness.

    d. The good of society.

    a. The mere possibility, the remote danger of one day dissolving partnership, weakens and robs of its chief charm, the friendship peculiarly characteristic of wedded life. Friendship is measured by its lasting qualities, and divorce is an enemy to conjugal steadfastness. Distrust is sure to poison every marriage contracted with the understanding that divorce is feasible. The woman will labor under a continual suspicion that the man is casting glances in another direction, and that freedom of confidence so essential to the happiness of married life will be entirely wanting. Some wives have been known to accumulate hidden wealth in preparation for emergencies created by the iniquitous law of divorce. Faithfulness which should be above suspicion is endangered. Wicked companionship with loose friends is rendered easy and possible. Unholy liberties are encouraged, and forbidden loves spring up in the hearts of the dissatisfied. Kent, a man of world-wide reputation in the domain of law, is authority for the statement, that adultery is full often committed to secure a decree of divorce. Mutual forbearance and patience with one another's faults have small or no ground for exercise. Absolute divorce provides the quarrelsome with a readier and more sweeping remedy. That prudence and caution, absolutely necessary for guidance in so serious and solemn a step, are utterly neglected. Young men and young women rush into marriage, satisfied that they can call the bargain off, if unforeseen difficulties arise.

    b. The education of children born to divorced couples must be sadly defective. To be complete, this education must be at the same time intellectual, moral, and physical. To be well balanced, it must be managed by father and mother alike. When this education is finished, the woman is so far on in years that divorce must prove for her injurious in the extreme and peculiarly aggravating. Children should, besides, learn from their parents that love and respect for father and mother, which are the crowning glory of childhood. Divorced fathers and mothers can hardly inspire their children with any such feelings of love and reverence. The child will necessarily side with either father or mother, and entertain a deadly hatred for one of the two or both.

c. In divorce woman is the sufferer. Dread of the untoward event can haunt her like a gaunt spectre. And when the step is taken, she is more at the mercy of fortune than the man. He is hale, hearty and accustomed to work. He can, besides, find new admirers with much more facility than the abandoned woman. A divorced woman, as some writer says, has far fewer attractions than a widow. Marriage on this account ceases to be a fair and equal contract. The woman, when divorce ensues, necessarily starts on an inferior footing. She has lost her virginity, her youth, her beauty, her reputation and good esteem. Men are slower to lose their attractive qualities than women. This unfair advantage procured by divorce to men, moved another writer, no doubt, to say that marriage is a partnership entered into for the exclusive utility of one of the partners.

d. One of the happy consequences, resulting to society from marriage, is the union and harmony promoted among families and their different members. St. Augustine is of opinion that nature forbids marriage between relatives primarily to tighten the bonds of friendship between individuals of the race, not otherwise united. Relatives are already close enough together without the addition of any further ties of union. Divorce breaks up families. It nourishes lasting hatred between the principals and all connected with them. It disgraces men and women of good reputation, who happen to bear the names of the divorced persons, and always spreads the reign of enmity and discord.

THESIS XI

Education of children belongs to parents first; to state, last.
Jouin, 185–193; 314–321.

QUESTION

Parents are in strict duty bound to procure the physical and moral education of their children. As between state and parents, the parents have prior rights to the child. They, not the state, are its makers, and to the maker belongs what he makes. Education means development, and a child's education means development of the whole child, body and soul. It means, therefore, development of body, food, raiment and preservation of health; it means instruction, or training of mind; it means morality, or training of will. The state's duty to train the child's mind and to train the child's will, to administer schools and inculcate virtue, is of a kind with the state's duty to supply the child with proper food and raiment, and safeguard its health. Its obligation in these several respects is to keep the parents to their duty, and supplement their weakness, when means or good will fail them. When parents are willing and able to proffer their children by themselves or others a measure of instruction suited to their rank in life, when they equip their children with a brand of morality above suspicion, the state's duty is at an end with respect to knowledge and virtue; and it has no more right to interfere with parents in the education of their children than it has to prescribe the cut of clothes they shall wear, the food they shall eat, or the rules of hygiene they shall follow.

TERMS

Education. Marriage bases a triple society, conjugal, parental and servant. Marriage is primarily between hus-

342

band and wife. Viewed this way, it constitutes conjugal society. Children are the natural outcome of marriage, and at their advent the family becomes parental society. Servants are needed helps to domestic management, and, when inserted as members in the family, constitute it servant-society. Education presupposes children, and becomes a duty only when the family grows to the proportions of parental society. Education is impossible without obedience; and this is true, whether there is question of developing the body, or the mind, or the will. It is a kindness their elders do the young, supposedly unable to care for their bodies and distinguish between true and false, good and evil. Apropos of this it is well worth remarking that father and mother in their relations with children are called parents, not parients. They are people to obey, not people who beget or produce; and usage itself lays more stress on the fact of obedience than on the fact of origin.

Instruction is, of course, a branch of education; but, when applied to children, instruction must not be confounded with mere information. And this would seem to be the difference between the two. Instruction in the case of children always connotes in the pupil obedience or submission of mind to the teacher's superior mind. Mere information carries no such obligation, it is altogether a transaction between equals, and no disorder results from its rejection. Between man and man information is the regular process, and it rests entirely with the person informed to accept or spurn aside his informant's views. No mere man, without some accompanying prerogative, is allowed to impose his views on others; and nobody can feel hurt, when the world refuses to adopt a theory or statement he is unable to prove to evidence. A teacher, without the authority needed to ratify his lesson, is no more a teacher than the morning-paper or a theatrical bill-board; and to endeavor to teach children after this manner, is to put them on an equality with grown men and grown women. Education of the kind would be a denial of education suited to children, and would make education the child's exclusive duty, and nobody else's.

Obedience, therefore, is an essential feature of education, and to say that the state, as compared with the parents, has prior rights in the child's education, is to assert that a child's obedience is first due the state and then his parents. States themselves take no such view of the thing. They deal with adults, not with children. They reach children through their parents. They hold parents responsible for their children, and by the very fact proclaim parents their children's immediate superiors, entitled first and foremost to their obedience. Citizens are the state's proper subjects, and children are only incipient citizens. They are on the way to full and complete citizenship, a fact accruing to them only when in large measure emancipated from the authority of their parents, and done with the process called education.

Of course, parents and children alike owe the state a measure of obedience in virtue of authority, without which government is an impossibility. But it would be folly to contend that the obedience owed the state is as sweeping as the obedience a child owes his parents. State authority is just as sacred as parental authority, but it is necessarily more limited. In both cases it is a means to an end; and its extent must be gathered from the purpose it is meant to secure. The state's solemn purpose is to promote the common good of its citizens; and it sins by excess, when by superfluous and harassing enactments it aspires to undue control of individual liberty and private rights. This is especially the case when it invades the domain of education or religion, because they are distinctively the concern of family and Church.

PROOFS

Education of children belongs to parents first; to state, last. Rights are based on duties; and priority of duty fixes priority of right. Viewed as a duty, the education of children touches parents first, the state afterwards. Therefore, in the education of children a parent's rights are prior to those of the state.

With Regard to the Minor: Parents were meant by nature to educate as well as produce children.

1°. For a long stretch of years after birth children are absolutely helpless with regard to the development of their bodies, their minds and their wills. This being the case, God must have appointed fixed and definite persons capable of carrying on the work of their education.

2°. Care of children involves hardship of the sternest sort, and men are not minded to embrace hardships except from a sense of duty. If the duty to educate children fell to the lot of no God-appointed person, everybody would shirk the responsibility, children would go without an education, and God's negligence would contribute to the destruction of the race.

3°. God has appointed either parents or the state to educate children, and we know from unmistakable signs that parents, not the state, are His choice. These signs are the natural love of parents for their children, the title of ownership vested in their very birth, and the child's tendency to look to his parents for help and support.

4°. The experience of ages and parallel conduct in the nobler specimens of brute creation strengthen our argument.

5°. It is preposterous to think that God exempts parents from the duty of education to impose it on a collection of strangers denominated the state. It would be far easier to believe that God wanted farmers to sit in idleness, while neighbors with fatuous generosity worked their fields and handed them the profits.

PRINCIPLES

A. The arguments alleged for state control of education are chiefly these.

1°. Children are born members of the state; and, therefore, subject to its control.

2°. The common good is involved in the education of future citizens.

3°. A good education in the case of every child is a necessary requisite for society.

4°. Parents get the right to educate their children from the state.

Answer: 1°. Members of the state are not subject in every particular to the control of the state. As individuals, they have prior and independent rights; and these rights must be respected, not absorbed by the state. Children are citizens not immediately, but mediately, in virtue of membership in a family, and care of children devolves first on parents, then on state.

2°. In the state many particulars are conducive to the common good; and yet, because of personal and antecedent rights, they must be left to private initiative. Instances are, eugenic marriages, clothing, food, residence.

3°. This good education can be secured without delivering up education to the state. In this matter the state enjoys only an indirect right; it can help parents by the erection of schools, by rewards and penalties; but it must not take from the parent what belongs to the parent.

4°. It is wholly wrong to think that parents get the right to educate their children from the state. The family is prior to the state, and enjoys prior rights, that the state must safeguard, but never absorb or usurp.

B. *The State and Education.* The word education, expressive of a parent's duty to his children, is a comprehensive term. It means support of body, food, raiment, and sanitary precautions. It means wise provision for his children's future. It means the bestowal of opportunities to acquire all the human knowledge necessary for success in life. It means incentives to morality in the shape of good example, rewards and punishments. It means early acquaintance with God and the things of God. Rousseau wants no mention of God till the child is twelve, and sufficiently grown to select his own religion; but that is only another tribute to the man's godlessness, and to his desire to make the world atheistic.

Regularly, then, and in the natural order, the right to directly and immediately educate their children belongs to parents alone. They have the right to say what branches their children shall learn, what teachers their children shall follow, what books they shall use, how many years they shall spend at school, and whatever minor details are connected with their education. If they object to state-schools on any of these several heads, they are at perfect liberty to withdraw their children and send them elsewhere.

Parents have duties towards their children in this matter of education; and, if they notably fall away from them, the state has a right to interfere to the extent of safeguarding the common good. It is of prime importance to the state to have educated citizens, and its own welfare is menaced when parents grossly abuse their prerogative, and deny their children all opportunity for intellectual improvement. In self-defense the state is obliged on such occasions to interfere, and by wise enactments arouse unnatural parents of the kind to a sense of their duty. Besides, it is the state's duty to safeguard individual rights; the child has rights in education against his parents, and the state is held to assist the child in the prosecution of his rights. These, however, are exceptional cases, scattered instances, and rare enough to leave unchallenged our statement, that regularly the right to educate their children belongs to parents alone.

Moreover, the state's rights in the matter remain always indirect and mediate. Its power is over the parent, not over the child's education. It has no right to educate the child, it has the right to hold the child's parents to their duty. It is to the state's own interest to help parents acquit themselves of their duty, to build schools everywhere, to equip them with capable teachers, to encourage study among the young by rewards in the shape of degrees, diplomas, certificates and political honors. But in last resort it rests with parents to use these state-schools or not, as they like. They have no duty towards state-schools, save payment of taxes; and the state has no power over the family's internal concerns. Their single duty is to educate their children, with the help of the state or without it. If the brand of education offered by the state is a serious menace to religion and morality, the parents enjoy no freedom. They are bound in conscience to reject all such instruction, and no law of God or man can compel them to subject their growing children to danger of eternal damnation.

C. *Compulsory Education and State Monopoly.* Hence we Catholics are uncompromisingly opposed to anything like government monopoly of education, reserving to the State the exclusive right to open schools, as to a thing against the natural law; and the sin is all the more grievous, when parents are compelled by law to send their children to these state-schools for a fixed period. More than this, we contend that the State has no right to compel parents to send their children a certain number of years to any school whatever, even if the school frequented be left to their own choice.

Monopoly in education is wrong on these several counts. It robs parents of their natural right to educate their children, and transfers it to the State; especially when parents, unequal themselves to the task, must perforce send them to some school. Instruction and education cannot possibly be kept apart. Instruction has to do with the training of the mind; and moral education is bound to be imperfect, if the mind from the beginning is developed along wrong lines, if a teacher's crooked notions regarding religion and morality are authoritatively impressed on the minds of the young. Moral education means more than the mere inculcation of right principles, it means the reduction of these principles to act; and pupils must be helped in this particular by the advice and example of their teachers.

Monopoly is an uncalled for restriction of the right to impart and receive instruction, viewed as mere information, implied in the gift of a tongue and ears, made every member of the race. In the natural order, the propagation of falsehood is the one limit to this freedom of instruction. In the supernatural order, the Church is of course supreme; and a profession of faith can with justice be exacted by the Church from the teachers of even profane sciences. Pius IX and Pius X insist with much vehemence on this right of the Church. The state has a right to only such measures as make for the common good, and the arbitrary exclusion of private instruction in the field of education is no such measure. On the contrary, it is the most deleterious of measures, because it kills all progress in letters.

Monopoly would make education dependent on some faction in government. Nobody could teach, unless approved of and educated by this particular faction; and all competition between teachers, so helpful to improvement, would be no more. Certainly, the Church would have no voice in the department of education, and supernatural truth would suffer.

Compulsory education is of two kinds; one with, the other without monopoly. Compulsory with monopoly is wrong, because it is the usurpation of parental rights, assuming direct and immediate control of the child's education, already proved the exclusive privilege of the parents. Besides, every such system savors of socialism. If the state is once allowed control of the child's education, nothing can prevent it from assuming control of family, property, and of the whole internal administration of the home.

Compulsory without monopoly is beside the power of the state, unless we maintain that a school education of a fixed kind belongs as a necessary right to the child, or that the common good demands such a course, inasmuch as defective education would contribute harm to the republic, or would prevent children from enjoying political and civic advantages. A school education is useful, not necessary. Even if necessary, children as such have no right in the name of rigorous or commutative justice against parents. Even if they had such right, reading, writing and arithmetic would be enough for the poor, without robbing parents of their children's help during long years.

D. *The Church and Education.* Religion and morality are not an affair of the state in direct sense, but of the Church; and the Church must manage for children, with help from the state. The Church has paramount rights in this business of education. It was established by Christ, to teach religion to the nations, and its authority bears equally on children, parents and state. According to the will of Christ, nobody in the world is exempt from its jurisdiction. In the supernatural order, in the order of faith and morality, it is regularly the direct and immediate teacher of all mankind, the one teacher vested with active and passive infallibility, empowered to control parents in the education of their children, and dictate terms to the state whenever and wherever the profane sciences, like history, physics, chemistry border on its domain.

Up to the time of the Reformation, it was educator to the world. That revolution substituted the state for the Church; and ever since history has been one long attempt to exaggerate state prerogatives at the expense of parental and ecclesiastical rights. Our public schools are but a baneful substitute for the cathedral and monastic institutions, established for children centuries before the appearance of Luther and the spread of his pernicious and destructive doctrines. Over these cathedral and monastic schools the Church exercised full and complete control. It was supreme arbiter in the field of education, sacred and profane. In sacred matters, with a direct bearing on faith and morality, it recognised no superior or rival. Whatever religion parents or state taught children, they had to take from the Church. In profane matters, considered apart from religion and morality, it viewed parents and state in the light of agents or helpers, attributing a fuller right to parents than to state. And all this, because profane matters are subservient to sacred interests. Parents were always reckoned agents born such and irremovable. It rested with them to choose teachers for their children, the branches of knowledge they were to pursue, the years they were to spend at school; and, as long as the child's eternal interests were not jeopardized, the Church confided everything to the prudence of parents.

It recognised no such sweeping power in the state, forbidding it to unduly interfere with parents in the conduct and management of their children. It welcomed with gladness every move made by the state in favor of right education, but consistently opposed every attempt on the part of the state to usurp prerogatives belonging to Church and parents. The Church can oblige parents to send their children to schools where religion is taught, can forbid them schools where religion is separated from instruction, because the Church's supernatural right weighs against the natural right of parents. The Church can likewise empower the state to insist on attendance at religious schools, and in this emergency the voice of the state is the voice of the Church, and the state as vested with the power of the Church is superior to parents. But without such authorization from the Church the state always ranks lower than parents in the education of children.

Hence the state is guilty of tyrannical usurpation against the Church, when it compels parents to send their children to neutral or mixed schools, condemned by the Church as hurtful to faith and morals. With certain restrictions Catholic parents are allowed to avail themselves of such schools, though they are solemnly exhorted to everywhere build and maintain parochial schools, where knowledge of religion and knowledge of letters keep equal pace together. Certainly, no Catholic can with a safe conscience help to the enactment of a law making the attendance of Catholic children at mixed or neutral schools obligatory. In countries, where Catholics must choose between compulsory education in godless schools and unlimited freedom in education, the latter alternative is the lesser evil and the more commendable course. It is another case of choosing between dogmatic toleration and political toleration.

Before the Reformation, state-schools were always under the direct supervision and control of the Church. After the Reformation, denominational schools came into use, and the Church had to be satisfied with the conduct and management of such schools as Catholic children frequented. Then came non-sectarian or mixed schools, in which religion was supposedly taught in such a way as to give no just offense to any pupil of whatsoever creed; and this would seem to be the complexion of our public schools. State-schools are rapidly becoming entirely lay or irreligious, with no concern for religion, teaching at most the broadest kind of humanitarianism, and the lay or independent morality introduced into philosophy by Kant.

E. *Controversy between Bouquillon and Holaind, S.J.* Education—To whom does it belong?

Bouquillon gives it to state first, to parents last.

Holaind, S.J., gives it to parents first, to state last.

Holaind, S.J. It is wrong to leave the Church out of the comparison. Its supernatural end ranks it above state and parents. Morality is an integral part of education, revelation is exclusively under Church control, and the moral impossibility of morality without revelation puts all education, in full and complete sense, at the mercy of the Church; makes state and parents subject to her jurisdiction in matters educational. The Church is empowered to teach human as well as divine science, at least in an indirect way, inasmuch as the human sciences are useful or necessary to religion and morality. Faith cannot hurt science, because its exponent, the Church, is infallible; the sciences can hurt faith, because their exponents, mere men, are not infallible.

The Church can share her prerogative as educator with state and parents; and, when they work under her control, they are her agents, and they enjoy rights that are far from belonging to them in their own private capacity. The Church counts state and parents her agents after a different manner. A father in virtue of paternity has rights over his child, that cannot be disputed by any claimant with a lesser title than paternity; and the Church, taking this fact into account, reckons parents her agents, born such and irremovable. The state's control of the child is based on no such intimate relation as paternity, and whatever educational prerogatives it enjoys, it gets by favor of the Church. The Church cannot be supposed to do favors to her enemies, to reckon agents her deadliest foes; and non-Catholic states, because they work outside her control, are usurpers when they attempt to educate children.

With these few needed remarks, we leave the Church. Our question is between parents and state. We maintain that education belongs to parents first, to state last. Our opponents are of opinion that it belongs to state first, to parents last. They recognize the right to educate in individuals, in the family, in the state, and in the Church; and the order they follow would lead one to think that they subordinate family to state in the matter of educational rights. It is simple nonsense to talk about the individual's right to educate. All individuals have the power to teach, to give useful information to others; but the others are free to accept or reject the information. The power to teach gives rise to no positive duty of a kindred color in the listener; and a power in me, that creates no such duty in others, can hardly be called a right. Education means more than mere teaching; it means teaching with authority. It embraces all those functions, which promote not only ꞓ preservation and development of the body, but also the perfection of the mind, and the evolution of intellectual and moral powers. To educate is to exercise jurisdiction, it supposes authority in the educator, submission in the pupil. Nobody has the right to educate the children of anybody else, unless their parents give him that power. Paternity is the foundation of jurisdiction in parents, and paternity can be found nowhere outside of parents. The Church can educate, because divine command is a higher title than paternity.

And this is the mistake Bouquillon makes in all the quotations from Catholic philosophers and theologians he urges to prove the right of the state to educate the young. They have in mind a state with the Church at its back; the state, whose claims he advocates, has no such support. The king they talk about is no mere king, he is a Charlemagne, with the unction of the Church on his forehead; a most dutiful son, actuated in all his conduct by childlike obedience to the Church's wishes. The king Bouquillon talks about is a non-Catholic, and therefore a non-Christian state, whose rulers would count it profanation to be touched by the Church's unction, with whom word from a Mexican rebel weighs about the same as, or even more than, word from a Pope. The truth may as well be told, our country is no truly Christian Country in the full and complete sense of the word, because it is not a Catholic country. "Extra Catholicismum non datur verus Christianismus." There can be no true Christianity without Christ, the Son of the living God. True Christianity means the profession of Christ's doctrine in its entirety, not in parts; it means membership in the Church Christ established, not mere toleration of its members.

F. *Holaind, S.J., on Family, State, Church and Education.*

Family. Duty and right of the parent. Education belongs to the parents first, to the state last. It belongs to the parents regularly, directly, and immediately; it belongs to the state in exceptional cases, indirectly, and mediately. Blackstone makes the duty of parents threefold, support, protection and education. Four reasons to prove that this threefold duty flows directly from natural law.

1°. Children result from free act of parents, and every moral agent is responsible for consequences of his free acts. Life would be a curse, and no blessing, without support, protection and education. Ergo, parents are held to this threefold duty, and the obligation is independent of all positive law.

2°. Nature's chief purpose in marriage is the continuance and perfection of the race. This purpose would be defeated, if parents neglected this threefold duty. Ergo, the obligation is imposed by nature itself.

3°. A universal impulse, rational, human, reproduced in

instinct of animals, is unmistakable token of natural law. But the accomplishment of this threefold duty is such an impulse. Ergo, it is imposed by natural law.

4°. A special and natural fitness indicates a special and natural duty. Parents have a special and natural fitness to educate their children. Ergo, it is their special and natural duty. Nothing can replace the love of a mother, the mild firmness of a father. Sparta never produced a single poet, orator or statesman of superior ability. Rome gave even too much authority to fathers, and had a long line of great men.

State. In parents this duty of education is a perfect duty, demanded by rigorous or commutative justice; not merely an imperfect duty, based on mere fitness and unenforcible by children. Government takes this latter view, because it wants to absorb individual and family. The state has right to keep education clear of moral poisoning; but it has no right to invade privacy of the home. Sphere of state's activity is fixed by its end or purpose, to maintain peace, protect rights, supply insufficiency of individuals. Its direct object is not individual, but social good. Wrong must be exterior and must visibly attack society, before state can invade the home.

Seven points to be kept well in mind.

1°. The family is a true and complete society.

2°. The family is exterior to the state, with rights and duties prior to those of the state, and closer in their origin to nature.

3°. Education is one of these rights, inalienable, suffering no abridgement or destruction.

4°. The state cannot at will invade the home.

5°. The state must help the family in case of extreme need.

6°. The state must ensure rights in family, when great disturbance arises.

7°. The state must do all this without absorbing rights of the family. It must oblige parents to educate their children, it must not itself educate them.

Church. Docete omnes gentes, fixes the Church's mission as a teacher. Its jurisdiction extends to human sciences, at least indirectly. Certainly, it has direct control of such natural moral truths as are morally impossible to unaided intelligence.

G. *Bouquillon's Argument*. Bouquillon seems to claim direct control of education for the state. Here is his argument, his apodictic syllogism. Major—"Civil authority has the right to use all legitimate temporal means it judges necessary for the attainment of the temporal common welfare, which is the end of civil society. Minor—Now, among the most necessary means for the attainment of the temporal welfare of the commonwealth, is the diffusion of human knowledge. Conclusion—Therefore civil authority has the right to use the means necessary for the diffusion of such knowledge, that is to say, to teach it, or rather to have it taught by capable agents," p. 12.

About the Major—If the parents refuse to agree, the means are not legitimate, because the rights of the family are invaded. If the parents agree, state education is not compulsory and the state's right to education is indirect, not direct, getting all its validity from the consent of parents.

About the Minor—The diffusion of human knowledge to such as are willing to receive it, is not education in strict sense. Jurisdiction is wanting. To teach or instruct the willing, is not to educate, excepting perhaps in part, because independent of revelation, without which morality is impossible. Revelation cannot be received or rejected at will.

About the Conclusion. To teach or instruct children against the will of their parents, is an illegitimate means to the diffusion of knowledge, because it is an invasion of family rights. The state's one legitimate way to diffuse human knowledge, is to build schools, employ capable teachers, furnish suitable text-books, all at the discretion and with the consent of parents; to help parents perform their duty, without robbing parents of their sacred right; and all this makes the state's power over education indirect, not direct. The Church is educator by divine command, parents are educators by nature, the state is educator by favor of Church and parents.

H. *Bouquillon and History*. Bouquillon's arguments from history prove nothing, because princes in question got their morality from Church, acknowledged right of inspection in bishops, and obeyed the Pope. The state has no more right to found mixed or neutral schools than agnostic schools. Such a state ignores revelation, and is incapable of education.

Pope Leo condemns all such schools, as well as Syllabus, 48.
Our rulers have on their hands a bad bargain, and they try to
meet conditions without hurting anybody. We condemn, not
our rulers, but the Catholics who send their their children
to such schools without need and without precautions.

The state has no authority to set aside parents in education. Injustice is not compatible with authority. The state's
rights are therefore limited to the repression of immoral
or treasonable teachers, and to the promotion of learning by
supplementing private enterprise, and encouraging letters; to
substituting for parents, when they are dead or notoriously
vicious, and when nobody is bound to the child by closer
ties of relationship. This control is, of course, indirect.

Church control is higher and more complete than even
parental. Her mission is supernatural, the mission of parents is natural. The state, in union with the Church, has
completer rights than when alone.

Education is not in state control, simply because the growth
of learning is conducive to the common good. Every such
argument proves too much, common ownership of property,
supervision of the kitchen, and the like. The state must
promote the common welfare by social means, without short-
ening individual activity or invading the home. Education
is an individual good, and the state has only indirect influence over it. Power over cases of neglect implies no power
to fix a minimum of education, except, perhaps, for neglected
children. Power to punish parents who starve their children,
implies no power to settle the number of ounces a child must
get. These matters are undefinable a priori, and must be
settled in each particular case by a competent judge.

I. *Bouquillon and Authority.* Authors Bouquillon quotes
are opposed to his theory, Costa-Rossetti; Jansen; Hammerstein.

Costa-Rossetti has this thesis, ''Considering natural law
only, parents cannot be compelled by civil authority to send
their children to an elementary school, but they may be
obliged to do so in particular cases.''

Three Theses of Jansen. (1) Parents alone have right;
(2) Lawful for nobody to instruct without authority from
parents; (3) Parents not subject to state-control.

Hammerstein says, Parents are before Church and state in concept and in fact, and without either, parents would have to educate. State has indirect right, namely to supply what is wanting in family, to found and endow schools where needed, to compel negligent parents, to take place of parents for orphans and abandoned children. State has no direct right, and therefore no compulsory, no monopoly, no minimum. Some wrongly hold that children belong to state before parents; and this is worse than Eminent Domain and conscription; it is Socialism. State can insist on necessary education some way; and this is not compulsory education. Church has direct power over religion; indirect power over natural knowledge.

SECTION III—CIVIL SOCIETY, OR THE STATE

THESIS XII

Man is by very nature a social being. Jouin, 204–212; Rickaby, 297–310.

QUESTION

Family, or domestic society, is not equal to man's full evolution. State or civil society is a further need.

State, or civil society, means a complete multitude of men, banded together to safeguard their rights and promote their common good.

It means new relations, a new bond, new duties, new rights.

Origin, scope and structure of State are our topics.

TERMS

By Very Nature. Protestants in general derive origin of civil society from compact. They contend that there was no civil society in the primitive state of nature. Hobbes and Rousseau are their standard-bearers.

Hobbes (1588–1679), instructor to Charles II.

Man's highest faculty, sensation. Its object, pleasure; opposed to society, and favorable to egoism or selfishness. Hence, solitude, not society in strictest accord with primitive state of nature. Might, the only claim to possession; war and quarrels, natural condition. Interminable disputes, because strength was met by trickery, fraud. Theory proved by conduct of two boys on first acquaintance. Fear, therefore, led to establishment of civil society; and passage from state of nature to political society had fear for motive. Authority needed, to repress turbulent. This authority without bounds or limit; the more sweeping, the better.

Multitude transfers individual rights and forces to representative.

Authority absolute and beyond law; unimpeachable, irresponsible, superior to justice itself; disobedience, invariably a crime; became Church and revelation for subjects.

With *Rousseau* (1712–1778), man's natural state is a wandering and solitary life, like that of wild beasts. Strength and ferocity from encounters with beasts. Imitate instinct of brute creation for herding together. No higher knowledge than that of sense. No worship, no notions of duty. Free will and intelligence acquired only after the lapse of many ages. Solitary life more in accord with human nature, because more favorable to freedom. Social contract fixed everything. Therefore, society accidental, no improvement, a mistake, a curse.

Absurdities of Hobbes and Rousseau:

Hobbes:

Man inferior to brutes; lions fight with other animals, not among themselves.

Example of small boy proves the contrary.

Nature and man's inclination counsel peace, not war; order is nature's first law, and peace is order.

Wars are fought to establish peace, and settle disturbed relations.

Hobbes' entire system is death to morality; petrified, adamantine tyranny.

Rousseau:

Some refuse to take Rousseau seriously, and regard his theory an elegiac poem in memory of his times' abuses.

Man has no reason and is limited to sensation.

Man enjoys freedom without intellect, freedom's foundation.

All mankind departed from man's natural and proper condition.

Absolutely no foundation, able to render the theory likely.

PROOFS

1. From facts.
2. From man's natural needs.

3. From speech.
4. From inborn kindness.
5. From notion of perfectibility.
6. From dictate of reason.

1. The oldest history at our disposal, monuments and kindred remains, testify that man always lived in society. Nature alone is motive for a fact so universal, so enduring, so constant.

2. The young of animals are born equipped for life's struggles, and little dependent for support on parents or others; the children of men are born absolutely helpless. St. Thomas compares. Food ready for animals; garments, teeth, horns, claws, wings, for defense or flight. Man has reason instead, to direct work of equipment; a man is not sufficient unto himself in the work of equipment; he needs others. Instinct helps animals to choose things beneficial, and avoid things dangerous or harmful; young sheep and wolf. Man knows in only a general way; many heads are required to reduce general knowledge to practical utility.

3. Man enjoys the gift of speech, an accomplishment denied the rest of animal creation. Dogs bark, to express passions in a general sort of way. Man alone is able to express himself with distinctness and precision. Speech is the bond of society, and can have for design nothing short of communication between man and man. This communication of ideas can have for result nothing short of the formation of families and societies.

4. Man is by nature prone to spend himself on others, and let them into his joys and griefs. The learned like to share their knowledge with friends. The fortunate add to their store by manifesting to others their success. The wretched derive comfort from the company and commiseration of their neighbors. In a word, man wants others to rejoice and be sad with him; and nothing more provokes uneasiness and dissatisfaction than distressing solitude and the privation of mutual intercourse.

5. Man is essentially perfectible. He is always on the road with progress, employing his energies to add to whatever wealth preceding ages have bequeathed. His sense of a want

of finish prevents him from ever resting or accumulating moss or rust. Condemned to the task of working out his plans alone and unaided, his lot would be a sorry one, inviting disappointment and despair. He must face a world of difficulties; and, to win in the end, must necessarily apply that age-old principle of successful generals, "Divide and conquer." No one man can hope to advance far into the secrets of a multitude of arts or occupations. Human weakness and limitations force us to devote our energies to some particular line of work, and trust to the activities of others for the rest. Progress would be practically impossible, unless the sons took up the task where the fathers left off; unless succeeding generations held fast to and improved on the results achieved by the men of old. Harmony of effort is a prime requisite for anything like remarkable success in human industry. And society is the most powerful engine of war put at man's disposal by nature.

6. Reason clamors for order in the various activities of men. And order without society is impossible in the matter of duties, rights, propagation of knowledge and the arts, and the exercise of all the virtues peculiar to humanity.

P.S. All six arguments indisputably prove man's membership in family, state and Church natural in strict sense, whether immediately or mediately; and we note in passing that this present thesis has a very important bearing on Thesis XIII and Thesis XIV, where authority is the topic discussed. Membership in society makes man a social being, and society is threefold, domestic, civil, ecclesiastical, or family, state and Church. Man is by very nature a social being, if these three societies are natural to man in strict sense. Recall what we said in General Ethics, Thesis II, about desire of complete happiness and desire of marriage. Natural in strict sense means inborn, prompted and imposed by nature, independent of man's choice and consent, unavoidable. Natural in wide sense means not inborn, not imposed by nature, not independent of man's choice and consent, not unavoidable; but in harmony with man's dignity as a human being.

All three societies are strictly natural to man, but in different ways. Costa-Rossetti, page 409, distinguishes three ways, immediately natural, mediately natural and remotely natural.

A society immediately or mediately natural is natural in strict sense, a society remotely natural is natural in wide sense. A society is immediately natural when its purpose and character flow immediately from man's nature; and the family is an instance. Every man is born into a family, he is always a son of some parents, nature wants parents to be married, marriage constitutes family, children born out of marriage are against nature, branded by the world as things of shame, no free will about entering family. A society is mediately natural, when immediately natural societies are its constituent parts, when its purpose and character flow from man's nature in such a way that the man's free choice has something to do with its organization; and the state and Church are instances. Man is born into a state, he is always a member of some family, family is always a unit in some state. Church is as natural a society as state, because as needful for spiritual prosperity as state is for temporal; men are born into it, nature wants all men to belong to the true Church, nature wants all men to be Catholic; it is against nature to be anything else, wrong churches are from compact and civil law, not true Church; God and nature settle that, no moral freedom is left, physical stands; too important to leave to men's choice, eternal salvation is at stake. A society is remotely natural, when not at variance with man's nature, though its purpose and character are fixed not by man's nature but by his free choice, not imposed by nature, not unavoidable; and a business-partnership is an instance. A society is unnatural when its purpose and character are wicked, when it is without moral union based on duties, when it is in reality no society and ought to be dissolved; and the Freemasons are an instance.

Nature definitely settles the family to which a man must belong, no man ever ceases to be the son of his parents. In definitely settling his family, nature definitely settles the state, into which he is born, without definitely settling the state, in which he must live. Though born into a fixed state, a man can change his allegiance from one country to another; though he cannot change his nationality, he can change his citizenship, but always in such a way that nature wants him to be always a citizen of some state, leaving the determination of the particular state to his own free choice.

PRINCIPLES

A. *Rousseau* says: a. To get down to man's natural condition, we must strip him of whatever ornaments and advantages the civilization of centuries added to his original perfections. Stripped of these ornaments, man is nothing more noble than what Rousseau paints him, a wandering beast, without reason, and without social aspirations.

b. Universal ideas are the immediate effects of language, and language is not at all natural to man, but the result of art and study. It would, therefore, seem that in the state of nature man was wholly destitute of universal ideas.

c. America and Africa are inhabited by tribes of human beings more like beasts than men, with no religion, no laws, no customs.

Answer: a. Man must not be stripped of his essence; and, as long as he remains in possession of that, he is the owner of a higher faculty than sense, viz., reason. He is by nature a rational animal, a species of being entirely and utterly distinct from brute creation.

b. In the supposition of the Nominalists Rousseau's theory about universals would be true; but that supposition is long since exploded. Universal ideas are independent of words, and owe their being to a process of abstraction founded on the reality of things. Language is no work of art, it is the product of nature, which fits men with organs nicely arranged and admirably intended for the production of articulate sounds. This language or that language in particular is, of course, a work of art; but nature evidently had in view the use of some language or other, subject to the choice of different peoples.

c. No barbarous nation is so poor as not to possess and employ reason in the ordinary affairs of life. Rousseau may endeavor to deceive his readers into believing that rude reasoning and dense ignorance are no higher essays at knowledge than sensation; but the man capable of such folly is, either unacquainted with the first rudiments of philosophy, or dishonest enough to impose on the credulity of others by downright lying. Neither is any nation so barbarous as not to acknowledge a deity and worship him in some way suited to its false and imperfect notions. The mistakes of barbarism in the matter of religion and laws are not a gift of nature, but an addition made to nature by the depravity and wickedness of free agents. Nature even in barbarians rebels against the wrong done her, but she is kept in check by the species of omnipotence resident in liberty's tyranny.

B. *Hobbes* says: In state of nature everything common, no private property. Therefore wrongs and universal quarreling. The arrogant and strong always adding to their stores by oppression and robbery; the mild and gentle in continual strife, to protect themselves and their goods. Differences of disposition beget hatred and contempt. Men travel laden with weapons, citizens lock their doors, the state supports policemen, sheriffs, troops.

Answer: Hobbes' whole mistake consists in foolishly supposing that human nature proceeds from the hands of the Creator with all the imperfections resulting to it from man's perverseness. Man's power for harm is immense, and the wicked are no true exponents of human nature. To form a fair estimate of what man would be in a state of nature, we must take the virtuous for standard; and surely their dispositions and methods of behavior tally exactly with the requirements of society. Individual defects ought not to be laid to the account of human nature, and saddled on the back of all mankind. Nature is not to blame for the precautions taken by citizens against danger to life and property, but the passions of men, greed of gain, anger, quarrelsomeness and qualities loudly condemned by nature. Even the wicked cannot shake off this inclination towards society, precisely because it is from nature.

C. If society is a dictate of reason, monks and solitaries are out of harmony with nature, and guilty of a grievous wrong.

Answer: Society is a dictate of reason meant for mankind as a collection, and as a help to the race's betterment. It is not a dictate meant for each and every individual, as an end of absolute and supreme importance. For higher purposes and motives a man can with praise abandon society and live apart from his fellows. Naturally speaking, however, and apart from the supernatural advantages accruing to the hermit, it must be said that normally life in solitude is far inferior to life in society.

D. Differences between Hobbes and Rousseau:

Hobbes, natural state opposed to society; Rousseau, natural state outside of society.

Hobbes, society bettered man's condition; Rousseau, society, a downright injury to mankind.

Hobbes, natural state, universal warfare; Rousseau, natural state, good, peaceful, happy.

Hobbes, society founded on egoism and fear. From egoism, universal war, because everything in common; fear of death and want of security, desire of society. Each transferred his will to one man or body of men; hence, Regal Absolutism.

Rousseau, man in natural state happy with the happiness of brutes, oaks, rivulets, trees. No need of society, but by degrees compacts were made at the expense of liberty. Hence, "Social Contract."

THESIS XIII

A multitude and authority, or subjects and a ruler, are elements essential to civil society, or the State. Jouin, 212–214.

QUESTION

The State's Purpose. The State has for object external order, actuated by internal righteousness, and all for common good of the citizens. Kant has another theory about the guiding purpose of political society. He assumes that man's freedom is nothing worth, unless it implies absolute independence of all restraint, moral as well as physical, depending solely on itself and on whatever reason, unbiassed by any outside recommendations or impressions, decrees. These impressions serving to destroy freedom are twofold in his hypothesis, inner and outer. The former have their origin in the mind's appetites and desires. The latter are due to outside forces at work against an agent's free choice. The first class of impressions are subject matter for what he styles moral law; the second class, subject matter for what he chooses to designate juridical or judicial law. Moral law is therefore a restraint on nature and inborn factors of disorder. Juridical law holds in check what enemies threaten an attack on freedom from without. To bring order out of the chaos liable to result from the conflict between will and will in the field of outward agencies, reason and nature made the establishment of the State, or political society, imperatively necessary. In establishing the State it imposed on the same the obligation of seeing to it that each man's freedom be confined within such limits as not to interfere with the freedom of others. The principle, therefore, of coexistence of individual liberties lies at the root of civil society, and constitutes civil society's sole purpose and aim. This theory of Kant is built from turret to foundation-stone on false principles. We call attention to these three statements in particular:

a. Man is absolutely independent, responsible to no one save himself.

b. Morality is an affair of abstractions, outside the sphere of concrete realities.

c. Human liberty, viewed externally, is illimitable and unconfined.

We beg leave to think that all three statements are unfounded and untrue.

a. Man is God's creature, and essentially dependent on his Creator, essentially responsible before God for his every act.

b. Morality's principles, though abstract in themselves, are founded on concrete relations, existent not in the mind solely, but alive and at work in the beings that surround us. Kant, it may be remarked, would blasphemously rate love of God unmoral, because, forsooth, God its object is outside the agent eliciting the act, and because love is accomplished not by reason, but by the will.

c. In the abstract, human liberty may be considered a thing without bound or limit; but in the concrete, in the everyday affairs of men, liberty is decidedly restricted. The object matter on which it exercises itself, the duties incumbent on the free agent in the use of his liberty, certainly operate to render human liberty anything but illimitable and unrestrained.

In Kant's system society would procure to mankind nothing higher than a negative good, the curbing of wicked violence and cessation of quarrels between man and man. If it once set about accomplishing any positive effect, it would at once degenerate to either individualism, or selfishness and despotism. It would either oblige every man to work for himself solely, or, relieving the State of all moral responsibility in its arbitrary enactments, would rob subjects of the protection now afforded by the salutary restraints morality exercises over even the State. The abuses arising from Kant's system are manifold:

a. All public morality would perish from the earth. The State would be able to prohibit only what actions of mine interfere with the full liberty of my neighbor. Suicide, blasphemy, sacrilege, unholy contracts, public scandals, if done with the full consent of parties concerned, would be no crimes at all.

b. Religious indifference, political atheism would be men's rights; and the Church would have no voice whatever in the affairs of men.

c. Finally, government, when closest to its end's fulfilment, would lose its usefulness, its very reason for existence. The State would slowly work out its own destruction, and would ever tend towards self-annihilation. Harmony once secured, men would have no further need of the State's directive and saving influence. In our theory, even with this harmony secured, the State would still be a need. Righteousness and common good demand state. State has indirect control of our thoughts and wishes.

Right System. The State has for object external order, actuated by internal righteousness, and all for the common good of the citizens. The end or object of a thing is that for which it exists, that towards which its energies must tend. We have already described the various classes of ends. To now apply. God's glory is the absolutely last end of society, as it is of everything else in the universe of existences. The relatively last end of society is external order, procured with a view to the common welfare of its members, and actuated by morality or rectitude. Society accomplishes this end, when it secures to citizens means to fully exercise their rights. The means themselves are said to be society's proximate or nearest end. Actual possession by the citizens of these means, or prosperity in first act, is society's remote or more distant end. The actual evolution of faculties and exercise of rights constitute civic prosperity in second act, or in its completeness. Order is taken in its philosophic sense, and means a becoming disposition of things, such as allots to each its own proper place. Righteousness is harmony with reason or objective order. If external order were not actuated with righteousness, society would be ethically wrong, and would be in direct opposition with man's natural tendencies. That society has no other purpose than the purpose we assign, is evident from the fact that men enter society with no other end in view. They regard it as an institution designed for the relief of individual deficiencies, an aid to the full and peaceful enjoyment of their rights; and, therefore, intended to establish external order, actuated by internal righteousness, for the common good of the citizens.

The scope of society determined, we can now proceed to *discuss its elements or structure.* By multitude we understand any large or small collection of individuals. Authority in the State is a moral right independent of every other right in its own order, to direct or guide the actions of citizens towards the common good. Scholastics, applying their theory of matter and form, regard the multitude its matter, the authority its form. Society is therefore a compound reality, and these two parts are indispensably necessary to its being.

PROOFS

Society, or the state, is an individual body, not physically, but morally speaking. It is likewise a peaceable and well ordered assembly of many. But we must recognize in every individual body parts blended together, and a principle effecting the union sufficient to constitute the body one. In the same way every peaceable and well ordered assembly necessarily involves the idea of individuals making up the assembly, and some principle capable of maintaining peace, and holding the different wills to harmony. Multitude means the persons forming the state. Authority means principle procuring unity and preserving order. Ergo.

PRINCIPLES

A. Subjects are the concrete expressions of multitude; rulers, the concrete expression of authority.

B. Difference between authority and dominion, or property: Dominion turns on things; authority, on persons. Use of dominion is a free act; exercise of authority, a duty. Dominion has for object the owner's private profit; authority is for good of community.

Difference between a subject and a slave: A slave as such is more like a thing or chattel than a person, in point of service; a subject as such has all the qualifications of a person, and enjoys a person's free rights and privileges. A slave is a person and a chattel, a subject is a person and no chattel. A slave is absolutely dependent on the wishes of his master, in point of service; a subject is moved to act not by the superior's will precisely, but by the authority it represents and by the appointment of reason. A slave works unto his master's gain; a subject aims at the advancement of the whole community.

C. It is a duty incumbent on the State to procure the prosperity of every single citizen, whether rich or poor, learned or ignorant, noble or plebeian. Any legislation aiming at the aggrandizement of a certain few to the injury of certain others, is against the first elements of political morality, and grievously wrong. To procure signifies to furnish means, the citizen himself must apply them.

D. Only admissible form of society, that in which liberty and equality are guaranteed, meaning equality of opportunities.

THESIS XIV

Authority proceeds immediately from God. In the nature of things, and ordinarily, authority is not conferred on the people. Ordinarily, and in the nature of things, the consent of the people fixes or determines the person in whom authority resides. This consent may be implied or expressed, immediate or gradual, and cannot always be withheld. Jouin, 214–226; Rickaby, 310–338.

QUESTION

Two questions:
A. *Whence comes authority?*
B. *How is authority conferred?*
One deals with the origin of authority; the other, with its recipient.

A. All Catholics are agreed about the origin of authority. Catholics are not a unit on the second question. Rousseau and Hobbes, on account of the theories already alluded to, are logically obliged to invent a false theory about authority's origin.

The word, immediately, needs explanation. Two ways: Cause immediate, when no other cause intervenes. Election, never a cause. It is a condition. The two ways are positive enactment and law of nature. Moses and Aaron in Holy Scripture received their authority from God in first way, because chosen and appointed by God without any free act on part of people. Positive enactment is likewise the method in force in case of the Sovereign Pontiff. God in revelation instituted the office in such sort that men are forbidden the liberty of changing, limiting or lessening the Pope's authority, though they are allowed the privilege of electing or choosing an individual for the office. Authority can spring from a law of nature, and, therefore, from God as its immediate cause, in a threefold manner.

a. It can belong to a subject by very force of creation, and in virtue of the natural order of things. A father's authority in the family is an instance.

b. It can be bestowed by God on a person determined by some such accidental fact as acquiescence or inheritance. The accidental fact is by no means a cause of the acquired authority, but at most an indispensable condition.

c. Finally, it can result from the free choice of a people, expressed by suffrage. Nature in this case advises and counsels the act, it gives the act all its force. It renders the act such a medium that in the event of its absence no authority would accrue to any individual. And yet, because of the influence nature exerts in the performance of the act, and because of the circumstance that the act operates merely to designate the person, on whom God afterwards bestows authority, God remains the immediate cause of political supremacy in even a republic.

B. The second question about the recipient of authority is more delicate and harder to settle. Apart from certain openly false opinions, the Scholastics themselves are divided on this topic, and proffer apparently different solutions. Everybody is agreed that a multitude, or the people as such, cannot exercise authority. It would be quite out of the question, and simply impossible, for each person to issue orders to his neighbor, and be in turn ordered by the neighbor. It would be impossible in the tumult of opinions to decide what person was invested with the prerogatives entitling him to the obedience of others. A multitude of the kind would be matter without form; and, therefore, no society at all. Everyone would have to know everything, and everyone would have to pass sentence on every measure and detail of government. Therefore, even if authority were first bestowed by God on the multitude or whole people, an individual ruler, in whom this authority would be centred, would be a necessity of nature, and as such indispensably necessary. By ruler we mean any person or body of persons legitimately constituted to exercise full dominion of jurisdiction. A multitude is a collection of individuals. A people is a multitude of citizens living under the same government. State authority is social power existent in particular and determined individuals. There can be no difficulty in understanding that no mere multitude, no people separated from its ruler, is a fit subject for authority. In fact, a multitude as such can never become the actual exponent and agent of authority. All the difficulty lies in determining whether a people can in first act, as they say, retain authority, immediately bestowed on the people by God and wielded by the sovereign in the State. To compare, state is the whole man, body and soul. Authority in ruler is the soul, multitude is the body.

Philosophy discusses four different systems, advocating each its own theory about the manner of authority's bestowal by God. *Their authors are:* [1] *James I,* [2] *Taparelli,* [3] *the Scholastic in general,* [4] *Hobbes and Rousseau.*

1. *James I,* supported for a long time in his opinion by the University of Oxford, contended that kings and Popes were on a level. Men, therefore, as he thinks, are as unable to tamper with the authority of secular princes as they are to tamper with that of the Sovereign Pontiff. They cannot in justice lessen or change the prerogatives of kings. They cannot frame laws setting bounds to royal wishes, nor can they with any show of right object when their rulers override the limitations of law. James appeals to the instances of Saul and David; but his appeal is vain, since revelation made their claims good. No modern king has revelation on his side. The divine right of kings is authority's only defense, in the opinion of James, against factions and rebellious subjects. Against James we maintain that apart even from the divine right of kings, a people is not at liberty to limit at will power once transferred to the ruler. It is far less able to abolish such power, unless the ruler, abusing his trust, descends to the meanness and injustice of open tyranny. This, too, is the case, in Bellarmine's opinion, though he favors the supremacy of the people to something of an excess. He thinks that a people never completely hands over its authority to a king; but, always retaining it in habit or potency, can in certain cases actually recover it and administer things.

2. *The second system, that of Taparelli* and many modern writers among Catholics, advocates God's immediate bestowal of authority on the ruler, and denies to consent of the people everything higher than accidental necessity or importance.

The ruler, according to these writers, is determined either by some antecedent concrete fact or by the free consent of the people. Hence they count consent of the people necessary only by accident, when the antecedent concrete fact is wanting. Ordinarily this fact settles succession, and dissent on the part of the subjects is out of the question. The all important fact is described as superiority from the standpoint of domestic headship. The state is in its first origin an outgrowth of the family. The father, from ruler in household concerns, grew by degrees to exercise political sovereignty over his own immediate family, and families connected with it. As he holds from nature the authority to govern his wife and children, so from nature he holds his right to manage the State. These authors, therefore, consider God's gift of authority immediate, inasmuch as it proceeds from a law of nature. They contend that, in the ordinary course of events, a people's consent is not absolutely necessary; admitting at the same time that contingencies can happen in which this consent becomes a reason why God vests some set person with authority. Different from doctrine of James I, who derives authority from positive divine enactment. Kings, therefore, are on a level with the Pope. People cannot establish, cannot change authority, because it is a divine institution.

3. *The system proposed by Scholastic philosophy* is complicated, and offers among others these characteristic points:

1. Authority universally considered comes immediately from God.

2. This authority rests immediately in the whole multitude.

(N.B. To at once refute this theory, we answer the three reasons alleged in its support.

x. Because it is of divine right and granted by God to no one in particular.

Answer: Impossible, because multitude unfit to govern. It is granted to ruler chosen by people.

y. Because no one is born a king. All are born equal.

Answer: True in the abstract, but circumstances surrounding birth make some infants kings. In this Scholastic sense no man could own property by law of nature. The ruler selected by the people is not born selected.

z. Because Society ought to be a perfect government, with prerogatives enabling it to protect itself and punish disturbers of its tranquillity.

Answer: This is true enough of a perfect society, consisting of ruler and people; not true of a half-society, consisting solely of subjects without a ruler. It is the ruler's business, not the business of separate individual citizens to protect the state and punish its disturbers).

3. The multitude can and must make over its authority to some king or governing body, with no vestige of a right to retain it.

4. The law of nations rules men's choice of form of government, because prior to government they are without other law.

5. Political power is from God, but through human counsel as a medium, not through multitude as medium, in which authority first resides.

(N.B. Difference between civil and ecclesiastical power. In general, civil power is from God by divine law; in particular, from God through the law of nations. Ecclesiastical power is always and in every case God's immediate gift, and positive divine law is its foundation. Political power is vested in the multitude; ecclesiastical power belongs to one man. In political, multitude controls prerogatives; in ecclesiastical, multitude is without control.)

6. Men dispose the material for the reception of the form infused by God, i.e., men designate the ruler, God vests him with authority. Suarez says as much in De Legibus, Bk. 3, c. 3, n. 2.

7. A people never makes complete surrender of its authority to the king. It always retains the authority by way of a habit, or capacity, or in quiet. After the appointment of a king, no two authorities remain capable to pass into act. Nevertheless, it is safe to say that two remain, one in the king, the other in his people; understanding always that the authority, resident in the people, is merely habitual, debarred from activity, as long as the king's authority endures. When the king's authority falls, then that of the multitude asserts itself. The people resumes its right to designate a ruler.

8. Suarez on the authority of Ulpian and St. Augustine in-

troduces the "Royal Compact," in virtue of which subjects are considered to transfer all their rights to the king, the king at the same time, or in return for the favor, assuming all the responsibility attaching to government.

9. A Dominican, Father Victoria, thus sums up the doctrine of the Scholastics: "By divine decree the government holds its power. This power resides by divine and natural right in the government itself, since it devolves on the government to rule and manage itself, and direct all its energies to the common good. Nature makes no difference between individuals in a community, before the assignment of a head. When the king is once established on his throne, he must be said to have his authority immediately from God alone, not from the people at all." These statements sound like a contradiction in terms; but a distinction may serve to reconcile the two Catholic schools of thought represented by Suarez and Victoria respectively. Victoria contends that the people create their king, not his royal authority; Suarez maintains that the people make some person ready and fit for authority. Molina admits that the king is above his people, even collectively taken.

To reconcile apparent contradictions in Suarez and others, we must only suppose that they view authority and society at one time in the abstract; at another, in the concrete. Abstractly considered, like that vague ownership denominated common and everybody's title before occupancy, authority exists in every member composing a society or state. Concretely speaking, and taking the state for an established institution made up of a king and subjects, authority exists again in every member comprised in the society or state, but only after such a manner that the people dispose or make ready the matter, choose a ruler, and God in turn impresses on the object of their choice the form of authority.

Resemblances:

a. Civil power comes immediately from God through nature, and what comes through nature comes from God.

b. Certain human acts are necessary to invest one man rather than another with authority.

c. When no prior right exists, when no right is endangered by such action, a people has from very nature the right, it is in fact bound, to specify its own form of government and appoint its own ruler.

Differences:

a'. Authority passes immediately from God to the people = abstract.

Authority passes immediately from God to the state = concrete.

b'. Ordinarily, and of itself, authority is the result of "Royal Compact"; of a variety of causes by accident = no ruler fixed, choose ruler.

Ordinarily, and of itself authority has its origin in family authority or a preceding right; by accident, in agreement = ruler fixed, no choice.

c'. No authority can accrue to a king without some sort of consent on the part of his people. Such consent may be immediate or gradual, implied or expressed. When a prior right is the foundation of the king's claim, no consent of the people is needed; but the people can in some cases be obliged to give consent.

4. *A fourth system is that introduced by Rousseau and Hobbes.*

Rousseau conceives authority as the result of a surrender of free will and rights, made by every member of the state or society. By this surrender every individual deeds over to the whole community his person, and puts under the direction and control of a general or universal will all his powers and faculties. Public or social authority is, therefore, with him a sum total of individual wills and liberties, and this sum total constitutes a general or universal will, which is authority, the state. The very act of alliance immediately produces, in place of the single persons closing and sealing this contract, a moral body, a collective group, composed of as many parts as the suffrages or votes represented at the meeting. This moral body assumes at the same time, and by the self-same act, its proper oneness, its personality, its life, its will.

Hobbes establishes a like compact, made out of fear and from sense of danger. He then vindicates to the state a power that puts it above conscience and all law, human and divine.

Against Rousseau and Hobbes:

1.. Contradiction. 2. Liberty inalienable. 3. Leaves no liberty in individual. 4. Transfer in favor of individuals; no society yet; same would command and obey. 5. Man would obey man—real slavery. 6. Authority would vary with sum of votes—arithmetical progression.

DIVISION

Four Parts—I, II, III, IV,

I.   Authority from God.
II. Not conferred on people.
III. People fix ruler.
IV. Consents.

PROOFS

I. Authority immediately from God.

1°. God makes to society immediate gift of that without which society cannot be even conceived of in thought, of that which belongs to the very essence of social order. But authority is a thing of the kind. Ergo.

With Regard to the Major: The essences of things moral, as natural to man as society, are supplied immediately by God.

With Regard to the Minor: A thing's essence is made up of its matter and form; and, of these two elements, form is always considered the superior and more important. Authority, we have seen, is the form; multitude, the matter of society. Man is made up of body and soul; state, of multitude and authority.

2°. The state receives authority either immediately from God or from the individuals composing the state. But the second member of this dilemma is absurd. Ergo.

With Regard to the Minor: St. Thomas says, and the world agrees with him, that nobody is born by very nature a king, because otherwise everybody would be born a king, since nature is the same in all men. Some men are born kings by accident of birth from royal parents. By birth or nature they are mere human beings, and no better than common children. By royal birth they are kings, and royal is an accident or quality superadded to birth or nature. It is no escape from this argument to say that men transfer to the king not authority properly so-called, but dominion over their own acts. The transaction is nowhere recorded. Besides, it would bind only parties to the contract, not their descendants. Apart from the man himself, God alone is master of a man's dominion over his own acts. The men of 1776 could never transfer to Wilson dominion over the acts of men living in 1918. And they never attempted the thing. They could transfer dominion over their own acts to Washington, and the obligation of obedience would bind only such men of 1776 as actually made the transfer, and Washington would have no authority over recalcitrants in the country.

Obedience to Washington like obedience to Wilson, is not rooted in any authority given them by the people, but in authority given them immediately by God. Authority is dominion over the conduct or free acts of others. No man of himself enjoys this dominion over others, God enjoys it over all. And God shares this dominion of His with the ruler, to make the state an established fact. Just as Washington in virtue of the dominion or authority immediately conferred on him by God, ruled all the men in America during his presidency, recalcitrants as well as friends, so Wilson rules all the men in America in 1918, dissatisfied republicans as well as satisfied democrats. Men of themselves have no right to impose obedience on others against their wishes. God has the right to impose obedience on all, whether they are willing or unwilling. In itself a majority has no more right in this matter than an individual. The thing is plain in the case of a king and his successors. The makers of a king could never transfer dominion over the free acts of their descendants to the king's successors. God alone has that power, and therefore God alone gave the king's successors authority.

Besides, God never gives authority to a ruler for his own personal advantage, but for the advantage of the state. The gift therefore endures as long as the state endures, and authority belongs as much to successors as to the original king. The state as such never transfers authority to the ruler, because no state exists till after the ruler is invested with authority by God. When members of a firm give its president certain powers, they give him what they first possessed. When individuals attempt to give authority to a ruler, they attempt to give what they never possessed, namely, dominion over wills different and distinct from their own.

3°. Positive divine law can be alleged to strengthen the position we take. "There is no power but from God, and those that are ordained of God. Therefore, he that resisteth the power, resisteth the ordinance of God." Rom. 13.1. If authority came from the people, disobedience would be direct resistance to an ordinance of the people, not to an ordinance of God.

II. *Authority is not conferred on the people.*

1°. Because such bestowal is not evident from nature. The only bestowal evident from nature is bestowal on the complete state, multitude and ruler together; and this bestowal is verified, whether immediate gift is made to ruler or people. Immediate bestowal on the ruler is not evident from the nature of the state, but it is evident from the nature of authority. From its very definition, authority cannot be exercised by the people as such, it can be exercised by the ruler.

When Bellarmine says that authority as a divine and positive right is bestowed on no man in particular, and therefore on the multitude, he means that no man in particular has a natural right to authority, that no man is born by very nature a king, that by the nature of the state authority is in the multitude, meaning multitude and ruler together, not separately; and with Bellarmine we stand for the same statement. We deny, however, that authority is in the multitude apart from the ruler, and contend that the very nature of authority demands that it be in the ruler. Intellect is in the man without being in his body, it is in his soul.

2°. It is absurd to consider the recipient of authority an agent wholly unfitted and unable to exercise it.

But the people are such an agent. Ergo.

With Regard to the Minor: Adversaries admit the people's incapability to exercise authority; and, to meet the argument, distinguish between ability in first act or radically, and ability in second act. But ability in first act always implies the remote possibility of passing from a present state of inactivity to a future state of full activity. No such possibility can be recognized in the multitude. If the distinction, "radically," means ability to choose the king, or determine the form of government, we readily grant to the people possession of such a power. The *people, therefore, and this is our doctrine, have a full right to create the ruler. They have no right to create or transfer the authority lodged in the ruler selected.*

A power in a person that the person himself cannot exercise is a contradiction in terms = power and not power. Authority in a multitude that the multitude itself cannot exercise is the same. If the king exercises authority only as the agent or instrument of the multitude, he is completely at the mercy of his subjects, and has no real authority at all.

3°. According to adversaries, e.g., Suarez, De Legibus, Bk. 3, c. 3, n. 2—men make ready the material, they furnish a subject for the reception of authority. God adds the form, confers authority on this subject. But he that merely prepares the material, cannot be said of himself to possess the form. Ergo, authority is not of itself and immediately in men or the multitude.

With Regard to the Major: This argument may be of little force to any but Scholastics, who are familiar with the theory of matter and form, current in the Schools. We introduce it, however, because of its peculiar strength and cogency, when used against such as admit the theory and accept the phraseology.

With Regard to the Minor: Form is always absent, until the matter is fully equipped and ready for its advent. As soon as it approaches the matter, complete substance results. If the supposition of our adversaries were correct, society or the state would exist long before they conceive it to begin. For the two elements would be a long while present together, and no obstacle would stand in the way of their union.

4°. Catholics all admit that the republic is not the essential and only natural form of government.

But whoso lodges authority in the multitude, and then in the ruler, must necessarily adopt this attitude. Ergo.

With Regard to the Major: Many writers, influenced by

Aristotle's opinion, hesitate not to affirm with him that republics are in some respects inferior to other forms of government. In point of stability history is emphatically in favor of monarchy. Witness the following table.

Monarchies:

Assyria,	1449 years		Constantinople,	1121 years
Egypt,	1675 "		England,	1071 "
Persia and Media,	417 "		France,	1373 "
China,	2000 "		Germany,	1000 "
Roman Empire,	344 "		Spain,	1426 "
Rome,	853 "		Rome,	525 "

Republics:

Carthage,	647 years		United States,	125 years
Venice,	1346 "		Athens,	397 "
Genoa	855 "		Rome,	290 "

With Regard to the Minor: A republic is, in a few words, a state conceding to the people or multitude the largest possible measure of influence in political affairs. If authority is first vested in the people, to be afterwards transferred by them to the ruler, a republic, or better still a democracy pure and simple, is the only form of government certain to commend itself to the mind of the philosopher. No man can fairly give what is not his own, and the principle holds good when applied to a people. The people, therefore, must be considered rightful owners of all the authority resident in the ruler, before its transmission and acceptance. Absolute democracy, or pure republicanism, is that manner of government which vindicates all authority to the people in joint assembly. Whatever different forms of government may now be in use, it is quite certain, according to our adversaries' way of thinking, that absolute democracy ought to have been the original form, because the form most in accord with the dictates of reason.

It is difficult, besides, for us to see why, if the people were so minded, they could not retain authority and lend it to no individual in particular. For, if in the moment preceding the loan, they were really capable of possession, nothing could possibly occur afterwards to divest them of that right. An attempt to wield power by the whole multitude in common might certainly be attended by innumerable and disagreeable inconveniences; but right would nevertheless be on their side, and reason is loud against any spoliation of rights. If the people were incapable of authority in the moment preceding the loan, then they attempted to give what was not their own, and were little better than thieves or robbers. It was easy for primitive peoples to see the need of submitting to the patriarch, because nature taught them that the ruler got his authority immediately from God, not from the people.

To reconcile the two seemingly opposite schools of Catholic thought, it is necessary to merely examine these two statements made by Victoria, one of our principal opponents, and see how well they can be made fit with our own doctrine: "Monarchy is not only just and legitimate rule, but kings have their authority in virtue of a divine decree, and by a natural right. They are not dependent for it on the government taken collectively, they are not dependent for it on men at all." (No. 8.) In No. 7 he has the following: "A government, therefore, has power by divine appointment. The material cause, or subject in which this power dwells, is by law of God and law of nature the government itself, because it belongs to the government to administer and manage itself and turn all its forces to the common good." Victoria certainly never intended to contradict himself. When, therefore, in his second statement he maintains that authority is vested in the government, he cannot mean the people separated from the ruler. When writers of his opinion come to explain themselves, they contend merely that authority resides in the people in root, and consists entirely in their being able, speaking philosophically, to prepare the matter and get ready the subject. They, that with us deny authority to the people, readily grant the people all the privileges contended for by the opposite side. We willingly recognize in the people the right to even determine, and appoint, and choose by election, the person on whom God will afterwards bestow the authority. But we emphatically deny that the people are on this account the immediate recipients of authority, we deny that authority properly so called rests in the multitude. The motive uppermost with writers of the school opposed to our view, is the fact that God never passes authority to the ruler without the intervention in some way

of popular will, human consent, or some other equally just
cause. We certainly pay due deference to the fact, denying
at the same time to such intervention the causalty claimed
for it by these others, and allowing it only the influence proper
to the designation or appointment of the candidate for authority. We follow Suarez, Victoria rightly understood follows Suarez; and we are all one.

To settle disputes about the title to authority in a state, and
decide between the rival claims of a lawful sovereign and a
usurper, these various opinions are advanced. Suarez insists
on his Royal Compact or Contract. Zigliara leaves everything
to election or choice, direct or indirect. Taparelli notes a
difference between three several classes of societies. Some
he calls natural, others free, others obligatory. In societies
of the first class, and the family is an instance, nature itself
appoints the ruler or head. In those of the second class,
consent is the all important factor. In those of the third
class, everything depends on preexisting rights. It must be
at first sight evident that consent of some sort or other is a
characteristic common to all three classes. In obligatory societies, such, for instance, as result from the subjugation of a
people by just process of war, this consent is an obligation
freely assumed by the conquered people at the beginning of
hostilities. They took up arms with the undestanding that
ultimate victory was to decide supremacy, and in agreeing
to preliminaries they agreed to the result. In like manner,
consent is an element entering into the family. Consent,
however, is here, as in the former case, obligatory and exacted
by a law of nature.

Morally necessary consent is as physically free as morally
free consent; and one kind is as much consent as the other.
Consent, therefore, has place in natural and obligatory societies as well as in free societies. In all three societies consent of the governed is title. In natural and obligatory societies this consent is physically free, morally necessary; in
free societies it is physically free and morally free.

Our position then is that taken by Zigliara. We simply
change the word, ''choice direct or indirect'' to ''consent of
the people, whether implied or expressed, immediate or gradual.'' And first, a word about these consents. *They are*

implied and expressed, immediate and gradual, direct and indirect.

Implied, manifest not from words, but from acts, that sufficiently declare the will of parties to the consent.

Expressed, manifest from words whether spoken or written.

Immediate, accomplished at once, without delay or interruption.

Gradual, given in parts, by some members of the community to-day, by others to-morrow.

Direct, willed in itself, not through the agency of a second event.

Indirect, not willed in itself, but in a cause freely assumed and working out the event as a consequence.

Thus a murderer, though at first sight far from consenting to or wishing his execution on the gallows, really makes deliberate choice of that manner of death, when he slays another. In the same way, a nation rushes into unjust war with a hatred for defeat and subjugation. But to wish the cause is to wish at the same time the effect. And, if the event of the war is defeat, the nation in the wrong must be said to have accepted defeat or consented to it, when it made ready to march against the enemy. At the dawn of history, children of the patriarchs, by the very fact of residence in territory occupied by their fathers, yielded implied and indirect consent to be politically controlled by them. These children after attaining their majority were by the law of nature constituted free to move off, settle elsewhere, and establish their own distinct government. Hence, even in patriarchal times, though the family or domestic society was in reality the origin of the state or civil society, that very freedom to withdraw from the patriarch's political influence rendered consent necessary to the constitution of individual authority. Families, intent on remaining within the bounds of a patriarch's kingdom, had their origin, of course, at different intervals of time, and paid him the homage of what we call gradual consent.

III. Consent of people determines person in whom authority resides.

1°. Moral obligations of obedience to another arise either

from nature or from free choice. We omit contingent facts, because they are reducible to nature or free choice. But man's moral obligations towards authority, vested in some set person, arise not from nature. Ergo.

With Regard to the Minor: Were the Minor false, some individuals, apart from accidental circumstances of heredity or election, would be born princes, and no such statement is borne out by sound philosophy. St. John Chrysostom on the text, "All power is from God," Romans, 13.1, says, "Not the king, but his power." He means that authority is from God, king is from people, by act of selection and free consent.

2°. A people has the natural right to organize itself into a society. But this right would mean nothing, unless the people's consent were necessary. Ergo.

With Regard to the Major: Some see an answer to this argument in the distinction between a free people and a people already held to preexistent obligations. But the distinction is vain. For the people surrendered their liberty by free consent. If they were unjustly and unwillingly deprived of their liberty, no rights of authority accrued to the despoilers.

3°. Taparelli's division of societies into natural, free and obligatory is complete and in harmony with Logic. But consent is a necessary element in each class. Ergo.

With Regard to the Minor: Natural society is that which arises from the family by the ordinary process of evolution. Without at least implied and gradual consent, no family, no number of families, can ever coalesce into a perfect and complete civil society. Without such consent, the children after attaining their majority are certainly free to migrate from the domains of their fathers, and cut entirely loose from ancestral authority. The fact that they remain at home, necessarily betokens an act of free consent. Free societies of their very nature suppose consent of the people, and offer no special difficulty. Obligatory societies arise, either like natural societies from the evolution of families, or from the vicissitudes of war; and in each case consent is essential.

4°. Were consent unnecessary, every family would by the very fact form a state or civil society.

But this is absurd.   Ergo consent is necessary.

With Regard to the Major: All the needed elements are present, multitude and authority, at least parental authority. If civil authority is independent of consent, the members of a family owe its head due and full obedience.   Civil authority is absent from family precisely because consent is needed. Children never consent to father's authority as civil ruler, and nature imposes no such obligation on them.

With Regard to the Minor: Domestic society is specifically different from civil or political.   Their scopes, constitutions and methods are quite distinct, and it would be a fatal mistake to endeavor to apply to the two the same rules for government.   Civil society, for instance, is endowed with the right to inflict capital punishment, wage war, raise taxes, privileges never even imagined in domestic society.   The difference between the two conditions is more than that of mere degree, it is specific.

IV. Consent may be implied or expressed, immediate or gradual, and cannot always be withheld.

1°. The people are obliged by nature to adopt government, without which order in the State is an impossibility.

But it sometimes happens that one certain ruler and one certain form of government are alone feasible.   Ergo.

2°. The people are not allowed to use their freedom to the detriment of preexisting rights.   But to refuse consent, is often to make such a use of their freedom.   Ergo.

With Regard to the Minor: The lawful heir has antecedent rights to the throne, and any violation of them is injustice.

3°. To wage unjust war with a neighbor, is to assume a lower position in the moral scale, and disturb the balance of morality.

But it can often happen that morality is impossible of adjustment, unless the wrong-doer accepts the rule of the injured party.

Ergo, consent is of obligation and morally necessary.

With Regard to the Major: The unjust aggressor indirectly chooses the punishment meted out to him, and the nation in the wrong worsted in a conflict of the kind has no ground for complaint, if subjected to the winner's jurisdiction.

THESIS XV

Woman suffrage, though legitimate in exceptional cases, is fraught with dangers. Jouin, 209–212; Cathrein, 415–419.

QUESTION

Family, State and Church are the only complete societies in the world. Society is a moral and lasting union of two or more persons pledged to promote a common aim or purpose. Multitude is matter; moral union or authority, the bond securing union, is form. Nature is efficient cause, and this is plain in family, from which nobody can escape. The same is true of state and Church, though the question calls for profounder study. Whatever multitude tallies with the above description is a true society. To be a complete or perfect society, the common aim or purpose must be peculiar and proper to the society in question, outside the domain of other societies, and requisite means must be within the society's reach. Family, state and Church are commonly regarded as complete and perfect, though the family of its very nature grows towards the state, and though state and Church must work together in mutual harmony. Their distinctive domains make them free and independent. They are mutual assistance of man and wife, the procreation and education of offspring; temporal prosperity of people; and spiritual welfare of faithful. This whole question of woman suffrage has to do with the woman's place in the state, and it can be most expeditiously settled by determining her place in the family. Again we pause to define things.

TERMS

Family is a moral and lasting union of husband, wife and children for mutual assistance, the procreation and educa-

388

tion of offspring. Its main purpose is domestic order and the education of children.

State is a moral and lasting union primarily of families, secondarily of individuals, banded together for the purpose of safeguarding their rights and securing temporal prosperity. Its main purpose is the suppression of injustice by law, and the procurement of opportunities for mental, moral and bodily improvement, hard or impossible in family and Church.

Church is a moral and lasting union of men banded together for purposes of eternal salvation by profession of the same faith, and by participation in the same sacraments, under the rule of duly accredited superiors, especially the Pope of Rome.

Like everything else, the state has four causes, *efficient, final, material and formal.* Though the State's material cause, multitude or citizens, is the thing of vital importance in this question of woman suffrage, it will be no waste of time to glance at the other three causes. They furnish Ethics with all the topics discussed in its treatment of civil society or the state. We give only the briefest summary of things.

Efficient cause is nature, not agreement among men. Opponents are Hobbes and Rousseau. Hobbes makes war man's natural condition, men surrendered all to king, absolutism of monarchy. Rousseau makes peace and individualism man's natural condition; people cheated into State, absolutism of democracy.

Final cause is public prosperity, security in rights, opportunity to improve mind and body beyond private activity. Opponents: Some minimize, coexistence of individual liberties; Kant, Fichte, Darwinists. Some exaggerate, public good in itself; Pantheists, Schelling, Hegel. Plato, State a superior man; Leibnitz, Hartmann, Ahrens, culture and civilization.

Kant's autonomy, despotism, atheistic state; consequences.

Material cause is people and implicitly territory; not individuals, but families compose state; state supposes family and ministers to its needs; only heads are citizens, men. Others are citizens mediately through head, women and children.　Only heads can have part in legislative, executive and judicial functions.　Church follows nature.　State is organism like plant, made up of heterogeneous, not homogeneous parts.　Hence woman suffrage is unnatural and wrong; women are not citizens in immediate sense.　Fixed territory is not of essence, but complementary and contributes to perfection of state.

Formal cause is authority.　Questions: Origin, extent, titles, kinds, functions.

Extent: morals, religion, Church and state; education, economic and social matters; Liberalism.

Titles: inheritance, election, war or conquest, purchase; loss of title.

Kinds: monarchy, aristocracy, democracy.

Functions: legislative, executive, judicial.

Returning now to the state's material cause, or multitude, the family is the seed of the republic.　From history it is plain that the first state had its origin in a group of families acknowledging the authority of Adam.　His sons settled in his neighborhood, and nature prompted them to do their father this honor.　The first state was, therefore, a species of patriarchal government; and can be best described as a perfect union of several families banded together for the purpose of safeguarding their rights and securing their common good.　In process of time these families became a village, a town, a city, and country; and the various other titles to authority successively came into play, inheritance, election, conquest and purchase.　But all through history states never lost sight of their primary origin.　Nature prevented that.　They were made up of men, women and children; but each class had its own fixed function in government.　Because the state had its rise in families, not in individuals, the functions of man, woman and child in government were settled by the rôle they played in the family.　Children have as much right to claim the suffrage as women, and the average boy is a better politician than his mother.

Woman's place in the family settles her place in the republic, and nature is clear about woman's place in the family.　Nature vests parents with power over their children.　This power is a necessary consequence from marriage's purpose, the education of children; and from the fact that family is impossible without authority, an essential element of every society. Besides, children get their being and support from their parents, and the circumstance bases a relation of dependence. This power resides in father and mother. One, however, must be first, husband or wife. As a general rule the husband has qualities of mind and body entitling him to the dignity. As compared with the wife, he is less dependent on others, he is more prudent, braver, stronger and firmer. Occasionally a wife surpasses her husband in these respects, but such wives and husbands are exceptions, and in questions of natural ordinances exceptions are neglected. The husband chooses the wife, and so starts the family. The wife is a man's companion, not his slave, nor yet his equal, excepting in her possession of a human nature. Husband and wife ought to work together in mutual harmony. Home is the wife's proper sphere, her kingdom. The father's power is limited to family's twofold purpose, education of children and the preservation of domestic order. He is empowered to use the rod, not to mutilate or kill his children. Education and order can be secured without recourse to the extreme measures legitimately employed by the state. In this matter of paternal authority, nature recognizes three distinct periods in a child's life:

Children of unripe and imperfect judgment owe their fathers full and entire obedience in every respect, save sin.

Children of ripe and perfect judgment, as long as they stay at home, owe their fathers full and entire obedience in matters touching domestic order.

Children of ripe and perfect judgment, emancipated or married, owe their fathers no obedience, though bound to love, reverence, respect and support them. Man's supremacy in the family is clear from these passages in St. Paul and St. Peter:

The head of every man is Christ, and the head of the woman is the man. 1 Cor. 11.3.

Let women be subject to their husbands, as to the Lord. Eph. 5.22.

Wives, be subject to your husbands as it behooveth in the Lord. Coloss. 3, 18.

Let wives be subject to their husbands. 1 Peter 3.1.

And as Catholics we must not disdain borrowing wisdom from the Scriptures. Scripture is word from God, the author of nature; and Scripture is, therefore, a safe source of information regarding natural and unnatural practices. In this sense the law of faith is the law of nature.

And now to resume, for the purpose of fixing woman's place in the state. The material cause of the state is composed not of individuals as such, but of families. Citizens, therefore, are not individuals as such, but heads of families, actually such or such in capacity, men. Women and children are citizens mediately through husband, and must vote and govern through husband. The State was meant from the start to minister to the needs of the family, not to the needs of the individual as such. Like the human body the state is an organic whole, not made up of individuals on the same footing but of families, and families in turn are made up of husband, wife and children. State supposes the family already constituted and mends its needs. Ergo, not all individuals in the state are citizens, but only family heads, and they alone have capacity to govern, the very essence of citizenship according to Aristotle. The state is as much an organism as the human body, and consists of heterogeneous, not homogeneous parts, men, and women and children. The man is the head, the woman is the heart; and the heart must never govern the head.

This whole question of woman suffrage is only one branch of a larger question, the emancipation of women. The slavery of women current with pagans and Turks was long ago abolished by Christianity, and that kind of emancipation is an accomplished fact, though Socialism purposes restoring the old order, and suffragettes are Socialism's helpers. The emancipation, that would make woman man's equal in family or state, is an utter impossibility, ruled against by nature and destined to forever remain an empty dream, unless the whole world turns monster, and men forget to think. Work away from home for a living is a species of emancipation now on trial, and with certain restrictions it is quite natural and right. Not all women can be wives, because adult women in the world are more numerous than adult men. Some women must therefore support themselves. Modern machinery lessens the value of work at home, and the one remedy is work abroad. As things stand at present, even married women must leave home to help support the family, and the new woman is much to blame for this sad condition of affairs.

Restrictions: Woman's virtue must not be endangered; time and place can be menaces. Woman's weak strength must not be overtaxed. With the married, care of home must be first consideration. Studies and the professions are a new field open to the activity of women. Medicine is not without its own peculiar dangers for women. Women entering the professions ought to submit to the same tests as men. Co-education is wrong in principle and regularly productive of harm. When woman enters the professions to compete with men, she steps down from her high pedestal. Our thesis, omitting the other phases of emancipation, declares emancipation in a political sense unnatural and wrong. Suffrage or the right to vote is the heart of the question. The right to hold office, to act as lawmaker, executive and judge is a logical consequence of the right to suffrage. In a man the right to vote is natural, in virtue of his capacity for headship in the family. In woman the same right is wholly unnatural. An unnatural right can be acquired with the connivance of wrong-headed law, and the exercise of every such right is bound to have disastrous consequences. Such consequences may be a long or short while working themselves out, but they must eventually show head.

Liberalism favors woman suffrage; but, with our knowledge of Liberalism's other wild notions, its advocacy of the cause produces no worry, and strengthens us in our position. The strongest conceivable argument against a theory, is its acceptance and championship by wrong philosophy. John Stuart Mill is on the side of woman suffrage, and we know from Utilitarianism what importance attaches to his opinion. Now and then a Catholic priest or layman raises his voice in its favor. *Catholics are, of course, free to take one side or other in the controversy. Our Church has made no doctrinal decision in the matter,* even though the spirit of Catholicity revolts at the idea, and all our history is opposed to the practice. The Blessed Virgin Mary is our ideal woman, and nothing in her sublime life countenances conduct of the sort. *Some of these Catholics live in corners of the world where woman suffrage is by law established, and in these circumstances common wisdom advises Catholic authorities to urge Catholic women to avail themselves of the unnatural prerogative, and so neutralize the harm.* It would be decidedly wrong for Catholic women in countries of the kind to allow their wrong-headed sisters to control affairs, and turn the government topsy-turvy. Other Catholic advocates of woman suffrage among clergy and laity are few in number, and, while truth on rare occasions fails the majority, it seldom or never rests with the minority.

PROOFS

We divide women into (a) married, and (b) single. Our thesis is clear with regard to the married, and only a little less clear with regard to the single.

(a) (b) We argue from custom. There ought to be no departure from universal custom of long standing without good reason. Woman suffrage is such a departure. Ergo.

With Regard to the Minor: The reasons alleged assume the shape of objections, and we meet them in our Principles. *Reasons against woman suffrage:* Women, whether married or single, are not citizens immediately, but through family; and man is head of the family. Wife would be exempt from husband's jurisdiction, quarrels would be multiplied, rights would collide, man's authority would go, and peace would disappear.

(a) Family would be hurt. Woman's place is home, care of household and children her special charge. Devotion to politics would be as much a duty with women as with men.

(a) (b) Woman's native modesty would suffer, and propriety would be offended. Witness suffragette meetings, parades, campaigns, polls, journeys from home, absence from family. Woman has no head for business of the sort. State affairs are weighty, and call for deep thought and far reaching foresight. Women are proverbially changeable, more open to sentiment than to reason.

Suffrage is not an inborn right, but a means of government. Natural has two senses, inborn and becoming. Inborn in neither man nor woman; becoming in man, unbecoming in woman. It is an acquired right even in man. It is a question of expediency, of the proper. Not that woman is inferior to man, but different from man. Men adapted by nature to some functions, women to others. Hurts woman, politics is modified war, strife, contention, bitterness. Duty and right of protection rest with the male. True government in family. Woman's true functions superior to man's, to form conscience of child, influence will, control impulses. Cardinal Gibbons says: "Mary model of women, not Amazon, not Spartan, not Venus, not Juno." Spiritually, woman is same as man. Equal rights, not similar rights. Suffrage alienates from home. To debar woman from vote is not to degrade, to restrict her to home is not to fetter her aspirations to higher and better things. Home is more a factor in republic than court or congress. Mothers mould presidents, legislators and judges; woman's noblest work is to care for children.

PRINCIPLES

A. Women have same right as men to good government. Ergo, right to suffrage and office.

Answer: Argument proves too much. Infants have same right. Pure democracy would be only legitimate rule. Right to be well governed is different from right to govern. Woman suffrage would be worst government in world, because unnatural and wrong.

B. Women are burdened with taxes and other obligations same as men. Ergo.

Answer: Equality of burdens is different from equality of rights. Women are not soldiers, sailors. Women are independent and sui juris by accident. They ought to be members of a family and subject to its head. Exceptions never count in ethics.

C. Women have been queens. Ergo.

Answer: Cases are rare and exceptional, and happen without harm to family. Women queens for common good, to keep succession in family and smother ambition. Queens govern through men.

D. No argument against voting for candidate selected by men. Ergo, suffrage at least.

Answer: Suffrage means universal rights of citizenship. With suffrage women could extend privilege to selection of candidates and every other function of government.

E. Women make good doctors, lawyers, managers. Ergo, they can vote.

Answer: Nothing follows. Professions are different from suffrage. In the professions men make contracts with them, and are content to use their services. Universal suffrage is different and open to blame; it is unnatural and wrong.

F. Unclean houses, impure food, risk of disease, immorality on street, bad plumbing, fire escapes.

Answer: Woman must leave something for the man to do. If she is much away from home, the house must take care of itself, or the man must turn housekeeper. In her eyes the man, with no care of home to distract him, is unable to regulate outside conditions. Will she be able to manage things inside and outside? Division of labor. Let her urge the husband to manage neighbors, grocers, plumbers, inspectors, policemen. Men are responsible for outside abuses, only when women stay at home and mind their own concerns. Every woman has her own house to care for. No woman is housekeeper to the city. Men are the city's housekeepers, its citizens.

G. Women are citizens, mediately, not immediately; and they ought to do their civic duty mediately through men. In civic matters women must be protected by the men. Men have the interests of their mothers, sisters, wives and daughters at heart. Men must regulate the city's sanitary conditions, not women. Men are as much opposed to unsanitary conditions as women. Men are as fond of their children as women. Other and better ways than woman suffrage to remedy abuses, more natural, less damaging. Independent women are exceptional; no father, no brother, no husband, no son.

H. No taxation without representation.

Answer: Representation is possible without vote. Heads of families represent women. Representation is not personal and immediate management. The colonists never wanted to enter parliament and vote. They wanted an agent on the ground to present their views. Women have such agents in men. Nature, not election, fixes their agents. Men who imposed taxes on colonies did not have to pay them. Men who impose taxes on women have to pay them.

The above principle is per se wrong. In case of law or custom it can happen to be right; and this is true of England.

I. Woman must help man in civic matters by her advice, not by ballot. Suffrage is none of her civic duties.

THESIS XVI

The State enjoys full Legislative, Executive and Judicial rights, the prerogative of Eminent Domain and the War Power. Jouin, 265–284; 351–362; Rickaby, 338–355.

DIVISION

Three Parts. I, Legislative, Executive, Judicial; II, Domain; III, War Power.

I. *Legislative, Executive, Judicial.*

TERMS

Legislative rights are the power to make laws and fix penalties in general.

Executive rights are the power to enforce laws, to punish and pardon.

Judicial rights are the power to decide between right and wrong, and fix penalties in particular.

Judicial rights are civil and criminal.

Civil, to render decision in civil suits, determine to which of two parties a right belongs.

Criminal, to render decision in criminal cases, determine the nature of a fact at variance with law, and settle the penalty.

Penalty is the pain or privation inflicted on the criminal to avenge the wrong done law, and establish anew the disturbed reign of justice. In wrong might does violence to right; in punishment right asserts its supremacy, and brings might to grief.

Punishment ought to be, as far as possible, reparative, medicinal, corrective.

Reparative is calculated to mend disturbed relations and reestablish order.

Medicinal is calculated to cure men and reform them.

Corrective is calculated to act as a deterrent from evil.

PROOF

All three rights are necessary means to state's end or purpose. Confusion would reign in state without Legislative. Legislative would be a dead letter without Executive and Judicial.

PRINCIPLES

A. For three reasons Aristotle thinks it better to rule by written laws than by judge merely.

1°. Fewer wise men are needed. A few lawmakers would be enough, many judges would be needed.

2°. Lawmakers have plenty of time to study and reflect; judges must decide in a hurry.

3°. Lawmakers deal with future and universal contingencies; judges, with present facts and particular cases. No chance for greed, hatred, anger, revenge with lawmaker; judges, open to all these emotions.

B. Rules for lawmakers: 1°. Let your laws be as few in number as possible. 2°. An unjust law is no law. 3°. An impossible law is no law.

C. Capital punishment is just:

1°. Right to amputate limb that threatens harm to whole body. S.T.2.2.q.64.a.2. State is the body, a bad citizen, like a murderer, is such a limb. Ergo.

2°. Right to inflict penalty in proportion with harm done or attempted, e.g., treason, arson, murder.

3°. All civilized peoples, God Himself in laws of Hebrews, sanction capital punishment, e.g., Exodus 22.18. Wizards thou shalt not suffer to live. Ps. 100.8, In the morning I put to death all the wicked of the land. David.

4°. It is lawful to kill animals for man's use. By abuse of free will, the criminal virtually though not formally loses the dignity of a man, descends to the low level of an animal, and ceases to be sui juris.

5°. God takes life when state takes life, because God arms state with the prerogative.

II. *Eminent Domain.*

TERMS

Eminent Domain means power to make whatever use of citizens' property the existence and welfare of the government demand. Hobbes vests in the state thorough ownership of its citizens' goods. He makes citizens, viewed as proprietors, like sons with regard to their father. Sons have no ownership against father, citizens have none against state. Hobbes is wrong, [1] because state can claim only what is necessary, and mere use without full ownership is sufficient; [2] because state-ownership of everything would create indifference, and hurt prosperity and progress; [3] because the state is altogether different from the family; citizens get only well-being from the state; sons get being from their father; citizens are less dependent on the state than sons are on their father.

PROOF

State enjoys Eminent Domain, because it is a means necessary to the state's end and a means not otherwise available.

PRINCIPLES

A. Taxes are contributions made the state by citizens or subjects to advance common interests and defray public expenses. Instances are property tax, customs, revenues, personal tax and the like.

B. State is vested with the right to impose taxes, 1°, because they are necessary means to state's end; without taxes revenue would be uncertain and precarious, while debts would be fixed, certain and steady; 2°, because citizens ought to pay for advantages the state secures to them.

C. Only the supreme power in the state can lawfully impose taxes, 1°, because means belong to him alone, who procures end; 2°, because private citizens would otherwise enjoy others' goods.

D. This power is limited to strict necessity, because otherwise a perversion and abuse of means.

E. No taxation without representation. Per se, this saying is wrong. Per accidens, in case of law or custom it can be right. Charles I and Parliament. American Colonies and England.

III. *War Power.* Four parts, a, b, c, d.

a. *War Power vested in state extends to offensive as well as defensive war.*

b. *Right to declare war is prerogative of supreme power.*

c. *Sedition is intrinsically wrong.*

d. *Precautions before, during and after war.*

TERMS

War Power is power to protect the commonwealth against enemies.

War is state or condition of nations forcibly contending for right.

Defensive war is war waged to keep off an enemy. *Offensive war* is war waged to avenge wrong and establish security.

N.B. War without any real or apparent right is murder.

Sedition is a rising in arms as between people and ruler, or as between factions among the people.

N.B. The belligerency of rebels is recognised only after they have by certain signs proved themselves capable of autonomy. International law is obscure and unsettled on this point.

Sedition is offensive warfare of people against legitimate ruler. Two kinds of tyranny are of rule and of title.

Tyranny of rule is abuse of power, title intact; and it is no legitimate excuse for offensive warfare, which would be sedition.

N.B. It is legitimate excuse for defensive, if ruler attacks, because citizens have same rights as individuals.

Tyranny of title or right means no title, no legitimate ruler; and it is legitimate excuse for offensive warfare, which is then no sedition. Tyranny of rule leads to loss of title, without being actual forfeiture.

PROOFS

a. *Defensive war:*

1°. Nations enjoy rights of individuals and self-defense is a personal right.

2°. Often it is the only means of securing safety to the republic.

Offensive War:

1°. Justice among nations is necessary. Otherwise natural law as between nations would be without sanction; no future life for nations; international law of no force, because nations are sovereign. Often war is only available means; order must be reestablished by its violators or by the wronged.

2°. Safety insecure, if defensive war is alone legitimate; wrongs could never be repaired; wicked would prosper and grow in power after each attack.

3°. Enemy must often be attacked in midst of preparations; otherwise defeat is certain.

b. *War is prerogative of supreme power.* Order demands as much.

1°. If private citizens exercised war prerogative, nations would be kept busy settling feuds and personal quarrels.

2°. Individuals are prone to exaggerate their petty grievances.

3°. Jurisdiction over people belongs to ruler, not to individuals; call for volunteers belongs to supreme power.

c. *Sedition is intrinsically wrong.*

1°. Against common good; it attacks the very form of society, authority.

2°. Done without right; war prerogative belongs to ruler.

N.B. Same arguments hold for factions. Defensive war is not wrong—because subjects have same rights as individuals.

d. *Precautions before, during and after war.*

Before war, three things, 1°. Grave and just cause. 2°. Just motive. 3°. Probable success.

1°. *Some grave and just causes:*

Puffendorf mentions:

1. Protection of self and property against attempts at injury and destruction;

2. Insistence on clear rights denied by others;

3. Recompense for wrongs suffered at the hands of an enemy;

4. Demand of pledges against future insult and injury.

Suarez mentions:

1. A nation's refusal to observe the common law of nations.
N.B. Refusal to promote commerce is no good excuse.

2. Serious wrong done a nation's reputation and good name.
N.B. Indignity done an ambassador.

3. Danger threatening an allied nation, when that nation has a right to wage war and intends to do so.

Some weak and insufficient reasons:

1. Suspicions founded on no external facts, and wholly destitute of moral certainty.

2. Violations of natural law perpetrated at home, with citizens for victims.

3. Monarch's religion, if without oppression and tyranny.

4. Zeal for true religion and progress of civilization.

5. Desire to seat a certain family on throne, even to the advantage of other nations.

2°. *Motive must be right*—Suarez assigns two. a, to make good injuries done by another, and b, to punish offenders. If offender stands ready to make satisfaction, war is out of the question.

N.B. The ruler of the wronged republic fixes the penalty.

3°. *Hope of success*—Necessary for offensive war, of less moment for defensive. Reason is evident. Otherwise nation would be exposed to certain danger.

Precautions during war:

1. Plots are legitimate; lies and violations of treaties are not legitimate. Plots involving lies are wrong. Deception is quite possible without a lie.

2. International law must be respected.

3. The innocent must never suffer direct injury, indirect injury can be legitimate.

4. Evils not calculated to help along the cause must be avoided.

5. Poisoning of water, death by treachery and the like are forbidden by international law.

Precautions after war:

By strict right the winner can inflict on the loser whatever punishment is necessary to repair his losses, secure himself against the recurrence of difficulties, and establish himself in peace. The instinct of Christianity has done much to moderate the cruelties formerly practised in the name of strict right. Certainly the victor is not now allowed to slay the defenseless or sell captives. The law of nations sets salutary limits to the right of conquest.

THE END

INDEX